The Authors

CARRIE FORMAN ARNOLD is an artist and businesswoman who has made a study of the history of the Palace of the Governors.

ADRIAN H. BUSTAMANTE is an ethnohistorian and head of the Arts and Sciences Division at the Santa Fe Community College.

STANLEY M. HORDES, a historian, was formerly the New Mexico state historian.

JOHN L. KESSELL, professor of history and editor of the Vargas Project at the University of New Mexico, is the author of *Kiva, Cross, and Crown: The Pecos Indians and New Mexico, 1540–1840.*

JANET LECOMPTE, a historian, is the author of *Rebellion in Rio Arriba, 1837,* and of several articles on republican New Mexico.

FRANCES LEVINE is an ethnohistorian specializing in Spanish Colonial New Mexico.

DAVID GRANT NOBLE is an author, editor, and photographer and former director of public information at the School of American Research.

JOSEPH P. SÁNCHEZ, a historian and the director of the Spanish Colonial Research Center at the University of New Mexico, is the author of *The Rio Abajo Frontier, 1540–1692: A History of Early Colonial New Mexico.*

MARC SIMMONS, a historian specializing in New Mexico and the Southwest, is the author of *Along the Santa Fe Trail, New Mexico: An Interpretive History,* and many other books and articles.

JOHN P. WILSON is an anthropologist who currently runs a business specializing in innovative historical and anthropological research.

SANTA FE

History of an Ancient City

The School of American Research
wishes to thank the
Kirkpatrick family and the Inn at Loretto in Santa Fe
for their generous support of this book

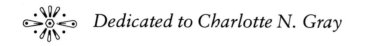 *Dedicated to Charlotte N. Gray*

SANTA FE

History of an Ancient City

Edited by

DAVID GRANT NOBLE

School of American Research Press

SCHOOL OF AMERICAN RESEARCH PRESS
P.O. Box 2188, Santa Fe, New Mexico 87504

Assistant editor: Tom Ireland
Designer: Deborah Flynn Post
Typographer: Casa Sin Nombre
Printer: Dai Nippon Printing Co.

DISTRIBUTED BY UNIVERSITY OF WASHINGTON PRESS

Library of Congress Cataloging-in-Publication Data:

Santa Fe: history of an ancient city
edited by David Grant Noble

p.   cm.   Bibliography: p.   Includes index.
ISBN 0-933452-26-8. -- ISBN 0-933452-27-6 (pbk.)
1. Santa Fe (N.M.)--History.   I. Noble, David Grant.
F804.S257S26   1989
978.9'5602--dc19   89-4214
CIP

Front cover: "The End of the Trail," oil painting by Gerald Cassidy, 48" x
60," ca. 1930. Courtesy Fine Arts Museum, Museum of New Mexico.
Frontispiece: Palace of the Governors, ca. 1900. Photo by
Christian G. Kaadt. Courtesy Carrie Forman Arnold.

Contents

Acknowledgments

The School of American Research is grateful to
the following people for their assistance and
support of this book: Margaret Arrott,
Renee and John Benjamin, Charles Bennett,
Nancy Bernard, Tom Chavez, Robin Farwell Gavin,
Charlotte N. Gray, Peggy Grinnell, Roy Grinnell,
Jonathan Haas, Laura Holt, Stanley M. Hordes,
Wilson Hurley, Paul Andrew Hutton,
Byron A. Johnson, James F. Kirkpatrick,
Lester B. Loo, Timothy D. Maxwell,
Barbara Mauldin, Arthur Olivas,
A. Lincoln Pittinger, Stephen S. Post,
Orlando Romero, Richard Rudisill,
James Russell, Curtis Schaafsma,
Albert and Barbara Simms, Cordelia Snow,
David Snow, Don Spaulding, Louise Steiner,
Rosemary Talley, Charles Venrick,
and Samantha Williams.

We would also like to express our
appreciation to the following institutions for
their assistance: the Albuquerque Museum; the
Museum of New Mexico's Fine Arts Museum,
Laboratory of Anthropology, Museum of
International Folk Art, Palace of the Governors,
and Photo Archives; the New Mexico
Records Center and Archives; and Sunwest Bank
of Santa Fe.

Foreword

When I moved to Santa Fe in the early 1970s, my neighbor told me of her childhood, when she and her family followed the winding trail up Santa Fe Canyon to the mountain meadows of Aspen Ranch. Here they summered, grazing their goats and returning only occasionally to town to sell the cheese they made.

Oral history, which recalls the events of a lifetime and recounts the collective memory of several more, gives us an intimate and often colorful sense of where we live and the generations that preceded us. Old timers in Santa Fe tell of the burros that brought firewood to town from the surrounding hills. And they remember when you could build a house for "ten dollars a thousand, made and laid"—ten dollars to have a thousand adobe bricks made and laid up in the walls.

But it is equally fascinating to take the longer view of the past, the perspective of centuries surviving in the papers of officialdom, church documents, the journals and chronicles of the major players, and the archaeological record. Here the sweep of centuries supersedes the passage of mere generations.

The earliest era of Santa Fe history is difficult to resurrect because warfare, which swept through New Mexico in 1680, destroyed all local documents and erased most traces of Spanish settlement and culture. Today, historians regularly travel to Mexico City and Seville in their attempts to reconstruct the life and times of seventeenth-century Santa Fe and New Mexico.

One intriguing question that may never be fully answered is exactly how the site for Santa Fe was chosen in 1609 by Don Pedro de Peralta. In 1598, Don Juan de Oñate had settled his colonists at San Juan Pueblo along the Rio Chama, later moving to nearby Yunge Oweenge, which the Spaniards called San Gabriel. Unlike these first locations, the site along the Rio Santa Fe was not occupied by Native Americans. After twelve years of close interaction with and dependency upon Pueblo Indians, the Spaniards may have needed the independence that the Santa Fe site offered.

San Miguel Church, 1873.

But certainly other factors were taken into account. Peralta's people needed a reliable water supply and a topography allowing irrigation. They also required good land to farm, meadows in which to graze their stock and grow hay, a supply of wood for fuel and construction, and nearby areas offering hunting and other resources. And finally, the site would have to provide security from potential attack. Santa Fe seemed to satisfy all these requirements.

In the nearly four centuries since Peralta and his company surveyed the site for Santa Fe, the town has been ruled by Spaniards, Pueblo Indians, Mexicans, and Americans. For many generations, its basically rural character was complemented by the energy of a political center and military headquarters. Later, Santa Fe thrived as a marketplace and thoroughfare for international trade. The city has seen its measure of history.

Today, Santa Fe's historical ambiance draws visitors from around the country and abroad. The city's history is no less than an economic resource from which spring the livelihoods of many people. Indeed, "Santa Fe style" has become a small national industry. Like past travelers who came over the Camino Real or the Santa Fe Trail, today's visitors come with a stirring image of the city. This image has been created, although with some romantic embellishments, from a truly intriguing past.

As we approach Santa Fe's four hundredth anniversary, we would do well to look closely at the city's historical foundation and reappraise its value from various perspectives—educational, scholarly, artistic, economic. Are we adequately nurturing Santa Fe's history? Are archaeological sites being responsibly investigated and interpreted? Do our history libraries need support? How much do our students know about their ethnic past? Is scholarly research being encouraged? Does the city adequately protect architectural integrity? How will the next generation of tourists respond to the Santa Fe they will experience? Santa Fe's history supports Santa Fe, but does Santa Fe support its history?

Some four centuries ago, Governor Peralta selected a site along the Santa Fe River for the establishment of his colony. Although we have no record of his thoughts, we can assume that he carefully considered how the place would serve the needs of his followers. He probably walked along the banks of the river, tasted the water, tested the soil, and explored the foothills. Certainly, he prepared for the oncoming winter and planned for the following spring. And he must have pondered the fate of the future generations he would not see. Perhaps his faith in the site inspired the name he gave it, *Santa Fe*, Holy Faith.

Four centuries later, as we ourselves look to Santa Fe's future, we can benefit by knowing its past and by assessing, as did Peralta, the resources that future generations will need to thrive. Santa Fe's historical heritage should be counted among them; like the city's precious water supply, it must be both used and conserved.

It is my hope that the present essays, which represent the latest thinking of some of New Mexico's most distinguished historians, will help deepen public understanding and appreciation of Santa Fe's fascinating past and stimulate wise planning for its future.

David Grant Noble

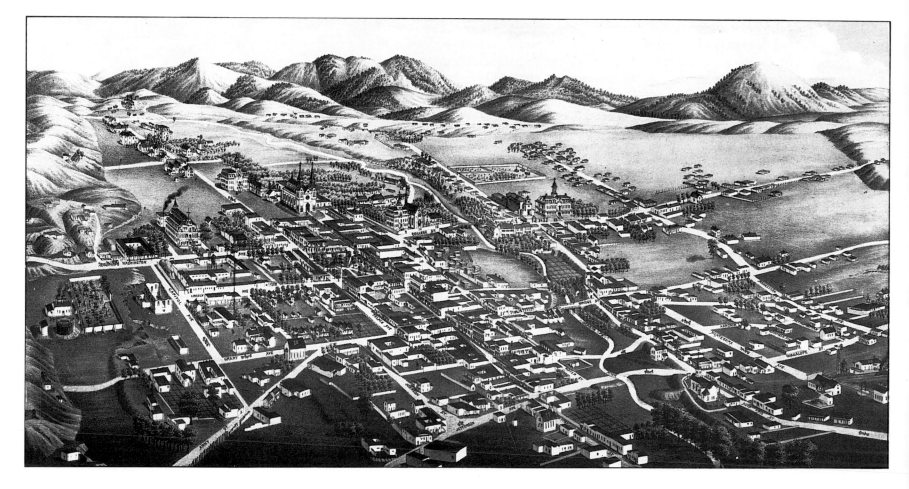

Bird's-eye view of Santa Fe in 1882.

Introduction:

A History of the Histories of Santa Fe

STANLEY M. HORDES

One could scarcely imagine a town more deserving of a historical volume than Santa Fe. Established in 1610, it stands as the oldest capital city in what is now the United States. For almost two and a half centuries, it represented the administrative, military, and commercial center of the Spanish and Mexican far northern frontier—first as the terminus of the Camino Real, or Royal Highway, which stretched over one thousand miles from the viceregal capital in Mexico City, and later as the destination of Anglo traders carrying goods from the United States along the Santa Fe Trail. Even today, Santa Fe maintains an international reputation as a historically significant city, whether based on its rich architectural and archaeological resources or on its "Pueblo Revival" buildings.

This volume draws together the talents of a distinguished group of New Mexico historians to examine the history of Santa Fe from a variety of fresh scholarly perspectives, ranging from the occupation of the area by prehistoric Indian groups, through the Spanish and Mexican periods, to the early years of occupation by the United States. Indeed, the collective efforts of these scholars fill a large void in the historical literature on the city's heritage. Until recently, only two attempts have been made to offer a comprehensive historical account, one by Ralph Emerson Twitchell in 1925, and the other by Father Stanley Cracciola in 1958, both inadequate by today's standards. The remainder of the works consist of a few monographs and journal articles on various aspects of Santa Fe's history. These tend to fall into three general categories: descriptions and translations of documents; arguments over dates of

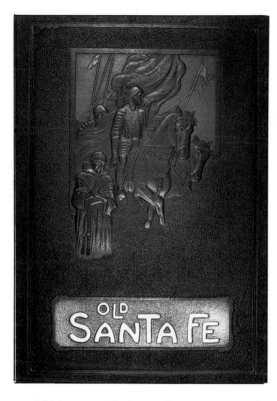

Old Santa Fe: The Story of New Mexico's Ancient Capital, by Ralph Emerson Twitchell.

buildings or events; and site-specific studies, more often than not, prepared in response to physical threats to the resource.

Twitchell's *Old Santa Fe: The Story of New Mexico's Ancient Capital* (1925) represented a noble effort on the part of the prolific lawyer / historian to piece together a chronicle of the city from its origins until the early years of the twentieth century. While this work must be respected as a pioneering attempt and remains the most utilized book on the topic, it has its share of problems, including an anecdotal narrative style, significant chronological gaps, and the absence of Hispanic figures in its treatment of the Territorial period. Less satisfying still is Father Stanley Cracciola's *Ciudad Santa Fe* (1958), a long, rambling essay that includes very little material on Santa Fe itself, concentrating on New Mexico history in general. Moreover, Father Stanley maintained a strongly anti-Hispanic bias in his approach to history, leading the reader to conclude incorrectly that the Spaniards came to New Mexico exclusively to rape and pillage.

Fortunately, Susan Hazen-Hammond's *A Short History of Santa Fe* (1988) offered an excellent synthesis of both the classical authors and more recent research, recounting Santa Fe's past from prehistory to the present. As it was based almost entirely on secondary works and edited translations of original documents, the work broke little new ground, and to a certain extent, it perpetuated the perspectives of its sources. But for the first time, the reader can benefit from scholarship produced during the mid and late twentieth century.

Several monographs and journal articles published over the course of the past sixty years shed considerable light on Santa Fe's past. Two journals in particular—*El Palacio* (published jointly by the School of American Research, the Museum of New Mexico, and the Archaeological Society of New Mexico until the 1950s) and the *New Mexico Historical Review*—have taken the lead in this direction. In the 1920s, Lansing Bloom started the tradition of publishing annotated translations of significant documents illustrating key historical developments in the history of Santa Fe. His article on the trading activities of Mexican-period merchant Manuel Alvarez (*El Palacio*, 1923) and his translation of the royal instructions to Governor Pedro de Peralta in 1609 regarding the establishment of the capital at Santa Fe (*El Palacio*, 1928) established the precedent for later scholars to share their newly discovered documents with the public—for example, Marc Simmons's translation of "Antonio Barreiro's Proclamation of Santa Fe City Government" (*El Palacio*, 1970) and Clevy Lloyd Strout's "The Resettlement of Santa Fe, 1695: The Newly Found Muster Roll" (*New Mexico Historical Review*, 1978).

A considerable share of the articles written about Santa Fe in the early part of the twentieth century tended to focus on the dating of particular buildings and events or the city's name. In a protracted debate, Benjamin M. Read claimed that Juan de Oñate established Santa Fe as the capital of New Mexico ("The Founder of Santa Fe," *El Palacio*, 1927), and Lansing Bloom contended (correctly) that Pedro de Peralta did ("Instructions for Don Pedro de Peralta . . . in the Place of Don Juan de Oñate," *El Palacio*, 1928; "When Was Santa Fe Founded?" *New Mexico Historical Review*, 1929). Bloom also tackled the controversial issue of the name of Santa Fe, favoring "La Villa de Santa Fe" over the more romantic and flowery "La Villa Real de la Santa Fe de San Francisco de Asis," which is still the official name according to the city ("What is Santa Fe's Name Historically?" *New Mexico Historical Review*, 1945). Still other articles dealt with the age of San Miguel Chapel, which some people claim to be the oldest church in the United States (e.g., Fray Angelico Chávez, "How Old is San Miguel?" *El Palacio*, 1953).

The recognition of the need to protect and interpret Santa Fe's architectural and archaeological treasures stimulated another genre of historical scholarship. Beginning in the 1930s and continuing through the 1980s, historians and archaeologists documented significant buildings and sites in downtown Santa Fe. The city's churches attracted the attention of most of these writers, led by historian Fray Angelico Chávez, whose many articles in the *New Mexico Historical Review* in the 1940s, 1950s, and 1960s shed new light on Santa Fe's past. Among others instrumental in documenting the history of these structures were Eleanor Adams (with Chávez, the coauthor of *The Missions of New Mexico, 1776*), A. von Wuthenau, José D. Sena, and Bruce Ellis. Of particular value is Mary Jean Straw's *Loretto: The Sisters and Their Santa Fe*

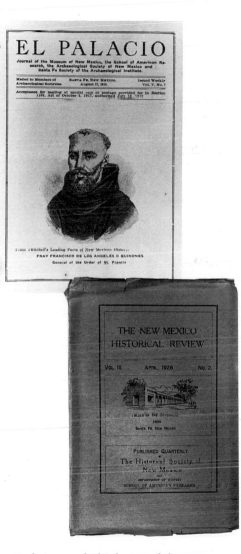

Early issues of *El Palacio* and the *New Mexico Historical Review*.

Double-barred cross
excavated from the Palace of
the Governors.

Chapel, which went considerably beyond a mere building history to encompass the people associated with the structure.

For many years, threats from intrusive development have stimulated studies of Santa Fe's built environment. As long ago as the 1920s, Twitchell wrote a short essay, *The Conquest of Santa Fe, New Mexico, and the Building of Old Fort Marcy, A.D. 1846*, to generate interest in the restoration of the old fort. Civic organizations formed to protect the architectural heritage of Santa Fe, such as the Old Santa Fe Association (1926) and the Historic Santa Fe Foundation (1961), supported historical research on structures throughout the city. The two groups sponsored a series of essays in the *New Mexican* entitled "Let's Keep Our Heritage," edited by architect John Gaw Meem, and in 1966 published *Old Santa Fe Today* (republished in 1972 and 1982), containing architectural histories of significant buildings in Santa Fe and biographical sketches of their former occupants. With new threats of instrusive development in the 1970s and 1980s came a renewed interest in the underground resources of Santa Fe and their historical contexts. *El Palacio* featured the work of Cordelia Snow, Bruce Ellis, David Snow, Stewart Peckham, and Curtis Schaafsma, writing about their excavations at the Palace of the Governors, the Museum of Fine Arts, Nusbaum House, and La Garita (see bibiliography).

Not surprisingly, the plaza and its surrounding buildings have attracted a large share of scholarly attention. Bruce Ellis's "Santa Fe's Seventeenth Century Plaza, Parish Church, and Convent Reconsidered" (1976), Max Moorehead's "Rebuilding the Presidio of Santa Fe, 1789-1791" (*New Mexico Historical Review*, 1974), and J. K. Shishkin's *The Palace of the Governors* (1972) are but a few of these studies.

This brief review of the scholarship dealing with the history of Santa Fe suggests that with few exceptions the literature has been either too broad, treating the larger unit of New Mexico and neglecting the history of the city, or too narrow, focusing on site-specific topics to the exclusion of the larger municipal context. Although the Hazen-Hammond history partially fills this void, a considerable amount of archival material remains untouched.

Much significant material may be found in repositories such as the Archivo General de Indias in Seville, the Archivo Histórico Nacional in Madrid, the Archivo General de la Nación and the Biblioteca Nacional in Mexico City, and various regional archives in northern Mexico. But the richest sources exist in local archives and libraries, most notably at the New Mexico Records Center and Archives and the Museum of New Mexico History Library. Contained among these tens of thousands of pages of official and private papers are administrative, judicial, military, and church records documenting the activities not only of the movers and shakers of the community, but also of the more humble residents of Santa Fe. By examining civil proceedings and land records, for example, one can begin to discern patterns of urban and rural land ownership in the area—who was accumulating wealth and power at whose expense. By analyzing criminal trials, scholars can begin to better understand standards of behavior and morality during the Spanish and Mexican periods of Santa Fe's history. Church baptismal, marriage, and burial records, together with civil and ecclesiastical census records, can yield a considerable amount of information on Santa Fe's changing demographic profile in the seventeenth, eighteenth, and nineteenth centuries.

The articles assembled in this volume are an example of the level of research and analysis that can be achieved when scholars cultivate the fertile fields of Santa Fe history. Frances Levine offers an overview of prehistoric and historic archaeological resources in the Santa Fe area, analyzing the cultural chronology revealed by these resources and reviewing efforts to interpret their significance. Joseph P. Sánchez, director of the National Park Service's Spanish Colonial Research Center at the University of New Mexico, tells how a struggle between civil and ecclesiastical authorities in the seventeenth century influenced life in the young Spanish capital and details the harrowing events of the Pueblo Revolt of 1680. The story of the reconquest of Santa Fe thirteen years later is recounted by University of New Mexico Professor John L. Kessell, and Adrian Bustamante, of Santa Fe Community College, examines the ethnic and social diversity of the city in Spanish Colonial times.

South side of the Santa Fe plaza.

Janet Lecompte, Marc Simmons, and John P. Wilson investigate the Mexican period of Santa Fe's history. Lecompte discusses the changing lifestyle of Santa Feans in the wake of Mexican independence from Spain in 1821 and the influx of Anglo-Americans brought about by the opening of the Santa Fe Trail. The trail is the focus of Simmons's article, which analyzes the interdependent roles of Anglo and Mexican merchants and the impact of their relationship on the community. Wilson recounts the invasion and occupation of Santa Fe in 1846 by General Stephen Watts Kearny and fifteen hundred U.S. troops, ending nearly two and a half centuries of Spanish and Mexican administration and causing dramatic changes in the lives of Santa Fe's residents.

Encompassing all periods of Santa Fe's history, Carrie Forman Arnold traces the evolution of the Palace of the Governors from its construction in 1610 to its most recent renovation in the 1980s. The *casas reales*, or *palacio real*, as the structure was once known, represents Santa Fe's transition over the course of four centuries—the architectural manifestation of its transformation from frontier backwater capital to tourist mecca.

The history of Santa Fe is reflected in the wealth of architectural, archaeological, and documentary resources of the community. The scholars whose work is represented in this volume have gone a long way towards realizing the tremendous research potential of these precious resources. It is hoped that the scholarship presented here will serve not only to enlighten the community about its past but also to stimulate other researchers to delve into primary archival materials with the end of better understanding Santa Fe's unique heritage.

A Short Chronology of Santa Fe

Interior of Loretto Chapel showing spiral staircase, ca. 1935.

Ca. 1150–1325	Coalition period. Pueblo Indian villages thrive along the Santa Fe River.
Ca. 1325–1600	Classic period. Indians abandon the area by the early 1400s.
1598	Establishment of the first permanent Spanish colony in New Mexico at San Juan Pueblo.
1610	Founding of Santa Fe by Spaniards. The building of the Palace of the Governors begins.
1680	Pueblo Revolt. Spanish colony exiled.
1693	Santa Fe reconquered by Spaniards under Vargas.
1821	Mexico wins independence from Spain. Santa Fe Trail opens.
1846	Conquest of Santa Fe and New Mexico by the United States.
1880	Railway reaches Santa Fe. The end of commerce on the Santa Fe Trail.
1912	New Mexico achieves statehood.

Down Under an Ancient City

An Archaeologist's View of Santa Fe

FRANCES LEVINE

Santa Fe recently commemorated its three hundred seventy-fifth year as the capital of New Mexico and its proud heritage as one of the oldest cities in the nation. But Santa Fe has an even longer legacy. Scattered throughout the city are archaeological remains of Pueblo Indian villages that were occupied over a span of more than seven centuries.

Between about A.D. 600 and 1425, ancestors of the modern Pueblos lived along the Santa Fe River. Why did they abandon the area that Spanish colonists later found so attractive for their capital city? In part, rainfall in the early fifteenth century may have been insufficient to support the farming communities in and around Santa Fe. We do not yet fully understand the reasons for this abandonment because the archaeological resources of Santa Fe have not been as systematically studied as those of many other parts of the Southwest. Yet the archeological remains of the Pueblo, Hispanic, and Anglo-American occupations of Santa Fe contain evidence of a fascinating and largely untold history of "the City Different."

Prehistoric Cultures of the Northern Rio Grande

The city of Santa Fe lies within the northern Rio Grande region. Archaeological remains of hunting camps and temporary shelters containing stone tools and utilitarian and crudely painted pottery are evidence of the mobile life-style of the Archaic people who lived in the region between about 3000 B.C. and A.D. 600. They lived in small, probably family-based bands, scheduling their frequent moves by the seasonal and local availability of edible wild plants and

Above, Red Mesa bowl. *Opposite page*, archaeological excavations at the building site of the First Interstate Bank on Washington Avenue in 1982.

Archaic campsite.

Santa Fe Black-on-white mug.

game. Archaic sites have not yet been recorded closer to Santa Fe than the Cochiti area, some twenty-five miles southwest of the city.

Beginning perhaps in the fifth century A.D. and certainly by the beginning of the seventh century, people in the northern Rio Grande began to shift their economy from foraging to farming. For some five hundred years, beginning about A.D. 400–600 and lasting until A.D. 1150–1200, these early agriculturalists lived in small villages of pithouses or in surface masonry houses. Red Mesa Black-on-white, Kwahe'e Black-on-white, and Chaco II Black-on-white—geometrically patterned, mineral-painted pottery styles—characterize archaeological sites of this so-called Developmental period. Some pottery was produced in the Santa Fe villages, but several kinds of ceramics seem to have been traded into this area from pueblos further to the west, perhaps from the flourishing cultural center of Chaco Canyon.

Few Early Developmental sites have been found in the northern Rio Grande, which suggests that the population was small, or perhaps that this area was not favorable for incipient agricultural practices. Sites of the Late Developmental period are more abundant.

As the Developmental period drew to a close, the population of the northern Rio Grande was expanding, using the major river valleys for villages and fields and the nearby mountains for game and wild plant foods. By the mid-twelfth century, a virtual population explosion had taken place in the northern Rio Grande. Archaeologists traditionally have attributed the growth to an immigration of people from the Mesa Verde area, Chaco Canyon, and the San Juan Basin of northwestern New Mexico, believing that people left those areas as the climatic and cultural conditions changed. Other evidence suggests that the local population may have been large enough by the mid-twelfth century to require new agricultural technology, economic practices, and settlement patterns.

Archaeological remains of the Coalition period, which began between A.D. 1150 and 1200 and ended at about A.D. 1325, are found widely throughout the northern Rio Grande. Coalition-period sites underlie parts of downtown Santa Fe and are found in the nearby settlements of Agua Fria and

Arroyo Hondo. During this period pottery production underwent a series of technological changes, and the inhabitants began to settle in fewer and larger villages. Archaeological sites of this age are identified by the prevalence of a locally made vegetable- or organic-painted pottery called Santa Fe Black-on-white and by the presence of a later variant known as Wiyo Black-on-white. Coalition architecture is variable, but most villages have multiroom masonry or adobe houseblocks built around plazas and include characteristic round, subterranean kivas.

Wijo canteen.

The transition from the Coalition to the Classic period (A.D. 1325–1600) is identified archaeologically by the appearance of pottery decorated with mineral-paint glazes and by a thick, porous pottery known as biscuit ware. Early in the Classic period, population seems to have increased, as evidenced by more and larger villages. Classic-period settlements are frequently associated with soil- and water-conservation features such as check dams and gridded gardens, indicating the extent to which the population was committed to farming. The appearance of kachina figures in rock art and ritual paraphernalia and the common occurrence of great kivas in Classic-period sites suggest that Pueblo society had complex regional social and political organizations. Village craft specialization also flourished during this period. Pottery styles produced in a number of the northern Rio Grande pueblos are found in archaeological sites throughout the Southwest and High Plains, indicating that some pueblos in the northern Rio Grande supplied goods to regional trade networks.

The Early Classic period seems to mark the end of Pueblo occupation in Santa Fe, Agua Fria, and Arroyo Hondo, although there was a brief interval of Pueblo reoccupation of Santa Fe following the Pueblo Revolt of 1680. In other parts of the northern Rio Grande, Classic-period archaeological sites, including the Tano pueblos of the Galisteo Basin, Tesuque Pueblo, and Pecos Pueblo, were still occupied at the time of Spanish contact.

Kachina mask petroglyph south of Santa Fe, thought to represent Hilili, the guardian kachina.

Toward the end of the Classic period and continuing into the seventeenth century, the population of the northern Rio Grande pueblos declined dramatically. Diseases introduced by the Spaniards decimated the Pueblos. A collapse of the aboriginal social and economic networks accompanied this

Adolph F. Bandelier at an archaeological ruin.

decline, leading to the abandonment of some villages and the concentration of population into others. Santa Fe was not one of the areas in which the Pueblo population concentrated. It would be more than two and a half centuries before Pueblo people again occupied Santa Fe, and then, their brief occupation was abruptly terminated when they were removed by Spanish troops.

Archaeological Investigations in Santa Fe

Archaeological studies along the Santa Fe River began in the late nineteenth century. During the 1880s, Adolph Bandelier, the father of southwestern archaeology and ethnology, recorded a number of late prehistoric and historic pueblos in Santa Fe County in his attempts to find the ancestral sites of the modern pueblos of the Rio Grande. He speculated that Santa Fe had been the site of one or two Tano-speaking villages related linguistically to the pueblos of the Galisteo area. He believed that the Tanos abandoned Santa Fe at least a century before the establishment of the Spanish capital in 1610. Bandelier placed one of the Tano pueblos in Santa Fe north of the city, near the later site of Fort Marcy. The other, he thought, had stood in the vicinity of San Miguel Church. Bandelier's Tewa-speaking informants from San Juan and Santa Clara pueblos called Santa Fe Kua'p'o-oge or O'gha po'oghe, meaning "the place of the shell beads near the water," or "bead water place."

In June of 1910, a skeleton was unearthed during construction of the Sylvanus Morley house on La Garita Hill, the area east of the Scottish Rite Temple bordered by Paseo de Peralta on the south and Washington Avenue on the west. Edgar Hewett, then director of the School of American Archaeology (later the School of American Research), used the occasion to prepare a brief review of the prehistory of Santa Fe for the *New Mexican*. Hewett believed that there were three pueblo ruins in the city—one underlying the ruins of Fort Marcy, a smaller one near San Miguel Chapel and a downtown tourist attraction that is touted as the "oldest house" in the continental United States, and a third underlying the Palace of the Governors. He vividly rendered the landscape of fifteenth-century Santa Fe as follows:

If one could have stood on the spot where the city now stands, looking east from the site of the Church of Our Lady of Guadalupe, five hundred years ago, there would have been seen on what we call Fort Marcy hill, an Indian town of considerable size, consisting of one large terraced pueblo and one or two smaller buildings near by, a kiva or sanctuary of the circular, subterranean type on the bench half way down the hill side; south of the river on San Miguel slope, a small pueblo two stories high, and passing back and forth from these two towns to the river, then considerably larger than now, the water carriers with their ollas on their heads. In the foreground, where the historic Old Palace has undergone the vicissitudes of nearly three centuries, would have been a cluster of ruined walls and rounded mounds, the remains of an earlier town, over which some of the earliest houses of Santa Fe were doubtless built.

Some months after Hewett's published description, the historian Ralph Emerson Twitchell responded in another *New Mexican* column, stating that no pueblo existed in the vicinity of San Miguel Church, although the "oldest house" was probably of Pueblo construction. Twitchell believed that the other Pueblo ruins in Santa Fe were attributable to Tano-speaking peoples. The debate between Hewett and Twitchell makes interesting reading, but their disagreements are largely moot. With more precise dating of archaeological remains, it is now clear that the population of Santa Fe was declining in the fifteenth century, and it is unlikely that the pueblos were as bustling as Hewett depicts. As for Twitchell's rejection of the idea of a pueblo near San Miguel Church, Coalition-period remains have been found under its earliest floor levels, underlying the PERA building, and in other construction sites east of the church.

The *New Mexican* contains the only record of archaeological materials removed during the 1916 demolition of the Fort Marcy barracks, which stood on the site now occupied by the Museum of Fine Arts. Wagon loads of Pueblo pottery and Spanish crockery, animal bones, assorted household and personal

Edgar Lee Hewett, 1911.

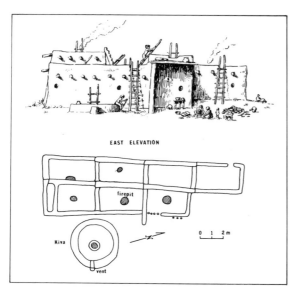

EAST ELEVATION

firepit

Kiva

vent

0 1 2 m

Reconstruction of a Coalition pueblo.

items, and as many as six human burials were found in cultural deposits extending more than ten feet below the street level in some places.

The first three decades of the twentieth century were seminal years for the development of southwestern archaeological methods and theories. The School of American Research and the Laboratory of Anthropology provided intellectual and logistical support to a distinguished group of scholars who came to study the archaeology and ethnology of the northern Rio Grande. Edgar Hewett, Harry P. Mera, Nels Nelson, A. V. Kidder, Anna O. Shepard, Kenneth Chapman, and many others developed the systematic classifications of ceramics and the site-recording procedures that remain fundamental to archaeological studies in the region. The continuum of culture in the later prehistoric, historic, and modern pueblos of the northern Rio Grande provided archaeologists with the laboratory they needed to refine their techniques. Excavations in the Galisteo Basin pueblos, at Pecos, and at La Cieneguilla established the procedures for using specific pottery designs to date the occupation of archaeological sites.

In Santa Fe the most significant archaeological study of the 1930s was the excavation of Pindi, a Late Developmental- and Coalition-period site in Agua Fria. Laborers hired by the Works Progress Administration excavated the site, and Stanley Stubbs and W. S. Stallings documented the work. The site is one of the larger Coalition sites in the northern Rio Grande. Until recent studies by the School of American Research in the Arroyo Hondo area, this was the only comprehensive excavation and reporting of a prehistoric site in Santa Fe.

In the 1950s a number of projects in and near Santa Fe focused on the Spanish Colonial archaeology of the city. Stubbs and Bruce Ellis excavated within the sanctuary of San Miguel Chapel to reconstruct the building sequence of the church. They also excavated what remained of La Castrense, the eighteeenth-century chapel that had stood on the south side of the plaza. During this time Ellis also excavated the architectural remains of La Garita, a Colonial fortification on the north side of the city. Also beginning in the 1950s, a study of Spanish Colonial and Mexican-period ranchos in the area between Cieneguilla and Agua Fria was carried out by E. Boyd over a period of some

Archaeological excavations at Pindi Pueblo showing outlines of turkey pens under the plaza. Pindi is located along the Santa Fe River west of downtown Santa Fe.

twenty years. Boyd, then curator of Spanish Colonial art at the Museum of International Folk Art of the Museum of New Mexico, performed limited test excavations at these sites to examine the range of Hispanic domestic artifacts.

Since the early 1970s, the number of archaeological excavations in Santa Fe has increased. Downtown and suburban development has been responsible for much of this research. Unfortunately, few of the excavation projects have had the funds necessary to completely analyze the materials recovered from the sites or to report these finds.

What was it about the location of Santa Fe that made it desirable to Pueblo Indians from the tenth to the fourteenth centuries and then, in the early decades of the fifteenth century, caused them to abandon their settlements here?

The initial Pueblo occupation in Santa Fe appears to date from the Late Developmental period. An early occupation level of Pindi Pueblo, on the west side of the Santa Fe River in Agua Fria; the Arroyo Negro site, in south Santa Fe; and a number of sites in the vicinity of Fort Marcy and the Hillside neighborhood have yielded evidence of Late Developmental pithouses and associated artifacts. The Arroyo Negro site covers an extensive area and may represent an important village of the mid-eleventh century.

Some of the most intriguing Developmental archaeological sites are located in the Tesuque and Cerrillos areas. The Pojoaque Grant site is an extensive settlement of small adobe and jacal houses and a great kiva located near the pueblos of Pojoaque and Tesuque. The site shows Chacoan influence in architecture and associated pottery types, traditionally attributed to migrants from Chaco Canyon who began to move into the Rio Grande area as cultural and environmental conditions in Chaco Canyon changed, and who may have occupied this settlement.

Recent work at the Bronze Trail site group, near Cerrillos, and intensive studies at Chaco Canyon have suggested alternative explanations for the apparent Chaco influences in the northern Rio Grande during the Developmental period. The Bronze Trail site group, the Pojoaque Grant site, and the Arroyo Negro site were occupied in the mid-eleventh century, when the influence of Chaco throughout the Southwest was at its greatest. All these sites contain pottery that was produced in the Chaco-Mount Taylor area or influenced by Chacoan ceramic designs. The Bronze Trail site group differs from the Pojoaque and Cerrillos sites in that it appears to lack houses and to have been used solely for mining and processing turquoise from the famous Cerrillos turquoise mines. Turquoise found in sites in the Mount Taylor area and in Chaco Canyon appears to come from the Cerrillos mines. It seems likely that the Chaco influence observed in northern Rio Grande Developmental sites is related to an

Storage jars under excavation at the Pojoaque Grant site.

exchange of Cerrillos turquoise for food or other natural resources, but the connection may have been ritual rather than material. With the limited evidence available, it can be argued either that Chaco migrants occupied these northern Rio Grande sites or that the local people were copying Chaco-like architectural details and pottery designs. Additional studies of Developmental sites in the Santa Fe area have much to contribute to our understanding of the complex social processes that were occurring throughout the Southwest in the tenth, eleventh, and twelfth centuries.

Coalition and Early Classic archaeological sites are the most impressive prehistoric resources in Santa Fe and the immediately adjacent villages. Pindi Pueblo, the adjacent Agua Fria School site, and Arroyo Hondo Pueblo are well-known Coalition sites in or near Santa Fe. Other archaeological remains from this period have been found in excavations in various parts of the city, including the vicinity of Fort Marcy and La Garita Hill and underlying the City Hall complex on Marcy Street.

Pindi is the Tewa word for turkey, so named for the abundance of turkey bones and droppings and the turkey-raising pens found during the excavation of the site. Pindi was constructed in at least three phases between about 1200 and 1350. Excavations revealed numerous rearrangments of the roomblocks, kivas, and outbuildings that constituted the Coalition-period occupation of the site; the final remodeling took place just before the abandonment of the site in 1350. Changes in ceramic technology seem to have accompanied many of the renovations of the site, perhaps indicating a period of intense economic or social change. Inhabitants of Pindi appear to have moved across the river to a pueblo now known as the School House site, where limited test excavations were conducted in 1988. The full extent and configuration of this prehistoric village are not yet known, but recovered potsherds point to possible relationships between the School House people and those living at other pueblos near Galisteo, Cieneguilla, and Arroyo Hondo. The pueblos of Pindi and School House may have been occupied contemporaneously in the mid-fourteenth century. Like Arroyo Hondo Pueblo, School House was abandoned in the early fifteenth century.

Cherie Scheick excavating a portion of the School House site, December 1988.

Ceremonial jar containing a shell necklace, excavated at Arroyo Hondo Pueblo in 1971.

Douglas W. Schwartz, 1972.

The School of American Research's Arroyo Hondo project, conducted in the 1970s under the direction of Douglas W. Schwartz, has provided stimulating information about past climate in the Santa Fe area and about the physical condition of the Pueblo population of Santa Fe in the fifteenth century. The pueblo of Arroyo Hondo was founded in about A.D. 1300, when the northern Rio Gránde population was settling into fewer, larger pueblos and beginning to use smaller tributary drainages of the Rio Grande proper. For about thirty years the village grew, and by about 1330 it had more than one thousand rooms in twenty-four houseblocks, surrounding ten plazas. Rainfall in the early fourteenth century was favorable to agriculture, native plant foods, and game. By 1335, however, Arroyo Hondo was in decline, and its Santa Fe contemporaries were also being abandoned. Much of Arroyo Hondo was dismantled systematically, and the entire site may have been abandoned for a time. The decline of the pueblo is dramatically visible in the high mortality rate among children under five and young adults, their skeletal remains clearly showing the ravages of malnutrition.

In the early 1370s, Arroyo Hondo began a second period of prosperity, and by 1400 or so the village consisted of nine roomblocks containing two hundred rooms, arranged around three plazas. This period of growth corresponds to another period of above-average rainfall. The second period of prosperity was over by 1410. A fire destroyed the pueblo in 1420. This event, coupled with a decimating drought between about 1415 and 1425, was no doubt responsible for the abandonment of Arroyo Hondo. Many other Classic sites in the northern Rio Grande were also abandoned at this time.

Historical Archaeology in Santa Fe

The Historic period in the northern Rio Grande is generally reckoned to begin with the contact between the Pueblos and the Vásquez de Coronado expedition of 1540; thus, the Historic period overlaps the end of the Classic period in the archaeological sequence. In Santa Fe, excavations of historic sites, largely occasioned by construction projects, are necessarily limited salvage

Aerial view of a portion of Arroyo Hondo Pueblo, 1971.

Objects excavated from the Palace of the Governors. *From left,* brass candle holder, unidentified, unidentified, double-barred cross, nail (?), needle.

Bandelier Black-on-cream jar.

projects. In most cases it has not been possible to recover more than a small fraction of the materials impacted by development.

The Santa Fe City Council recently passed an ordinance protecting archaeological resources within the city that are at least seventy-five years old. The council's unanimous vote of approval in the face of opposition from some developers was a significant gain for our community. Councilors and proponents who spoke in support of the ordinance emphasized the unique cultural history of Santa Fe and the importance of preserving the valuable information that has yet to be obtained from excavations in the city.

Historical archaeology has an important place in the history of Santa Fe. Much of our knowledge about seventeenth-century Santa Fe is drawn from eighteenth-century documents, earlier documentation having been destroyed during the Pueblo Revolt. Further, many aspects of daily life preserved in archival records are seldom recorded in official documents preserved in archives. The analysis of artifacts and food remains offers insight into Santa Fe's domestic life in much greater detail than is available from documentary sources alone. And when archaeological and historical investigations are combined, the details of daily life are placed in a larger cultural and historical context.

The plaza has been the central feature of European settlement in Santa Fe since 1610. Because of the longevity and intensity of land use around the plaza and as far north as the municipal office complex on Marcy Street, in some places more than ten feet of cultural stratigraphy underlie the street level. Within these deposits, which consist of structural debris, the bones of butchered animals, Puebloan pottery, and historic artifacts, exists a record of changes in diet, trade networks, and cultural practices during the course of Hispanic colonial and Anglo-American settlement.

In what is now the southwest corner of the patio of the Palace of the Governors, the Museum of New Mexico has reconstructed a well excavated by Marjorie Lambert in 1956. Lambert had hoped to be able to excavate a feature in the east part of the patio that she suspected was a domestic well dug some time around 1715. Museum officials were afraid that the well, described in colonial documents as 4 varas (about 11 feet) wide by 40 varas (almost 110 feet)

Marjorie F. Lambert and Bernie Valdez
excavating well in the patio of the palace,
1956.

deep, would, if opened, pose a hazard to visitors. Instead, they allowed Lambert to excavate a well in the southwest corner. The nails, bottles, and horseshoes recovered date the use of this well to the mid to late nineteenth century.

Archaeologists and historians have varied opinions about the size and extent of the seventeenth- and eighteenth-century plaza area. Some authors have suggested that it was twice as long, east to west, and twice as wide, north to south, as it is now. A number of excavations in the downtown area have offered evidence in support of or in opposition to this suggestion.

Excavations in the block now occupied by the First Interstate Bank building, between Washington and Lincoln avenues to the north of the Palace of the Governors, produced evidence of more than two hundred years of occupation in deposits less than four feet below the street level. At the lowest level of this excavation, archaeologists found eighteenth-century Pueblo pottery and deposits that seem to correlate with the mid-1760s location of gardens and corrals shown on a 1766-1768 map of Santa Fe by Joseph de Urrutia. Foundations of what may have been part of the 1791 presidio overlay the deposits. These walls were later incorporated into structures used for the commissary, carpenter's shop, and smithy of Fort Marcy. Ruins of Fort Marcy and underlying Spanish Colonial foundations were also found during the 1979 excavations of the addition to the Fine Arts Museum.

Test excavations in the Water Street parking lot failed to find any evidence that structures were built in this area until the late 1800s. The majority of the artifacts and architectural features revealed by the excavations showed that this property was used primarily for industrial purposes. Between 1882 and 1887, a lumber company occupied the site. From 1891 to the mid-1960s, Public Service Company of New Mexico had a power generating station on the property. The small number of Spanish Colonial artifacts and the absence of structural remains indicates that the project area was not a residential property in the seventeenth or eighteenth centuries, but farm land, as shown on the Urrutia map.

This excavation and one in the parking lot between Saint Francis Cathedral and La Fonda offer additional perspectives on the extent of the plaza in the Colonial period. The absence of substantial Colonial deposits in the Water Street excavations suggests that the plaza did not extend that far south. The presence of a deep deposit of Spanish Colonial trash in excavations in the La Fonda parking lot confirms that the plaza did extend at least as far as the cathedral. The excavations at La Fonda were not extensive enough, however, to determine whether this deposit was associated with Colonial houses, corrals, or garden areas. Neither excavation found evidence of the *muralla*, or wall, which some authors speculate was built around the plaza by Spanish colonists before or after the Pueblo Revolt or by the Pueblo Indians who occupied the plaza area before the Reconquest (1680–1696). This may support the argument made by others that only the *casas reales*, or the immediate vicinity of the palace, was walled.

The Palace of the Governors has had a complex history, as revealed by archaeological studies that have accompanied many of the renovations to this

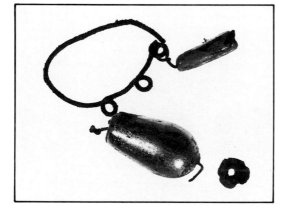

Earring excavated from the Palace of the Governors.

structure. Elsewhere in this volume, Carrie Forman Arnold traces its construction history. The excavations have yielded small amounts of jewelry, household objects of Spanish manufacture, and some personal items, but the bulk of material excavated has been comprised of animal bones, Puebloan pottery, and colorful Mexican majolica ceramics. Even within the palace, where one might expect to find evidence of how the wealthier residents of colonial Santa Fe lived, there is evidence of a rather Spartan life-style.

The plaza and the palace were not the only area of Spanish Colonial settlement. The ruins of La Garita, the Spanish Colonial fort built on the hill east of the Scottish Rite Temple, was once an important landmark in the folklore of Santa Fe. The ruins of the two adobe bastions of the fort were clearly visible as late as the 1920s. In 1954, portions of the little fortress-like structure were excavated by Bruce Ellis. The stone foundations showed that it was square, with pentagonal bastions on the northern and southern corners. At least three floor levels were revealed. Five pieces of rotted ponderosa pine were found, and tree-ring analysis of these timbers yielded dates of 1802 and 1805, closely coinciding with 1807 and 1808 documents that mentioned construction of a powder magazine, a granary, and a *sala de armas*, or arsenal. Beneath the lowest floor level of La Garita, archaeologists exposed the stone base of a *torreón* (defensive tower) that, on the basis of associated Pueblo pottery, they believe was built during the period of the Reconquest. The foundations of La Garita and the *torreón* had been dug into an earlier Indian pueblo on the hillside. Pottery associated with these ruins indicated a lengthy Pueblo occupation, ending in the Late Coalition or Early Classic period (ca. 1325–1350).

Along the Santa Fe River between Agua Fria and Cieneguilla are the remains of four of the ten Spanish and Mexican-period ranchos recorded by E. Boyd. The recent excavations at the Agua Fria School House site, mentioned above, produced pottery indicating a Spanish Colonial reoccupation of that area in the early to mid-eighteenth century. Other Colonial ranchos have been recorded in La Cienega. The artifacts recovered from rancho sites by Boyd, and from more recent tests at these sites performed under my direction and by David Snow, consist primarily of Pueblo-manufactured ceramics.

Fragment of a Pojoaque Polychrome *olla* showing unmistakable European influence. Excavated at a site near La Cieneguilla by E. Boyd and David Snow.

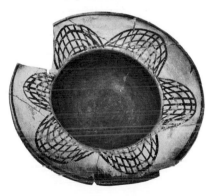

Tewa Polychrome soup bowl.

La Garita ruins, circa 1910.

To the lay person, archaeologists must seem to have an inexplainable fascination with potsherds. These Colonial sites are a good illustration of the importance of pottery. The ceramics from the Santa Fe River ranchos, as well as in the deposits dating to the Colonial occupation of the plaza, demonstrate the little-documented economic interdependence of Hispanic and Pueblo communities in seventeenth- and eighteenth-century Santa Fe. In the absence of an adequate supply of imports from Mexico, Hispanics turned to the Pueblos for many of their cooking pots and tablewares. In the Historic period, new Pueblo vessel forms such as the comal and rimmed soup bowl, new Pueblo design elements clearly derived from the Spaniards, and Mexican majolica patterns are found in the pottery recovered from Pueblo and Hispanic archaeological sites.

Ceramics continue to mark changes in trade practices in nineteenth-century archaeological deposits. The Santa Fe Trail, and later the railroad, brought new merchandise to the people of Santa Fe, introducing a wider variety of European ceramics, mass-produced glass, metal items, and other material goods. These changes are evident in the archaeological deposits of sites occupied after the opening of the Santa Fe Trail such as the foundations of the house underlying the Eldorado Hotel (formerly the Big Jo Hardware store) and some of the Santa Fe River ranchos investigated by this author. One of the most striking changes is the incorporation of American- and European-made ceramics into assemblages that, during the Spanish Colonial period, had consisted mainly of Pueblo-made ceramics. This change to mass-produced ceramic wares reflects a shift from the local exchange networks that had existed between and among Pueblo and Hispanic communities in Colonial times to the cash-based economy that began in New Mexico in the Mexican period and widened in the American period.

The Santa Fe Trail itself has been identified by archaeological surveys. Short segments of deeply rutted tracks found near the junction of the Old Las Vegas Highway and Old Pecos Trail are thought to be the remains of the trail.

Elsewhere in the city, archaeologists have recorded the remains of a brewery that flourished on Santa Fe's east side from about 1868 to 1896. They have also recorded the remains of acequias that served the farmsteads lining the Santa Fe River until not so long ago. Change is an inevitable part of the landscape, and archaeology is an essential tool for learning about the past and for preserving this knowledge for the future.

Visitors to Santa Fe are inspired by the multiethnic culture of the northern Rio Grande. Here the diversity of Native American, Hispanic, and Anglo-American cultures blends in distinctive regional foods, architectural styles, language, and life-styles. The archaeological resources of the northern Rio Grande are, like a fossil bed, a chronicle of the accommodations that these cultures have made between and among themselves. As we dig "down under" Santa Fe, we expand our understanding of the complex processes of cultural exchange and cultural change that have shaped this southwestern community over at least fourteen hundred years of human occupation.

Don Pedro de Peralta surveying the site for Santa Fe in 1610. Painting by Roy Grinnell. Courtesy, Sunwest Bank of Santa Fe.

The Peralta-Ordóñez Affair and the Founding of Santa Fe

JOSEPH P. SÁNCHEZ

Between 1610 and 1615, in the newly founded villa of Santa Fe, a dramatic story evolved that would affect its history throughout most of the seventeenth century. The theme of this story, ecclesiastical resistance to civil control, originated with two powerful adversaries—Governor Pedro de Peralta, who founded La Villa Real de Santa Fe in 1610, and Friar Isidro Ordóñez. It was a conflict that would continue to plague the government of the province until 1680.

The founding of Santa Fe on the north bank of the Rio Santa Fe occurred twelve years after Spanish frontiersmen led by Juan de Oñate had settled La Provincia de Nuevo Mexico at San Juan de los Caballeros, on the upper Rio Grande. By 1600, the Spaniards had moved downstream to a new capital at San Gabriel, at the confluence of the Rio Chama and the Rio Grande. Sometime in the spring of 1610, Governor Peralta and several settlers from San Gabriel selected a site on the southern end of the Sangre de Cristo Mountains, and in accordance with the viceregal instructions of March 30, 1609, marked out "six *vecindades* [districts] for the villa and a square block for government buildings [*casas reales*, later known as the Palace of the Governors] and other public works."

After ordering that the villa be built on the new site, Peralta allowed the residents to elect four *regidores* (councilmen), two of whom were chosen as *alcaldes ordinarios* (judges) to hear civil and criminal cases within the boundary of the villa for "five leagues around." Of the two judges, one would serve

Santa Fe's "oldest house," on East De Vargas Street.

as *justicia mayor* (senior judge) of the villa. Accordingly, the incumbent councilmen would annually elect the *alcaldes* and councilmen who were to succeed them.

To ensure the development of the villa, Peralta empowered the *alcaldes* and councilmen for a period of thirty years to "apportion to each resident two lots for house and garden, two contiguous fields for vegetable gardens, two others for vineyards and olive groves, and in addition four *caballerías* [about 133 acres] of land; and for irrigation, the necessary water." In return for the grant, the settlers were obligated to establish residency for ten consecutive years without absenting themselves, under penalty of losing everything. Permission would be required from the *cabildo* (town council) for absences of more than four months, or one's grant could be assigned to someone else. Peralta, moreover, instructed the *cabildo* to elect an *alguacil* (sheriff) and a notary. Next, Peralta clarified the role of the *cabildo* regarding the creation of ordinances for the villa and the province. He told them that every conciliar action would be subject to his confirmation in conformity with the Laws of the Indies.

Much of the villa was built between 1610 and 1612. Later additions formed a large government-military compound containing arsenals, offices, a jail, a chapel, and the governor's residence and offices. The outer walls of adjoining structures, which also served as the defensive walls of the compound, enclosed two interior plazas whose dwellings were three and four stories high. Throughout its early history, the villa had only one gate, with a defensive trench in front of it. Despite its military character, Santa Fe was inhabited by farmers, artisans, traders, missionaries, and other frontiersmen and their Indian servants.

All roads in the province led to Santa Fe. The fortified town posted sentries in each of its four towers, two on the south wall and two on the north side of the quadrangle, who could watch the roads leading to the villa. They could see the Jemez Mountains to the west, and to the southwest, a singular peak known as La Tetilla. It marked La Bajada, the descent on the Camino Real de Tierra Adentro (Royal Road of the Interior), which began in Mexico City, crossed the central Mexican plateau, passed the pueblos of the lower Rio

Detail of a 1656 French map of New Mexico showing the Rio Grande flowing to the Pacific Ocean.

Copy of a portion of the viceregal instructions of March 30, 1609.

Grande and La Cienega, and ended in Santa Fe. Other roads ran north from Santa Fe to Taos Pueblo, south to Galisteo, and southeast to Pecos.

Outside the enclosed plaza stood the homes of settlers, and on the southeast side, a Mexican Indian section called Barrio de Analco. *Analco* means "on the other side" in Nahuatl, referring to the other side of the Rio Santa Fe. Generally, Indian allies from Mexico who assisted missionaries or worked as servants to certain settlers resided there. Just south of Barrio de Analco were Las Milpas de San Miguel, the cultivated fields adjacent to the land of the chapel of San Miguel. The *milpas* were watered by the *acequia madre* (mother ditch), which was constructed to irrigate the fields south of the chapel of San Miguel. Before the Pueblo Revolt, Santa Fe's settlement does not appear to have extended southward beyond the *acequia madre*. On the north side of the villa, other fields had their attendant irrigation ditch.

The viceregal instructions of March 30, 1609, also advised Governor Peralta on the Indian policy for frontier New Mexico that had evolved since 1598. "No one shall have jurisdiction over the Indians except the governor or his lieutenant," wrote Viceroy Don Luis de Velasco. Regarding the *encomienda*, a grant to certain individuals to collect tribute from Indians, Peralta was permitted to make new grants if they did not interfere with those of the previous governor, Juan de Oñate. The orders to Peralta were explicit. Wrote Viceroy Velasco, "Inasmuch as it has been reported that the tribute levied on the natives is excessive, and that it is collected with much vexation and trouble to them, we charge the governor to take suitable measures in this matter, proceeding in such a way as to relieve and satisfy the royal conscience." The defense of Santa Fe and the province was the watchword of Peralta's Indian policy, as it would be for succeeding governors. "Under no circumstances," wrote the viceroy, "shall he give up the protection of the land and the colonists, but he shall try by peaceful means or by force to subdue the enemy or drive him out." Aside from military force, the pacification plan also enlisted the missionaries who already had been hard at work converting the Pueblo Indians to Christianity.

While Governor Peralta busied himself with establishing the villa, Friar Alonso de Peinado, Franciscan prelate of the New Mexico missions, supervised

Santo Domingo Pueblo.

the construction of a church for Santa Fe. Meanwhile, the settlers were content with a temporary church made of mud mortar and poles. In 1610 Friar Rosa Figueroa wrote that Peinado's church lasted a few years before it collapsed, whereupon the settlers had reverted to holding services in a makeshift church. There, noted Figueroa, the settlers and their servants gathered on Sundays and holy days of obligation in a wattled structure called a *xacalón* which also doubled as a *galerrón*, a granary. In 1627, under the watchful eye of Friar Alonso de Benavides, a new church called the *parroquia* was constructed.

Meantime, in 1610 Friar Peinado decided to establish the ecclesiastical headquarters for New Mexico at Santo Domingo Pueblo, south of Santa Fe. There, Franciscan prelates held their occasional chapter meetings and planned missionary activities throughout the seventeenth century. Once the civil and ecclesiastical capitals of the province had been established at Santa Fe and Santo Domingo, Governor Peralta and Prelate Peinado settled into an amicable administration of the province's temporal and spiritual needs. The halcyon days of 1610–1611, however, would not last long.

Spanish halberd.

Sometime in late summer of 1612, Friar Isidro Ordóñez arrived in Santo Domingo from Mexico City with twelve new missionary recruits. Before going to Santa Fe, he declared that he had orders to relieve Fray Peinado of his duties as prelate. Although the authenticity of Ordóñez's documents was questionable to Peinado, he accepted them as genuine. If they were not authentic, then the ambitious Ordóñez had deceived almost everyone in the province to gain control of the missions and force Governor Peralta to recognize him as the chief official of the province. Once at Santa Fe, Ordóñez presented Peralta with an order from the viceroy to direct his soldiers and settlers who so desired to leave New Mexico. To Peralta, the order was an incredible contradiction to his earlier instructions, which had authorized him to strengthen the area of Spanish occupation.

Everyone knew Friar Ordóñez's presence spelled trouble. When Governor Peralta heard Ordóñez had replaced Peinado, he was heard to exclaim, "Would to God the devil were coming instead of that friar!" The arrogant Ordóñez, who had served in New Mexico during the Oñate administration, was disliked by most of the friars as well. One of them, Friar Francisco Pérez Huerta, a notary, later examined Ordóñez's papers and declared them forgeries. The discovery of fraud came four years too late, however, for by that time Ordóñez had altered the character of the New Mexico province. His plan—to force the civil government out so that New Mexico would become exclusively a mission field—had almost succeeded.

The break between Friar Ordóñez and Governor Peralta occurred in May 1613, when the prelate interfered with the governor's privileged functions to collect the annual tribute of corn and blankets from the pueblos. As the tribute collectors bound for Taos went past Nambe Pueblo, north of Santa Fe, Ordóñez intercepted them, and under threat of excommunication, ordered them to return to the villa to hear mass, for the Feast of the Pentecost was at hand. Upon their return, Captain Pedro Ruiz, leader of the tribute collectors, reported to the governor, who ordered them back on the trail.

On Friday afternoon, May 24, 1613, Peralta and Ordóñez met in the plaza and publicly had words over the matter. Ordóñez had used the church calendar to countermand Peralta's authority, and the governor had responded by exercising his powers as captain-general to override his prelate's wishes. To strengthen his authority, Friar Ordóñez pulled out another surprise document from his robe. It named him as the agent of the Holy Office of the Inquisition for New Mexico. Angrily, he ordered the governor to bring back the tribute collectors under threat of excommunication. When Peralta refused, Ordóñez nailed a declaration of excommunication of the governor on the door of Santa Fe's church for all to read.

The settlers of the villa were in shock. They urged Peralta to seek absolution, but he refused. Friends and friars attempted to reconcile the two adversaries, but to no avail. One of the priests, Friar Luis Tirado, offered to absolve Peralta in the secrecy of the church so that he could be spared the humiliation of the ceremony before his peers, but he refused to do so on principle. Finally, under a truce the two men met, and in an abbreviated ceremony, Ordóñez absolved Peralta.

Before long trouble between the two men began anew. Everywhere Ordóñez looked, he found reason to criticize Peralta. Finally, Ordóñez met with Friar Tirado and hatched a plan to embarrass and discredit the governor in front of the citizenry of the villa. Closing the *convento* door, the two priests planned three Sunday masses, one of which was to be a main mass for captains and town officials. On Sunday Ordóñez and Tirado watched as the church filled with local dignitaries. Peralta's servants set the governor's chair on its platform in anticipation of his arrival. Suddenly, as the shocked congregation looked on, Friar Tirado stormed from the sacristy and ordered the chair thrown out of the church. When the governor arrived, he calmly ordered his chair placed immediately inside the rear of the church. While his political subordinates, nervous over the insult, sat toward the front of the church, friars Ordóñez and Tirado prayed the mass.

After Friar Tirado had read the gospel and was seated, Friar Ordóñez ascended the pulpit and delivered an impassioned homily against the governor,

Black wool embroidered manta (48" × 54") from Acoma Pueblo, made between about 1850 and 1860. Blankets of this nature were standard tribute items paid by the Pueblo Indians to the Spaniards in the seventeenth century.

Petroglyph of early Franciscan, south of Santa Fe.

much of it scandalous. Ordóñez claimed that his powers, granted through a papal concession, superseded those of the governor. He alone had the power to arrest, cast in chains, and punish anyone whom he considered an enemy of the church in New Mexico. "What I have told you," said Ordóñez, "I say for the benefit of a certain person who is listening to me who perhaps raises his eyebrows."

The congregation sat motionless. The ejection of the governor's chair, his presence at the rear of the church, and Ordóñez's stirring speech against Peralta's gubernatorial powers had made an indelible impression on those present. As soon as mass had finished, the villa was abuzz with new rumors of the friction between their governor and prelate.

That week a new confrontation occurred that permanently changed the political nature of colonial Santa Fe. The crisis reached a peak when Peralta heard that Ordóñez had called all his friars from the neighboring missions to the villa to arrest him for obstructing the business of the church. Previously, the two men had clashed over the collection of church tithes. One of Peralta's men-at-arms was also Ordóñez's syndic, a civilian representative of the church whose chief duty was to collect tithes. The governor ruled that the man's military duties came first, and, given the conflict of interest, the soldier could not fulfill his ecclesiastical obligations to collect the tithes. Ordóñez looked upon Peralta's decision as an offense against the church. A showdown was at hand, and Peralta decided to strike first.

Showdown at Morning Mass

On Tuesday morning, July 9, 1613, Peralta called upon loyal frontiersmen to grab their guns and meet at his quarters in the *casas reales*. When all had arrived, he explained that Ordóñez planned to arrest him and asked them to join him in ousting the friar from Santa Fe. After the meeting they followed him to the *convento* of the Santa Fe church.

Having watched the early morning commotion in the plaza from behind the *convento* walls, the priests warned their prelate. As Peralta's men walked across the plaza toward the *convento*, their wives, some of whom were crying lest Ordóñez excommunicate their husbands, entered the church for morning mass. Meanwhile, Ordóñez had entered the sanctuary, stood at the altar, and turned his gaze on Doña Lucía, wife of Bartolomé Romero, a Peralta supporter. "Shut up," he told the weeping woman, as Friar Pérez Huerta later wrote, "words that today still ring in the church." Calmly, Ordóñez began the mass.

Outside, near the *portería* (*convento* gate), Friar Huerta watched as Peralta and his men came toward him. As the noisy frontiersmen approached, the friars retreated to the patio of the *convento*. Then the governor, wearing a coat of chain mail, armed with a sword in his belt, and carrying a pistolet (pocket pistol) in his hand, entered the *portería* with his men.

Having finished mass, Ordóñez, aware of the governor's purpose, grabbed a wooden cane and went out to face him. Immediately, Peralta ordered Ordóñez to return to his ecclesiastical headquarters at Santo Domingo Pueblo. The two men exchanged curses. Raising his pistolet, Peralta ordered his soldiers to enter the room and confiscate all weapons they could find. Ordóñez threatened to excommunicate them all, and Peralta countered with a threat to arrest the prelate. A scuffle ensued. Peralta grabbed Ordóñez's cape, and the friar slapped away his hand. Other priests moved in to defend their prelate. Friar Tirado took a sword from one of the soldiers and thrust it at Peralta, ripping his cape. While Ordóñez tried to hit the governor with his cane, Peralta raised his pistolet, but someone grabbed him by the wrist and the gun went off. The loud noise made by the discharging pistolet and the pungent smoke which filled the room brought everyone to a standstill. Friar Pedraza fell to the floor; he had been shot. Luckily, he had only been superficially wounded, but the shocking sight of a priest lying in pain on the floor cast a different character on the governor's actions. Slowly, Peralta's followers began to drift out of the room and away from him.

Outside, women were crying. The fight was over. That afternoon, before leaving for Santo Domingo, Ordóñez again posted a notice of excommunication for Governor Peralta and certain of his followers.

Friar Ordóñez called a meeting of all friars at Santo Domingo to determine their course of action. Four days later, he returned to Santa Fe hoping to persuade the settlers to arrest the governor on charges of attempted murder. He

Zia Pueblo, 1890.

was unsuccessful, for the settlers wanted no part of the scandalous behavior of their civil and ecclesiastical leaders. Ordóñez waited. He knew that sooner or later, Peralta would try to get a message out to Mexico City or go himself. The friars and their Indian friends watched the Camino Real from Santa Fe to see what the governor would do. Soon, some of the settlers joined Ordóñez at Santo Domingo, and a trap was set for Peralta.

The Fall of Peralta

A few weeks later, Peralta made his move and somehow got past Santo Domingo. Ordóñez vowed to track him down. Finally, at a camp near Isleta Pueblo, the friar and his self-appointed posse surrounded Peralta and his men and arrested them.

The governor and his men were taken to Sandia Pueblo and held as prisoners. Eventually, Peralta's men were released, but Peralta remained imprisoned until he escaped from his cell eight months later. Still shackled, Peralta crossed the rugged hill country east of Santo Domingo. After three days and two nights, he arrived in Santa Fe and took refuge at a friend's house. He was in poor health, for he had not eaten during the whole time of his escape, and he was so badly bruised by the shackle on one of his ankles that he could hardly walk. The freezing temperatures and snowfall of March 22, 1614, had further debilitated Peralta.

The next day, Palm Sunday, Ordóñez learned of Peralta's escape from Sandia. Immediately, he ordered a search of the villa. Peralta was found, dragged from his hideaway, put on a horse, and covered with a hide for his journey to Santo Domingo. There, Ordóñez assembled the Indians to show them that colonial justice applied to all. After making a public spectacle of Peralta, he returned the humiliated governor to his cell at Sandia Pueblo. He remained there until April 6, when he was transferred to a cell at Zia Pueblo.

Another year passed before news traveled up the Rio Grande that a new governor, Bernardino de Ceballos, had been appointed for New Mexico. Ceballos, a former admiral of the Spanish navy, arrived at Isleta, where he rested for two days before resuming his journey northward along the Camino Real. Before Ceballos reached Santo Domingo, a nervous Friar Ordóñez went out to meet him. Ceballos accorded the prelate small respect: "Are you the same *padre missionero* who represents himself as most powerful and exacting, whom I have met before?" The indignant Ceballos told him that he knew that his predecessor was held prisoner and that he would "release him and honor him . . . as a governor deserves." Ceballos was little impressed by Friar Ordóñez, but the prelate was not one to trifle with.

At Santo Domingo, Governor Ceballos was received by the pueblo amidst cheers and the ringing of church bells. Organ music poured out from inside the church as the Indian choir chanted prayers the friars had taught them. Ceballos entered the church and graciously listened to the choir. Shortly, the new governor was taken to his quarters in the *convento*, where he rested for two days before pushing on to Santa Fe.

Once at Santa Fe, Ceballos sent a letter to Peralta, still imprisoned at Zia, telling him that he regretted his absence and that he would bring him to the villa and honor him. Oddly, Peralta's release from Zia did not take place for another month, and then without the ceremonial reception Ceballos had promised him. Instead, within two weeks after his arrival, Ceballos began the *residencia*, the customary audit and review of Peralta's administration. Peralta's enemies did not miss the chance to testify against him. Ordóñez attended each session to intimidate pro-Peralta settlers into staying away from the proceedings, hoping that his presence would discourage any statements in favor of Peralta. His strategy worked, and all who testified were extremely careful of what they said concerning Peralta's relationship with Ordóñez. It was evident to Ceballos, however, that Ordóñez lacked inquisitorial authority and justification to arrest the former governor, or any governor for that matter.

The *residencia* continued into August. Each day of testimony worked against Peralta and his followers, who soon found that Governor Ceballos was not on their side. The historical record does not give a clue about Ceballos's change in allegiance other than to indicate that he demurred in his promise to honor Peralta. Perhaps Ceballos found more in common with the beguiling

Seal of the Mexican Inquisition.

Friar Ordóñez. In early November, Ceballos permitted Peralta to depart New Mexico—but not before friars Ordóñez and Tirado relieved him of some of his property.

Peralta was yet to suffer the final indignity. Once out of Santa Fe, past the pueblos of the Rio Abajo along the Camino Real, he took the route later called the Jornada del Muerto (journey of death). At a place called Agua del Perillo, a little northeast of El Paso, four soldiers sent by Ceballos and Ordóñez caught up with him and ransacked his cart for documents that might incriminate them. They found nothing. He had hidden his papers well. Sometime in the spring of 1615, Peralta arrived in Mexico City, and as soon as he could, reported to Spanish officials.

The Mexican Inquisition of 1615 pronounced against Ordóñez's pretensions, and on October 6, 1617, after two years of charges and countercharges, Friar Ordóñez was brought to Mexico City and reprimanded. Peralta was vindicated. But in many ways, Ordóñez had altered the course of New Mexico's history. From 1615 to 1680, Santa Fe continued to be the stage of troublesome and dramatic events, and almost every governor without exception suffered the test of ecclesiastical resistance to civil control.

Twelve Days in August

The Pueblo Revolt in Santa Fe

JOSEPH P. SÁNCHEZ

At dawn on August 10, 1680, curly-haired Pedro Hidalgo and Friar Juan Baptista Pio set out from La Villa de Santa Fe for mass at Tesuque Pueblo. They reached Tesuque at daylight and found it abandoned. Friar Pio decided to search for his congregation. Not far from the pueblo, he and his guard caught up with them near a ravine, which some of the Indians had already entered. Approaching them, Hidalgo noticed that the warriors were armed with lances, shields, bows, and arrows, and they were wearing war paint. Holding up a shield he had found along the way, Friar Pio walked toward them saying, "What is this . . . are you mad? Do not disturb yourselves; I will help you and die a thousand deaths for you."

The Spaniards tried to persuade them to return to the pueblo, but to no avail. The friar followed the Pueblos into the ravine, while Hidalgo, on horseback, rode over the ridge of it to intercept the Indians on the other side. Moments later, Hidalgo saw some warriors emerge from the mouth of the ravine. One of them, El Obi, carried the shield Friar Pio had taken into the ravine. Another warrior, Nicholas, painted with clay, had blood splattered on him. The Indians quickly grasped the reins of Hidalgo's horse and tried to pull him down, grabbing his sword and hat, but he managed to stay mounted. Spurring his horse down the hill, he broke away, dragging along those who clung to him. Arrows zipped past him as he made his escape. Riding hard, Hidalgo warned his fellow colonials on the farmlands leading to the villa that the Indians had taken up arms against the Spaniards. Hidalgo was the first to spread the alarm of the Pueblo Revolt.

Interpretation of the Pueblo Revolt by Parker Boyiddle.

Tesuque Pueblo.

The Pueblo Revolt of 1680 represented an accumulation of Indian resentments against a Spanish colonial occupation that had assumed total sovereignty over them. Long-standing grievances caused by an oppressive colonial economic system and Indian policy had worked to undermine the religious, political, and social traditions of the pueblos. Colonial-native relationships had not been exclusively antagonistic. In the eighty years since Juan de Oñate's founding of New Mexico, Spaniards and Indians had intermarried, and religious kinships such as *compadrazgo* (godparenting) had been established. Friendships and social associations had been formed among Spanish frontiersmen and their Indian counterparts. But such relationships were not enough to stifle Indian resentment against the injustices of colonialism.

Long-standing grievances were renewed by recent events, which were the immediate causes for the revolt. Soon after the Pueblo Revolt had begun, an Indian named Pedro García told Governor Antonio Otermín that the Tanos from Galisteo had planned to rebel "for more than twelve years . . . because they resented greatly that the friars and the Spaniards should deprive them of their idols, their dances, and their beliefs." At San Felipe Pueblo, other Indians told the governor that they had rebelled because of the ill treatment they had received from three Spaniards: Francisco Javier, Diego López Sambrano, and Luis Quintana. They complained that the three colonials often "beat them, took away what they had, and made them work without pay."

The colonials knew the history of such grievances and of several previous attempts by the Indians to liberate themselves from their Spanish lords. Red-haired Diego López Sambrano, a Santa Fean who was lucky to survive the rebellion with his wife and six children, said he had witnessed attempted revolts and punishments of Indian rebels "since the time of the government of don Fernando de Argüello (1644–1647), who hanged more than forty Indians." In 1650, a plot in which Pueblo Indians attempted to unite against the Spaniards had been discovered and quelled. Governor Hernando de Ugarte y la Concha had many Indians arrested from most of the pueblos in the province. After an investigation, nine leaders from Isleta, Alameda, San Felipe, Cochiti, and Jemez were found guilty and hanged. Others, recalled López, were "sold as slaves for ten years."

López remembered another rebellion on the Rio Abajo near Socorro during the administration of Governor Fernando de Villanueva (1665–1668), when the Piros "rebelled." One Piro named El Tanbulita had joined six Christian Indians and a band of Apaches in the "Sierra de Madalena," where they ambushed and killed six Spaniards. El Tanbulita and five others were captured and hanged, and several "others were sold and imprisoned," recalled López.

Soon after, one of the most serious of the rebellions was led by the Spanish-speaking Don Esteban Clemente, governor of the Tanos and Salinas pueblos, whom the "whole kingdom secretly obeyed." Clemente was extremely influential among Spaniards as well as Pueblos. He spoke several Indian tongues, and he was literate in Spanish. Organizing a "conspiracy which was general throughout the kingdom," said López, Clemente ordered the Christian Indians to drive all the Spanish horse herds in all of the jurisdictions to the sierras and leave the Spaniards afoot. The insurrection was to take place on the night of Holy Thursday. Then the Indians were to strike, reported López, "not leaving a single religious or Spaniard" alive. Clemente's plot was found out, and he was tried, convicted, and hanged while the Pueblos looked on helplessly. With Clemente gone, no one dared step forward to conspire against the Spaniards.

During the term of Governor Juan Francisco de Treviño (1675–1677), reported López, the Spaniards attempted to suppress Indian religious practices in New Mexico, claiming they "had continued their abuses and superstitions" long enough. López claimed that the natives "had bewitched the father preacher, Fray Andrés Durán," guardian of the *convento* of San Ildefonso, along with his brother and wife and an Indian interpreter named Francisco Guíter, "who had denounced the said sorcerers." Forty-seven Tewa Indians were arrested, four of whom admitted to the "witchcraft" worked against Friar Durán and his companions. The four, said López, were sentenced to death for the "above crimes and for other deaths which were proved against them." One was hanged at Nambe; another at San Felipe; a third *"hechicero"* (sorcerer)

Pueblo religious dance.

hanged himself while alone; and the fourth man was hanged at Jemez, remembered López.

The narrative of the 1675 "witch trial" did not end there. López explained how the execution and suicide of the four *hechiceros* and the detention of the remaining forty-three men had almost started a rebellion. Of the forty-three *hechiceros*, Governor Treviño ordered some released with a reprimand, and others "he condemned to lashings and imprisonment," recalled López. Among the prisoners was an angry headman known as Popé, who grew in resentment against the Spaniards.

Soon after the sentences were pronounced and the hangings had taken place, López recalled, "more than seventy Indians armed with *macanas* [clubs] and leather shields" entered the governor's office in the *casas reales* at Santa Fe. Filling two rooms, the warriors crowded together to hear the governor's response to their plea. As a sign of peace, the leaders presented him with an offering of "some eggs, chickens, tobacco, beans and some small deerskins." At first Governor Treviño refused the gifts, whereupon one of the Indians defiantly called out, "Leave them there if he does not want them." Wisely, the governor ordered Captain López to accept the gifts, and the natives got to the point of their visit. They asked the tough-minded colonial administrator to release the prisoners to them, requesting "that he should pardon them," and promising that "they would make amends." Treviño responded condescendingly: "Wait a while, children; I will give them to you and pardon them on condition that you forsake idolatry and iniquity." As a gesture of magnanimity, the governor gave them some woolen blankets and ordered the prisoners released to their pueblos. The Indians were satisfied and withdrew from his office.

A few days later, López saw some of the warriors who had pleaded for the prisoners' release. In a friendly way, López asked "why so many of your people came armed to see the governor." One of them replied, "We came determined to kill him if he did not give up the said prisoners, and on killing him, to kill the people of the Villa of Santa Fe as well." López learned that an ambuscade had been left in the nearby hills to support their escape. López asked where they would have gone, for the Apaches, who had intensified their raids against the pueblos and outlying Spanish farms, would have killed them in the sierras. The proud warriors gave him a chilling reply. "In order to defend the prisoners whom they asked for," wrote López, "they would have gone to the sierras even though the Apaches would kill them." That was how strongly they felt about colonial injustices.

Rebellion

The lessons of past attacks, conspiracies, and rebellions were not lost on Popé. Fleeing harrassment from Captain Francisco Javier, a tribute collector, early in 1680 Popé hid in one of the kivas at Taos Pueblo. There, he communicated with spirits and formulated his plan to drive the Spaniards from New Mexico. Pedro Naranjo, a Keres Indian from San Felipe Pueblo, later recounted what he knew of the already legendary Popé. "It happened in a kiva at the pueblo of Los Taos," swore Naranjo. "There appeared to the said Popé three figures...called Caudi, another Tilini and the other Tleume." In awe, Naranjo described how Popé "saw these figures emit fire from all the extremities of their bodies." They told him to make a cord of maguey fiber "and tie some knots in it which would signify the number of days that they must wait for the rebellion." The cord was passed from one pueblo to the next, each of which accepted the righteousness of the revolt. After delivering the mandate to rebel, exclaimed Naranjo, the three spirits "returned to the state of their antiquity."

Convinced that secrecy was of utmost importance, Popé ordered the death of his brother-in-law, Juan Bua, because he had threatened to tell the Spaniards of the plot. Bua, from San Juan Pueblo, was not alone in his misgivings concerning the chances for a successful rebellion against the Spaniards. Some Pueblos thought Popé's plan was insane and refused to support it. Others warned their Spanish friends and relatives to prepare for a general uprising. When it finally occurred, some Indians helped Spaniards escape, and others fled with them.

The rebellion began with full fury on August 10, 1680. At a gallop, Pedro Hidalgo, with a cut on his neck from his escape near Tesuque Pueblo, pushed

Kiva, Taos Pueblo.

Pueblo runners between Zia and Jemez, August 6, 1980, in the tricentennial celebration of the Pueblo Revolt.

his jaded horse into the Santa Fe plaza and told of the death of Friar Pio at the hands of heavily armed Pueblo warriors. Angrily, Governor Otermín convened a council of war. The day before, having received warnings of a possible rebellion, he had started an investigation and devised a plan of attack should an uprising occur. Now it was too late, for he had not had time to call together his frontier men-at-arms who lived in the outlying farms, ranches, and haciendas near Santa Fe, who had also been caught off guard. The rebellion had begun, and the slaughter of Spanish women, children, friars, and other colonial frontiersmen had already taken on horrific proportions.

Those who could in the Rio Arriba region, between Cochiti and Taos pueblos, fled to the walled safety of Santa Fe. Luckily, Otermín had completed repairs on the villa's walls and gates eight days before the rebellion. Settlers in the Rio Abajo, between Cochiti and Socorro, were likewise caught unprepared. Many of them fled to the friendly pueblo of Isleta. On the eastern fringes of the Pueblo world toward the Great Plains, as on the western side of the province from Zia and Jemez across to Zuni and Oraibi, Spanish friars and settlers fell victim to the rebels.

Within four hours of Pedro Hidalgo's midday ride to warn Santa Fe of the rebellion, Governor Otermín acted to determine the extent of the revolt and protect the surviving settlers and their servants. He sent messengers to warn all settlers in the outlying districts to defend themselves. Meanwhile, he ordered the official of the armory in the villa to distribute "harquebusses, blunderbusses, swords, daggers, shields, and munitions" to all males who had none to defend the capital. Sentries were stationed on the rooftops and at the gates of Santa Fe and even in the church "for the protection and custody of the holy sacrament and the images, sacred vessels, and things pertaining to divine worship," wrote Captain Javier, secretary of government and war.

Detailed preparations were made for an Indian assault. In the next few days, particular attention was given the defense of the *casas reales*, presently known as the Palace of the Governors. Javier reported that the *casas reales* were "to be immediately intrenched, embrasures are to be made in the walls, watches set, and harquebusiers stationed on the roofs. The two small pieces of ordnance will be placed in the doors of the *casas reales*, charged and mounted on their carriages, and aimed at the entrances of the streets."

Throughout the ordeal, Governor Otermín continued to receive accounts of harrowing episodes experienced by survivors who reached the villa. Among the first to report the rebellion were Nicolas Lucero and Antonio Gómez, who arrived in Santa Fe at five o'clock on the afternoon of August 10, 1680. They told the governor that they had been sent by the *alcalde mayor* of Taos to warn Santa Fe of the conspiracy. On the way there, they discovered that the *camino real* between Taos and the villa had been blocked by Pueblo warriors from Taos and Picuris—their first indication that a rebellion had begun. Forced to flee through the mountains, Lucero and Gómez reached La Cañada (Santa Cruz) and learned that the rebellion had spread to Santa Clara Pueblo, where two of eight men under Captain Francisco de Anaya had been killed as they were attending to a horse herd. Anaya and his men escaped, but herds of horses and cattle were driven off by mounted warriors from Santa Clara and Jemez pueblos. Lucero and Gómez also reported that the rebels had taken property from the fields and houses of Spaniards. Tight-lipped Otermín now knew that Taos, Picuris, La Cañada, Santa Clara, Tesuque, Jemez, and their vicinity were under attack.

To learn the extent of "the damages and atrocious murders" which had taken place, wrote Javier, Governor Otermín ordered his high-ranking officer, Maestre de Campo Francisco Gómez Robledo, and a squadron of soldiers to La Cañada to investigate the rebellion at Tesuque, Cuyamungue, Pojoaque, and the rest of the pueblos on the road to Taos. As soon as they had collected their gear and supplies, they departed Santa Fe that evening.

Having reconnoitered the Indian pueblos and Spanish settlements on the road to Taos, Gómez Robledo and his men returned to Santa Fe on August 12 and confirmed the extent of the rebellion in the north. He reported that all of the pueblos from Tesuque to San Juan were in rebellion. A large number of warriors were fortified at Santa Clara, others were in the mountains near Tesuque, and the rest were scattered along the *caminos reales*, the various roads leading to the pueblos, to intercept Spaniards who fled on them. He reported

Spanish coat of mail.

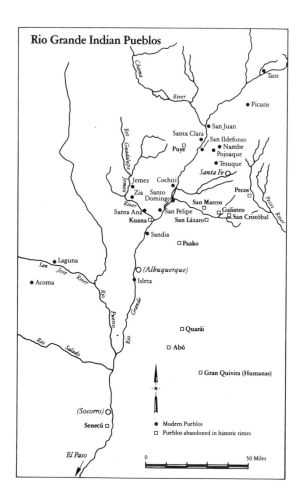

Rio Grande Indian Pueblos

Chama River

Taos

Picuris

Rio Guadalupe

San Juan
Santa Clara
San Ildefonso
Puyé • Nambe
Pojoaque
• Tesuque

Rio Jemez

Jemez Cochiti
Zia Santo
Domingo
San Marcos
Santa Ana
Kuana San Felipe
San Lázaro

Santa Fe

Pecos

Pecos River

Galisteo
San Cristóbal

Sandia

☐ Paako

• Laguna

San Jose River

• Acoma

Rio Puerco

Rio Grande

○ (Albuquerque)

• Isleta

☐ Quarái

☐ Abó

☐ Gran Quivira (Humanas)

Rio Salado

—N—

(Socorro) ○
Senecú ☐

• Modern Pueblos
☐ Pueblos abandoned in historic times

El Paso

0   50 Miles

that he had learned of the deaths of several friars and that many settlers had been killed at Pojoaque, Santa Clara, Nambe, and the outlying haciendas in the area. He also informed Otermín that many other Spaniards had been taken captive by the rebels.

Throughout the next few days, Otermín heard from the rest of his scouts whom he had sent out to assess the revolt in the Rio Arriba. From friendly Indians and captive rebels, the Spaniards learned that in a line south and west from Pecos to La Cienega by way of the Galisteo Basin, the Pueblos had rebelled and killed their Franciscan ministers as well as many settlers. Indeed, the picture looked grim for the settlers in Santa Fe, who now found themselves cut off from all routes of escape, for the rebels controlled all roads leading to the villa. The Spanish colonial capital seemed isolated and doomed.

From all the reports he had received, Otermín feared the imminent destruction of Santa Fe. He recommended that Friar Francisco Gómez de la Cadena, guardian of the church in the villa, consume the Holy Eucharist, take down the images and statuary, remove all sacred vessels and other religious paraphernalia for safekeeping in the *casas reales*, and close the church. Realizing the province had been lost, Otermín sent messengers through the rebel-held countryside to seek all survivors and bring them and whatever herds they could to the fortified villa.

Despite the onslaught, large numbers of Spaniards had been able to group together for common defense against the rebels and managed to stay alive. At Los Cerrillos, Sargento Mayor Bernabé Márquez and his men had been able to hold out, but they would not be able to do so for much longer. Otermín sent a small squadron to break the siege at Márquez's hacienda and escort the survivors to Santa Fe. Similarly, messengers reached Captain Luis Quintana and the besieged settlers at La Cañada, urging them to fight their way to the villa. Although the initial blow of the revolt had been devastating, through his scouts and messengers Otermín was able to account for various strongholds of Spanish settlers and summon them to the capital for their mutual protection.

Oddly, no word from the Rio Abajo had yet reached Otermín. Unknown to him, the three messengers he had sent to Lieutenant General Alonso García, in command of forces on the Rio Abajo, had all been killed. García and his settlers were under heavy attack between the pueblos of Alameda and Cochiti and were unable to get past the latter to assist Santa Fe. Deceived by the rebels that Santa Fe had fallen and that no one had survived, and realizing the extent of destruction in the Rio Abajo, García began to believe them. Likewise, Otermín thought that García and his settlers had been wiped out. The message to García was in the hands of the Pueblo warriors, who sensed victory. They had succeeded in splitting the Spanish command in New Mexico into two groups: one in Santa Fe, the other at Isleta.

The Siege of Santa Fe

Because the Pueblos first sought to control the countryside, the Spaniards had time to pull in survivors from their outlying strongholds. Two Christian Indians whom Otermín had sent with a message to García returned with the shattering news that the road to the Rio Abajo was held by the rebels, and five hundred Indians from Pecos, Galisteo, La Cienega, and other pueblos were on their way to attack Santa Fe. Shouting "God and Santa María are dead!" the rebel warriors had begun their march on Santa Fe with one aim: to kill the governor, the priests, and all the settlers.

The situation appeared even more ominous yet, when the Spaniards learned that the Apaches, motivated by revenge, had joined the pueblo rebels. Their grievances, although historical in nature, were sparked by a more recent event. Shortly before the general uprising, Captain Javier and a group of frontiersmen had seized a number of Apaches trading at Pecos Pueblo under a promise of safe conduct. Some were kept as slaves, and others were sent to Parral, in southern Chihuahua, to be sold in slavery. The Apaches were outraged, as were the Pecos, who feared reprisal from them and other Plains tribes. More importantly, the Pecos had depended on trade with the Apaches.

On the morning of August 13, Spanish sentries at Santa Fe spotted a host of rebel Indians in the fields of maize near San Miguel Church. Shortly, another group of warriors took Barrio de Analco and sacked the houses of Christian

De Vargas Street and San Miguel Church.

Mexican Indians. The besieged colonials recognized one of the Pueblo leaders, a man called Juan, a Tanoan from Galisteo. Wearing a sash of red taffeta from a missal and armed with a harquebus, a sword, a dagger, and a protective leather jacket, Juan approached the gates of Santa Fe on horseback to give Governor Otermín a message under a sign of truce. After some discussion, he was persuaded to enter the plaza to speak to the governor. Juan confirmed that all deaths and reports of destruction reported previously to the governor were true. He told him that the rebel army was on its way to offer the Spaniards the choice of one of two crosses, one red, the other white. The red cross meant continued war; the white cross, that the Spaniards would abandon the province.

Otermín responded that the Spaniards did not seek war and that the Indians could never cease to be Christians or forsake Spanish sovereignty. If they laid down their arms, Otermín said sternly, he would pardon the crimes they had committed. He admonished Juan and the rebels for what they had done, and he reiterated his demand that they disarm quietly. Nonplussed, Juan wheeled his horse around and left the plaza.

When Juan returned to Barrio de Analco, he told his warriors of the governor's response. Amidst sounding trumpets and shouts, they ridiculed the governor. Then, ringing the bells of the hermitage of San Miguel, they set fire to the small church and ransacked the houses near the walls of Santa Fe.

Meanwhile, Otermín, on the advice of his council of war, ordered an attack on the rebels before they could be reinforced by those whom Juan said were coming with the red and white crosses. As the Spanish soldiers left the gates, they were spotted by some other Indians, who swiftly fell upon them. Seeing that his men needed help, Otermín arrived with reinforcements to drive the Indians off. Then the Spaniards turned on the rebels who had set fire to San Miguel. They rushed the houses and killed many of the rebels in a fight that lasted most of the afternoon. Although many of the Spaniards were wounded, they were able to take back small herds of animals and some weapons to the villa.

Just as the Spaniards set fire to the houses so the rebels would not be able to use them, a large army of Taos and Picuris Indians attacked the villa from the other side, forcing Otermín to turn his attack against them. They were able to hold their positions, however. By dark the rebels had captured a number of houses behind the *casas reales* and set fire to the church, which Friar Gómez de la Cadena had abandoned earlier. Also, the Taos and Picuris bands had captured the cultivated fields and a few herds of cattle and sheep. The desperate colonials realized that part of their food supply had been lost to the enemy.

The siege of Santa Fe lasted nine days. Short of fodder and unable to spare water for their livestock, the colonials, who numbered about a thousand, let a number of their animals die. Worse still, the rebels cut off the water supply to the plaza and the *casas reales*. After two days without water, the colonials had to make a decision. Addressing the demoralized Spaniards in the plaza, Governor Otermín explained that their position was untenable and offered them their only alternative. Even if only a few of them should survive, they would have to fight their way out. It would be better to die fighting, he told them, than to die slowly of hunger and thirst, fearfully cooped up in the *casas reales* with the stench of the dead animals. Not only had the Spaniards lost control of the fields and water supply, but the rebels had actually captured a corner of the plaza and boldly lodged within the villa. By attacking at dawn, Otermín reasoned that they at least had a chance to escape.

The Battle of Santa Fe

At sunrise on August 20, 1680, the governor advanced with a small force of hand-picked veterans. Taken by surprise, the rebels were routed with great losses. By eleven o'clock, the siege had been broken. The Spaniards claimed to have slain three hundred rebels and put the rest of the Indian army to flight. Forty-seven rebels were captured, interrogated, and executed. The Spanish attack, bold as it appeared, was an act of desperation, for the rebels had numbered over 1,500 warriors.

After the battle, the Spaniards warily came out of the *casas reales*, leading the surviving livestock from the rooms where they had been kept for protection to the ruined fields to feed and water them. People and animals alike

The Acequia Madre, circa 1915. This irrigation ditch, which is still maintained, may date to Santa Fe's earliest decades.

had a chance to regain their strength. When the Spaniards saw their burnt homes, their ruined fields, and their desecrated church and hermitage, any hopes they may have had of remaining in Santa Fe were dashed.

Governor Otermín called a council of war to determine their course of action. Officers, soldiers, and priests filled the plaza. The priests, led by Friar Gómez de la Cadena, requested that Santa Fe be abandoned, for it would be impossible to hold it. Otermín's officers stated that the safety of the people, horses, and cattle could not be guaranteed if they remained in the gutted town. They had best leave before the rebels recovered from their setback.

On August 21, 1680, Otermín ordered that all clothing and livestock be divided among the defenders and their families and servants. Then an affidavit was signed to certify that Santa Fe had been abandoned after the council of war had collectively decided to rendezvous with Alonso García at Isleta. There, they

The front of the Palace of the Governors, circa 1920. Original construction of the palace dates to 1610.

would make a stand against the rebels. Marching in full military formation, more than one thousand men, women, and children departed Santa Fe. Otermín, who had been wounded twice, led his settlers southward on the Camino Real, which eighty-two years earlier had brought the Spaniards to New Mexico. Arriving at Isleta, they found the pueblo abandoned, for García had already retreated toward El Paso.

For more than a year, Otermín planned to reconquer the province. During the winter of 1681–1682, he led an expedition north to evaluate the destruction by the rebels. They reached Cochiti. In February 1682, suffering from his wounds and complaining of continuous headaches and eye problems, Otermín asked to be temporarily relieved to travel to Parral, Chihuahua, for treatment. His request was denied. In 1683 his gubernatorial term ended, and he rode out of El Paso as quietly as he had ridden into New Mexico.

Looking back on the Pueblo Revolt, colonial officials declared that the loss of New Mexico had tarnished Spanish pride. That pride had to be restored. Aside from the loss of the province, 21 clergymen and 380 settlers had been killed, and an undetermined number of colonists had been left behind as captives of the rebels. For the next twelve years, however, the Spaniards' principal accomplishment would be the establishment of El Paso.

The rebel Indians had also sustained significant losses during the revolt. Spanish accounts indicate that large numbers of warriors were killed and wounded. But for the Pueblos, the blow that had been delivered against a colonialism won by their subjugation and maintained by military superiority was worth the Pyrrhic victory. The fall of Santa Fe signaled the end of the first phase of Spanish colonial control of New Mexico. Twelve years later, after several attempts to regain the province, Governor Diego de Vargas led the army of the Reconquest from El Paso and once again took Santa Fe and New Mexico for Spain.

By Force of Arms

Vargas and the Spanish Restoration of Santa Fe

JOHN L. KESSELL

To Don Diego de Vargas, proud son of the illustrious house of Vargas of Madrid and twenty-year veteran of the royal service in the Indies, Santa Fe was a paradox. The mudbuilt capital of a poor kingdom—in Vargas's words, "last on earth and remote beyond compare"—Santa Fe had been lost to the rebellious Pueblo Indians for a dozen years, from 1680 to 1692. It offered him the promise of reconquest. And it became his prison. He loathed the place.

As reward for his heroic restoration of Santa Fe to the Spanish Crown in the early 1690s, Vargas expected promotion to Manila, Santiago de Guatemala, or Havana. But circumstances entrapped him. He aspired to improve his post, to escape what he termed the *zozobra*, the wrenching anguish, brought on by "the adversities and perils of that government of New Mexico." Yet, in 1704, when death overtook him, they buried Diego de Vargas in Santa Fe.

Today, we have more questions than answers about Santa Fe's physical appearance at the time of Vargas. What did the Indian pueblo superimposed on the former Spanish government buildings look like in 1692? What form had the villa taken by 1697, when Don Diego reluctantly surrendered authority to his successor? Where did the "parish church" stand in 1704? We do not even know at present the site of Diego de Vargas's grave.

A strutting aristocrat, the forty-seven-year-old Vargas acceded to the governorship of New Mexico in exile on February 22, 1691, at miserable, unkempt El Paso. He proved decisive, fearless, and vain. Described twenty years earlier, on the eve of his departure from Madrid, as a young nobleman of aver-

Don Diego de Vargas Zapata y Luján Ponce de León.

Spanish petroglyph at El Morro, New Mexico. "Gen. Don Diego de Vargas was here, who conquered all New Mexico for our Holy Faith and the Royal Crown, at his own expense, in the year 1692."

age stature, straight hair, and broad face, Don Diego had a distinguishing feature. He could not pronounce certain words correctly. He lisped.

Appointed to the New Mexico post for his outstanding record in two mining districts of New Spain and an appropriate payment to the Crown, Vargas enjoyed the full confidence of the viceroy in Mexico City, the Conde de Galve, a personal acquaintance. Galve's grand design to expand and defend the borderlands of New Spain encompassed the explorations of Jesuit Father Eusebio Francisco Kino on the Sonora-Arizona frontier, west of New Mexico, and the occupation of east Texas and the Gulf Coast to thwart French colonization of Louisiana. Restoration of New Mexico, as a buffer to safeguard the silver mines of northern New Spain, was crucial to the plan.

The lightning first round in 1680 of the Pueblo-Spanish War, which saw the Spaniards driven from the colony to wretched exile in the El Paso district, had not been avenged. During the second round, an ill-advised attempt at reconquest in 1681 failed ingloriously. More recently, two of Vargas's predecessors had led forays up the Rio Grande, resulting in bloody Spanish victories at the pueblos of Santa Ana in 1688 and Zia in 1689.

The next round of the Pueblo-Spanish War was up to Vargas. The new governor planned a two-stage reconquest: first, a military reconnaissance to repossess the pueblos, by force of arms if necessary, and then a larger colonizing expedition to reoccupy Santa Fe and the former kingdom of New Mexico.

Frustrated for a year and a half by problems of supply, recruiting, Apache warfare to the west, repair of the diversion dam at El Paso, and a hundred other details, Don Diego delayed publicly proclaiming the first expedition until the feast day of St. Lawrence—August 10, 1692, the twelfth anniversary of the Pueblo Revolt. Then, he moved with dispatch.

Ritual Repossession, September 13, 1692

In the early morning darkness of Saturday, September 13, Vargas cautiously led a slender column of forty mounted soldiers, ten armed citizens, fifty Indian auxiliaries, and two blue-robed Franciscan friars through the fields adjoining the plaza of the former Spanish capital. No one was to open fire, on pain of death, unless Don Diego unsheathed his sword.

North of the plaza loomed the massive pueblo and stronghold that the Indian occupants—mostly Tanos from the Galisteo Basin and some Tewas—had built over the top of the rambling old governor's "palace" and *casas reales*. The Spaniards' cry in unison, "Glory to the Blessed Sacrament of the Altar!" sent the Indians inside scurrying to the parapets.

With the aid of Spaniards who knew the native language, Vargas called out that he had come in peace to pardon them and accept their renewed obedience to God and king. The defenders could just make out the cross and the banner of the Blessed Virgin as the first thin light of morning shone over the mountains to the east. They were defiant. At the sound of the Spaniards' trumpet and drum, they began shouting obscenities.

Vargas, dividing his small force to surround the stronghold, stationed himself before the main gate and tried to negotiate. Armed natives from other pueblos gathered on the hills nearby. The grimly determined Spaniard now ordered the ditch supplying water to the stronghold cut and a small cannon and a mortar brought up.

A less decisive commander might have withdrawn. Vargas relied instead on extraordinary boldness and personal diplomacy to exploit the Indians' disunity. Narrowly averting battle, he won the day. As the native leaders came out to make peace, Don Diego dismounted to embrace them. The anxious confrontation had lasted from four in the morning until late that afternoon.

Next day, in the first of two enclosed patios of the high, multistoried stronghold at Santa Fe—and later in most of the other pueblos of the kingdom—Diego de Vargas, resplendent in European court dress, proclaimed the ceremonial repossession before hundreds of wary Pueblo Indians. The Franciscans then absolved the Indians of their apostasy, celebrated the Mass, and baptized the dozens of children born since 1680. Vargas stood as godfather to daughters and sons of Pueblo leaders, thereby, in Roman Catholic terms, binding the latter to him as *compadres*.

Remnants of a rosary found in the graveyard of the church (circa 1700) at Pecos National Monument.

Statue of Nuestra Señora del Rosario, known as La Conquistadora.

Halfway through his symbolic reconquest, an exultant Don Diego wrote to the viceroy from Santa Fe, enclosing a copy of his campaign journal to date, a chronicle of hardship and heroics. The same day, October 16, he penned a letter to his son-in-law in Madrid, Don Ignacio López de Zárate, a well-placed royal bureaucrat. He wanted to make certain the king learned promptly of "such a triumph and glory." Surely his majesty would wish to reward him appropriately. "I therefore give him the news of this conquest, of the pueblos and districts I have restored to his royal crown, and the number of people baptized."

Conveyed by fast courier to Mexico City, the news set off a grand celebration. The celebrators, including the Conde de Galve, seemed not to care that this was no more than a ceremonial reconquest. By Christmas of 1692, Diego de Vargas and his weary force would be back in El Paso, but at the time no one could foresee the desperate clashes to come.

Even today, despite our historical vantage, we tend to forget what happened next. By commemorating only the "bloodless" reconquest in the annual Santa Fe fiesta, we do neither the Pueblo Indians nor Vargas and the colonists the honor they deserve. By ignoring the bloody sequels to 1692 and the end of the Pueblo-Spanish War, we distort the past and disregard the sacrifices demanded of others to achieve the plural culture we cherish so much.

There is no reason to believe that the Pueblo leaders duped Don Diego in 1692 or that he failed to recognize the difference between ritual repossession and actual occupation. With characteristic zeal, he threw himself into the recruitment and supply of a colonizing expedition, generously supported by Galve and the royal treasury, and, with characteristic impatience and overconfidence, he led it north in 1693 too late in the year.

But Vargas knew that the Pueblo Indians were capable of repeating their violent acts of 1680. He had advised the viceroy in 1692 that to reoccupy the kingdom with fewer than five hundred families and a hundred soldiers would be "like casting a grain of salt into the sea." Still, in the motley caravan that forded the river at El Paso and crawled north in October of 1693, there were only seventy families. None would forget the suffering of that journey.

Wagons broke down, provisions ran so low that the people were reduced to trading their belongings to Indians for food; rumors of ambush abounded; and, worst of all, winter came early with freezing wind, snow, and deadly, cold silence. In contrast, smoke from a hundred fires rose above the secure Pueblo Indian stronghold in Santa Fe, at the base of towering, gray-blue mountains.

Ordering colonists, soldiers, and friars to make camp on the frozen field where Rosario Chapel stands today, Vargas tolerated two agonizing weeks of negotiations. Nuestra Señora del Rosario, the small statue still venerated as La Conquistadora, waited in a wagon to be restored to her throne in Santa Fe. Meanwhile, malnutrition and exposure took a ghastly toll. Infants died and were buried under the snow. Bitter resentment gripped the Spanish camp. The Pueblo Indian occupants of Santa Fe, it was obvious, had no intention of vacating their homes.

The Battle of Santa Fe, December 29, 1693

The fiercely fought battle for Santa Fe broke out on the morning of December 29, 1693. Had the Pueblo Indians of New Mexico united against Vargas, as they had in 1680, the outcome would have been different. Instead, motivated by their traditional enmities and the advantages of honors, protection, and trade offered by the returning Spaniards, they split. One hundred and forty fighting men from Pecos Pueblo, enemies of the occupants of Santa Fe, arrived just in time to join the Spanish assault. Taking the parapet above the main entrance, the attackers burned the heavy wooden gate and rushed into the first patio, overrunning the round, partially subterranean kiva. The previous year, at Vargas's orders, this kiva had been whitewashed for use as a temporary chapel, but the friars, objecting to the heathen rites that had taken place within, had refused to consecrate it.

That afternoon, having secured one entire houseblock and the front patio, the attackers repulsed outside two assaults by Indian allies of the defenders, probably Tewas. Inside, they constructed ladders. Night interrupted the fighting. Before dawn on December 30, Spaniards scaled and won all the

Statue of Spanish conquistador in full armor.

rooms facing on the first patio. From the rooftops of the houseblock separating the two patios, they could look down into the second one, where the defenders had fortified another kiva. It, too, was overrun. In a room nearby, José, the wounded native governor of Santa Fe, garroted himself. By mid-morning the battle was over. Vargas ordered a cross erected above the main entrance and the royal banner flown from the walls. The Spaniards had won back their capital.

It took twenty soldiers and thirty Indians the rest of the day to inspect and inventory all the rooms of the four houseblocks. More than a thousand people, they estimated, could be housed within. The maize, beans, and other provisions they discovered were carried to a kiva that had been swept out to serve as the temporary public granary. Vargas ordered seventy of the defenders, who had refused to surrender, taken out behind the stronghold and executed. Some four hundred others, who had given themselves up, he distributed among the soldiers and colonists for ten years of servitude. Although soldiers would set out in the future from Santa Fe to fight under the banners of successive sovereigns—Spain, Mexico, and the United States—never again after its restoration was the capital of New Mexico the scene of a major battle.

Vargas Imprisoned

In the flush of victory, Vargas could not have imagined how his fate would change. On September 30, 1698, evidently somewhere in the remodeled complex known as the governor's palace, confined to quarters and desolate, Don Diego found two blank pages in a book and wrote a desperate letter to his son-in-law in Madrid. He had been held prisoner for eighteen months, a fate he compared figuratively to captivity in Algiers, where Spain's traditional enemies in the Mediterranean, the Turks, often cast Spaniards into prison. His clothing, his slaves, and his mules had been sold at auction. Even the Franciscan friars were prevented from visiting him. He felt utterly forsaken. His particular patron, the Conde de Galve, had retired as viceroy more than two years earlier and died in Spain. Vargas himself, considering his periodic bouts of typhus and other maladies, feared that he might not live much longer.

Historic-period leg irons.

"May God keep Your Lordship and my daughter, Isabel, and the grand-children, to whom I give my blessing," he wrote, "for I do not know if I shall see them again." Because his jailers had taken even paper from him, this one letter would have to suffice for all the relatives. "I made my will in Madrid in 1672," he reminded his son-in-law. If God should take him, he wanted his wishes carried out. The reconqueror of New Mexico had lost all hope.

In large part, Vargas had himself to blame for his imprisonment. Early in July of 1697—more than sixteen months after his five-year term of office as governor of New Mexico had expired—Don Diego, so convinced that the Crown had rewarded him, at the very least, with an extension in office, had turned over authority to his successor grudgingly.

Of relatively humble origin, the forty-year-old Don Pedro Rodríguez Cubero had worked his way up through the ranks. His royal appointment to succeed Don Diego, which had been challenged in Mexico City by Vargas's lawyer and delayed, was completely in order. Furthermore, he was empowered to conduct the mandatory judicial review of his predecessor's administration. After that, he heard criminal charges against Vargas, purportedly brought by the six-member Santa Fe municipal council. Misuse of royal funds, abuse of authority, favoritism, fomenting sedition among colonists and Indians—the accusations were serious. On October 2, 1697, Don Pedro jailed Don Diego.

Whether or not Rodríguez Cubero coerced the council members and others to testify against their former governor, as Vargas charged, not a few of the colonists hated the haughty, unbending Don Diego. He had held the power of life or death over them for six years. He should never have led them upriver from El Paso so late in 1693. And three years later, he should have listened to the friars and anticipated the second rebellion of the northern pueblos. On both occasions, his arrogance had cost the lives of their relatives. For his part, Don Diego considered the council members "of very low class and menial offices—tailors, a shoemaker, and a lackey—poor and base people." New Mexicans, he assured his son-in-law, were "people of very bad qualities and worse behavior . . . given to swear falsely, perjuring themselves in exchange for a young goat."

Jemez Pueblo, 1847.

In Spain, meanwhile, Vargas's notable accomplishments were being discussed in the king's councils. After the brutal battle and executions at Santa Fe—which the Conde de Galve, upon review, had judged unavoidable—Vargas, using Santa Fe as a base of operations, had carried his reconquest, the final stage of the Pueblo-Spanish War, to Indians fortified on steep-sided mesas. Aided by the Pecos and other Pueblo auxiliaries, he had won two pivotal victories on or about July 25, feast day of St. James, Spain's patron saint—first against the Jemez Indians in 1694 and then against the Tewas near Santa Clara in 1696. He had vowed to make a pilgrimage to the saint's shrine at Santiago de Compostela whenever he returned to Spain. Following in the footsteps of his father and most of the males in his family, Don Diego sought knighthood in the military Order of Santiago. But he failed, evidently because of the opposition of an influential member, a first cousin of Pedro Rodríguez Cubero.

Vargas had ridden out from Santa Fe to reinstall Franciscan missionaries at as many as fifteen of the pueblos and to personally encourage the Indians to rebuild their mission churches. He had welcomed two delayed contingents of colonists. The first, 60 families, some 225 people, were recruited in Mexico City and reached Santa Fe on June 23, 1694. These the governor led north the following spring to found the colony's second chartered municipality, Santa Cruz de la Cañada, near present-day Española. Forty-four more families brought up from Sombrerete, Zacatecas, and other mining towns by Juan Páez Hurtado, Vargas's trusted lieutenant, finally entered the capital on May 9, 1695.

The winter of 1695–96 was a time of suffering. Food shortages, an epidemic of "plague," and rumors that the northern pueblos were plotting war again kept the colonists on edge. By this time, between 1,500 and 2,000 men, women, children, and Indian servants were concentrated in and around Santa Fe; Santa Cruz de la Cañada, twenty-five miles to the north; and Bernalillo, forty miles down the Rio Grande. Outnumbered by the Pueblo Indians ten to one, many of the colonists were thoroughly disillusioned by the hardships of New Mexico and wanted to desert. That December, Vargas summoned Santa Fe officials to his sickbed in the governor's palace and dictated a will. But his time had not yet come, and he recovered.

Early in June 1696, the Franciscans' dire predictions came true. The Pueblo Indians of the north rose again with all the fury of 1680, killing five missionaries and twenty-one civilians. Don Diego and his soldier-colonists, aided by men from five allied pueblos, fought back fiercely. By November, the fighting had ended. Pueblo Indian resistance was broken. Authorities in Mexico City, jolted by the prospect of losing New Mexico again, now committed further aid to the beleaguered colony. By 1697, the Reconquest had at last been achieved, and the Pueblo-Spanish War, which had erupted so furiously in 1680, was finally over.

While he languished in captivity in Santa Fe, Don Diego was belatedly honored in Spain. In 1698, the king granted him a noble title of Castile, Marqués de la Nava de Barcinas, a name Vargas took from two of his family's rural properties near Granada. Recipient as well of a considerable annuity, he failed to win promotion in the royal service. Instead, he was reappointed to succeed Rodríguez Cubero as governor of New Mexico. Not until the summer of 1700, after he had been held in leg irons for five months, did Vargas secure his release. The reconqueror, after "three lost years," wiped the dust of Santa Fe from his boots. Reanimated, he rode south not to a hero's welcome, but to answer in Mexico City the charges against him.

Three leagues north of the viceregal capital, the former governor experienced an emotional reunion. He was met by a dashing, twenty-nine-year-old Spanish cavalry officer, formerly a noble page to two queens of Spain. Don Diego had last seen the captain as a twenty-month-old infant. His only surviving legitimate son and heir had grown up in his absence. Don Juan Manuel had journeyed to New Spain to get to know his father and to convince him to come home. The elder Vargas, wrote Juan Manuel admiringly, looked "so fit that those who had known him were amazed, for the hardships he has undergone were enough to have put him in his grave." Now, beholding his son, Diego de Vargas could not speak.

For three years, Vargas resided again in Mexico City, accepting the generosity of wealthy friends and pursuing his exoneration. He already had a residence there. Since the late 1670s, he had provided a home in the capital for a woman companion. His wife in Spain, Doña Beatriz Pimentel de Prado, had died in 1674, the year after he had sailed. Even though he was a widower, he had chosen not to marry the woman in Mexico City, who may have been Nicolasa Rincón, even though he had three children with her. He would never give up the hope, he later admitted, of returning honorably to Spain and again marrying someone of his temperament and social station.

Securing passage home for Don Juan Manuel in 1702, Vargas went further in debt to outfit the captain "as if he were the son of a grandee of Spain." He indulged his son. When Juan Manuel's lover died in childbirth, Don Diego paid the funeral expenses and took care of the baby, who, he confessed, was "the very image" of him. Then, tragic news arrived from Havana. Vargas's beloved son had contracted a respiratory illness aboard ship and died. Utterly disconsolate, for a brief time Don Diego contemplated suicide. Then, drawing on his deep sense of honor and family responsibility, he pulled himself together to face the charges against him in court.

Vargas Exonerated

With the advent late in 1702 of a new viceroy, the Duque de Alburquerque, who knew Vargas's daughter and son-in-law and who personally attended the hearings, the proceedings moved more swiftly. The verdict, read in the spring of 1703, elated Don Diego. He was fully exonerated; he owed nothing to the royal treasury; in fact, a considerable balance remained in his favor. The authorities had dropped all charges against him and assessed Rodríguez Cubero and the villa of Santa Fe court costs.

Free at last to put his reappointment into effect, Vargas swore that, despite the injustices he had suffered, he would not govern vindictively. That summer, accompanied by his two natural sons, Don Diego rode north again for Santa Fe, where, at the age of sixty, he took office a second time on November 10, 1703.

To hear Vargas tell it, Rodríguez Cubero had all but ruined the colony. He had let Vargas's defensive works in Santa Fe fall into disrepair. He had allowed the presidial garrison to disperse, implying that the men had previously lived

Don Francisco Fernández de la Cueva Enríquez, duke of Alburquerque and viceroy of New Spain, 1702–1711.

in barracks. The church was in abhorrent condition. Leaving New Mexico by a westerly route to avoid meeting his antagonist on the road, Don Pedro hastened to Mexico City to prepare for his next assignment. But he died there in 1704. Meanwhile, the humble people of New Mexico welcomed the restored Don Diego, first Marqués de la Nava de Barcinas, in his words, "with applause and general acclamation."

Two months after his reinstatement in Santa Fe, Diego de Vargas had a premonition of death. In mid-January, he wrote a series of letters to family members in Spain, putting his affairs in order. "After all," he mused, "we are mortal." By mid-April, he was dead. He had gone on campaign. Pursuing Apaches in the bosque some forty miles south of Bernalillo, "he suffered," according to Juan Páez Hurtado, "a severe attack of fever caused by stomach chills." It may have been dysentery. Carried back to Bernalillo, he hung on for four days. Then, on April 8, 1704, at about five in the afternoon, Vargas expired.

In his final will, he had asked to be buried in the church of Santa Fe "in the main chapel beneath the platform where the priest stands." Unfortunately, the site of the church in 1704 is unknown. It may be that Vargas's bones were transferred ceremonially to the new parish church in use a dozen years later in the vicinity of the nineteenth-century cathedral. Wherever the reconqueror's remains came to rest, it is unlikely, given successive reconstructions, that they lie undisturbed.

In many ways, New Mexico was different in the years after Vargas from what it had been before. Out of the tumult and shifting for survival, a gradual if sometimes fitful change in human relations had begun to take place—from crusading intolerance to pragmatic accommodation. The names of native peoples and colonists who found themselves forced to coexist in the 1690s and in succeeding generations are still present in New Mexico three centuries later.

By restoring Santa Fe, seat and symbol of government authority since 1610, Don Diego de Vargas reestablished Spain's presence in the kingdom of New Mexico. No matter that he never liked the place. Here, at least, his memory lives on.

Coat of arms of General Vargas.

De Yndio y Mestiza
Coyote.

Españoles, Castas, y Labradores

Santa Fe Society in the Eighteenth Century

ADRIAN H. BUSTAMANTE

Friar Francisco Atanacio Domínguez, recently appointed father visitor of New Mexico, and his small retinue passed through Quemado (now Agua Fria) on a windy day in March 1776. There he was told that they were only one league from the villa of Santa Fe. Friar Domínguez, who had been raised in Mexico City, expected Santa Fe to have the conveniences that other capitals of the viceroyalty of New Spain afforded. But as the travelers continued, they saw only oxen, horses, and burros grazing on dried corn stalks and wheat stubble, and at the edge of the fields, adobe houses where the owners of these small ranches lived. Even when they reached the villa itself, they found little to distinguish Santa Fe from the other rural settlements they had passed since leaving north central Mexico. Fields lined the river and even surrounded the main plaza. This, the seat of government for Spain's northernmost province in the Americas, was to him nothing but a village practicing subsistence agriculture.

In his official description (published in 1956 in *The Missions of New Mexico, 1776*) Friar Domínguez noted,

> This villa . . . in the final analysis . . . lacks everything. Its appearance is mournful because not only are the houses of earth, but they are not adorned by any artifice of brush or construction. To conclude, the Villa of Santa Fe (for the most part) consists of many small ranches at various distances from one another, with no plan as to their location, for each owner built as he was able, wished to, or found convenient, now for the little farms they have there, now for the small herds of cattle which they keep in corrals of stakes, or else for other reasons.

Opposite page: Eighteenth-century Spanish illustration of New World *castas,* or racial mixtures. Depicted here, an Indian man with his "mestiza" wife and their "coyote" child.

This 1865 photograph of East San Francisco Street gives a sense of how Santa Fe may have appeared a century earlier. *Opposite page,* map of Santa Fe by José de Urrutia, 1766.

In spite of what has been said, there is a semblance of a street in this villa. It begins on the left facing north shortly after one leaves the west gate of the cemetery of the parish church and extends down about 400 or 500 varas. Indeed, I point out that this quasi-street not only lacks orderly rows, or blocks, of houses, but at its very beginning, which faces north, it forms one side of a little plaza in front of our church. The other three sides are three houses of settlers with alleys between them. The entrance to the main plaza is down through these.

Friar Francisco's observations on the layout of the village are confirmed by a map of Santa Fe drawn by Joseph de Urrutia in 1768. It was totally unlike farming communities in Europe and Mexico, which consisted of rows of houses surrounding a central plaza. Many medieval European villages had been walled for protection, and in the seventeenth century, Santa Fe too had been a walled town. But by the eighteenth century, the defensive wall was gone, and the people spread out to pursue their livelihood. Up and down both sides of the Santa Fe River, they built homes near their fields to keep marauding bears, raccoons, porcupines, and other wildlife from laying waste to the crops. They also had to guard themselves against their fellow citizens; in some cases, the governor sentenced those caught stealing their neighbors' produce to be pilloried on the plaza, with the stolen fruits and vegetables hung around their neck.

This decentralized settlement pattern caused many problems for the governors of New Mexico, who wanted to fortify Santa Fe against attacks by hostile Indians. In 1768, when Comanches persistently threatened the colony, Governor Pedro Fermín de Mendinueta ordered Santa Fe's residents to move closer to the plaza. Possibly because no Indians had attacked the villa since the Pueblo Revolt of 1680, the populace refused, staying close to fields and livestock in their *ranchitos.*

When Mexico City officials sent Don Juan Baptista de Anza to Santa Fe to deal with the Indian problem in 1777, the new governor initiated what historian Marc Simmons has called "the first attempt at urban renewal in Santa Fe." Anza wanted to move the plaza, the *casas reales* (Palace of the Govenors),

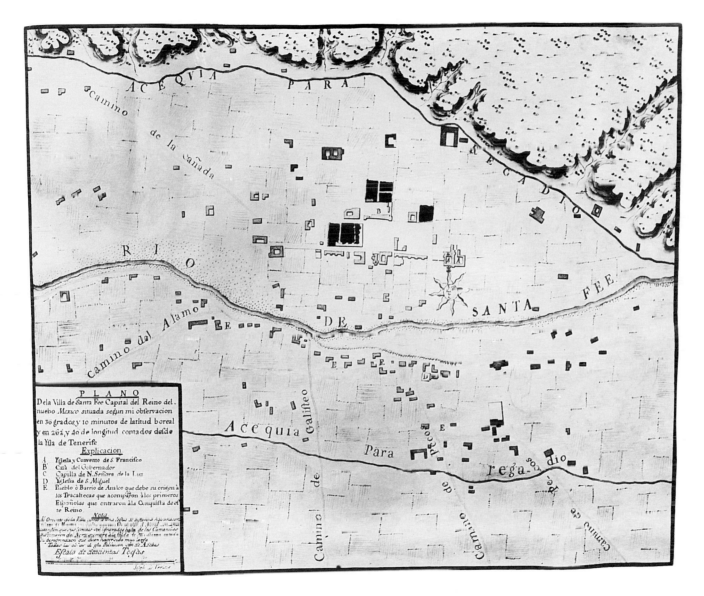

and all other public buildings across the river to Barrio de Analco, which surrounded San Miguel Church, and which shows clearly on Urrutia's map. Anza felt that the higher ground south of the river was easier to defend than the area around the plaza. Again, the citizens refused to move. Anza abandoned the project, and the locals continued to build their homes where it was convenient for their livelihood.

Santa Fe Society, 1790

The 1790 census of New Mexico, the most complete of the period, shows that farming was the most common occupation in Santa Fe, which had a population of 2,542. Out of 564 heads of family, 262 (46 percent) were listed as full-time farmers (*labradores*). Day laborers, accounting for another 60 heads of household, also contributed to the farming economy.

For some reason, the census did not give the occupations of many of the heads of household, but those mentioned—adobemakers, carpenters, blacksmiths, barrelmakers, lumbermen, muleskinners, shoemakers, weavers, and tailors, to name a few—demonstrate the self-sufficiency of the villa. Interestingly, the census names two hunters, but no butchers. Families probably did their own butchering, as they do to this day in the villages of northern New Mexico, although not to as great an extent.

The census lists only one schoolteacher, who was probably hired as a tutor by the few families who could afford to pay for his services. As farmers, most Santa Feans saw little value in formal education. Boys were expected to learn farming or some other practical trade, and girls learned how to take care of the household. The few families who did send their children to Mexico to be formally educated were very much in the minority. Literacy was the exception. If someone needed a document written, they went to a scribe, who worked for a fee. The lack of educational facilities would always be endemic to colonial Santa Fe. As far as the needs of the society were concerned, a good farmer or herdsman was worth ten scribes.

Typical *carreta*, or cart, formerly used by New Mexico farmers.

Until relatively recent times, sheep and goats were commonly used to thresh wheat.

It is not surprising that the census also lists only one full-time merchant. In 1790, New Mexico suffered from an imbalance of trade with Mexico. The merchants of Chihuahua and other parts of the Mexican interior charged more for their goods than Santa Feans could for theirs. However, local trading had always been important in New Mexico in late fall and winter, after the crops were in. At well-attended trade fairs in Pecos and Taos, people bartered for goods, and very little money circulated. For example, a bridle could be had for two buffalo hides, a horse cost twenty deerskins, and a female slave between twelve and twenty years old cost two good horses and some clothing or woven saddle blankets. Corn was exchanged directly for meat. Colonists also bartered among themselves with chile, *punche* (tobacco), sheep, and other products and animals, which were exchanged for services, goods, and even land.

By 1790, the colonial government may have been making some attempt at economic development, for the census mentions twenty-five *obrajeros* in Santa Fe. An *obraje* was a sweatshop that hired people to weave or produce other articles for sale. In the seventeenth century, sweatshops using Indian labor and run by the Franciscan friars supported the missions. Using forced Indian

New Mexico farmers husking corn.

labor, some governors also ran *obrajes* for their own benefit. *Obrajes* survived for a short time into the eighteenth century, died out, revived towards the end of the century, and then died out again.

Eighteenth-century Santa Fe was a socially stratified society. The governor and his staff of high-ranking officials, along with the officers of the presidio, belonged to the top echelon. The Franciscan clergy in Santa Fe, although seen as a separate group as men of the cloth, were also included at this level of society. But as members of a religious order that stressed the virtue of humility, most friars did not aspire to social prominence. Also, the province had no bishop to create a real hierarchy among the clergy. When Santiago Roybal, New Mexico's first native-born clergyman, was stationed in Santa Fe as vicar and as the local ecclesiastical judge for the diocese of Durango in 1730, he was considered a member of the upper level of society, but the native clergy did not really develop until the nineteenth century.

The next social level consisted of farmers and artisans who were relatively better off than their peers. Then came the common people, with little or no social prominence. The soldiers of the presidio, another separate group, had no special social privileges. In fact, judging from their complaints, they were a poverty-stricken lot whose pay was usually late, and when it did arrive, it went directly to their creditors.

The *Casta* System

Like Spain's other colonial settlements, the population of Santa Fe was multiethnic, as it had been since its founding, and social distinctions often broke along racial lines. The term *casta*, broadly defined as a person of mixed blood, referred to the people of eighteenth-century Santa Fe who were not considered *españoles*—that is, who were not credited with pure Spanish blood, or *pureza de sangre española*.

After King Ferdinand and Queen Isabella's expulsion of the Moors and national unification in 1492, Spaniards began to think of themselves as *españoles* for the first time. Previously, Spain had been divided, not just between Spaniards and Moors, but also among their own petty kingdoms (*patrias chicas*) such as Castile, Leon, and Aragon. The *españoles* began viewing themselves as members of a single nation while still preserving some loyalty to their respective regions. The new spirit of Spanish nationalism was accompanied by an affirmation of Roman Catholicism, which became the state religion. The *españoles* had been fighting not only to regain their peninsula, but also to cast the "infidel Moslems" out of Christian lands. The Catholic religion called for militancy, and the *españoles* saw themselves as defenders and propagators of the Holy Faith (*Santa Fe*).

Religious militancy led to the persecution of non-Christians in Spain, as it had in most European countries up to that time. Jews became special victims of this fervor. The *españoles* never forgot that the Jews had signed a pact with the Moors when they invaded the peninsula and formed cadres in certain towns. The year 1492 witnessed the beginning of a policy to expel Jews who would not convert to Christianity. When many of the Jews converted rather than leave Spain, some of the *españoles* still regarded them with suspicion or condescension, and they were recognized as not being *"de pura sangre española."* Thus the consciousness of *pureza de sangre* was born among Christian Spaniards. The Jews who converted suffered from the stigma of being New Christians, a distinction that gave rise to a new status group, *cristianos viejos*, or Old Christians. The elite among the *españoles*, then, were *"cristianos viejos y de pureza de sangre."* The persistent idea that some of the families who colonized Santa Fe and other areas of New Mexico were descendants of converted Jews has not been documented.

In the sixteenth and seventeenth centuries, *españoles* brought the concept of *pureza de sangre* with them to the New World, where they found themselves facing a new social reality—miscegenation. They intermarried with Aztecs, Tlascalans, and other tribes of Mexico, producing offspring who went on to mix further with *españoles* or Indians. To complicate matters, late in the sixteenth century, a new Spanish law forbid the use of Indians for forced labor. When New Spain began importing African slaves to work the mines and do other labor, blacks also began to contribute to the developing genetic pool.

Casta illustration.

Women at Rancho de las Golondrinas, a Spanish colonial museum near Santa Fe, reenact household chores as they were done in the eighteenth century.

Some blacks did come to the colonies as free men and women, but they were very much in the minority.

By the seventeenth century, a social system for classifying New World ethnic mixtures was evolving. One's social position was determined by the degree of *pureza de sangre española* that flowed in one's veins. To have been born in Spain, especially in Castile, gave one the highest classification possible— *peninsular*. Pure *españoles* who had been born in the New World had the marginally lower status of *criollos* (creoles). The more prestigious offices of government were usually given to *peninsulares* and *criollos*.

Within the growing mixed-blood population, the pecking order was determined by the degree of Spanish blood one possessed, or whether one was pure Indian or black. Indians, especially if Christianized, were of higher status than blacks. In an attempt to make sense of all of this mixing and cross-mixing, the *españoles* developed complex racial categories. People who belonged to any of these mixed-blood categories were members of the *castas*. To help colonists understand the *castas*, illustrators depicted the characteristics of each pairing and their offspring.

The 1790 census of Santa Fe recognized six categories of *castas* (Table 1). *Color quebrado* (literally, "broken color") sometimes replaced the wider range of classifications that appeared on typical *casta* lists of the day (Table 2), perhaps because the census taker did not want to do a complete genealogy or just did not believe in the *casta* system. Most of the people living in Barrio de Analco were listed as *color quebrado*, and most of the residents on the plaza side of the river as *españoles*.

In New Mexico, the term *genízaro*, used differently in the rest of the Spanish colonial world, meant a full-blooded Indian who had been captured at a young age by warring Plains Indian tribes and sold to Spanish colonists. *Genízaros* benefitted the colonists economically, for they represented cheap labor in a labor-intensive society. These children, raised as *criados* (servants) in Spanish households, took the names of their Spanish families and went on to start their own families under those names. Well-to-do and poor families

Table 1. The Population of Santa Fe in 1790 *

Category	Male	Percent	Female	Percent
Españoles	820	67.38	875	66.04
Color quebrado	185	15.20	195	14.72
Mestizo	101	8.30	121	9.13
Mulato	42	3.45	43	3.25
Genízaro	31	2.55	5	0.38
Indio	36	2.96	85	6.42
Coyote	2	0.16	1	0.08
Total	1,217		1,325	

Note: These figures do not include the presidio, which numbered about ninety-five soldiers.

alike had *criados*. The Franciscan friars advocated the purchase of these young people to bring them to Christianity.

The census takers also used *genízaro* to mean "civilized Indians who were not Pueblo." Friar Domínguez recorded that forty-two families of *genízaros*, comprised of 164 persons, lived in Santa Fe in 1776, but by 1790, only thirty-six were listed. Friar Morfi, Domínguez's superior, cajoled the governor into giving *genízaros* land of their own so that they would lead independent and productive lives. During this time, New Mexico governors planned to settle *genízaro* families in outlying communities as shock troops, and although the plan was not successful, it may partially account for the decrease in their numbers in Santa Fe. Also, former *genízaros* may have been listed under the general term, *color quebrado*, in 1790.

Casta illustration.

* Janie Louise Aragon, "The People of Santa Fe in the 1790s," *Aztlan: International Journal of Chicano Studies Research* 7, no. 3, (1976): 397.

Coyote, also used differently in New Mexico than in the rest of Latin America, seems to have been used almost interchangeably with *mestizo*. Both terms referred to people of mixed Hispanic and Indian blood. It may well be that *coyote* denoted someone who had not achieved the social status of a *mestizo* as defined in Mexico, but who was considered to be of an acceptable *casta* in New Mexico.

It is surprising that 66 percent of the population of Santa Fe in 1790 was classified as *españoles*, high compared to other provinces in New Spain. Undoubtedly, some Santa Fe families were pure *criollo*, and a few were even *peninsulares*. However, it is also possible that some of the people listed as *españoles* were actually *mestizos* who had earned enough distinction politically and financially to be promoted. Domínguez alluded to this possibility by mentioning that some New Mexico citizens "passed" for *españoles*.

The *casta* classification was not as strictly enforced in the frontier provinces as it was in the interior of New Spain. Because *españoles* stood at the top of the social ladder, it seems logical that many would aspire to achieve that category if the social system allowed it. Likewise, the descendants of blacks or *mulatos*, at the bottom of the social scale, may have striven to improve their social condition by working their way into the *color quebrado* category, or even better, that of *mestizo*.

For a *casta*, social acceptance was one thing, but being able to hold high office was quite another. No *casta* ever became governor during this period, for example, or was ordained as a priest to say mass or dispense the sacraments. The attitude of the civil and ecclesiastical authorities was that a *casta* would not be respected by the people and that he might even lapse into a primitive (*cimarrón*) state and cause a scandal. Among farmers, muleteers, shoemakers, and carpenters, however, the common hardships of the frontier served as a

---

* Pedro Alonzo O'Crouley, *A Description of the Kingdom of New Spain, 1774*, translated by Sean Galvin. (San Francisco: John Howell, 1972), 19.

[1] These *castas* are mentioned in the documents pertaining to New Mexico. In New Mexico, *mestizo* or *español* x *india* = *coyote*.

[2] In New Mexico, as explained in the text, the term was used differently.

Santa Fe, July, 1776. Painting by Wilson Hurley, from map by Joseph de Urrutia.

Eighteenth-century Segesser hide painting depicting the Pedro de Villasur expedition to eastern Nebraska. Painting shows Spanish troops and Pueblo Indian auxilliaries being attacked by Pawnee and Oto Indians on August 14, 1720.

social equalizer, and there seems to have been little ethnic discrimination in such occupations.

In the meting out of justice, *españoles* received more lenient sentences than *castas*. For example, *españoles* caught trading with the Utes without government permission were fined ten pesos and their goods were confiscated, but *castas* and *indios* caught breaking the same law were given ten lashes in addition.

Like New Mexico's other settlements, La Villa de Santa Fe struggled to survive during the 1700s. Its only advantage was that as the capital of the province, it had a higher official and social standing. Its citizens were in closer contact with government operations and could enjoy watching the militia going and returning from military operations in the field. Later writers would romanticize Santa Fe's history and its beautiful physical setting. The eighteenth-century citizens of the villa certainly appreciated the beauty of their surroundings, but they would not have made any sense of later romantic notions about their lives as *conquistadores*. By the nineteenth century, the dream of wealth and empire was dead. Whatever their ancestry and social standing, the people of Santa Fe had set their roots deep in a harsh, marginal land. Their lives there had grounded them in a practical approach to life and laid the foundation for their descendants to meet new challenges in the years ahead.

East De Vargas Street in the Mexican period probably closely resembled this 1884 photograph.

When Santa Fe Was a Mexican Town

1821 to 1846

JANET LECOMPTE

When Santa Fe was a Mexican town it had a population of only about five thousand, but it was the provincial capital of a huge area that included all of present New Mexico and Arizona and parts of Colorado and Utah. In former centuries the center of town was the presidio, with barracks for a hundred federal soldiers and a large parade ground extending from present Palace Avenue to Federal Place and from Washington Street to Grant Avenue. By the Mexican period only a few soldiers lived in the presidio, much of which was in ruins. The military commander complained that the foundations of the dilapidated barracks were being destroyed by stray chickens, cows, horses, and donkeys. The city council discussed selling the remaining adobe bricks of La Muralla, the wall that surrounded the presidio, to raise a little revenue, for most of the bricks had already been hauled off by townspeople to make new structures.

The Palace of the Governors formed the south side of the presidio. Its west end, where the Museum of Fine Arts now stands, had been lopped off during colonial times, reducing the size of the palace by nearly a third. It was still a long adobe rectangle with a flat roof, shaded on the south by a *portal* (portico) supported by pine pillars. The walk under the *portal*, where Pueblo Indians now sell their wares, was used for a public meeting place and led to the market at the west end of the palace. The adobe palace was often in disrepair. Throughout the seventeenth and eighteenth centuries it was patched and propped up, and its interior partitions were rearranged. In Mexican times it housed the quartermaster, commissariat, and other civil offices, a granary for

The La Castrense *reredos,* or altar piece, presently at the Church of Cristo Rey.

tithes paid in grain, a warehouse for confiscated merchandise, the customs house, the jail, and the guardhouse. It also provided a meeting room for the Provincial Deputation (later the Departmental Assembly) and an office and private quarters for the governor's family.

The man who spent the most time in the palace during the Mexican period was Governor Manuel Armijo. His office was described as a small, plain room about sixteen feet square with two calico-covered sofas against the walls. The floor was covered with a cheap homespun carpet, and the governor's desk was a small table in the center of the room with four crude chairs around it. On the walls were a bill of lading from an American steamship company and dinner plates of various American manufacturers, indicating the governor's interest in trade with the United States.

Downtown Santa Fe

South of the palace was the town plaza. Originally it had been twice as large as it was in the Mexican period. For most of its history the plaza was a rectangle of sunbaked mud where traders parked their wagons and animals, and visiting Indians camped. In the 1820s Governor Antonio Narbona built a rock sundial on an adobe base about eight feet high in the center of the plaza. The sundial bore a Latin inscription, *"Vita fugit sicut umbra"* ("Life flees like a shadow"), and like a shadow it disappeared before 1832, probably knocked down by traders' wagons.

One-story adobe buildings surrounded the plaza. On the east side were government offices, private homes, and a squalid, ruined house where the town council met. On the south side (San Francisco Street) were adobe houses and stores rented in the summer by American traders and the military chapel of La Castrense, considered the handsomest building in town. It was decorated with Spanish paintings brought from Cadiz in 1812 by Don Pedro Pino, the only delegate from New Mexico ever to attend the Spanish Cortes, or national assembly. La Castrense's exquisite altar piece was saved and now adorns the Church of Cristo Rey at the top of Canyon Road. Governor Armijo used to march his presidial soldiers across the plaza to attend services at La Castrense once a week, but by 1846 the chapel was in ruins.

Buildings on the west side of the plaza included Don Juan Vigil's house and his beautiful chapel of the Holy Trinity, which an observer distinguished from other Santa Fe buildings as "immaculate." At the east end of San Francisco Street stood the adobe *parroquia*, or parish church. It was the third church to occupy that spot since the early seventeenth century and was replaced by Bishop Lamy in 1869 with the present stone cathedral. The *parroquia* had faced the plaza before the latter was reduced to its present size in colonial times.

In the Mexican period, Santa Fe was divided into seven districts, each named for a parish church or other familiar landmark. These landmarks were old when New Spain became part of Mexico in 1821, and some are still standing. The district of San Francisco surrounded the *parroquia* and included the plaza and governor's palace. The district of San Miguel centered on the old Indian settlement of Analco surrounding San Miguel Church, now known to tourists as the "oldest church" in the United States. The district of Nuestra Señora de Guadalupe was named for the adobe Guadalupe Church, later demolished and rebuilt in stone by Bishop Lamy. La Muralla district, referring to the remains of the old presidio wall, included Calle de la Muralla (present Washington Street). The road to Albuquerque ran through the district of Agua Fria, as it still does.

Santa Fe during the Mexican period had little of the charm it has today. American visitors called it squalid and ugly, and contemporary records confirm their judgement. Minutes of its *ayuntamiento* (town council) meetings describe dusty streets obstructed with rocks and holes and fouled with piles of garbage thrown from houses. Council members complained that public health was threatened by stagnant pools and undrained marshes and by animal excrement and dead dogs floating in irrigation ditches. At night, vagrants, drunks, and wayward children roamed the streets, as well as traveling strangers whose business was unknown and therefore suspect. Often the silence was shattered by

The *parroquia*, or parish church, stood at the site of the present-day St. Francis Cathedral.

A Santa Fe fandango.

the whoops and yells of revelers at *fandangos* (informal dance parties) and by the ominous crack of American rifles.

Santa Fe's streets were probably no dirtier than those of Mexico City, and much safer. The people of Santa Fe, with a few exceptions, had never seen the streets of a real city with its beggars, criminals, abandoned children, the deformed, and the insane. Santa Fe took care of its own marginal people within its capacious family structures; no one remained homeless or hungry for long.

The People of Santa Fe

Before American traders arrived with their goods, the people of Santa Fe were mostly self sufficient. They built their houses of adobe bricks, using pine beams to hold up the flat roofs, sheets of mica for window lights, and leather for hinges. Few of their houses had tables, chairs, or bedsteads. They spread mattresses on the floor at night and rolled them up against the walls to serve as settees during the day. Their hard earth floors were covered with homemade *jerga*, a coarse woven fabric so inexpensive that traders used it to wrap bales of goods.

Their clothing was simple. Men wore pantaloons of leather or cotton, with plain homespun shirts. Women wore short, full skirts and full, low-necked blouses, with *rebosos* (shawls) over their heads and shoulders. Before the Americans came, New Mexicans imported a few expensive manufacturered goods from Mexico—sugar, shoes, fine cottons, and iron—but their land and labor provided them with everything else.

The people of Santa Fe valued honesty, generosity, hospitality, courtesy, loyalty to one's family and community, and obedience to authority when it did not conflict with their passionate individualism. They worked no harder than completion of the task required, and they lightened their labor by working with others, sometimes making a joyous game of it. Social occasions such as church festivals, weddings, and nightly *fandangos* were fully attended, for New Mexicans were a gregarious people.

The Mexican period began in the spring of 1821, when revolutionaries in Mexico set up a republic independent of the Kingdom of Spain. Because Santa Fe was located 1,600 miles north of Mexico, its people did not hear of the new government until September 11, when a horseman arrived with a mail pouch of official correspondence demanding that New Mexico's governor and other officials take an oath of allegiance. The people of Santa Fe received the news calmly. As a sequestered colony of Spain, New Mexico had been isolated for centuries from the rest of the world, and her people had little understanding of what a republic was.

In their isolation, New Mexicans had assumed a degree of local autonomy and a habit of resistance to central control. When in October the government sent a decree ordering New Mexicans to celebrate independence immediately, the people complied, but not until January. Their celebration included processions, orations, patriotic dramas, music, masses, ringing of church bells, firing of muskets, dancing of Pueblo Indians, and a ball in the governor's palace. Governor Melgares reported that the celebration was a very genteel affair and just what the government had ordered, but an American visitor described the street celebration as "licentiousness of every description," with crowds of gamblers enjoying "unrestrained vice" at dice and faro tables. Gambling, though illegal, was described as "the national sport of Mexico."

In 1821 Americans were trading with Indians on the borders of New Mexico. When they heard that Mexico's new government welcomed foreign commerce, as Spain had not, they entered Santa Fe and sold their goods quickly. By early 1822 William Becknell had already returned to Missouri for more goods to bring along the Santa Fe Trail. The trade between Missouri and Santa Fe was, in the end, the most signficant result of Mexican independence for New Mexico. At first, Americans and their goods were not much more than a diversion in Santa Fe. On Sundays after church people gathered in the plaza to shop, drink, dance, and gamble. Along San Francisco Street and around the plaza American traders rented stores to sell their calicos and muslins to the natives, and the natives responded by opening wineshops and monte tables for Americans.

Mexican girls.

Before long Americans and their goods had altered many aspects of everyday life in Santa Fe. Most rooms now had dadoes of calicos and ginghams, a profusion of American mirrors on the bare, whitewashed interior walls, and an occasional clock or piece of American furniture. For special occasions women put aside their peasant blouses and skirts to appear at balls in tight-waisted American gowns, and men who wore homespun shirts, buckskin breeches, and moccasins for work, dressed up in muslin shirts, imported trousers, and boots. Besides luxuries, traders' imports included useful things such as tools, medicines, newspapers, primers for schools, and a printing press. Some Americans built distilleries and made whiskey from wheat grown in the Taos Valley; others had sawmills or flour mills, or practiced their skills as carpenters, trappers, hatters, surveyors, gunsmiths, and blacksmiths, and taught these skills to New Mexicans.

Americans became indispensable, not only for their goods and skills, but also for the customs duties they paid, which supported both the civil officers of the territory and the presidial soldiers. Some Americans became citizens and lifelong residents, serving in municipal offices and as valued advisors to the governors. Many volunteered to fight Indians in the citizen-militia. Americans loaned money to the New Mexico treasury when it was empty and set up schemes for profit that further enriched the rich men of Santa Fe and provided jobs for the poor.

Although some Americans became respected citizens of New Mexico, others were arrogant and lawless. American hunters trapped beaver illegally in Mexican streams from New Mexico to California and south into Chihuahua and Sonora. American merchants cheated their customers with short weights and measures and sold guns to Indians. Traders smuggled in contraband goods and filled their wagons, returning to Missouri with contraband gold and silver bullion, specie, and illegal beaver pelts. In a land where courtesy was the first rule of conduct, Americans were often rude. They jeered at New Mexican folkways, broke up *fandangos* with drunken violence, and seduced and then abandoned both wives and maidens.

West San Francisco Street in 1881.

American trapper.

For better or worse, Americans influenced the lives and thoughts of New Mexicans. Contemporary Mexicans observed that the American work ethic, with its emphasis on accumulation of land and capital, began to undermine the leisurely quality of New Mexican life. American-style liberty and independence made some New Mexicans critical of their government and church and eager to choose their own political parties and leaders, as we shall see in the rebellion of 1837. Mexicans' perceptions of American wealth, freedom, and power was a factor in the ease with which Colonel Stephen W. Kearny conquered New Mexico in 1846. The cultural and ideological contributions of Americans were more influential in New Mexico than all the confused policies of the failed Mexican republic.

Nevertheless, it would be an error to assume that New Mexicans did not already have freedoms similar to those that Americans enjoyed. The constitutional government that the Republic of Mexico adopted in 1824 provided for a national congress of representatives from states and territories and citizenship for both Indians and blacks, although not for criminals and women. The 1824 constitution was modeled on that of the United States in its provisions for free trade and free speech, but in other ways it was different. It tolerated only the Roman Catholic Church, and it promised laws for New Mexico and other territories that were never promulgated. Through much of the Mexican period, New Mexican officials were forced to use Spanish laws passed by the Cortes of 1812, with suitable and often arbitrary changes to fit local conditions.

The governor (*jefe político*) was often made military chief as well. He was appointed by the president of Mexico with consent of the Mexican Congress, as were the secretary, treasurer, district judge, and *asesor* (legal advisor to the government). The latter two positions were rarely filled in New Mexico for lack of qualified men. The Territorial Deputation or Assembly consisted of seven men who met in Santa Fe and acted upon territorial matters, including the choice of a deputy to the Mexican Congress. The town council consisted of unpaid citizens who passed local ordinances and elected an alcalde to serve as its chairman and as mayor and municipal judge.

One of the permanent changes made by the Republic of Mexico was the abolishment of the old Spanish caste system, based on supposed degree of Hispanic blood. Now every respectable man could hold the title of "don," and native New Mexicans replaced Spanish knights as governors.

Governor Manuel Armijo

Manuel Armijo was the best known of the Mexican governors of New Mexico, and he was no Spanish knight. Born into a rich Albuquerque family in 1793, a mestizo of Spanish, Mexican Indian, and Plains Indian stock, he grew up to be handsome and portly, arrogant and charming, quick tempered and tough. Although he served three separate terms (1827–29, 1837–44, and 1845–46) and proved to be a fine administrator and clever politician, he was not popular, especially with Americans. Two contemporary American writers, Josiah Gregg and George Wilkins Kendall, both published books about New Mexico in 1844 portraying Armijo as a tyrant, a monster of lust and greed, an enemy to Americans, and a coward. Their best-selling books established a reputation for Armijo that was worse than he deserved.

Governor Armijo was hated by Americans for, among other things, his hostile confrontations with their well-armed countrymen. In 1827, during his first term as governor, he was determined to stop illegal fur trapping by Americans in Mexican territory. One day American trappers impudently cleaned their contraband beaver pelts in the plaza in front of the governor's palace, in full view of all Santa Fe. Armijo ordered his guard to seize the furs and arrest the trappers, but when the trappers began loading their guns, Armijo became uneasy and ordered the guard to retreat. The trappers escaped with their furs and jeered Armijo as a coward.

Armijo and other Santa Fe officials had good cause to fear armed Americans. In all New Mexico there were probably no more than 250 operable muskets, and usually fewer than 100 trained presidial soldiers. The hundreds of frontiersmen accompanying a single American caravan (such as the 1843 caravan of 230 wagons) would have had more and better guns than all New

General Manuel Armijo.

José Antonio Laureano de Zubiría, bishop of Durango.

Mexicans put together, and far more skill in using them. It was possible that a caravan of traders with their superior guns could have caught Santa Fe unawares and captured the city—or so Armijo feared. The governor and other responsible men of New Mexico continually warned the central government of the possibility of foreign invasion, and begged in vain for more money, soldiers, arms, and ammunition.

Armijo's fears were vindicated when 350 well-armed Texans arrived on New Mexico's eastern border in 1841 to capture Santa Fe in the name of the Republic of Texas, then at war with Mexico. Armijo met them on the eastern frontier, professed friendship, and persuaded them to lay down their arms. Without their guns the Texans were helpless. Armijo tied them together and sent them on foot to Mexico for the disposition of the president.

The Republic in Disarray

In this emergency and others, the central government of Mexico was powerless to help New Mexico, for its own affairs were in chaos. Between 1821 and 1837 the presidency turned over twenty-seven times, often violently. With such turmoil at the center, the outlying provinces suffered neglect and privation. Santa Fe showed the strain of poverty in its institutions, its buildings, and in the frustrations of its people. At one point the assembly disbanded for lack of travel money, and government offices closed for lack of paper, ink, and wood for heating the rooms in winter. In 1833 the government withdrew its support for churches and clergy. Henceforth the old churches, built by Franciscan friars with Indian labor in past centuries, were maintained only by donations. The buildings became dilapidated, their sacramental linens threadbare, their silver plate dented and tarnished, and their vestments shabby. Franciscan priests became scarce. Most of them were natives of Spain, and in 1827, during a quarrel with Spain, Mexico banished Spanish-born citizens. During the Mexican period only five to eight secular priests remained in New Mexico, far too few to administer sacraments to all the people.

No bishop visited New Mexico between 1760 and 1833. Confirmations all but ceased for half a century, baptisms decreased in number, and couples lived together without benefit of marriage. When Bishop Zubiría finally made the journey to Santa Fe from his diocese in Durango in 1833, the people were overjoyed. They sprinkled the streets with water to keep down the dust, constructed arbors of pine branches over the route of the episcopal procession, whitewashed buildings, and decorated bridges that would meet His Worship's eyes. The results of the bishop's visit were hardly worth the trouble of cleaning up Santa Fe. After administering sacraments and tendering his blessings, he departed, but not before offending everyone by outlawing the *penitentes*. This lay brotherhood provided many parishioners of northern New Mexico with their only source of religious ritual and comfort, in the absence of a sufficient number of priests. After the bishop's visit, the church continued to neglect New Mexico as usual, but the *penitentes* thrived.

New Mexico *penitentes*, circa 1890–96.

The military also suffered in the nineteenth century. The 120 presidial troops formerly allotted to New Mexico were sometimes reduced to about 60 in the Mexican period. Their uniforms were tattered and incomplete, lacking hats, coats, or jackets. A few were armed with ancient and barely serviceable muskets and scanty ammunition, but most had only clubs, lances, or bows and arrows. The soldiers were entitled to succor (provisions and shelter) and a salary, usually paid in grain. Some were owed twenty years' pay but remained in service for lack of land or other employment. They were drilled in European maneuvers and drawn battle lines, making their training useless against the hit-and-run warfare of Indians.

As their numbers declined in the Mexican period, the presidial troop served only to lead American caravans into Santa Fe to prevent smuggling, to escort the mail through Indian country, and to provide a ceremonial guard for the governor. They also served as Santa Fe's police, performing such degrading duties as killing stray dogs on the streets and flushing gamblers out of private homes in the dead of night.

The real soldiers of New Mexico were its ragtag militiamen, sometimes commanded by officers of the presidial troop, who fought in the miserable

Life on Santa Fe's plaza in the nineteenth century.

campaigns against Navajos and Apaches in the 1830s. Militia were requisitioned by the alcalde; they received no succor or salary, and they furnished their own arms, mounts, and provisions for three-month enlistments. As paltry compensation, they shared the spoils captured in battle. Rich men often paid poor men to substitute for them in the militia, but even so, the expense of campaigns often ruined the small farmers and Pueblo Indians who composed it.

The Society of Mexican Santa Fe

In previous centuries, New Mexico had been in constant danger from hostile Indians. Government aid was rarely forthcoming, and citizens of all classes were forced to pool their efforts to survive. Consequently, New Mexico developed its own version of a democratic society and a spirit of independence unique to the frontier. In Santa Fe, the stratifications of society were blurred, at least on social occasions. At Governor Armijo's ball at the palace in 1839, an American reported, "All the beauty and fashion attended and all the rabble, for, true to their republican principles, none can be refused admission." Another wrote, "It was not anything uncommon or surprising to see the most elaborately dressed and aristocratic women at the ball dancing with a peon dressed only in his shirt and trousers."

By virtue of Spanish and Indian tradition and the influence of the frontier, the independence of New Mexicans was especially apparent in their women. Every Sunday after church, women gathered in the plaza to sell vegetables, cheese, and American whiskey, or to deal cards in games of monte. Women had their own businesses and were not required to turn profits over to their husbands, as they were in the United States. They could own rental property such as a house or a billiard table, and they owned flocks of sheep which they entrusted to a shepherd in return for a percentage of the lamb crop.

The most famous woman in Santa Fe was Gertrudes Barcelo, known as La Tules. In the 1830s and 1840s she ran a bar and gambling casino that stretched the length of Burro Alley. Although not beautiful, she was a very bright, witty, and elegant woman, "the height of fashion," wrote one American. She was said to be Governor Armijo's mistress; at the least she was his close friend and advisor. She became so rich that after the occupation of Santa Fe she loaned money to the United States Army to pay its soldiers.

In an era when most wives of the world were mere chattels of their husbands, married women of Santa Fe kept their own wages and their maiden names. Their legal rights were such that they could even sue their husbands. Women also enjoyed sexual freedom. During the Mexican period fewer than half the couples of Santa Fe were married. Men and women lived together and raised children in relationships sanctified by society if not by the church.

Another independent group were the *genízaros*, Plains Indians captured as children and brought up as Mexicans in Mexican communities. In the nineteenth century they were allowed their own settlements and government; the towns of San Miguel and Abiquiu were first populated by *genízaros*. In Santa Fe, *genízaros* settled in Barrio de Analco with descendants of Indians brought from Mexico as servants of early Spaniards. They were finally absorbed into the mestizo population.

Although the citizens of New Mexico were generally patriotic, docile, and obedient, New Mexico's officials often acted independently of the central government, ignoring federal laws and edicts when they were not in the best interests of New Mexico. For instance, Governor Armijo refused to obey an order from the central government to make war against the Comanches because the tribe was at peace with the people of New Mexico. This notoriously independent governor exceeded the rights of his office by hearing appeals from dissatisfied litigants in the alcalde courts because there was no judge in New Mexico. New Mexico received no money from the central government for public works—roads, bridges, hospitals, and schools. Its presidial soldiers were paid out of customs house receipts that the national government allowed Santa Fe to keep, but when customs receipts were low, the soldiers were dismissed. The people paid no federal income or property taxes in New Mexico, however, in acknowledgment of their militia service on the frontier.

La Doña Tules

Mexico's neglect of New Mexico was symptomatic of that government's failure, and by the mid-1830s the Republic of Mexico was plainly not working well at the center. In 1835 conservatives drew up a new constitution dividing the country into departments with governors directly responsible to the president. All departments were to be governed alike, with autonomy for none and taxes for all. The departments that suffered most were those farthest from central Mexico, and many of them rebelled, including New Mexico.

In 1835 the central government appointed Albino Pérez as governor of New Mexico to put centralism and taxation into operation. New Mexicans disliked not only the new policies but also the new governor, who was handsome and brave but entirely too sophisticated for them. He did not bother to conceal his taste for luxuries—fur capes and fancy clothes, silver-mounted saddles and camp chairs, an imported American carriage, and a Santa Fe mistress in the absence of his wife in Mexico. During his governorship the plainly furnished palace was filled with extravagances such as gilded mirrors, a large table clock, and calico-covered sofas. Pérez gathered sycophants about him and amassed debts he could not pay.

Angry at the excesses of the new governor and the threat of taxes, men of the northern part of New Mexico sought to throw out the new constitution and establish a popular government. They formed a mob that savagely murdered seventeen civil and military officers, including Governor Pérez. The rebels then occupied Santa Fe, camping in the open field near the Rosario Chapel. As governor they elected one of their own, José Gonzáles, a simple, honest, illiterate man. While Gonzáles occupied the governor's palace and tried to bring tranquility to Santa Fe, secret plans were being made to get rid of the unruly rebels. In the town of Tomé, near Albuquerque, former governor Manuel Armijo organized a small army, marched to Santa Fe, and persuaded the rebels to go home. Then Armijo executed the leaders of the rebellion and assumed the governorship. Early in 1838 he was confirmed in the office and prepared to serve his second term as governor.

Armijo was a good governor. From 1838 to 1843 he worked to reduce the department's debt to soldiers, civil servants, and Americans who had loaned money to put down the revolution. He constantly badgered the central government for money, soldiers, and guns, defying directives and laws that did not meet the needs of New Mexico. By 1841 he had reduced depredations of the Navajos and made a treaty with them that was at least partly effective. He supported the demoralized priests and ordered parishioners to help repair and clean up their churches. He also encouraged teachers and wrote often on the people's need for literacy.

Armijo recognized the American traders as the economic salvation of New Mexico. In 1839 he illegally lowered duties on goods imported from the United States. The number of American traders multiplied, as did customs duties, and the financial state of the department improved. He also made illegal concessions to Mexican merchants, increasing their participation in the Santa Fe trade to the extent that Mexican wagons along the Santa Fe Trail outnumbered those of Americans by 1843.

Then Armijo made an error that ended his second term as governor. In 1843 he led an army of citizens against Texan pirates gathered on the Arkansas River to the north, but at the first danger of confrontation, he ordered a retreat. His cowardice was duly reported to Mexico, and he was ordered to give up his military command. Early in 1844 he resigned his civil office as well and retired to his home in Albuquerque.

Armijo was replaced by General Mariano Martínez de Lejanza, a man from central Mexico with good intentions and military experience. But like Governor Pérez, Martínez de Lejanza was not familiar with the people and problems of New Mexico, and he made mistakes. During an argument with some Ute Indian allies in the reception room of the palace, he hit one of the chiefs with a chair. The chief died, and the Utes began a war with New Mexico. Martínez de Lejanza also raised customs duties, to the detriment of the Santa Fe trade, and infuriated the people by trying to collect direct taxes. He was recalled to Mexico, and his only memorial in New Mexico were the cottonwood trees he had planted in the Santa Fe plaza.

Monument to Governor Albino Pérez on Agua Fria Street, since moved to the patio of the Palace of the Governors.

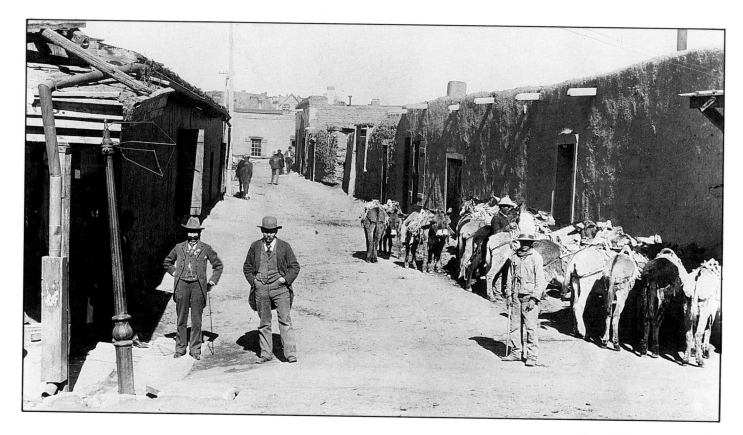

Burro Alley, circa 1895–98.

In November 1845 Manuel Armijo began his third, shortest, and last term as governor and military commander of New Mexico. New Mexico received word in June 1846 that the United States had declared war on Mexico a month earlier, putting Armijo in a difficult position. New Mexico's only financial support—its only business—was the Santa Fe trade with Americans. Yet, as a general in the Mexican army, Armijo was obliged to fight Americans if ordered to do so.

On July 7 news arrived in Santa Fe that an American army was camped at Bent's Fort on the Arkansas River, prepared to invade New Mexico. The people were terrified, for their priests had told them that Americans would rape women and brand men on the cheek like cattle. Many families abandoned their homes and fled to the mountains. At Armijo's call to arms, more than 4,000 men from all over gathered in Santa Fe. Frantically, Armijo collected money to succor them, ordering the church to turn over its silver plate and livestock and demanding funds from the city council and Departmental Assembly.

On August 15, as General Stephen W. Kearny and his army marched ever closer, United States agents secretly met Armijo at the palace, begging him to give up New Mexico peacefully. It was said that the agents offered him a bribe, but there is no good evidence of it. Still undecided, Armijo ordered his citizen-army to march out and fortify Apache Canyon, a steep-sided, narrow gap on Kearny's route to Santa Fe. The next day Armijo followed with the presidial troop. At Apache Canyon, he finally made up his mind and ordered the people to return to their homes. He continued south with his presidial troop to meet Mexican forces coming north to defend Santa Fe. In Mexico City Armijo was tried and acquitted of treason. He returned to New Mexico, where he died in 1853.

General Kearny and his army marched into Santa Fe with drawn sabres. They met no opposition, only sullen faces and downcast eyes. The wail of women rose above the din of the horses' hooves. As cannons boomed, soldiers raised the American flag on a newly constructed pole in the plaza. One soldier wrote later that he saw black eyes peering from behind latticed windows, many filled with tears, but a few gleaming with joy. The moment held both despair and hope—sorrow that Santa Fe was no longer a loving child of Spain and Mexico, and anticipation that the United States would prove a more attentive parent.

The American Occupation of Santa Fe

"My Government Will Correct All This"

JOHN P. WILSON

On August 18, 1846, Brigadier General Stephen Watts Kearny led his 1,500-man Army of the West into Santa Fe to claim New Mexico for the United States. Some residents greeted the American occupation of their ancient city with sullen looks and muttered curses, others with winsome smiles. Kearny's troops welcomed the bloodless conquest at the end of their long march, one that climaxed a convoluted series of political events.

Prelude: 1836–1846

For roughly 240 years, the boundaries of New Mexico had generally been set by the most remote line of settlements in the province. In 1819, when New Mexico's frontiers still lay at Taos and the villages along the upper Pecos River, the United States signed a treaty recognizing all of the lands south and west from the Arkansas River as belonging to Spain, and later, to Mexico. Texas complicated this situation in 1836 when it declared independence from Mexico and claimed the Rio Grande to its source, then northward to the forty-second parallel, as a western boundary. The Texas claim, which lacked any historical basis and included half of New Mexico, set the stage for conflict.

New Mexico Governor Manuel Armijo recognized the threat and managed to forestall one invasion from Texas. U.S. dragoons under Captain Philip St. George Cooke disarmed another set of raiders. The president of Mexico reacted by closing the northern ports of entry to commerce, which had the

Opposite page: General Kearny's Army of the West entering Santa Fe plaza, August 18, 1846. Painting by Don Spaulding. Courtesy, Sunwest Bank of Santa Fe.

General Stephen Watts Kearny, circa 1847.

unintended effect of depriving Armijo of his only revenue source, import duties. In mid-January 1844, Armijo resigned as civil governor. For two years, government in New Mexico ranged between confusion and chaos.

The United States meanwhile elected a new president, James K. Polk, who entertained decidedly expansionist views. The United States annexed Texas, and in December of 1845 Texas became a state, with its western boundary designated as the Rio Grande. President Polk's intentions went beyond Texas. He wanted to acquire California as well and squelch any British designs on either area. New Mexico may or may not have been an afterthought, but by September 1845 he was ready to ask for cabinet approval of a plan to settle the claim to Texas and also to "adjust a permanent boundary between Mexico and the United States" by negotiating with Mexico to purchase the country north of a line drawn west from El Paso to the Pacific Ocean. The cabinet agreed unanimously, and in November Polk sent John Slidell as his minister to Mexico with secret instructions to offer a graduated scale of payments for increasing amounts of the country north of the thirty-second parallel.

The Mexican government refused to receive Slidell, who never got to present Polk's proposals; nevertheless, rumors spread to Santa Fe that Mexico had agreed to sell New Mexico to the United States. This garbled story provoked a protest from New Mexico's leading citizens, who denied Mexico's right to sell the province and swore to defend it. Slidell meanwhile reported the Mexican government's refusal to receive him. When this news reached Washington on January 12, 1846, Polk ordered Brigadier General Zachary Taylor to advance his 4,000-man "Army of Observation" from Corpus Christi, Texas, to a point on the disputed boundary along the Rio Grande. With this movement, only a spark was needed to set off a war.

Polk was a president who engaged in brinksmanship. He never explained his strategy, and as a result, several interpretations of the causes for the Mexican War have grown up. One school of thought laid the blame on American territorial ambitions and the desire to provoke a war of conquest against a weak and divided Mexico. Not surprisingly, this theory has had a congenial reception in Mexico. Another thesis placed the onus upon Mexico for its unwillingness to accept the annexation of Texas, a step that by 1846 was irreversible. More recent studies suggest that neither side wanted war, but that Polk's attempts to negotiate a purchase while simultaneously exerting military pressure, combined with his lack of understanding of Mexico and the stresses within it, placed that country in an impossible situation.

For Mexico's leaders to have negotiated and surrendered territory at a time when the country's national existence appeared to be at stake would have ensured a rebellion. A refusal to negotiate was certain to bring on a war that most Mexican officials probably did not want. War, on the other hand, would at least preserve the national honor while providing a means to unite a seriously divided nation and perhaps setting the stage for a series of reforms. In the end neither country adopted a conciliatory position. The Mexicans continued their refusal to receive Slidell, and Polk, seeing no alternative to war, began to plan accordingly. The first overt action, a skirmish between Mexican troops and an American detachment near present-day Brownsville, Texas, took place in late April 1846. It may have come as a relief to both sides.

Slidell reported back to Washington personally on May 8, 1846. One day later, word arrived of the fight between Zachary Taylor's dragoons and some Mexican cavalry. The president drafted a message to Congress, and on May 13, Congress passed an act recognizing the existing war with Mexico and authorizing 50,000 volunteers to fight it. By this time American and Mexican soldiers on the lower Rio Grande had fought three engagements.

New Mexico and the Army of the West

On May 13 the president and the secretary of war directed Colonel Stephen Watts Kearny, stationed at Fort Leavenworth, on the Missouri River, to protect the trade caravans then en route from Missouri to Santa Fe. They also agreed to dispatch a column to seize New Mexico, calling upon the governor of Missouri to raise 1,000 mounted volunteers as a supplement to Kearny's First U.S. Dragoons. As usual the authorities in Santa Fe were well informed; in early June they understood that a war was imminent, and by June 24 at the

Hall's breechloader, type used by Kearny's soldiers.

Kearny's troops crossing the New Mexico
mountains. *Opposite page:* map of Santa
Fe, 1846–47, by J. F. Gilmore.

latest they had learned that an American army was advancing across the plains
from Fort Leavenworth, distant some 856 miles by way of the Santa Fe Trail
and Bent's Fort on the Arkansas River.

In fact, Kearny's march to Santa Fe with his Army of the West was based
on a plan forwarded to the adjutant general of the army on September 4, 1845.
Major Richard B. Lee had recently returned from Santa Fe, and the U.S. War
Department solicited detailed information and recommendations from him.
Lee's response was a handbook for the conquest of Santa Fe, complete with distances, routes, numbers, the proposed composition of the army itself, rendezvous points, rations, costs, and much more. He recommended only a thousand
men in all with a single artillery company (four guns), and naively thought that
"by a cautious approach and a night march" his force could advance undetected
at least as far as San Miguel del Vado. Indeed, Major Lee mapped out the conquest of New Mexico ten months before it happened. When Kearny set off he
had a copy of Lee's report in his pocket.

New Mexico in the spring of 1846 was a province already under attack
from the neighboring Ute and Navajo Indians. They raided with impunity, and
the frontier settlements were nearly defenseless against their assaults. The local
militia lacked horses and weapons, the presidial soldiers had not been paid in
a long time, the treasury was empty, and the central government in Mexico
offered encouragement but little or no real help.

Manuel Armijo returned to office for his third term as civil governor of
New Mexico in November of 1845, and in March 1846 he was appointed commanding general as well. He established a new militia system and organized
reconnaissance parties to patrol the frontier regions while making all manner
of futile appeals for money to meet New Mexico's urgent financial needs.
When his pleas failed, the governor was reduced to issuing proclamations and
circulars to stir the national pride.

Under these conditions, it is understandable why the first news about an
American army crossing the plains caused great consternation in Santa Fe. It
was not clear whether the advancing forces were Texans or Americans, though
by this time Armijo was fully aware of the ambitions of the United States and

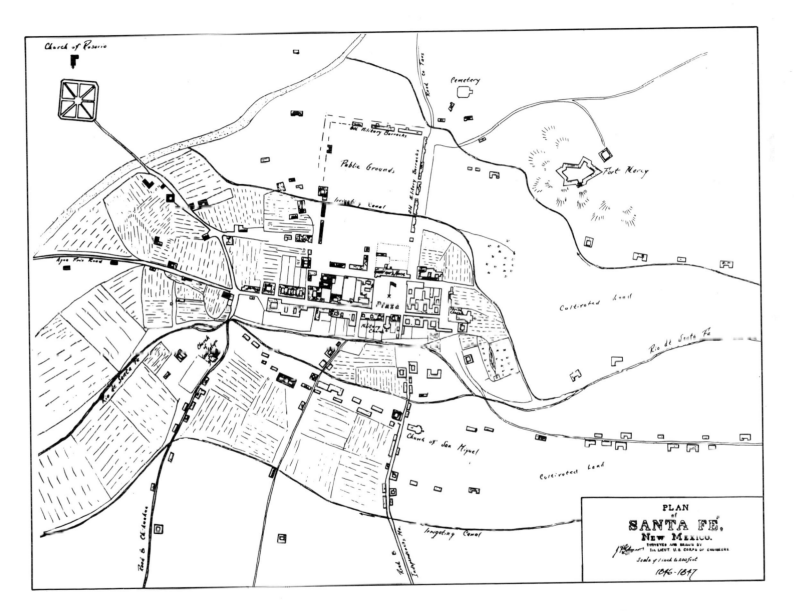

Church of Rosario

Road to Taos

Cemetery

Old Military Barracks

Public Grounds

Fort Marcy

Old Military Barracks

Irrigating Canal

Agua Fria Road

Cultivated Land

Plaza

Rio de Santa Fe

Rio de Santa Fe

Church

Church of San Miguel

Cultivated Land

Road to Galisteo

Road to Albuquerque

Irrigating Canal

PLAN
of
SANTA FE,
NEW MEXICO.
SURVEYED AND DRAWN BY
1st LIEUT. U.S. CORPS OF ENGINEERS
Scale of 1 inch to 200 feet
1846-1847

Colonel Alexander W. Doniphan, 1881–82.

that country's assumption of the Texas claim to the Rio Grande as its boundary with Mexico. Within New Mexico there were mixed sentiments about both Mexican sovereignty and Armijo himself, at least while the enemy remained out of sight. A greater concern lay with the economic consequences of delays in the summer caravan's arrival from Missouri. The forty wagons that finally rolled into the city included the train brought by Albert Speyer, Armijo's business partner, with thousands of pesos worth of goods consigned to the governor. After this, Armijo's decisions heavily favored his personal business interests.

Everything the governor heard during July indicated that the North Americans were coming with no less than 2,500 troops, all well equipped, and accompanied by upwards of twenty-four artillery pieces. Around August 1 or 2 a newly arrived merchant doubled the estimate of the number of American soldiers. Manuel Armijo's 200 regulars and poorly armed, untrained militia would be swept aside by a force of that size. His resolution now wavering, Armijo authorized himself to conduct the annual caravan south to Chihuahua, then drew up a power of attorney giving a trusted friend the authority to settle his affairs in the future. To the public he continued to put up a bold front, but by now it was a bluff. With the Americans only days away he ordered out the militia, bringing to Santa Fe as many as 4,000 citizen-soldiers. He assured them that "your governor is willing and ready to sacrifice his life and all his interests in the defense of his country," but with the moment of truth approaching, Don Manuel had already made his decision to abandon New Mexico.

War preparations were also going on at Fort Leavenworth, near the eastern end of the Santa Fe Trail. The U.S. Army had one of its ablest officers in Colonel Stephen W. Kearny, and in little more than a month he assembled nearly 1,500 men and had them ready to march. Most were volunteers—all Missourians—with Colonel Alexander Doniphan's regiment of First Missouri Mounted Volunteers constituting over half of the force. In addition there were two companies of volunteer infantry, the LaClede Rangers from St. Louis, two companies of artillery (sixteen guns in all), and five companies from Kearny's own First Dragoons. The volunteers began to move out on June 22, 1846, followed by Kearny with his staff and the artillery on June 30. The army required most of July to march the 537 miles to Bent's Fort, a private trading post on the upper Arkansas River a few miles east of present-day La Junta, Colorado.

While at Bent's Fort, Kearny issued a proclamation to the citizens of New Mexico, sounding the themes that he was to repeat during the next several weeks. He was entering New Mexico to seek union with its inhabitants and ameliorate their condition. People who remained quietly at their homes would be protected in their rights, both civil and religious. Those who took up arms would be regarded as enemies and dealt with accordingly. Nothing was said about a boundary or any other unresolved differences between Mexico and the United States.

The same day that the Army of the West broke camp at Bent's Fort, Kearny sent Captain Cooke and a prominent Santa Fe trader named James Magoffin on ahead with an escort of dragoons to try and negotiate a peaceful surrender from Governor Armijo. When this party arrived in Santa Fe on August 12, Cooke found the plaza crowded with thousands of soldiers and countrymen called out to resist the American invasion. The envoys' reception was hospitable, nonetheless. Cooke was shown to the governor's palace, where, as he recollected,

> I entered from the hall, a large and lofty apartment, with a carpeted earth floor, and discovered the governor seated at a table, with six or eight military and civil officials standing. There was no mistaking the governor, a large fine looking man. . . . He wore a blue frock coat, with a rolling collar and a general's shoulder straps, blue striped trowsers with gold lace, and a red sash.

Captain Cooke then presented a letter from Kearny stating that by virtue of the annexation of Texas, he had come to take possession of the country. Armijo politely declined to accept this version of events but offered to negotiate. That evening, James Magoffin conferred with General Armijo, and the two men then met secretly with Cooke.

Magoffin never understated his own importance in these negotiations.

Woodcut of Bent's Fort, 1847.

James W. Magoffin.

What he claimed at the time was recorded in the diary kept by Lieutenant William H. Emory, Kearny's chief engineer officer, in a paragraph edited out from the published version of the diary:

> Mr. McGriffin [Magoffin], an American, says that the night Armijo's messenger returned from General Kearny with the news that the latter had refused to stop, but was still advancing, he (Armijo) was thrown into the greatest trepidation: that he sent for him, (Mr. McGriffin), embraced him, and asked him for God's sake to go out and use his influence with General Kearny, to *stop* him. When Mr. McGriffin told him that was impossible, he gave way to the most uncontrollable despair.

On the other hand, there is circumstantial evidence that a bribe was offered and accepted and that Armijo's second-in-command, Colonel Diego Archuleta, was disaffected of his intention to fight the Americans by an offer of control over New Mexico *west* of the Rio Grande. Not for another ten days, on August 22, was anything said publicly about the claim of the United States to lands beyond the river. When Cooke and his party left Santa Fe to return to the army, they may have borne the knowledge that Armijo was not going to fight. They rejoined Kearny two days later at Tecolote, New Mexico.

Accounts of what happened in the New Mexican camp over the next several days are contradictory. Governor Armijo was apparently embarrassed and surprised by the huge turnout his call to arms brought. On August 14 he ordered the throngs of people to leave the city and take up positions at Apache Canyon, fifteen miles to the east. Two days later the general rode out to join his troops, where he convened a junta to decide what to do. The consensus was to fight, but Armijo declined to lead this array and ordered the militia to return to their homes. One young officer later said that there was little choice because the army had no leaders or food supplies and lacked military training. The governor himself fled south to Chihuahua accompanied by seventy of the Vera Cruz dragoons, who had been sent to help with the defense.

General Kearny (he received his commission at Las Vegas, New Mexico)

Dress parade, Fort Marcy, 1897.

repeated the contents of his earlier proclamation when the Army of the West passed through Las Vegas, Tecolote, and San Miguel del Vado. The alcalde of Pecos rode out to greet them and said, with a roar of laughter, "Armijo and his troops have gone to hell, and the cañon is all clear!" Kearny required the community leaders to take oaths of allegiance and reminded them of the ravages by Apaches and Navajos. His promise, "My government will correct all this," would haunt future military commanders in New Mexico.

On the night of August 17 the Americans camped twenty-nine miles short of Santa Fe, resolved to push on to the capital city the next day. The army broke camp early and pushed on until the head of the column came in sight

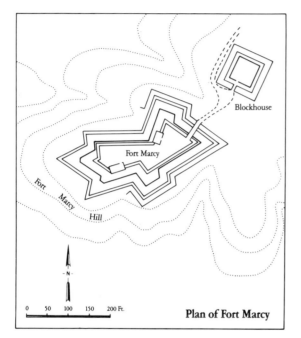

Blockhouse

Fort Marcy

Fort Marcy Hill

- N -

0   50   100   150   200 Ft.

Plan of Fort Marcy

of the town about three o'clock, the last units arriving around six. They marched through Santa Fe to the governor's palace, where General Kearny and his staff were received by the acting governor, Juan Bautista Vigil y Alarid, and other dignitaries and conducted inside.

Vigil had wine and brandy set out for refreshments. As one officer described it, "During the repast, and as the sun was setting, the United States flag was hoisted over the palace, and a salute of thirteen guns fired from the artillery planted on the eminence overlooking the town." Ceremonies over, the officers were invited to dinner by "a Mexican gentleman," a Captain Ortiz. The dinner "was served very much after the manner of a French dinner, one dish succeeding another in endless variety," all washed down with more wine from El Paso del Norte. Captain Cooke drew provost duty that night, however, and he witnessed the taverns and saloons of Santa Fe being overrun by the hungry and thirsty volunteers until he had to drive them all out.

What did New Mexicans think about this change of national allegiance? A Santa Fe trader told Kearny when he was still east of Bent's Fort that the populace was ready to accept occupation, but not so the leaders. The army's rapid advance had given no one in New Mexico much time to think about what to do, and when confronted with a choice of losing their office or swearing allegiance to the United States, the local alcaldes all took the oath, however reluctantly. In Santa Fe on the morning following the occupation, Kearny once more announced his peaceful intentions and "proclaimed" the people American citizens, subject to a new government. In a graceful response, the acting governor accepted their new situation on behalf of the inhabitants of New Mexico, asking that the general not find it strange if there were no manifestations of joy or enthusiasm.

Three days later General Kearny published a new proclamation, elaborating slightly upon the one he had issued at Bent's Fort and making it clear that he claimed "New Mexico, with its original boundaries (on both sides of the Del Norte) as a part of the United States, under the name of the Territory of New Mexico." This announcement evidently brought little reaction, consistent with the resignation that people had shown thus far. There would be serious trouble later, but for now the caravans were rolling, and money was circulating in Santa Fe. Kearny's creation of a territory of New Mexico and conferral of U.S. citizenship on the residents were both quietly disallowed by the powers in Washington, D.C., until such time as a peace treaty had been signed. But for the present, the offers were made and accepted in good faith.

The Building of Fort Marcy

On August 19, 1846, General Kearny sent lieutenants Emory and Jeremy F. Gilmer off to find a site for a fort. They selected an elevated site about 600 to 700 yards northeast of the plaza, the only point that commanded a view of the entire town.

There are number of brief descriptions of Santa Fe in 1846, none of them very flattering. A British visitor compared it to "a prairie dog town." Houses were universally built of adobe and one story high. Only the governor's palace had glass windows. In ordinary dwellings the window openings had shutters fastened on the inside with a heavy bar or else small windows closed with sheets of selenite, a translucent mineral. Room walls were whitewashed, and the smooth, earthen floors were partly covered with a locally woven black and white wool carpeting known as *jerga*. Calico tacked to the walls prevented the whitewash from rubbing off. For heating and cooking there were corner fireplaces. In addition to any furniture, room furnishings consisted of small mirrors, a few *retablos*, and perhaps a *bulto*, a carved statue of a saint. The wealthier homes had a wooden bedstead; poor families slept on the ground and rolled up their mats or blankets during the day for seats.

From their vantage point, Emory and Gilmer would have observed that Santa Fe was compact only in the vicinity of the plaza. Elsewhere the houses were interspersed among fields of corn, wheat, beans, and chile. In the neighborhood of present-day Grant Avenue and Griffin Street there were a half-dozen residences, "quite grand houses for the time." East Palace Avenue had

Jerga.

three residents, including Don Juan Sena, the owner of what is now known as Sena Plaza. The *parroquia*, the principal church in Santa Fe, stood on the present site of St. Francis Cathedral.

The center of the city was its public square or plaza, where Kearny would soon have a tall flagpole erected. An acequia, adjoined by a row of small cottonwood trees, ran along each side of the plaza. The west side was nearly all residences, near the center of which stood the post office and the store for tobacco sales, under the Mexican government's tobacco monopoly. La Castrense, the old military chapel that occupied the center of the plaza's south side, had been abandoned for some years, and part of the roof had already fallen in. On the east side about midway in the block was the *casa de cabildo*, used by the city council or *ayuntamiento* of Santa Fe. Other buildings on the east side were government offices, except for a store occupied by Don Juan Sena on the southeast corner. Sena's *tienda*, "the second best store in town" by one authority, boasted the only wooden plank floor in Santa Fe.

Elsewhere on the southeast corner there were other stores and a large residence that within a few years became a hotel, the precursor of La Fonda. On the north side, then as now, stood the long, low adobe structure known as the Palace of the Governors. The northeastern corner of the plaza had the old government storehouse, used to store merchandise brought over the Santa Fe Trail while the goods were examined by customs officials. Other buildings held shops, nearly all of them kept by American traders. Portals fronted the buildings on three sides of the plaza.

General Kearny approved his lieutenants' selection of a fort site and their plan for an earthwork enclosure or "star fort" with associated buildings. According to Lieutenant Emory, the fort was intended as a citadel to which troops could retreat "in case of extremities" and hold out until help arrived, but its chief object was the effect it would have upon the morale of the newly subjugated population of Santa Fe. Indeed, "their own guns [i.e., the artillery captured from Armijo] will be chiefly used to garrison the fort; and with them every house in Santa Fe could be levelled on the least appearance of revolt." Fortunately, this was never necessary.

Street scene in front of the Exchange Hotel (precursor of La Fonda), 1885.

Santa Fe plaza, circa 1867.

Construction on the fort began on August 23 with a work force of one hundred soldiers, later supplemented by thirty-one Mexican brick masons. The plan of this enclosure featured ten sides, generally aligned with the sides of the hill. The embankments were built up of earth and their slopes faced with sun-dried bricks, the embrasures for the guns likewise being built of adobes. The parapets had sufficient space for mounting seventeen cannons, most of which faced towards the town. A huge ditch surrounded the whole, and the vertical distance from the bottom of the ditch to the top of the parapet was seventeen feet. General Kearny named the fortification Fort Marcy in honor of the secretary of war, William L. Marcy.

Lieutenant Gilmer directed the construction, and by early November he had the fort in a defensible state. By the end of that month the earthworks had been completed. Gilmer also started work on an arsenal, which was finished the following spring. An adobe-walled blockhouse, laid out some sixty yards from the earthworks, may have been left uncompleted. There was never any

Donaciano Vigil, territorial governor of New Mexico, 1847–48.

thought of housing a garrison on top of this hill, and no shot was ever fired from the fort itself.

Until 1850 the officer who commanded the Ninth Military Department (New Mexico) occupied the Palace of the Governors, and his men lived in the old Mexican barracks in the downtown area then known as the Post of Santa Fe. In time, the old Spanish and Mexican buildings were replaced, and the name Fort Marcy was transferred to the facilities at the Post of Santa Fe. The earthwork on the hill gradually went to ruin. Santa Fe retained a garrison until 1894, and two of the old Fort Marcy officers' quarters yet remain.

The Early Months of American Occupation

General Kearny established a temporary civil government in New Mexico based upon a set of laws known as the Kearny code for governing the newly acquired territory. He also appointed a set of territorial officials, including the well-known trader and Taos resident, Charles Bent, as governor, and a prominent New Mexican, Donaciano Vigil, as secretary. With everything quiet and Colonel Sterling Price due to appear at any time to garrison the territory with his Second Regiment of Missouri Mounted Volunteers, Kearny prepared to advance on California.

The general left Santa Fe on September 25 accompanied by about 300 troopers of his First Dragoons. Colonel Price arrived in the capital a week later, followed by his regiment of Missourians and five companies of volunteers known as the Mormon Battalion. Price then relieved Alexander Doniphan's men, who set off to restore peace in the Navajo country before heading south into Chihuahua. In the meantime, Kearny detached Captain Cooke from his own command to lead the Mormon Battalion on to California. By late October, Sterling Price and the officers of the new civil government were in charge of New Mexico's affairs, the Second Missouri Regiment providing most of the military force.

Even as the other columns marched away, local tensions were rising. The new volunteers lacked discipline, and there were frequent altercations between

Ruins of Fort Marcy, circa 1915.

them and townspeople. In Santa Fe, priests and wealthy New Mexicans who saw their influence being reduced began to talk of revolt. Periodically, until Doniphan's regiment defeated and dispersed a Mexican force just north of El Paso on Christmas day, rumors flew that Mexico intended sending an army from Chihuahua to retake New Mexico. This unholy combination of rumors, disorderly conduct by the soldiers, and increasing resentment among New Mexicans led a number of leading citizens in Santa Fe and elsewhere into actively plotting the overthrow of the new government. For their part, these men considered themselves to be patriots.

Led by Tomás Ortiz, Pablo Montoya, Manuel Cortez, and the ex-colonel, Diego Archuleta, the conspirators set the evening of December 24 for a general uprising. All Americans throughout the territory and natives who had accepted positions in the territorial government were to be massacred or driven out. The wife of one conspirator leaked these plans to Colonel Price, who immediately

Diego Archuleta, 1884.

arrested a number of persons suspected of complicity and suppressed the rebellion. The two ringleaders, Ortiz and Archuleta, managed to make their escape. By early January, about the time that news of Doniphan's victory reached Santa Fe, Americans began to think that the spirit of revolt had been crushed. Governor Bent urged New Mexicans to disregard the libels spread by would-be revolutionaries and to remain quiet and support their government.

The Taos Rebellion

Two weeks after making his proclamation, Governor Bent was dead. The insurrectionists who escaped the Christmas eve roundup in Santa Fe continued to incite New Mexicans and found another opportunity when Bent and several other officials rode up to Taos in mid-January. Pablo Montoya and Tomasito, a Taos Indian leader, were already at Taos. Once they learned of the governor's presence, they enlisted anti-American Taoseños and Pueblo Indians to the cause of revolt. On the night of January 18, 1847, they roamed the streets of Taos; the following morning the insurrectionists murdered Bent and five others in the Bent home, then paraded the former governor's scalp through the town.

The same band of attackers moved a few miles north of Taos and killed seven Americans at Turley's Mill. Manuel Cortez carried news of the murders across the mountains to his home at Mora and stirred up the people there. Two Santa Fe traders happened to ride into Mora that same day and were shot as soon as they gave up their arms. Word of these murders reached the small American garrison at Las Vegas and Colonel Price in Santa Fe on January 20.

Price immediately ordered up most of the troops from Albuquerque to add to his own units, then set off to meet the rebels as soon as possible. The latter had been rousing the countryside and were advancing on Santa Fe. The American commander met them on January 24 near the town of La Cañada, now known as Santa Cruz, a few miles southeast of modern Española. He opened fire with artillery and charged the enemy's positions. Within a few minutes, he wrote, "My troops had dislodged the enemy at all points, and they were flying in every direction." He continued in the direction of Taos, and by January 28 his ranks had swelled to almost 480 regulars and volunteers. The following day they met the rebels again in the pass at Embudo. After a stiff fight, Price drove the enemy away and resumed marching on Taos.

At Taos Pueblo, the insurrectionists had fortified themselves in the church. Colonel Price's artillery finally breached the church walls, and his men stormed the rebel position. This broke the back of the defense, and the remaining insurrectionists fled or laid down their arms. The battle ended near nightfall on February 4 with some 150 of the enemy and 7 soldiers killed. The prisoners were held for trial; later that spring six of them, including Pablo Montoya, were hanged for their crimes.

The other principal action took place at the village of Mora. Hearing that the murderers had remained there after killing the traders, Captain Israel Hendley collected eighty soldiers at Las Vegas and started for Mora. They found the insurgents, and a pitched battle followed. After three hours of fighting, Hendley was shot down, and his lieutenants called off the attack. On February 1 some 200 of the Missouri volunteers returned and torched every building in Mora, destroying foodstuffs and everything else that would burn.

The Taos rebellion was the last organized revolt against American authority in New Mexico. Isolated raids and skirmishing continued through 1847; one of the raiders, Manuel Cortez, was found to have a captain's commission in the Mexican army. Partisan attacks on Price's grazing camps and retribution by the soldiers led to substantial casualties on both sides, including six inhabitants from one small village who were hanged after their conviction by a military court.

The signing of a peace treaty in February 1848 brought the war between the United States and Mexico to a close. New Mexico was now indisputably a part of the United States. Guerilla raids and threats by insurrectionists faded away, leaving the army and civilians free to face the centuries-old problem posed by the hostile Indians, particularly the Navajos, who surrounded the territory. It would be almost forty years before General Kearny's prophecy that his government would "correct all this" could be fulfilled.

Charles Bent, first territorial governor of New Mexico.

Arrival of a caravan at Santa Fe.

Santa Fe in the Days of the Trail

MARC SIMMONS

If any single event of the nineteenth century can be said to have shaped the character and determined the future of New Mexico's capital city, surely it would have to be the opening of the Santa Fe Trail in 1821. When an uneducated Missouri adventurer named William Becknell reached the plaza on November 16 of that year with a handful of companions and a string of pack mules loaded with trade goods, he had no way of knowing that his epic-making trip had launched a spectacular chapter in Southwestern history, one that would ultimately transform the lives of Santa Fe's citizenry.

At that date, the capital, population 5,000, was an unlovely huddle of one-story adobe buildings grouped around a plaza, a weathered governor's palace, and several chocolate-brown churches whose numerous bells daily created a din, according to one traveler, that could wake the dead. On the bare and dusty plaza, devoid of any hint of greenery, rose a single pole from which fluttered the flag of the new nation of Mexico. It had been the consummation of independence from Spain, in September of 1821, that allowed Missourian Becknell to enter the city freely and subsequently dispose of his wares at a large profit.

Under the Spanish colonial regime, commerce between the outlying province of New Mexico and foreign merchants from the United States had been strictly prohibited. The tight monopolistic policy of the king obliged New Mexicans to purchase all their manufactured goods at Chihuahua City, or points south, so that sales and profits could accrue to the benefit of the empire. The result was that many people on the frontier had to do without, so great was the cost of transportation and the markups of innumerable middle men.

Young Lieutenant Zebulon Pike, who had strayed into Spanish territory back in 1807 and was briefly held a prisoner in Santa Fe, saw the shining commercial possibilities that awaited American businessmen should the barriers to trade ever be dismantled. When they were, following directly upon the break with Spain, Santa Fe and neighboring towns north and south entered a new and quite unaccustomed era of prosperity.

In giving William Becknell a courteous welcome, Governor Facundo Melgares signaled the change in attitude and the beginning of a laissez-faire policy that would make possible the rapid rise of the lucrative Santa Fe trade. Americans, heretofore excluded from New Mexico, would now be at liberty to import merchandise and conduct business and even to settle permanently, said the governor. That was the word Becknell carried home to the Missouri border, and when it spread, many townsmen and farmers who had never thought of themselves as merchants decided to try their hand in the new overland trade with Santa Fe.

A Thoroughfare of Commerce

In the years that followed, the trail to New Mexico became a major international thoroughfare of commerce and a funnel by which not only foreign goods but foreign ideas, habits, and tastes were introduced to the isolated peoples of the Southwest. The American trader, questing for profits, scarcely perceived that his business ventures were fueling the beginnings of a cultural transformation among the Spanish-speaking New Mexicans. For him, Santa Fe had taken on the aspect of an exotic Eden—one where a man could go, indulge his hunger for novel experiences in a place whose customs were utterly strange, and, if he was lucky and the markets were brisk, make a small fortune in the bargain. That simple motivation drove him to risk the ever dangerous crossing of the prairies. The long-range effects of his activity upon New Mexico and the New Mexicans was probably something he never even considered.

In 1824 the first large freight caravan reached Santa Fe, consisting of twenty-three wagons and a small cannon, with eighty-one men. A member of

Lieutenant Zebulon Pike.

the party, Augustus Storrs—postmaster of Franklin, Missouri, turned trader—records that the value of their goods upon purchase at home was $35,000. When his stock was sold or traded at Santa Fe it returned $180,000, mostly in Spanish milled dollars but including some gold and silver bullion, beaver pelts, and mules. Storrs, who would soon be named the first U.S. consul for Santa Fe, also informs us that the American merchandise was made up of cotton and woolen items, light articles of cutlery, silk shawls, looking glasses, and "many other articles necessary for the purposes of an assortment." Afterward, we know that such things as books, paper, pens, religious medals, and colored prints of the saints formed a part of every merchants "assortment."

To a greater or lesser degree all imports had an impact upon cultural life as well as the provincial economy. An example can be found in the small printing press with its fonts of type, the first ever seen in New Mexico, which was carried to Santa Fe by famed merchant Josiah Gregg in 1834. It was probably a special order, placed by a prominent citizen of the capital, Ramón Abreu. At least he was soon listed as publisher of Santa Fe's first newspaper, *El Crepúsculo de la Libertad* (the dawn of liberty), which attracted fifty subscribers but folded after four issues. Ramón Abreu fared no better, dying in the short but bloody revolution that engulfed Santa Fe three years later. His little press ended up in a room of the governor's palace, where it was occasionally used to print handbills and dodgers. Then it fell into the hands of Padre Antonio José Martínez, who moved it to Taos.

Observant travelers who came over the Santa Fe Trail and were moved by the beauty of the city's natural setting and the novelty of the architecture and local custom often set down detailed descriptions of what they saw. One such early-day writer was Matt Field, a Santa Fe visitor in 1839 and later an assistant editor of the New Orleans *Picayune*, which published serially his articles on New Mexico. Field thought Santa Fe's adobe residences resembled "an assemblage of mole hills," and he noted that buildings were all one story, simply because land was cheap and the practical inhabitants preferred rooms six to a row rather than apartments piled on one another since it was easier to go through a doorway than climb a flight of stairs.

Instituciones De Derecho De Castilla Y De Indies by José María Álvarez. Published by Padre Antonio José Martinez, printed by Jesus María Baca, in Taos, New Mexico, in 1842 on the first printing press to be brought to New Mexico. Courtesy, Clark Kimball, the Great Southwest Books, Santa Fe.

East San Francisco Street at the plaza, 1868–69.

The situation with regard to two-stories, however, was soon to change, particularly on the plaza, as the pressure grew from American merchants to acquire summer store space in this central location. The eastern side of the plaza was taken up by the Mexican customs house and associated storerooms (where the Catron Building is today), and next to that the *ayuntamiento*, or municipal offices. Opposite, on the west side stood the post office, and on the south in the center of the block was the Castrense, or military chapel. In between, other structures were mostly private homes whose owners profited from the booming overland trade by seasonally renting their front rooms to foreign store keepers. Even Governor Manuel Armijo, himself heavily invested in the commerce with Missouri, was not above renting out rooms in the palace when demand was especially heavy.

By the 1830s it was the habit of the Missouri merchants to leave Independence or Westport (now part of Kansas City) in the spring so as to arrive in Santa Fe by early summer. At the customs house on the plaza they paid the required duties on their freight, and then many of them scurried to rent a store and commence retailing. Others sold at wholesale to local businessmen or those from neighboring towns or Mexico. In any case the aim was to sell out as quickly as possible and return home with the profits before the first snowfall swept across the plains.

The Chihuahua Trade

It was not long, however, before a serious trade imbalance appeared. The flow of goods from the States was so large in volume that little Santa Fe could not conveniently absorb it all. Some of the Americans, finding themselves stuck with surpluses, tried spending the winter in hopes that a trickle of sales during the off season would finally deplete their stock. But many others attempted a different course: from Santa Fe they directed their freight wagons down the old Camino Real to Chihuahua City, which had a population twice as large and was also rich, owing to nearby silver mines. For the more daring and enterprising, Santa Fe thus became a mere way station on the long trail to the Chihuahua market.

That Santa Fe did not entirely lose its place as a vital trade center can be attributed mainly to the entry of the New Mexican merchant class into this far-flung commerce. Members of the Pino, Ortiz, Delgado, Otero, Chávez, and other patrician families decided not to be left on the sidelines. They organized their own wagon trains and went east on the trail to buy directly from wholesalers. Returning with their freight to the Santa Fe customs house, they paid duties at a rate substantially lower than that imposed upon Americans. This favoritism, shown Mexican merchants, allowed them to undersell their foreign competitors and prosper.

The New Mexicans further enlarged their success by intensifying the trade with Chihuahua that had existed since colonial times. Santa Fe under Spanish rule had stagnated as a small and isolated market at the terminus of the Camino Real. But now, with the opening of the trail from the United States,

Aristocratic New Mexico don.

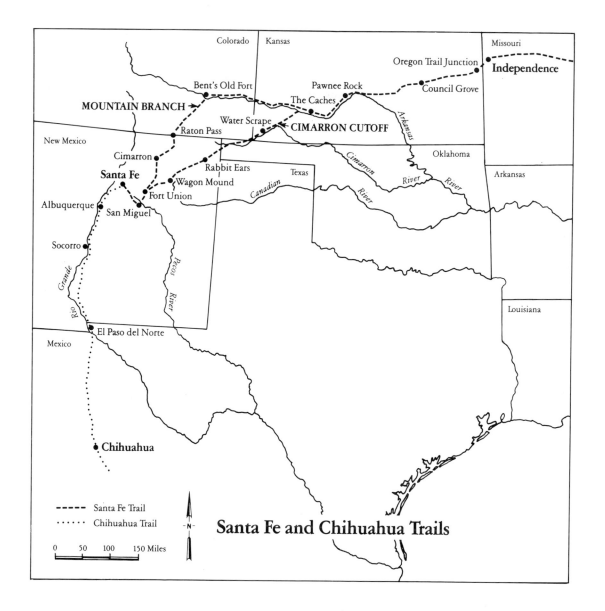

Colorado | Kansas | Missouri

Oregon Trail Junction • • Independence

Bent's Old Fort | Pawnee Rock
MOUNTAIN BRANCH → | The Caches | Council Grove

Water Scrape | Arkansas
Raton Pass | ← CIMARRON CUTOFF | Oklahoma

New Mexico

Cimarron | Rabbit Ears | Texas | Cimarron | Arkansas

Santa Fe | Wagon Mound | Canadian River | River

Fort Union

Albuquerque | San Miguel

Socorro | Pecos River

Rio Grande

El Paso del Norte

Mexico | Louisiana

• Chihuahua

- - - Santa Fe Trail
· · · Chihuahua Trail

N

Santa Fe and Chihuahua Trails

0   50   100   150 Miles

New Mexico's capital suddenly found itself in the center rather than at the end of the flow of overland traffic. The native merchants of Santa Fe, thereby, were well positioned to become middlemen and, in so doing, build personal fortunes. By 1843, according to several contemporary sources, New Mexicans outnumbered American travelers on the Santa Fe Trail, and that, added to the brisk Chihuahua trade, meant that the provincial economy had begun a recovery from the earlier imbalances.

In 1846 Private John T. Hughes, a member of the invading United States Army, was able to describe Santa Fe as "the great emporium where the merchants of central Mexico annually met the American caravans, to purchase their stocks. It is a city of considerable trade." Just how considerable is suggested by some figures available for that year. Caravans reaching Santa Fe had a total of 636 wagons, engaging 750 teamsters and drovers, and carrying $1 million worth of goods. While true that a significant portion of the freight continued on to Chihuahua and other interior cities, the import duties collected in Santa Fe and the stimulation of local business as a result of the booming international commerce directly benefited New Mexicans.

Josiah Gregg.

The dramatic aspect of this activity, particularly that associated with the arrival of a caravan from the plains, is best depicted by trader Josiah Gregg in his classic book, *Commerce of the Prairies*, first published in 1844. Approaching the limits of Santa Fe, the merchants and teamsters engaged in "clamorous rejoicings." And Gregg adds, "Even the animals seemed to participate in the humor of their riders, who grew more and more merry and obstreperous as they descended towards the city. I doubt, in short, whether the first sight of the walls of Jerusalem were beheld by the crusaders with much more tumultuous and soul-enrapturing joy."

As the huge wagons rumbled slowly down the last half mile of the Santa Fe Trail to the plaza, the air was filled with sharp pops, not unlike bursts of Fourth of July firecrackers. For the occasion, the wagoners had tied brand new "poppers" to the end of their whips, and they vied with one another to make the most noise. Crowds lined the dusty thoroughfare and added to the bustle and excitement by shouting, *"Los Americanos! Los carros! La entrada de la*

The Elsberg-Amberg wagon train in Santa Fe's plaza, October 1861. This is the oldest known photograph of the plaza.

caravana!" In short, it was a spectacle that now belongs to history and can never be repeated.

Part of the allure of Santa Fe for the first generation of American newcomers lay in the fact that it was a foreign capital. Most of the men from Missouri had never ventured outside of their own country, and the prospect of a trip to New Mexico—with its different language, strange customs, and distinctive architecture—held all the trappings of a romantic adventure. It offered the chance to escape from the humdrum at home and perhaps get wealthy in the bargain.

American Conquest and Its Impact

That side of the trail experience, however, was irrevocably altered by the turbulent events of 1846. With the outbreak of the Mexican War, Colonel (later General) Stephen W. Kearny marched over the trail and on August 18 unfurled the Stars and Stripes from the rooftop of the governor's palace. All at once the Santa Fe Trail was no longer the international road that it had been since 1821. Now both ends of the trail were in the hands of the United States, and while the atmosphere of Santa Fe remained foreign, its politics and economy began to move in directions familiar to Americans.

One of the most visible signs of change was the presence of English-speaking soldiers throughout the city, there to keep order but also to protect the citizenry from Navajos and Apaches who occasionally raided on the outskirts of Santa Fe. They were attached to Fort Marcy, an earthworks begun by General Kearny and located on a hill northeast of the plaza. About them, Susan Magoffin, wife of veteran trader Samuel Magoffin, wrote, "What an everlasting noise these soldiers keep up—from early dawn till late at night they are blowing their trumpets, whooping like Indians, or making some unheard of sounds, quite shocking to my delicate nerves."

Many of the troops who garrisoned Santa Fe over the next two years were short-term enlistees who had signed up during the heated excitement at the beginning of the Mexican War. When their enlistments were up, the majority of them returned to Missouri over the Santa Fe Trail, but some decided they liked the easy, colorful ways of the capital and remained. Several of them founded the first American newspaper in New Mexico, the *Santa Fe Republican*, which was printed in both English and Spanish. The initial issue appeared in September 1847 and came from a press the army had freighted over the trail from St. Louis earlier that year. On May 13, 1848, the paper gave a graphic account of changes that had overtaken Santa Fe in the two years since the Kearny conquest.

One of those changes made a strong impression on young Francisco Chávez after his return to Santa Fe following several years' schooling in Missouri. "Money was now more plentifully distributed in and about Santa Fe,

A banquet at Headquarters Building, Fort Marcy, circa 1890.

than at any other time in its long history," he declared. "Every man that wished to be employed had some sort of occupation, for which he was being regularly paid." The reason, he observed, was that the paymaster regularly brought the army payroll under escort from Fort Leavenworth, not only to pay the troops but also to furnish the sums for purchase of foodstores, hay and grain, mules, construction supplies, and labor. The influx of outside cash stimulated local business as much as the continued expansion of civilian commercial traffic.

Another innovation in Santa Fe life that soon made its appearance was regular mail service. In former days mail had come up the Camino Real from Mexico once a month, if the Apaches did not interfere. After the American occupation, military couriers and private travelers on the Santa Fe Trail carried mail from the States in a rather haphazard fashion until 1850, when the first government contracts were let to transport the mail on a regular basis. On one of the inaugural runs, the post wagon, bearing eleven riders, was attacked and burned by Utes and Jicarilla Apaches at Wagon Mound, in eastern New Mexico. The men all died, but a military patrol was able to recover much of the mail that lay scattered across the plain.

The "Mountain Pride" stagecoach on display at the Palace of the Governors Museum.

David Waldo of Independence, the initial mail contractor, was also a chief investor in the first stage line to link Missouri with New Mexico. In the Spanish and Mexican periods, Santa Fe had not enjoyed the blessings of stagecoach service to anywhere. So, when a monthly run from Independence began on July 1, 1850, it was a sign that New Mexico's capital had taken another step toward casting off the bonds imposed by isolation and provincialism. In 1857 the service was upgraded to twice a month, and a new contracting company, Hockaday and Hall, announced in the Santa Fe press that their coaches were "entirely new and comfortable for passengers. Travelers to and from New Mexico will doubtless find this the safest . . . and cheapest mode of crossing the plains. Provisions, arms and ammunition furnished by the proprietors."

During the last thirty years the Santa Fe Trail was in existence, the volume and value of goods shipped increased enormously. Much of this was in the form of military freight destined for new forts that sprang to life along the trail, but the Santa Fe and New Mexico markets also absorbed their share owing to

"Santa Fe Plaza in the 1880s," painting by Francis X. Grosshenney.

The American influence on Santa Fe's architectural style is apparent in this 1880s picture of Fort Marcy officers' quarters along Lincoln Avenue.

the rise in purchasing power that accompanied economic growth in the new territory. Some idea of the magnitude of the activity in these later decades can be gathered from figures recorded for 1860: engaged in the overland trade that year were 5,948 men, 2,170 wagons, and 17,836 oxen. Each wagon bore on the average 5,500 pounds of freight. The total value of transported goods for the year was estimated at $3,500,000.

The impact of this vigorous enterprise upon Santa Fe's society and traditional culture was necessarily profound. Those Hispanic residents of the mercantile class who profited from the new economic and political order adapted quickly to American fashions in dress, foods, household furnishings, and even architectural styles. Changes affecting the poorer classes were less pervasive. Among them the older customs and original patterns of domestic life persisted alongside the foreign introductions that symbolized the dawn of a new era. As a result, Joseph P. Allyn, upon completing a journey over the trail in 1863, could see the town with the fresh eyes of a newcomer and proclaim, "Santa Fe is a strange chapter torn out of the past and stuck in between the leaves of American progress."

Another observer of this period, Marian Sloan Russell, first saw Santa Fe as a child of seven in 1852, having come with her mother in a caravan led by the celebrated wagonmaster Francis X. Aubry. Approaching the eastern outskirts as Josiah Gregg had done a generation before, she exclaimed, "How our hearts waited for a sight of the Santa Fe of our dreams. We thought it would be a city and waited breathlessly for the first sight of towers and tall turrets. We crossed a water ditch . . . then passed through a great wooden gateway that arched high above us. We were in Santa Fe."

Marian made other trips on the trail, and despite her close familiarity with Santa Fe, the dove-colored adobe town never lost its image as a place filled with romance and adventure. She even had her first meeting alone with her future husband, Lieutenant Richard Russell, under the tall welcoming arch that spanned the trail somewhere east of the plaza. Only Marian, among thousands of travelers, mentions the presence of that arch. But many others succumbed to the charms of an old-world Santa Fe, just as she did.

By 1870, when the advancing railroad reached southeastern Colorado, it was clear that the days of the Santa Fe Trail were numbered. Early in 1879 the tracks of the AT&SF descended from Raton Pass onto the plains of New Mexico, and by the Fourth of July they were in Las Vegas. The trail, thereby, was reduced to a mere sixty-five miles, from the railhead to Santa Fe. One stage line, Barlow, Sanderson & Co., and one freighting outfit remained in operation throughout the remainder of the year and into January of the next.

Finally, on February 9, 1880, the first engine steamed into Santa Fe on a spur from the main line, which had bypassed the capital eighteen miles to the southeast. The *Weekly New Mexican* that day hailed the red-letter event with these bold headlines:

"Baby" on Glorieta summit, October 1880.

SANTA FE'S TRIUMPH!
THE LAST LINK IS FORGED IN THE
IRON CHAIN WHICH BINDS THE
ANCIENT CITY TO THE
UNITED STATES

And The Old Santa Fe Trail
Passes Into Oblivion

It was perhaps a fitting epitaph for the sixty-year-old trail. The flow of traffic during its long life had brought with it new people, new goods, new ideas, all serving to transform Santa Fe and connect it, however tenuously, to events in a far and alien world. The trail, as a forerunner of the railroad, helped prepare the way for the inevitable changes that would accompany the westward march of technology. But in the end, the Santa Fe Trail was to be remembered best for a rich and lively history, which after all may be its most enduring legacy.

The Palace of the Governors

CARRIE FORMAN ARNOLD

The Palace of the Governors in Santa Fe is probably the oldest public building in the United States. Still useful as a museum of the Southwest and exhibition hall, it is the city's centerpiece. The portal of the palace, overlooking the plaza, daily shelters a lively mix of Pueblo Indians and visitors.

The palace has been known by several names during the last 370-odd years. At the turn of the twentieth century, when interest in Spanish history began to overcome Anglo distaste for "mud" construction, writers increasingly began using the term *el palacio* instead of *adobe palace*. After the building became a museum, the name was formalized to today's *Palace of the Governors*. For several hundred years in the Spanish records, it was most often referred to as the *casas reales* (royal houses) or *palacio real* (royal palace). Indeed, the *palacio real* may have been quite royal for its day on the far frontier.

Beginnings: 1609–1680

Under King Philip III of Spain, Don Pedro de Peralta was appointed governor and captain general of the province of Nuevo Mexico in 1609. He engineered the design of the capital city on a sheltered bank of the Santa Fe River. Under Peralta's direction during the winter of 1609–10, the seat of government was moved from San Gabriel (near present-day Española) to Santa Fe.

Peralta had to bring in supplies, animals, and staff from Zacatecas, Mexico. Since the supply caravan did not leave until the fall of 1609, little if any construction was probably accomplished that year. But a fortified shelter must have been a priority as soon as any major construction began.

Opposite page: The Palace of the Governors, 1868.

Chess pieces (above) and majolica bowl (below) found in excavations at the Palace of the Governors.

During those first difficult and fearful years, rough buildings of simple construction probably provided immediate shelter. Spanish regulations decreed that the design of frontier settlements should be "defensive," particularly because the local Indians had few reasons to love the Spanish strangers.

Archaeological examination of the southeast room of the palace has shown evidence of ancient walls. Some were *jacal*, a palisade of upright timbers set into a trench with mud caulking for solidity. Buildings of this type still exist in New Mexico. The old walls may have been roofed for living spaces or left open to the sky as corrals for the stock. There is also evidence of old adobe walls at the palace. In any case, between 1609 and 1680, a palatial building did arise on the north side of the plaza, built at least in part of massive adobe walls.

The *casas reales* in Santa Fe probably seemed impossibly distant to the royal Court of Madrid. Still, Nuevo Mexico was the property of the Spanish Crown. The governors of New Mexico were the king's direct representatives via the viceroy of Mexico. Thus, the royal houses of Santa Fe reflected the prestige and power of the king of Spain. The governor's home enhanced his noble position and served the needs of administration and defense. Indeed, although many records were destroyed in the Pueblo Revolt of 1680, there are hints that in the seventeenth century the palace was quite an impressive structure, considering its remoteness on the New Mexico frontier.

Around 1657, the governor, Don Bernardo López de Mendizábal, and his lady, Doña Teresa, ran afoul of the Inquisition. In those days, the expense of the suspect's jail stay was met by the sale of his or her property. Lists of the governor's possessions made when the couple was carted off to Mexico City under arrest and the trial records provide an intriguing glimpse of life within the *casas reales* of Santa Fe.

Governor López de Mendizábal had several figures of Christ. "One of these was on a altar in his wife's drawing room, under a canopy so high that a ladder was required to reach up to clean it. The other statue was under a canopy at the head of his bed, where it was more accessible." In a peculiar room arrangement, there was a room of horse equipment between Doña Teresa's dressing room and the office of the secretary. Among their possessions were writing desks, books, silver tableware, rich clothes, and a private carriage.

Inhabitants of the adobe palace of the seventeenth century certainly enjoyed some luxuries. An idea of the quality of life at the palace before 1680 may be found below the level of today's floor in the west end of the palace. Archaeological excavations uncovered remains of a floor of adobe bricks beautifully laid in a diagonal pattern. They also yielded parts of a finely carved chess set dating from before the revolt. Pieces of Chinese porcelain are also likely to date from the same time.

Scholars have differing points of view concerning the location of the *casas reales* in the seventeenth century. Traditional theory holds that these public buildings formed a square compound extending into the property north of the back wall of the present Palace of the Governors. Until the middle of the nineteenth century, the front of the building was approximately 350 feet long. If square, the structure would have extended to the south edge of the First Interstate Bank Building. The present museum administration building at 113 Lincoln Avenue would have been well inside the interior patio. Workrooms, stables, and storage rooms are likely to have been located along the back wall and sides. Perhaps soldiers were garrisoned there too. If so, the central enclosed patio was probably more than four times the size of the palace patio today. At the southeast corner, the palace had a massive tower containing a chapel with at least one exterior door. Other towers also may have existed.

A typical *zaguan* (a double-doored entrance wide enough for a wagon to pass through) opened from the center of the palace off the main plaza into the huge interior patio. Metal grates were available and may have protected some windows. By 1650, the main entrance featured a pair of small cannon.

An alternate theory concerning the early location of the palace, proposed by Cordelia Thomas Snow, has it surrounding the plaza to the south. This rectangular plaza, probably 731 feet in length by 480 feet across, was much larger than the plaza of today and would have extended from its present western boundary east to St. Francis Cathedral and from the present Palace of the Governors south almost to Water Street.

Typical Santa Fe *zaguan,* or covered entrance way.

Since no copy of the complete plan of seventeenth-century Santa Fe is known to exist, and since downtown construction activity has disturbed archaeological remains, there is insufficient evidence to prove either theory.

Revolt and Change: 1680–1692

At any period in the history of the palace, one can find references to rebuilding or repair. Its walls, like those of all adobe structures, could be remarkably durable if protected and maintained. In the spring of 1680, Governor Otermín found the palace compound "in ruins and falling down, with many gates open and without even doors at the principal entrances." He spent several months supervising the repair and fortification of the *casas reales,* and his repairs proved timely. Beyond the walls of his palace, several years of drought and poor crops had aggravated existing conflicts with the Pueblo Indians. In August 1680, these grievances fueled the bloody Pueblo Revolt. Otermín later wrote that the repairs were finished only eight days before the revolt erupted.

The size of the structure during the siege is indicated in Otermín's papers, in which he mentions that about a thousand Spaniards and their servants gathered in the *casas reales.* In addition, it sheltered 5,000 sheep and goats, 430 horses and mules, and 300 head of cattle, all without crowding.

After the Spaniards abandoned the city, the Indians destroyed much that they felt showed evil Spanish influence. In the process, they remodeled the *casas reales* into a large pueblo. Visible today, a thick center wall runs most of the length of the palace. During the revolt, the roof over rooms to the north of this wall, in the west part of the palace, was destroyed. In the 1970s, archaeologists uncovered deep storage pits under a floor north of the center wall. Discovered in an area that seems to have been an outdoor area when they were constructed, the pits were usually bell shaped and up to six feet deep. Some had been plastered inside. The pits are now thought to have been built by the occupying Indians for storing foods such as dried grains.

Ceramic bowl excavated from under the palace.

Above, archaeological excavations at the palace in mid-1970s. *Below:* projectile points found under the palace.

Rooms to the south of the great center wall on today's plaza side of the building also offered revelations to the archaeologists. There is evidence that during the Indian occupation, many rooms—including the one with the fine brick floor—were divided into typical, small, pueblo-style rooms. Doors and presumably windows were filled in with adobe. Ladders leading down from roof openings were used for access. Evidence of fires in pueblo-style fireplaces was also found.

Another fascinating feature found by the archaeologists may be evidence of a rudimentary running water system, apparently built while the Indians occupied the palace. A mysterious little trench, discovered leading from the protected inner plaza into the Indians' living quarters, seems to have been lined with wood and fine sand. Although the purpose of this feature is not entirely clear, Don Diego de Vargas mentioned water conduits leading into the building in his reports to the king after the Reconquest of 1692–93.

Acequias flowed from high on the Santa Fe River northwest into Santa Fe; with the help of a few springs in the *ciénega* (swamp) northeast of the palace, they provided water for the people and their gardens. One acequia flowed in front of the palace as late as the American period (after 1846). Another flowed through the area generally covered by Marcy Street today. A plan of the palace property drawn by the Historic American Buildings Survey during the 1930s shows buried evidence of an acequia in the palace patio, approximately where the walkway in front of the Press of the Palace of the Governors is today. Various trenches in streets and driveways near the palace have shown evidence of old acequias in the area, running generally east to west. Small trenches could have brought water directly into the building from one of these acequias to the north.

One thing is clear from the archaeological investigations: in the seventeenth century, the *casas reales* did not look at all like the building that we see today. While the great center wall seems to have been built by 1680, many earlier walls do not align with later walls at all. Sadly, so little remains of pre-revolt walls, especially outside the existing building, and so few records seem to have been saved, that the appearance of the earliest *casas reales* may never be known.

Reconquest and Reconstruction: 1692–1789

In 1692, Don Diego de Vargas, leading a military expedition from El Paso, arrived at Santa Fe on the morning of September 13. He later described an amazing sight: the former *casas reales* had been turned into a multistoried Indian pueblo occupied by members of the Tewa and Tano tribes. Ruins of Spanish dwellings had been connected to form a walled fortress enclosing two large plazas. Archaeology and the historical shape of the city suggest that the *casas reales* became the base of a multistoried structure.

Historians differ about the shape and arrangement of the early plazas of Santa Fe, and the historical and archaeological references are vague. It seems quite possible that the palace separated the two plazas. If so, the south plaza

Opposite page, modern-day aerial view of downtown Santa Fe showing probable extent of the palace and presidio in the late eighteenth century.

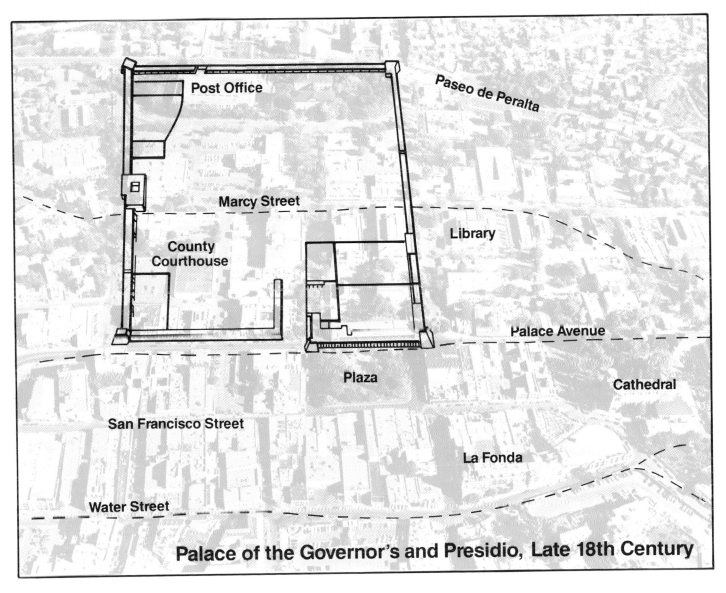

Post Office

Paseo de Peralta

Marcy Street

Library

County
Courthouse

Palace Avenue

Plaza

Cathedral

San Francisco Street

La Fonda

Water Street

Palace of the Governor's and Presidio, Late 18th Century

Portal of the Palace of the Governors.

would correspond generally with the one that exists today. The north plaza was probably the patio of the Spanish *casas reales,* where the refugees' animals had been gathered and later where the Indians dug storage pits. This pueblo fortress was further protected by towers at its corners. Providing the only access, a door in the center of the south wall, facing the river, could be defended from a fortification above. A walled passage to limit access and provide cover for defending the structure led to the door. It must have been an awe-inspiring structure.

During this mostly symbolic visit, the Spaniards had their first look at the changes that the Indians had made in the city. Some time later, after Vargas and a group of colonists had actually reoccupied it, he described the walled pueblo to the king. "There were so many living quarters, including those that had been built over the palacio, that it took a whole day to take a complete inventory." At least some of Vargas's account has been corroborated by other evidence, such as the archaeological discovery of early Spanish rooms divided into pueblo-style cubicles and reached by ladders through the ceilings.

Governor Vargas favored a defendable fortress, but the colonists evidently preferred separate home sites. Vargas went to jail (not necessarily because of that issue), and while he was incarcerated, the Indian fortress was dismantled. Sometime after the Reconquest, the Indian storage pits were filled with trash and debris, and rooms were built again on top of them in the inner plaza. Once again, the shape of the *casas reales* had been drastically changed.

In the eighteenth century, the aging building needed frequent repairs. How much was only repair and how much was new construction is difficult to determine from the records. Tree-ring dates from some of the vigas in the palace range from 1711 throughout the eighteenth century. Governor Marqués de la Peñuela even petitioned the Crown for permission to demolish the building in 1708. He apparently gave up, and eight years later Governor Don Felix Martínez reported that the *casas reales* were barely standing—and then only with the aid of many buttresses and timber props. Several south entrances were mentioned. One led through the governor's quarters into a patio, probably a walled-off segment of the large, old north plaza. Another entrance, a typical *zaguan,* opened to another patio. It is difficult to tell how many courtyards were behind the building at that time. One had a stable with a small, two-wheeled carriage and a dry well with a wooden bucket. Two towers, one of which contained gunpowder, were in particularly miserable condition.

While properly maintained adobe can be remarkably durable, lack of constant maintenance can quickly weaken a structure. In addition, the archaeological investigations revealed that the fill in the storage pits and other holes evidently was not allowed to settle before the impatient Spaniards rebuilt walls, causing them to slump. Numerous postholes uncovered in the areas of investigation indicate that the building was indeed propped up in rooms dating to the Reconquest.

Lieutenant Governor Pedro de Villasur probably saw the building in this condition as he led an ill-fated expedition against the French and Pawnees in June 1720. The Spaniards, wearing broad-brimmed hats, and their Pueblo Indian allies, wearing their long hair tied behind, rode off to meet the enemy. The disastrous battle that ensued in present-day Nebraska was depicted by an unknown artist on tanned hides. This remarkable painting, now known as one of the Segesser paintings, is proudly displayed today in the Palace of the Governors.

When Bishop Tamarón stayed in the *casas reales* in 1760, he noted that it had no fortress. In fact, the entire town was so spread out along the river that defense would have been difficult. Governor Juan Bautista de Anza, an able soldier and diplomat, decided that a new fortress and government building should be constructed in Barrio de Analco, on the higher south side of the river. During his term as governor (1777–89), he planned to destroy the palace, abandon the plaza, and rebuild in the barrio in a more compact and defendable manner. Some of the citizens were so incensed by the idea that they covertly left town and took their complaint to a higher authority in Mexico. In Arizpe, the commandant general agreed to block the move, and Anza gave up.

About the same time, King Charles III wanted some elk for his royal zoo in Madrid. Governor Anza managed to capture eight New Mexican elk, and while he awaited further orders, the elk apparently were corralled behind the

The death of Pedro de Villasur as depicted in the Segesser hide painting.

palace. Communication with Spain was slow, and the royal elk were less than ideal guests. They attacked people and had such large appetites that the governor was forced to tap an emergency military fund to feed them. Finally, orders arrived, and the elk were sent by caravan to Mexico City. Governor Anza was then ordered to capture a new herd of elk in the event that misfortune should befall the first bunch. Historian Marc Simmons has speculated that Governor Anza enjoyed a royal elk dinner in the palace when word came that some of the original animals had finally arrived safely at the Court of Madrid so that the others would not be needed.

Frontier Presidio: 1789–1821

Perhaps Governor Anza's concern about defense also traveled back to the king, who ordered a study of the frontier posts. A group of royal engineers was sent into New Mexico, directed by the Marqués de Rubí. In 1766, a member of the corps, Joseph de Urrutia, prepared a detailed map of Santa Fe. The document contains the earliest known mapped image of the palace and clearly records its relationship to other buildings in the city at that time.

The map shows a long building fronting the plaza and featuring slight projections at each end—perhaps towers or bastions. The depth of the building was fairly uniform except for the western third, where the palace may have had a sheltered passageway, and the building narrowed to the north. The indented passage may have indicated a *zaguan* or gate through the building into the north patio. Gardens were shown beyond the north patio. Other buildings in the town clustered along San Francisco Street, bordered the plaza, or were scattered along the Santa Fe River.

Probably in response to the Rubí reports, and concerned about territorial claims of other foreign powers in the New World, Spain determined to strengthen frontier defenses. In Santa Fe, the palace was to become the cornerstone of a mammoth new fortress—the presidio. Despite terrible rain storms that melted many of the adobes intended for its construction, it was started in 1789 and completed in 1791.

A plan of the Santa Fe presidio, drawn in Chihuahua from descriptions by people familiar with the structure, shows that in the new fortress, the old palace formed the extreme southeast corner of a huge quadrangle. A great wall extended north from the corner of today's Palace Avenue and Washington Street all the way to the front of the Scottish Rite Temple at Paseo de Peralta. There the wall turned west to enclose the site of today's post office complex, then south along the present site of Grant Street, then east toward the palace, on what is now Palace Avenue, in front of the current location of the Museum of Fine Arts.

The presidio had towers on the corners. In the middle of the south side of the presidio, just east of today's Museum of Fine Arts, a large entrance allowed access to the open fields within the structure. In times of danger, the garrison horses could be corralled there for easy availability. A jail occupied the west end of the palace next to this entrance. Soldiers' quarters built all around the inside of the quadrangle walls seem to have been in neglected condition in 1807, when they were duly noted by a young American, Lieutenant Zebulon M. Pike, when he arrived in Santa Fe as a prisoner. His report was the first American eyewitness account of Santa Fe. Before he and his men were sent on to Chihuahua, Pike dined with Governor Joaquin de Real Alencaster in the palace. He described the dinner as "rather splendid." They were served "wines of the Southern Provinces," wrote Pike, "and when His Excellency was a little warmed with the influence of the cheering liquor, he became very sociable, and expressed his opinion freely."

The Palace of the Governors, 1880s.

Mexican Transition: 1821–1846

The celebration of Mexican independence was led in January 1821 by Governor Facundo Melgares. As a young soldier, he had escorted Pike and the American soldiers as prisoners. Now, however, Americans were welcomed and even took part in the festivities, which culminated in a *baile* (ball) in the palace.

Mexico had too many financial problems at home to incur expenses on distant frontiers, and from 1821 to 1846 the fortunes of the palace depended upon the finances of its governors. Some of them did very well as a result of duties placed on trade goods arriving over the Santa Fe Trail from the United States. Before he was beheaded by a mob in 1837, Governor Pérez brought large gilded mirrors, a big table clock, and sofas upholstered in calico to the palace.

The walled presidio and the palace were again neglected, but occasionally, the governors spent money on renovations. Expensive glass windows were installed before 1832. Archaeological studies suggest that in the nineteenth century, more of the floors were carefully prepared with a layer of fine adobe over adobe brick than they had been.

A small acequia ran in front of the main doorway, which was evidently large enough for a mounted rider to enter. One of the governors, General Mariano Martínez de Lejanza, planted cottonwood trees in the plaza. These were watered by an acequia. Shortly after dawn one morning in 1844, a party of disgruntled Ute Indians attacked Governor Martínez in his palace office. While he held the attackers off with a chair, his wife brought a sword and called the guards. Workmen who were building a bullring in the plaza at the time joined in the fight. At least one Ute leader, Panacilla, was killed before the mayhem ended.

American Territory: 1846–1909

When Manuel Armijo returned to the palace for his third term as governor, the United States Army of the West, led by General Stephen Watts Kearny, was marching from Missouri toward Santa Fe. The troops occupied the city in August 1846. The triumphant Kearny slept on the floor of the palace the first night of occupation.

In 1846, the building was about 350 feet long on the plaza side, or about twenty-five percent longer than it is now, so it must have stretched westward almost to the sidewalk at the corner of the Museum of Fine Arts.

The principal door to the governor's residence was probably centered in the face of the building. Traditionally, Spanish architecture was symmetrical. This door is no longer in the center because the building has been shortened

Old Adobe Palace Santa Fe

Wittick Photo

at the west end, but it is in line with the central monument in the plaza. At the patio end of the corresponding entrance hall, Victorian woodwork was built to fit the angles of an ancient, slanting lintel. Philip St. George Cooke, on a spying mission just before the Americans entered in 1846, described the governor's carpeted earth floor, and several visitors mentioned spacious rooms with lofty ceilings.

The west end of the building was occupied by the ruined colonial jail. Its few small windows were grated and may have had wooden shutters.

The palace as recorded in the 1880s by photographer Ben Wittick.

Interior hallway of the palace, 1893.

Some of the small, old windows in the palace were probably glazed with selenite (a translucent stone) or thick sheets of mica. Evidence of this type of window was found during renovation in the mid-1970s. When the American army arrived in 1846, Santa Fe's only glass windows faced the plaza from the palace. In June of that year, Alfred S. Waugh, an artist, wrote that the windows in the palace were large, although the doors were not, and at least part of the building was whitewashed.

After Kearny's arrival, the U.S. Army took over the old presidio and remodeled some of the buildings to suit its needs, claiming the area as federal property. In the palace, several rooms were "fitted up" to accommodate both houses of the legislature. One of the larger rooms, which had been used for fandangos, was later converted into a theater under the auspices of Governor Charles Bent in 1846.

In the spring of 1982, an archaeological investigation of the area north of the palace, now covered by the First Interstate Bank Building, revealed Spanish-period structures from the presidio which had been remodeled and used by the Americans. In the area of the dig, the Spanish buildings were first adapted into a commissary storehouse. About 1859, these buildings were again remodeled, this time into a carpenter's work area and blacksmith shop.

The palace rooms soon contained the offices and archives of the governor and secretary of the treasury, as well as the legislature. Some of the government's most valuable weapons were also stored there. About this time the first American-style portal of sawn wood replaced the Spanish-style portal. Some Americans considered the local adobe architecture barbaric and were quick to update it with a simplified neoclassical style. The first American portal at the palace had a plain cornice over squared wooden columns. Sawn lumber characterized the trendy new territorial style.

In 1861, the government carpenter and blacksmith shops burned. When the fire threatened to spread to the palace and the post office, which seems to have replaced the government printing office, a building in between was pulled down, forming a successful firebreak.

During Governor David Meriwether's term in the 1850s, construction began on a fine, stone government building and a jail in the north area of the old presidio. Although the buildings remained roofless and unfinished for many years, the Americans connected the government building to the plaza with a wide street. This route went through part of the old *casas reales* jail. The jail end was certainly in miserable condition by that time. We do not know for certain what other rooms in that end of the palace were removed, but one of these rooms may have been used to host visiting Indians or for making treaties. We do know that some twenty years after Santa Fe became a United States territory, about a quarter of the palace was removed to make way for Lincoln Street, which led to the stone building—eventually completed as the Federal Courthouse.

As the structure of the government became more complex, ownership of the palace was divided to meet new needs. The federal government built a vault in the west end, an area that at various times housed the House of Representatives, the Office of Indian Affairs, the U.S. Depository (1869–76), the Receiver of the U.S. Land Office, the Office of the U.S. Marshall and the U.S. Attorney (1882), and the Second National Bank. By 1883, it was the site of the post office. The central section was traditionally used by the governor for his office and home. In the 1850s the east end was described as being in ruins. It seems to have been remodeled in 1867 into two long, adjoining rooms to house the legislature. These rooms were also used for public meetings. Nearby, a room was repaired to house the Territorial Library, and a series of rooms between the library and the governor's apartments were used as offices. The rights to these offices were sometimes hotly contested between the governor, the territorial secretary, and others.

A series of ever more elaborate porches replaced the portal, and each bureaucratic entity vied for attention with turnings, spindles, and balustered railings. In 1877 a large brick cornice was added to the east end, matching moulded brick chimneys were built, and the outside of the palace was plastered with white lime and sand with imitation stone blocks painted on it.

Interior of the U.S. Post Office in the palace, circa 1894–96.

Ben Hur Room.

Each tenant complained of the cost of upkeep on the old structure. Cotton sheeting was tacked to the vigas to catch the dirt sifting down from the roof. Worse, the vigas began to rot and sag, and the occupants sometimes feared for their lives. Of one such room, Governor Lew Wallace wrote, "the cedar rafters, rain-stained as those in the dining-hall of Cedric the Saxon, and overweighted by tons and tons of mud . . . had the threatening downward curvature of a shipmate's cutlass. Nevertheless, in that cavernous chamber I wrote the eighth and last book of Ben-Hur." After the book's tremendous success, the room became known as "the Ben Hur Room."

Technically, the palace was the property of the U.S. Department of the Interior, but in 1898 Congress "donated" it to the territory of New Mexico. The seemingly unending need for repairs had a strong influence on the donation. Governor Miguel Antonio Otero was hardly enthusiastic about the gift but urged that it be accepted and repaired.

Once under the ownership of New Mexico, the palace was offered to the Smithsonian Institution as a western branch of the national museum. Exciting new finds of prehistoric ruins in the southwest, such as those found by Edgar Lee Hewett at Puye and the Pajarito Plateau, had stirred national interest in archaeology. Hewett had begun to work at the Smithsonian in 1904. Theodore Roosevelt may have been the sole member of the Smithsonian's board in favor of acquiring the building or who understood its historical significance. In any event, when he assumed the presidency and left the board of the Smithsonian, the idea died. There was talk of selling the property for the value of the real estate, but a few people, such as former Governor L. Bradford Prince and Hewett, recognized the historical value of the ancient building.

The Palace in the Twentieth Century

Finally, in 1909, the New Mexico legislature established the Museum of New Mexico under the School of American Archaeology, later to become the School of American Research, and turned the responsibility of maintaining the building over to that organization as its permanent headquarters. The New Mexico Historical Society, headed by Prince, was already using the east end of the palace, and the legislature intended the two organizations to share the building as neighbors. However, the arrangment stipulated that the School would repair the entire building, giving it a large stake in the future of the palace. Eventually the Historical Society moved out, and the whole building came under the supervision of Edgar Lee Hewett, who had directed the School since its founding in 1907.

One of Hewett's protégés, Jesse Nusbaum, accepted the huge task of remodeling the palace. During repair of a wall near the area of the building in which archaeologists would later find the buried storage pits, he discovered a column and corbel embedded in an adobe wall. Later studies identified this feature as one of a series of old portals in that area. Nusbaum used the column and its corbel as the prototype for a replacement portal on the plaza side of the building in the process of eliminating the Victorian gingerbread and returning the palace to its Spanish-Pueblo style. Some of the changes were so successful that a new school of architecture, which would become known as "the Santa Fe style," was influenced by the design. The new facade was completed in 1913.

Today the palace generally retains the style it assumed under Nusbaum's direction. Interior rooms have been changed over the years, but they still follow the old Spanish plan of rooms surrounding a patio. In the mid-1970s a room was restored, with murals by Carl Lotave, to look much as it had early in the twentieth century under Hewett's direction. Showcases again displayed pieces of prehistoric pottery, and the ceiling was restored with great beams and inverted Indian bowls in the corners. This room commemorates Hewett's long guidance of the Museum of New Mexico and the School of American Research in the palace until the institutions were split off by the legislature in 1959 and the School moved to new quarters.

An award-winning restoration of the building under the direction of architect John Conron was completed during the 1980s. The entire roof, some of it dating back a hundred years, was replaced. New heating, ventilation, and

San Ildefonso potter Maria Martinez in the patio of the palace.

Rough Riders giving oath of allegiance in front of the palace.

security systems were installed within a roof and chimneys that faithfully replicated the former design. Provision was made for a fire-suppressant system to protect the irreplaceable building and its contents, with the hope that funding will become available to install it. When the exterior was restuccoed, the old surface revealed the plaster lined to simulate stone of the Victorian period, and sections were framed by glass panels for display.

The remarkable old palace continues to unveil its secrets. It represents the Indian heritage from prehistoric times to the present, as Pueblo Indians continue to sell handmade wares under its wide portal. It recalls the might of the Spanish Empire in its very form—the strong adobe walls that protected those who brought their books, laws, religion, and technology from Mexico and distant Europe. In front of the palace, Melgares proudly raised the Mexican flag. From here, expeditions began and ended, until the name "Santa Fe" came to mean the ultimate limit of the frontier to Americans. As the home of the School of American Research for many years, the palace contributed to the study of the past cultural riches of the Southwest. Today, the Palace of the Governors continues to offer the rich experience of former times to visitors of this ancient and remarkable place.

Firewood vendor on Palace Avenue, circa 1911.

This essay is based on "The Museum's Adobe Palace" by Carrie Forman Arnold, which appeared in El Palacio 90, no. 2 (1984): 36-45.

Suggested Reading

References to Santa Fe appear in countless books on the history of New Mexico and the Southwest; however, few books focus on the history of Santa Fe itself, and most sources are highly specific or scholarly. Two good resources for researchers are the Museum of New Mexico's History Library and the New Mexico State Records Center and Archives, both in Santa Fe. The *New Mexico Historical Review* and *El Palacio* are periodicals recommended for the multitude of articles they contain on specialized topics relating to Santa Fe history. Persons seeking archaeological data may wish to refer to the Arroyo Hondo Archaeological Series, published by the School of American Research Press. The following titles, which do not include technical or esoteric literature, will help readers pursue further studies on the subject.

Adams, Eleanor B., and Fray Angelico Chávez.
The Missions of New Mexico, 1776: A Description of Fray Francisco Atanacio Dominguez with Other Contemporary Documents. Albuquerque: University of New Mexico Press, 1956.

Drumm, Stella M., ed.
Down the Santa Fe Trail and into Mexico: The Diary of Susan Shelby Magoffin, 1846–1847. Lincoln, Nebraska: University of Nebraska Press, 1982.

Espinosa, J. Manuel.
First Expedition of Vargas into New Mexico, 1692. Albuquerque: University of New Mexico Press, 1940.

Hackett, Charles Wilson, ed., and Charmion Clair Shelby, trans.
Revolt of the Pueblo Indians of New Mexico and Otermin's Attempted Reconquest 1680–1682. Albuquerque: University of New Mexico Press, 1942.

Hazen-Hammond, Susan.
A Short History of Santa Fe. Lexicos, 1988.

Horgan, Paul.
The Centuries of Santa Fe. Santa Fe: William Gannon, 1976.

La Farge, Oliver, and Arthur N. Morgan.
Santa Fe: The Autobiography of a Southwestern Town. Norman, Oklahoma: University of Oklahoma Press, 1959.

Simmons, Marc.
Yesterday in Santa Fe. San Marcos Press, 1969.

Twitchell, Ralph Emerson.
Old Santa Fe: The Story of New Mexico's Ancient Capital. Chicago: Rio Grande Press, 1963. Originally published in 1925.

Picture Credits

Abbreviations: AN artifact number; LA-MNM Laboratory of Anthropology, Museum of New Mexico; NN negative number; PA-MNM Photo Archives, Museum of New Mexico; PGM-MNM Palace of the Governors Museum, Museum of New Mexico; SAR School of American Research.

Page *ix:* PA-MNM (NN10110). *xii:* PA-MNM (NN23306). 2: photo by Rod Hook. 3: photos by Rod Hook. 4: LA-MNM. 5: from *The Undeveloped West. . .*, John H. Beadle, Philadelphia, 1873. PA-MNM (NN144637) 7: PA-MNM (NN51395), photo by T. Harmon Parkhurst. 8: LA-MNM. 9: collections LA-MNM (AN17646), photo by Rod Hook. 10 top: From *Bandelier National Monument,* David Grant Noble, SAR, Santa Fe, 1980, drawing by Richard W. Lang. 10 bottom: collections LA-MNM (AN43863), photo by Rod Hook. 11 top: collections LA-MNM (AN19509), photo by Rod Hook. 11 bottom: photo by David Noble. 12: PA-MNM (NN31328). 13: PA-MNM (NN61150), photo by Valle de Vano. 14: drawing by Richard W. Lang. 15: LA-MNM archaeological site records. 16: LA-MNM. 17: photo by David Grant Noble. 18 top: SAR, photo by David Noble. 18 bottom: SAR, photo by David Noble. 19: SAR, photo by A. Stoker. 20 top: collections of the LA-MNM. 20 bottom: collections of the LA-MNM (AN47026), photo by Rod Hook. 21: PA-MNM (NN6821), photo by Arthur Taylor. 22: LA-MNM. 23 top: collection of David Snow, photo by Rod Hook. 23 bottom: collection of the LA-MNM (AN1955), photo by Rod Hook. 24: PA-MNM (NN12227), photo by Aaron B. Craycraft. 28: from Harpers Weekly, September 13, 1879. PA-MNM (NN133403). 29: PA-MNM (NN145015). 30: Special Collections, General Library, University of New Mexico. 31: from

The Story of New Mexico, Horatio Ladd, Boston, 1891. PA-MNM (NN133133). 32: collections PGM-MNM, PA-MNM (NN51249), photo by Ken Schar. 33: collections SAR, photo by Deborah Flynn. 34: photo by Karl Kernberger. 36: PA-MNM (NN82387), photo by M. C. Stevenson. 37: from *Kiva, Cross, and Crown,* John L. Kessell, Washington, D. C., 1979. 39: poster by Parker Boyiddle, courtesy Alfonso Ortiz. 40: from *Official Report of the Territory of New Mexico,* William Ritch, Santa Fe, 1882-83. PA-MNM (NN133140) 41: from *The Marvelous Country,* Samuel W. Cozzens, Boston, 1876. PA-MNM (NN133131). 43: PA-MNM (NN135333). 44: photo by Karl Kernberger. 45: collections of PGM-MNM, PA-MNM (NN505), photo by Wyatt Davis. 46: map by Katrina Lasko, adapted from "Pueblos Abandoned in Historic Times," Handbook of North American Indians, Vol. 9, Albert H. Schroeder, Washington, D. C., 1979. 48: from Official Report of the Territory of New Mexico, William Ritch, Santa Fe, 1882-83. PA-MNM (NN89210) 50: PA-MNM (NN11047), photo by T. Harmon Parkhurst. 51: Rod Hook, photo by H. C. Tibbetts. 53: PA-MNM (NN11409). 54: Bureau of Ethnology 55: Pecos National Monument (NN841). 56: PA-MNM (NN73815). 57: collections of the Albuquerque Museum, photo by Rod Hook. 58: collections PGM-MNM, PA-MNM (NN5736), photo by Wyatt Davis. 60: PA-MNM (NN2796), lithograph by R. H. Kern, 1847. 62: PA-MNM

(NN47997). 64: postcard from 18th-century painting at Museo de America, Madrid, Spain, courtesy Adrian Bustamante. 66: PA-MNM (NN11330). 67: PA-MNM (NN15048). 68: PA-MNM (NN11826). 69: PA-MNM (NN12583). 70: PA-MNM (NN71218), photo by Ed Andrews. 71: see p. 64 credit. 72: photo by David Noble. 73: see p. 64 credit. 75: painting by Wilson Hurley, 36"x30", collection of Albert G. Simms II. 76: PGM-MNM. 78: PA-MNM (NN76031), photo by J. R. Riddle. 80: PA-MNM (NN11645), courtesy Ernest Knee family, photo by Ernest Knee. 81: Amon Carter Museum, Fort Worth. 82: from *The Undeveloped West...*, John H. Beadle, Philadelphia, 1873, PA-MNM (NN144638). 83: Amon Carter Museum, adapted from *Narrative of the Texas Santa Fe Expedition,* Vol. II, George Wilkins Kendall, Harpers Bros., New York, 1844. 85: PA-MNM (NN11354), photo by William H. Jackson. 86: from *Century,* January, 1889, PA-MNM (NN144634). 87: PA-MNM (NN50809). 88: PA-MNM (NN13140). 89: PA-MNM (NN125551). 90: from *Harpers,* April, 1880, PA-MNM (NN133247). 91: from *Harpers,* April, 1854, PA-MNM (NN50815). 93: PA-MNM (NN36391), photo by Ina Sizer Cassidy. 94: PA-MNM (NN11070), photo by Christian G. Kaadt. 98: PA-MNM (NN7605), engraving by T. B. Welch (from a daguerreotype). 99: collections PGM-MNM, photo by Rod Hook. 100: from *Harpers,* New York, July, 1880, PA-MNM (NN133221). 101: PA-MNM (NN101912), map by J. F.

Gilmore. 102: PA-MNM (NN7174), photo by Bennett and Brown. 103: Amon Carter Museum, woodcut based on drawing by L. A. Maclean in *Doniphan's Expedition* by John T. Hughes (Cincinnati, 1847) 104: PA-MNM (NN10310). 105: PA-MNM (NN1727). 106: map by Katrina Lasko. 107: collections PGM-MNM, photo by Rod Hook. 108: from *Aztlan,* William Ritch, Boston, 1885, PA-MNM (NN10672). 109: PA-MNM (NN103021), photo by Nicholas Brown. 110: PA-MNM (NN11405). 111: PA-MNM (NN1725), photo by H. H. Dorman. 112: PA-MNM (NN50323). 113: PA-MNM (NN7004). 114: from *The Commerce of the Prairies,* Josiah Gregg. Denver Public Library Western Collection. 116: from *Massacres of the Mountains,* J. P. Dunn, Jr., New York, 1886, PA-MNM (NN7757). 117: Photo by Rod Hook. 118: PA-MNM (NN11329). 119: from *Harper's,* New York, July, 1880, PA-MNM (NN71387). 120: map by Katrina Lasko. 121: Kansas Collection, University of Kansas Libraries. 122: PA-MNM (NN11254). 123: PA-MNM (NN1706). 124: PA-MNM (NN11954). 125: collections Fine Arts Museum-MNM, oil on canvas, 36¼"x60½" 126: PA-MNM (NN30824). 126: collections Fine Arts Museum-MNM, PA-MNM (NN37916). 127: SAR collections at the PA-MNM (NN15870), photo by Ben Wittick. 128: PA-MNM (NN45819), photo by Nicholas Brown. 130 top: LA-MNM archaeological site records. 130 bottom: collections PGM-MNM, photo by Rod

Hook. 131: PA-MNM (NN40929). 132, 133: LA-MNM archaeological site records. 135: photo by Paul Logsdon, overlay by Katrina Lasko from information supplied by Carrie Forman Arnold. 137: PGM-MNM. 139: from *Marvels of the New West,* William Thayer, Norwich, Connecticut, 1888, PA-MNM (NN11212).
141: SAR collections at the PA-MNM (NN15376). Photo by Ben Wittick. 142: PA-MNM (NN46776). Photo by Thomas J. Curran. 143: PA-MNM (NN16659), photo by Adolph Fischer. 144: PA-MNM (NN12175). 145: PA-MNM (NN42317). 146: PA-MNM (NN5989). 147: PA-MNM (NN16731).

Index

"RIVETING ... DEVIOUS ... FASCINATING ...

Another gem in her Charlotte and Thomas Pitt *oeuvre* ... Extraordinarily rich in detail and the fog-laden atmosphere of the time, Perry brings to life the quirky society folk of London.... Her work soars with pathos and humor and, of course, a crackerjack mystery."

—*Mobile Register*

"[The] historical background is carefully presented."

—*The Boston Globe*

"Perry writes with both flowery overstatement and the kind of formality and restraint that befits her Victorian setting."

—*San Francisco Chronicle*

"Their fifteenth suspenseful turn through the wealthy front parlors and deadly back alleys of Victorian England demonstrates once again a fictional world rich with historical atmosphere and weav[es] a tale of mystery, corruption, detection, and justice as complex as the colorful characters who populate its pages."

—*Mystery News*

By Anne Perry
Published by The Random House Publishing Group:

Featuring Thomas and Charlotte Pitt:
THE CATER STREET HANGMAN
CALLANDER SQUARE
PARAGON WALK
RESURRECTION ROW
BLUEGATE FIELDS
RUTLAND PLACE
DEATH IN THE DEVIL'S ACRE
CARDINGTON CRESCENT
SILENCE IN HANOVER CLOSE
BETHLEHEM ROAD
HIGHGATE RISE
BELGRAVE SQUARE
FARRIERS' LANE
THE HYDE PARK HEADSMAN
TRAITORS GATE
PENTECOST ALLEY
ASHWORTH HALL
BRUNSWICK GARDENS
BEDFORD SQUARE
HALF MOON STREET
THE WHITECHAPEL CONSPIRACY
SOUTHAMPTON ROW
SEVEN DIALS

Featuring William Monk:
THE FACE OF A STRANGER
A DANGEROUS MOURNING
DEFEND AND BETRAY
A SUDDEN, FEARFUL DEATH
THE SINS OF THE WOLF
CAIN HIS BROTHER
WEIGHED IN THE BALANCE
THE SILENT CRY
A BREACH OF PROMISE
THE TWISTED ROOT
SLAVES OF OBSESSION
FUNERAL IN BLUE
DEATH OF A STRANGER

TRAITORS GATE

ANNE PERRY

BALLANTINE BOOKS • NEW YORK

A Fawcett Book
Published by The Random House Publishing Group

www.ballantinebooks.com

Library of Congress Catalog Card Number: 95-90828

ISBN 0-449-22439-2

Manufactured in the United States of America

First Hardcover Edition: March 1995
First Mass Market Edition: March 1996

OPM   20   19   18   17   16   15   14   13   12

To Donald Maass—with thanks

1

$P_{ITT SAT BACK}$ on the wooden seat and watched with profound pleasure as the sun faded on the old apple tree in the center of the lawn and for a few moments gilded the rough bark. They had only been in the new house a matter of weeks, but already it had a familiarity about it as if he were returning rather than moving in for the first time. It was many small things: the light on the patch of stone wall at the end of the garden, the bark of the trees, the smell of grass deep in the shade under the branches.

It was early evening and there were moths fluttering and drifting in the early May air, which was already cooler as twilight approached. Charlotte was inside somewhere, probably upstairs seeing the children to bed. He hoped she had also thought of supper. He was surprisingly hungry, considering he had done little all day but enjoy the rare full Saturday at home. That was one of the benefits of having been promoted to Superintendent when Micah Drummond had retired: he had more time. The disadvantages were that he carried far more responsibility and found himself, rather too often for his wishes, behind a desk in Bow Street instead of out investigating.

He settled a little lower in the seat and crossed his legs, smiling without being aware of it. He was dressed in old clothes, suitable for the gardening he had done through the day very casually, now and then.

1

There was a click as the French doors opened and closed behind him.

"Please sir . . ."

It was Gracie, the little waif of a maid they had brought with them, and who was now filled with importance and satisfaction because she had a woman in five days a week to do the heavy scrubbing and the laundry, and a gardener's boy three days. This fell under the heading of a considerable staff. Pitt's promotion had been hers as well, and she was immensely proud of it.

"Yes, Gracie," he said without getting up.

"There's a gentleman to see you, sir, a Mr. Matthew Desmond. . . ."

Pitt was stunned, motionless for a moment, then he shot to his feet and turned to face her.

"Matthew Desmond?" he repeated incredulously.

"Yes sir." She looked startled. "Shouldn't I 'ave let 'im in?"

"Yes! Yes, certainly you should. Where is he?"

"In the parlor, sir. I offered 'im a cup o' tea but 'e wouldn't 'ave it. 'E looks awful upset, sir."

"Right," he said absently, brushing past her and striding to the doors. He pulled them open and went into the sitting room. It was now filled with the last sunlight and looking oddly golden, in spite of its green and white furnishings. "Thank you," he added over his shoulder to Gracie. He went into the hall, his heart beating faster and his mouth suddenly dry with anticipation and something not unlike guilt.

He hesitated for a moment, a confusion of memories teeming through his mind and stretching as far back as consciousness would take him. He had grown up in the country, on the Desmond estate, where his father had been gamekeeper. He was an only child, as was Sir Arthur's son, a year younger than Pitt. And when Matthew Desmond had longed for someone to play with in the huge and beautiful grounds, Sir Arthur had found it natural enough to choose the gamekeeper's son. It had been an easy friendship from the beginning, and in time had extended to the schoolroom as well. Sir Arthur had been pleased enough to include a second child and watch his own son's application improve, with someone to share his lessons and to compete against him.

Even with Pitt's father's disgrace when he was unjustly accused of poaching (not on Sir Arthur's lands, but those of his nearest neighbor), the family were permitted to remain on the estate, with rooms in the servants' quarters, and Pitt himself had not been denied his continued education while his mother worked in the kitchens.

But it had been fifteen years now since Pitt had been back, and at least ten since he had had any contact with Sir Arthur or Matthew. As he stood in the hallway with his hand on the doorknob, it was not only guilt that stirred in his mind but a sense of foreboding.

He opened the door and went in.

Matthew turned from the mantelshelf, which he had been standing near. He had changed little: he was still tall, lean, almost narrow, with a long, erratic, humorous face, although all the laughter was bleached out of him now and he looked haggard and intensely serious.

"Hello, Thomas," he said quietly, coming forward and offering his hand.

Pitt took it and held it firmly, searching Matthew's face. The signs of grief were so obvious it would have been offensive and ridiculous to pretend not to have seen them.

"What is it?" he asked, sickeningly sure he already knew.

"Father," Matthew said simply. "He died yesterday."

Pitt was completely unprepared for the sense of loss which swept over him. He had not seen Arthur Desmond since before he had married and had children. He had only written letters to mark these events. Now he felt a loneliness, almost as if his roots had been torn away. A past he had taken for granted was suddenly no longer there. He had kept meaning to return. At first it had been a matter of

3

pride which had kept him away. He would go back when he could show them all that the gamekeeper's son had achieved success, honor. Of course it had taken far longer than in his innocence he had supposed. As the years passed it had become harder, the distance too difficult to bridge. Now, without warning, it had become impossible.

"I . . . I'm sorry," he said to Matthew.

Matthew tried to smile, at least in acknowledgment, but it was a poor effort. His face still looked haunted.

"Thank you for coming to tell me," Pitt went on. "That was . . . very good of you." It was also far more than he deserved, and he knew it in a flush of shame.

Matthew dismissed it almost impatiently with a wave of his hand.

"He . . ." He swallowed and took a deep breath, his eyes on Pitt's face. "He died at his club, here in London."

Pitt was going to say he was sorry again, but it was pointless, and he ended saying nothing.

"Of an overdose of laudanum," Matthew went on. His eyes searched Pitt's face, seeking understanding, assurance of some answer to pain.

"Laudanum?" Pitt repeated it to ascertain he had heard correctly. "Was . . . was he ill? Suffering from—"

"No!" Matthew cut him off. "No, he was not ill. He was seventy, but he was in good health and good spirits. There was nothing wrong with him at all." He looked angry as he said it and there was a fierce defensiveness in his voice.

"Then why was he taking laudanum?" Pitt's policeman's mind pursued the details and the logic of it in spite of his emotions, or Matthew's.

"He wasn't," Matthew said desperately. "That's the point! They are saying he was old and losing his wits, and that he took an overdose because he no longer knew what he was doing." His eyes were blazing and he was poised ready to fly at Pitt if he even suspected him of agreeing.

Pitt remembered Arthur Desmond as he had known him: tall, ineffably elegant in the casual way of those who have

4

both confidence and a natural grace, and yet at the same time almost always untidy. His clothes did not match each other. Even with a valet's best attention, he managed to select something other than whatever was put out for him. Yet such was his innate dignity, and the humor in his long, clever face, that no one even noticed, much less thought to criticize. He had been highly individual, at times eccentric, but always with such a basic sanity, and tolerance of human frailty, that he should have been the last man on earth to resort to laudanum at all. But if he had, then he was quite capable of absentmindedly dosing himself twice.

Except that surely once would have sent him to sleep anyway?

Pitt had vague memories of Sir Arthur's having long wakeful spells even thirty years ago, when Pitt had stayed overnight in the hall as a child. Then Sir Arthur had simply got up and wandered around the library until he found a book he fancied, and sat in one of the old leather chairs and gone to sleep with it open in his lap.

Matthew was waiting, staring at Pitt with mounting anger.

"Who is saying this?" Pitt asked.

Matthew was taken aback. It was not the question he was expecting.

"Uh—the doctor, the men at the club . . ."

"What club?"

"Oh—I am not being very clear, am I? He died at the Morton Club, in the late afternoon."

"In the afternoon? Not at night at all?" Pitt was genuinely surprised; he did not have to affect it.

"No! That's the point, Thomas," Matthew said impatiently. "They are saying he was demented, suffering from a sort of senile decay. It's not true, not even remotely! Father was one of the sanest men alive. And he didn't drink brandy either! At least, hardly ever."

"What has brandy to do with it?"

5

Matthew's shoulders sagged and he looked exhausted and utterly bewildered.

"Sit down," Pitt directed. "There is obviously more to this than you have told me so far. Have you eaten? You look terrible."

Matthew smiled wanly. "I really don't want to eat. Don't fuss over me, just listen."

Pitt conceded, and sat down opposite him.

Matthew sat on the edge of his chair, leaning forward, unable to relax.

"As I said, Father died yesterday. He was at his club. He had been there most of the afternoon. They found him in his chair when the steward went to tell him the time and ask if he wished for dinner. It was getting late." He winced. "They said he'd been drinking a lot of brandy, and they thought he'd had rather too much and fallen asleep. That's why nobody disturbed him before."

Pitt did not interrupt him but sat with an increasing weight of sadness for what he now knew would come.

"Of course when they did speak to him, they found he was dead," Matthew said bleakly. The effort of control in his voice was so naked that for anyone else Pitt would have been embarrassed; but now it was only an echo of what he himself was feeling. There were no questions to ask. It was not a crime, not even an event hard to understand. It was simply a bereavement, more sudden than most, and therefore carrying a kind of shock. But looked on with hindsight it would probably be a loss such as happens in most families sooner or later.

"I'm sorry," he said quietly.

"You don't understand!" All the rage built up in Matthew's face again. He looked at Pitt almost accusingly. Then he drew in a deep breath and let it out with a sigh. "You see, Father belonged to some sort of society—oh, it was benevolent, at least he used to think it was. They supported all sorts of charities. . . ." He waved his hand in the all to dismiss the matter. "I don't know what, precisely. He never told me."

Pitt felt cold, and unreasonably betrayed.

"The Inner Circle," he said, the words grating between his teeth.

Matthew was stunned. "You knew! How did you know, when I didn't?" He looked hurt, as if somehow Pitt had broken a trust. Upstairs there was a bang and the sound of running feet. Neither took notice.

"I'm guessing," Pitt replied with a smile that turned into a wince. "It is an organization I know a little about."

Matthew's expression hardened, almost as if some door had closed over his candor and now he was wary, no longer the friend, almost brother, that he had been.

"Are you a member? No, I am sorry. That's a stupid question, isn't it? Because you wouldn't tell me if you were. That's how you knew Father was. Did you join with him, all those years ago? He never invited me!"

"No I did not join," Pitt said tartly. "I never heard of it until recently, when I tangled with them in the course of my work. I've prosecuted a few of their members, and exposed several others for involvement in fraud, blackmail and murder. I probably know a great deal more about them than you do, and just how damnably dangerous they are."

Outside in the corridor Charlotte spoke to one of the children, and the footsteps died away.

Matthew sat silent for several moments, the emotions that churned through his mind reflecting in his eyes and the tired, vulnerable lines in his face. He was still suffering from shock; he had not accustomed himself to the knowledge that his father was dead. Grief was barely in check, the sudden loneliness, regret, a little guilt —even if he had no idea for what: simply chances missed, words unused. And he was terribly tired, wrung out additionally by the anger which consumed him. He had been disappointed in Pitt, perhaps even betrayed; and then immensely relieved, and again guilty, because he had accused him wrongly.

7

It was no time to require apologies. Matthew was near to breaking.

Pitt held out his hand.

Matthew clasped it so tightly his fingers bruised the flesh.

Pitt allowed him a moment or two of pure emotion, then recalled him to his story.

"Why did you mention the Inner Circle?"

Matthew made an effort, and began again in a more level voice, but still sitting far forward in his chair, his elbows on his knees and his hands under his chin.

"Father was always involved only with the strictly charitable side, until quite recently, the last year or two, when he rose higher in the organization. More by accident than design, I think. He began to learn a lot more about them, and what else they did, who some of the other members were." He frowned. "Particularly concerning Africa . . ."

"Africa?" Pitt was startled.

"Yes—Zambezia especially. There is a lot of exploration going on there at the moment. It's a very long story. Do you know anything about it?"

"No . . . nothing at all."

"Well naturally there's a great deal of money concerned, and the possibility of unimaginable wealth in the future. Gold, diamonds, and of course land. And there were all sorts of other questions as well, missionary work, trade, foreign policy."

"What has the Inner Circle to do with it?"

Matthew pulled a rueful face. "Power. It always has to do with power, and the sharing out of wealth. Anyway, Father began to appreciate just how the senior members of the Inner Circle were influencing policy in the government, and the South Africa Company, to their own advantage, regardless of the welfare of the Africans, or of British interests, either, for that matter. He got very upset about it indeed, and started to say so."

"To the other members of his own ring?" Pitt asked, although he feared he knew what Matthew would reply.

"No . . . to anyone who would listen." Matthew looked up, his eyes questioning. He saw the answer in Pitt's face. "I think they murdered him," he said quietly.

The silence was so intense they could hear the ticking of the walnut clock on the mantelshelf. Outside in the street, beyond the closed windows, someone shouted and the answer came back from farther away, a garden somewhere in the blue twilight.

Pitt did not dismiss it. The Inner Circle would quite readily do such a thing, if it felt the need great enough. He doubted not its resolve or ability . . . simply need.

"What was he saying about them, exactly?"

"You don't disbelieve it?" Matthew asked. "You don't sound shocked that distinguished members of the British aristocracy, the ruling classes, the honorable gentlemen of the country, should indulge in the murder of someone who chose to criticize them in public."

"I went through all my emotions of shock and disbelief when I first learned about the Inner Circle and their purposes and codes of conduct," Pitt replied. "I expect I shall feel anger and outrage all over again sometime, but at the moment I am trying to understand the facts. What was Sir Arthur saying that would make it necessary for the Inner Circle to take the dangerous step of killing him?"

For the first time Matthew sat back in his chair, crossing his legs, his eyes still on Pitt's face. "He criticized their general morality," he said in a steadier voice. "The way they are sworn to favor each other secretly, and at the expense of those who are outside the Circle, which is most of us. They do it in business, banking, politics and socially if they can, although that is harder." His smile twisted. "There are still the unwritten laws that govern who is accepted and who is not. Nothing can force that. You may impel a gentleman to be civil to you, if he owes you money, but you can never force him to look on you as one of his own, whatever he owes you, up to and including his life." He did not find it curious, nor did he seek words for the indefinable quality of assurance which made a gentleman. It had nothing to do with intelligence, achievement, money or title. A man might have all these and yet still fail to meet the invisible criteria. Matthew had been born to it; he understood it as some men know how to ride a horse, or to sing in tune.

"It includes too many gentlemen," Pitt said sourly, memory returning of past cases and his bitter involvement with the Circle.

"That is more or less what Father said," Matthew agreed, his eyes on Pitt's face with a deepening intensity. "Then he went on quite specifically about Africa and the way they are controlling banking, whose interests control the funds for exploration and settlement. They are hand-and-hand with the politicians who will decide whether we try for a Cape-to-Cairo domination or concede to the Germans and concentrate on the south." He shrugged with a quick, angry gesture. "As always the Foreign Secretary is hovering around, saying one thing, and meaning another. I work in the Foreign Office, and I don't know myself what he really wants. There are missionaries, doctors, explorers, profiteers, big game hunters and Germans swarming all over the place." He bit his lip ruefully. "Not to mention the native kings and warrior princes whose land it is anyway . . . until we wring treaties out of them for it. Or the Germans do."

"And the Inner Circle?" Pitt prompted.

"Manipulating behind the scenes," Matthew replied. "Calling in old loyalties secretly, investing quietly and reaping the reward. That's what Father was saying." He slid a little farther back in the seat and began to relax fractionally; or perhaps he was just so tired he could no longer sit upright. "What he objected to most intensely was the way the whole thing is secret. To give charity anonymously is fine and a perfectly honorable thing to do."

10

They were both oblivious of the sounds of movement in the passage beyond.

"That's what he originally thought the society was for," he went on. "A group of men banded together to have a better knowledge of where help was needed, and not to do it piecemeal, but with sufficient means to make a real difference. Orphanages, hospitals for the needy, and for research into specific illnesses, almshouses for old soldiers ... that sort of thing. Then just recently he discovered the other side to it." He bit his lip, almost apologetically. "Father was a trifle naive, I think. You or I would have realized there was more to it a lot sooner. He thought the best of many people I would not have."

Pitt recalled what he knew of the Inner Circle.

"Didn't they warn him very quickly that they do not take criticism kindly, in fact they don't take it at all?"

"Yes! Yes they did. They warned him in gentlemanly and discreet terms, which he misread completely. It never occurred to him that they really meant it." Matthew's eyebrows rose and his hazel eyes looked at once amused and bitterly hurt. Pitt had a curious sensation of respect for him, and realized the depth of his resolve, not only to clear his father of any suggestion of weakness, but perhaps also to avenge him.

"Matthew," he began, leaning forward spontaneously.

"If you are going to warn me to leave it alone, you are wasting your time," Matthew said stubbornly.

"I ..." That was precisely what Pitt had been going to do. It was disconcerting to be read so easily. "You don't even know who they are," he pointed out. "At least stop and think very hard before you do anything." It sounded feeble, desperately predictable.

Matthew smiled. "Poor Thomas, so much the elder brother. We are not children now, and one year doesn't make your seniority worth anything. It hasn't since we were ten! Of course I shall think carefully. That's why I've come to you. I know perfectly well I can't wound the Circle. It's

11

a Hydra. Cut off one head and two more will grow." His face hardened again and all the light vanished out of it. "But I'm going to prove Father was not senile, or get killed in the attempt myself." He looked at Pitt very levelly, meeting his eyes without a flicker. "If we allow them to say such things about a man like Father, to silence him with murder, and then discredit him by saying he had lost his wits, then apart from anything else, what have we left? What have we made of ourselves? What honor can we claim?"

"None," Pitt said sadly. "But we need more than honor to win that battle; we need a great deal of tactical skill as well, and some sharp weapons." Pitt grimaced. "Or perhaps a long spoon will be more appropriate."

Matthew's eyebrows rose. "To sup with the devil? Yes, well put. Have you a long spoon, Thomas? Are you willing to join me in the battle?"

"Yes of course I am." He spoke without even thinking about it. Only the moment after did all the dangers and the responsibilities come closing in on his mind, but it was too late. And even if he had thought about it and weighed every one, he would still have made the same decision. The only difference would have been the sense of anguishing over it, the fear and the understanding of risk, and the margin of success that could be hoped for. Perhaps that would have been only so much time wasted anyway.

Matthew relaxed at last, allowing his head to rest against the antimacassar behind him. He smiled. Something of the tiredness and the look of defeat had been ironed out of his features. At a glance he almost resembled the youth Pitt had known so long ago, with whom he had shared adventures and dreams. They seemed both immensely wild, full of impossibilities—journeys up the Amazon, discoveries of the tombs of Pharaohs—and at the same time boyishly tame, still with the gentle, domestic ideas of right and wrong, children's notions of wickedness: theft of goods and simple violence the worst they knew. They had not imagined corruption, disillusion, manipulation and betrayal. It all seemed very innocent now, the boys they had been long ago.

"There were warnings," Matthew said suddenly. "I can see that now, although at the time I didn't. I was up here in London when they happened, and he made light of it each time."

"What were they?" Pitt asked.

Matthew screwed up his face. "Well, the first I cannot be sure about. As Father told it to me, he was traveling on the underground railway, at least he was intending to. He went down the steps to the platform and was waiting for the train—" He stopped abruptly and looked at Pitt. "Have you ever been on one of those things?"

"Yes, frequently." Pitt pictured the cavernous passages, the long stations where the tunnel widened to allow a platform alongside the train, the dark curved roof, the glaring gaslights, the incredible noise as the engine rattled and roared out of the black hole into the light and came to a halt. Doors flew open and people poured out. Others waiting took their opportunity and pressed in before the doors should close and the wormlike contraption be on its way back into the darkness again.

"Then I don't need to explain the noise and the crowds pushing and shoving each other," Matthew continued. "Well, Father was fairly well towards the front and just as he heard the train coming, he felt a violent weight in the middle of his back and was propelled forward almost over the edge of the platform onto the lines, where of course he would have been killed." Matthew's voice hardened and there was a harsh edge to it. "He was grasped and hauled back just as the train appeared and came hurtling in. He said he turned to thank whomever it was, but there was no longer any person there he could distinguish as his helper—or his assailant. Everyone seemed to be about the business of boarding the train, and no one took the least notice of him."

13

"But he was sure he was pushed?"

"Quite sure." Matthew waited for Pitt to express some skepticism.

Pitt nodded barely perceptibly. With someone else, someone he knew less closely, he might have doubted; but unless he had changed beyond recognition, Arthur Desmond was the last man on earth to believe he was being persecuted. He viewed all men as basically good until he was forced to do otherwise, and then it came to him as a shock and a sadness, and he was still ready to find himself mistaken, and delighted to be so.

"And the second?" Pitt asked.

"That was something to do with a horse," Matthew replied. "He never told me the details." He sat forward again, his brow creasing. "I only knew about it at all because the groom told me when I was home. It seems Father was riding down in the village when some unexpected idiot came down the road at a full gallop, completely out of control of his animal. He was careering all over the place, one side of the road to the other, arms flying, whip in his hand, and he just about drove Father into the stone wall alongside the vicarage. Caught his horse a terrible blow about the head with his whip. Terrified the poor beast, and of course Father was thrown." He let out his breath slowly, without moving his eyes from Pitt's face. "It could conceivably have been an accident; the man was either drunken out of his senses or a complete imbecile, but Father didn't think so, and I certainly don't."

"No," Pitt said grimly. "Neither do I. He was a damn good horseman, and not the sort of man to imagine things of anyone."

Suddenly Matthew smiled, a wide, generous smile that made him look years younger. "That's the best thing I have heard anyone say in weeks. Dear God, I wish his friends could hear you. Everyone is so afraid to praise him, even to acknowledge his sanity, never mind that he might have been right." There was sudden hurt in his voice. "Thomas, he was sane, wasn't he? The sanest and most honorable and innately decent man ever to walk the land."

"Yes he was," Pitt agreed quietly and with total honesty. "But apart from that, it doesn't rest on his sanity. I know the Inner Circle punishes those who betray it. I've seen it before. Sometimes it is social or financial ruin—not often death, but it is not unknown. If they couldn't frighten him, and they obviously couldn't, then there was nothing else for them to do. They couldn't ruin him financially because he didn't gamble or speculate. They couldn't socially because he didn't curry favor with anyone, or seek any office or alliances, and he couldn't have cared less about being accepted at court, or in the social circles of London. Where he lived his standing was unassailable, even by the Inner Circle. So there was only death left to them, to silence him permanently."

"And then to nullify all he said by dishonoring his memory." Matthew's voice was filled with anger, and pain flooded back into his face. "I can't bear that, Thomas. I won't!"

There was a knock on the parlor door. Pitt suddenly became aware again of where he was, and that it was nearly dark outside. He had not eaten, and Charlotte must be wondering who his visitor was and why he had gone into the parlor and closed the door without introducing her, or inviting the visitor to dine.

Matthew looked at him expectantly, and Pitt was surprised to see there was a flicker of nervousness across his face, as if he were uncertain how he should behave.

"Come in." Pitt rose to his feet and reached to open the door. Charlotte was standing outside looking curious and a little anxious. She had finished reading to the children and from the faint flush in her cheeks and the stray hair poked into a misplaced pin, he knew she had been in the kitchen. He had even forgotten he was hungry. "Charlotte, this is Matthew Desmond." It was ridiculous that they had never met before. Matthew had been closer to him than anyone

15

else except his mother, at times closer than even she. And Charlotte was closer to him now than he had imagined anyone could be. And he had never taken her back to Brackley, never introduced her to his home, or to those who had been more than family to him before she was. His mother had died when he was eighteen, but that should not have cut the ties.

"How do you do, Mr. Desmond," Charlotte said with a calm and confidence Pitt knew was the product of her birth, not of any inner emotion. He saw the uncertainty in her eyes and knew why she moved a step closer to him.

"How do you do, Mrs. Pitt," Matthew replied, and his voice lifted very slightly with surprise because she answered his look squarely. In that brief second, with no more than a sentence and a meeting of glances, they had taken a certain measure of each other, understood the precise niche in society which they filled. "I am sorry to intrude, Mrs. Pitt," Matthew went on. "I am afraid it was most selfish of me. I came to tell Thomas of my father's death, and I regret that all consideration for anyone else went straight out of my head. I apologize."

Charlotte looked across at Pitt this time, her face full of shock and sympathy, then back to Matthew. "I am sorry, Mr. Desmond. You must be feeling quite terrible. Is there anything we can do to be of practical assistance? Would you like Thomas to go back to Brackley with you?"

Matthew smiled. "Actually, Mrs. Pitt, I wanted Thomas to find out precisely what happened, and that he has already promised to do."

Charlotte took breath to say something else, then realized perhaps it was inappropriate, and changed her mind.

"Would you like some supper, Mr. Desmond? I imagine you do not feel like eating, but you may feel worse if you leave it too long."

"You are quite right," he agreed. "On all counts."

She looked at him closely, at the distress and the weari-

16

ness in his face. She hesitated on the edge of decision for a moment, then made her judgment.

"Would you like to stay here overnight, Mr. Desmond? It will be no inconvenience whatever. In fact you would be our first guest since moving here, and we should like that very much. If there is anything you need, and have not with you, Thomas could lend it to you."

He did not need to consider it. "Thank you," he said immediately. "I would far rather that than return to my rooms."

"Thomas will show you upstairs and have Gracie prepare the bedroom for you. Supper will be served in ten minutes." And she turned, with only a glance at Pitt, and retreated towards the kitchen.

Matthew stood for a moment in the hallway looking at Pitt. All sorts of half thoughts were plain in his face: surprise, understanding, memories of the past, of long talks and even longer dreams when they were boys, and some of all the distance between then and now. No explanations were necessary.

Supper was a light meal anyway: cold roast chicken and vegetables, and a fruit sorbet afterwards. It was hardly a time when it mattered, but Pitt was glad Matthew had come after his promotion, and it had not been during the time when mutton stew and potatoes, or whiting and bread and butter, were all they could have offered.

They spoke little, and that merely of unemotional subjects such as plans for the garden, what they hoped to grow in the future, whether all the fruit trees were likely to bear, or how badly they were in need of pruning. It was only to fill the silence, not any attempt to pretend that all was well. Charlotte knew as well as Pitt that grief must be allowed its time. To prevent it by constant diversion only increased the pain, like a denial of the importance of the event, as if the loss did not matter.

Matthew retired early, leaving Charlotte in the green-and-white sitting room with Pitt. To have called it a withdrawing room would have been pretentious, but it had all the charm and cool ease that would serve such a purpose.

"What did he mean?" she asked as soon as Matthew had had time to be up the stairs beyond hearing. "What was wrong with Sir Arthur's death?"

Slowly, finding words harder than he had expected to, he told her all that Matthew had said about Sir Arthur and the Inner Circle, the warnings he felt they had given him, and finally his death from laudanum at the Morton Club.

She listened without taking her eyes from his, and without interruption. He wondered if she could see in his face, as transparently as he felt them, both his grief and his sense of guilt. He was not even sure if he wanted her to know it. It was a bitterly lonely thing to hide, and yet he did not wish her to see him as the thoughtless man he felt, careless of so many years of past kindness that he had not been back, and now all he could do was repay a fraction of the debt by trying to redeem Sir Arthur's name from a dishonor he knew it did not deserve.

If she perceived it in him, she did not say so. Charlotte could be the most wildly tactless of people at times. And yet when she loved someone, her commitment was such that she could keep any secret, and refrain from judgment in a way few people matched.

"He is the last man to have taken laudanum at all," he said earnestly. "But even if he had, for some reason we know nothing of, I can't let them say he was senile. It's—it's an indignity."

"I know." She reached out her hand and took his. "You don't speak of him often, but I do know you feel very deeply for him. But regardless of that, it is an injustice one should not let by for anyone at all." Her eyes were troubled and for the first time since he had begun, she was uncertain of his reaction. "But Thomas . . ."

"What?"

"Don't let emotion . . ." She chose the word carefully, leaving the implication of guilt unsaid, although he was cer-

18

tain she knew that was what he felt. "Don't let emotion prompt you into rushing in without thought and preparation. They are not enemies you can afford to take lightly. They have no honor in the way they fight. They won't give you a second chance because you are bereaved, or rash, or motivated by loyalty. Once they realize you mean to fight them, they will try to provoke you into those very mistakes. I know you will remember Sir Arthur's death, and that will fire you to want to beat them: but also remember the way in which they killed him, how successful it was for their purposes, and how completely ruthless."

She shivered and looked increasingly unhappy, as if her own words had frightened her. "If they will do that to one of their own, imagine what they will do to an enemy, like you." She looked for a moment as if she were going to add something—perhaps a plea for him to think again, to weigh the chances of achieving anything—but she changed her mind. Probably she knew it would be pointless now, of all times. He did not suspect her of duplicity ever—she had not the heart for it, nor the temper—but possibly she was learning a little tact.

He answered the unspoken question. "I have to," he said gently. "The alternative is intolerable."

She did not say anything, but held his hand more tightly, and sat still beside him for a long time.

In the morning Matthew slept late and Charlotte and Pitt were already at breakfast when he came into the dining room. Jemima and Daniel were already dressed and had walked to school with Gracie. This was a new task in which she took great satisfaction, stretching up to every fraction of her four feet eleven inches and smiling graciously to people she either knew or considered she would like to know. Charlotte suspected she also had a brief word with the butcher's assistant on the corner on her return, but that was neither here nor there. He seemed quite a respectable youth. Charlotte had made a point of going in on one or two occasions herself, in order to have a good look at him and estimate his character.

Matthew looked rested, but there were still dark circles of shock under his eyes, and his thick brown hair with its fair streak across the brow looked tousled and ill cut, although it was probably only the result of having combed it with haste and inattention.

The usual courtesies were exchanged and Charlotte offered him bacon, eggs, kidneys, and toast and marmalade. Automatically she poured tea for him and he drank it while it was still too hot, burning his mouth.

After several minutes of companionable silence, Charlotte excused herself and withdrew to the kitchen about some domestic chore, and Matthew looked up at Pitt.

"There's something else I really ought to speak to you about," he said with his mouth full.

"Yes?"

"This is in your official capacity." He took another sip of the tea, this time more carefully. "And mine too."

"The Foreign Office?" Pitt was startled.

"Yes. It's Africa again." He frowned in concentration. "I don't know if you know anything about our treaties . . . no? Well it doesn't matter a lot for what I'm going to say. But we did make an agreement with Germany four years ago in 1886, and we are looking towards another this summer. Of course it's all been altered by Bismarck's losing power and the young Kaiser taking over everything. He's got this wretched fellow Carl Peters, who is as sharp as a knife and tricky as a load of monkeys. And Salisbury not making up his mind what he really wants doesn't make anything easier. Half of us suppose he is still looking for British domination of a corridor from the Cape to Cairo. The other half think he prefers to let that go as too costly and too difficult."

"Difficult?" Pitt questioned with puzzlement.

"Yes," Matthew said, taking another slice of toast. "For a start it's over three thousand miles between British South

Africa and British-controlled Egypt. That means taking Sudan, Equatoria—currently held by a slippery customer called Emin Pasha—a corridor west of German East Africa: not so easy in the present climate." He regarded Pitt seriously to make sure he was following. Then to explain more clearly he started drawing on the kitchen table with his forefinger. "The whole area north of Transvaal, and that includes Zambezia and the territories between Angola and Mozambique, is still held by native chiefs."

"I see," Pitt said vaguely. "And the alternative you mentioned?"

"Cairo to Old Calabar," Matthew replied, biting into his toast. "Or Niger to the Nile, if you like. That's through Lake Chad, then westwards nearly to Senegal, taking Dahomey and the Ivory Coast from the French. . . ."

"War?" Pitt was incredulous, and appalled.

"No, no, of course not," Matthew said hastily. "In exchange for the Gambia."

"Oh, I see."

"No you don't, not yet. There's also the question of German East Africa, where there's been a lot of trouble, uprisings and several killings, and Heligoland. . . ."

"I beg your pardon?" Now Pitt was totally confused.

"Heligoland," Matthew repeated with his mouth full.

"I thought Heligoland was in the North Sea. I can remember Mr. Tarbet saying it was. I'd no idea it was anywhere near Africa."

"It is in the North Sea, just as Tarbet said." Mr. Tarbet had been Matthew's tutor as a child, and thus also Pitt's. "Ideally placed for a naval base to blockade all the principal German ports on the Rhine," Matthew explained. "We could trade Heligoland to the Germans for some of their lands in Africa. And believe me, they would be glad enough to do that, if we managed it really well."

Pitt smiled wryly. "I can see that you have an extraordinary number of highly complex problems. But what exactly

21

do you wish to consult the police over? We have no writ in Africa, or even in Heligoland."

"But you do in London. And London is where the Colonial Office is, and the German Embassy. . . ."

"Oh." In spite of himself, Pitt was beginning to see, or to fear that he did.

"And the British Imperial South Africa Company," Matthew went on. "And the various banks who fund explorers and missionaries, not to mention the adventurers, both literal and financial."

"Unarguable," Pitt conceded. "Why is that relevant?"

The faint flicker of amusement died out of Matthew's eyes and he became serious.

"Because there is information disappearing from the Colonial Office, Thomas, and turning up in the German Embassy. We know that because of the bargaining issues the Germans are aware of, and they shouldn't be. Sometimes they know things almost before we do in the Foreign Office. It hasn't done any great damage yet, as far as we know, but it could very seriously jeopardize our chances of a successful treaty if it goes on."

"So someone in the Colonial Office is passing information to the German Embassy?"

"I cannot see any alternative explanation."

"What sort of information? Could it not have come from some other source? Surely they have men in East Africa too?"

"If you knew a little more about African affairs you wouldn't ask that." Matthew shrugged. "Every report one gets is different from the last, and most accounts are open to a dozen interpretations, especially where the native chiefs and princes are concerned. It is our Colonial Office version the Germans are getting."

"Information about what sort of thing?"

Matthew drank the rest of his tea.

"So far as we know, at the moment it is mostly about mineral deposits and trading negotiations between various

22

factions and the native chiefs. In particular one in Zambezia called Lobengula. We were very much hoping the Germans were unaware of the stage of negotiations we had reached in that matter."

"But they are not?"

"Difficult to say, but I fear not."

Pitt finished his own tea and poured more, helping himself to another slice of toast out of the rack. He had a deep liking for homemade marmalade. Charlotte had a way of doing it that was so pungent the flavor seemed to fill his whole head. He had observed that Matthew liked it as well.

"You have a traitor in the Colonial Office," he said slowly. "Who else is aware of what you have told me?"

"My immediate superior, and the Foreign Secretary, Lord Salisbury."

"That's all?"

Matthew's eyes widened. "Good heavens, yes. We don't want people all over the place to know we have a spy in the Colonial Office. Nor do we want the spy himself to know we are aware of him. We need to clear up the whole matter before it does any real damage, and then keep quiet about it."

"I can't work without authority," Pitt began.

Matthew frowned. "I will write you a letter of authority if you like. But I thought you were a superintendent now. What more authority do you need?"

"My assistant commissioner's, if I am to start questioning people in the Colonial Office," Pitt replied.

"Oh, well, him of course."

"You don't believe this has any connection with the other matter, do you?"

Matthew frowned for a moment, then his face cleared as he understood.

"Good God, I hope not! The Inner Circle is pretty low, but I had not imagined it was involved in treason, which is what this amounts to. No. So far as I know, and from everything Father said, the Inner Circle interests are best

23

served by Britain remaining as powerful and as rich as possible. Britain's loss in Africa would be theirs as well. Their robbing us is one thing; the Germans doing it is quite another." He smiled bitterly at the irony of it. "Why do you ask? Do you think there are Inner Circle members in the Colonial Office?"

"Probably, but I'm quite sure there are in the police. Of what rank I have no idea."

"As high as assistant commissioner?" Matthew asked.

Pitt ate the last of his toast and marmalade.

"Certainly, but I meant of what rank in the Inner Circle. The two have no connection, which is one of the things that makes it so appallingly dangerous."

"I don't understand you."

"You can find that someone in a position of great financial or political power," Pitt explained, "is quite junior in the Circle, and owes some kind of obedience to an Inner Circle member who appears to be nobody significant in the world. You don't ever know where the real power lies."

"But surely that . . ." Matthew began, then trailed off, his eyes puzzled. "That would account for some very strange discoveries. . . ." he started again. "A web of loyalties under the surface, conflicting with, and stronger than, all the ones you can see." His face was pale and tight. "God, that's very frightening. I hadn't perceived it quite like that. No wonder Father was so distressed. I knew well enough why he was angry, but not the helplessness, at least not the depth of it." He stopped and sat silent for several moments. Then he went on suddenly. "But even if it is all hopeless, I shall still try. I can't let it . . . just lie like this."

Pitt said nothing.

"I'm sorry." Matthew bit his lip. "You were not trying to dissuade me, were you? I'm a little frightened of it myself. But you will take up the matter of the information from the Colonial Office?"

"Of course. As soon as I go in to Bow Street. I assume

you are making the official Foreign Office request? I may use your name?"

"Yes, certainly." He put his hand in his pocket and pulled out an envelope. He passed it to Pitt. "Here is a letter of authority. And Thomas . . . thank you."

Pitt did not know what to say. To brush it aside as a small matter also dismissed their friendship and reduced it to mere good manners.

"What are you going to do now?" he asked instead.

Matthew looked so inwardly weary, the night's sleep, if indeed he had slept, was merely a superficial relief. He set his napkin aside and stood up.

"There are arrangements to be made. They—" He took a deep breath. "They are having the inquest the day after tomorrow."

"I'll be there."

"Thank you."

"And . . . the funeral?"

"Two days after that, on the sixth. You'll be there, won't you? It's in Brackley, naturally. He'll be buried in the family vault."

"Of course I will." Pitt stood up also. "Where are you going now? Back to the Hall?"

"No. No, the inquest is here in London. I still have things to do."

"Is there anyone . . . if you want to come back here?"

Matthew smiled. "Thank you, but I really should go and see Harriet. I . . ." He looked faintly embarrassed.

Pitt waited.

"I recently became betrothed," Matthew went on with a faint color marking his cheeks.

"Congratulations!" Pitt meant it. He would have been delighted for him at any time, but now it seemed particularly fortunate that he had someone who could support him and share this time of loss. "Yes of course you should see her, tell her what has happened before she sees it in some newspaper, or hears it from someone else."

Matthew pulled a face. "She won't be reading newspapers, Thomas!"

Pitt realized with a jolt that he had committed a social gaffe. Ladies did not read newspapers, except for the court circulars or fashion columns. He had become accustomed to Charlotte and her sister, Emily, who, since leaving their father's home, accepted no restrictions whatever upon what they would read. Even Lord Ashworth, Emily's first husband, had allowed her that unusual latitude.

"Of course. I should have said until someone who has read a newspaper mentions it to her," he apologized. "That would seem a thoughtless way of allowing her to hear of it. I am sure she would wish to be every support to you that she can."

"Yes . . . I . . ." Matthew shrugged. "It seems so heartless to be happy in any respect now. . . ."

"Nonsense!" Pitt said fervently. "Sir Arthur would be the first person to wish you any comfort you can find, and happiness too. You really don't need me to assure you of that. You must know it for yourself, unless you have forgotten completely what manner of man he was." It seemed strange and painful to speak of him in the past, and suddenly without warning he was caught by grief again.

Matthew must have felt something of the same emotion. His face was very pale.

"Of course. I . . . can't . . . just yet. But I will go and see her, of course. She is a very fine woman, Thomas. You will like her. She is the daughter of Ransley Soames, at the Treasury."

"Again, congratulations!" Pitt held out his hand; it was an automatic gesture.

Matthew took it, smiling briefly.

"Now we had both better go," Pitt said. "I to Bow Street, and then to the Colonial Office."

"Yes indeed. I must find Mrs. Pitt and thank her for her hospitality. I wish . . . I wish you had brought her to meet Father, Thomas. He would have liked her. . . ." He swal-

26

lowed hard and turned away to hide his sudden loss of control.

"So do I," Pitt agreed intensely. "It is one of the many things I shall regret." He went out of the room tactfully, to permit Matthew the privacy in which to compose himself. And he went upstairs to look for Charlotte.

In the Bow Street police station he was fortunate to find Assistant Commissioner Giles Farnsworth present. He came only occasionally, being in command of a very considerable area, and this was an unusual time for him to visit. Pitt had expected to reach him only after a considerable effort.

"Ah, good morning, Pitt," Farnsworth said briskly. He was a handsome man in a smooth, well-bred manner, with sleek fair hair, clean-shaven face, and clear, very level blue-gray eyes. "Glad you are here in good time. Nasty robbery last night in Great Wild Street. Lady Warburton's diamonds stolen. Haven't got a full list yet, but Sir Robert will have it ready by midday. Most unpleasant. See to it personally, will you. I promised Sir Robert I'd have my best man on it." He did not bother to look at Pitt to receive his answer. It was an order, not a suggestion.

When Micah Drummond had retired he had recommended Pitt to take his place with such fervor that Farnsworth had accepted it, but with considerable reservations. Pitt was not a gentleman, as Drummond had been, nor had he any previous experience of commanding men, such as a commissioned rank in the army, again, as Drummond had had. Farnsworth was accustomed to working with men of Drummond's social rank in the position of superintendent. It made matters so much easier. They understood each other, they knew the rules as lesser men do not, and they were comfortable as something approaching equals.

Pitt would never be socially equal with Farnsworth, and there would never be friendship between them. The fact that Drummond had regarded Pitt as a friend was one of those inexplicable lapses that even gentlemen make from time to time. Although usually it was with people who had some particular skill or art to recommend them, such as the breeding of fine horses, or the design of a great garden with follies, parterres of box or lavender, or some brilliant new mechanical device for waterfalls and fountains. Pitt had never before encountered anyone who had such a lapse of judgment over a professional junior.

"Mr. Farnsworth," Pitt stopped him as he was about to leave.

"Yes?" Farnsworth was surprised.

"Naturally I will attend to Lady Warburton's diamonds if you wish me to, but I would rather put Tellman onto it and leave myself free to go to the Colonial Office, where I have been informed there is a leak of vital information about African affairs."

"What?" Farnsworth was appalled. He swung around, staring at Pitt. "I don't know anything about this! Why did you not report this immediately? I was available all yesterday, and the day before. You could perfectly easily have found me if you tried. You've got a telephone here. You should have one installed in your own home. You must keep up with the times, Pitt. Modern inventions are here for our use, not just to entertain those with more money and imagination than sense. What's the matter with you, man? You are too old-fashioned. Stuck in your ways!"

"I only heard of it half an hour ago," Pitt replied with satisfaction. "Immediately before leaving my home. And I don't think it is a suitable subject to discuss on the telephone, but I do have one."

"If it is not a suitable subject to discuss on the telephone, how did you hear about it?" Farnsworth demanded with a flash of humor and equal satisfaction. "If you wish to be discreet about it, you should have gone around to the Colonial Office to ascertain the situation before coming here. Are you really sure it is important information at all? Perhaps in your zeal to be discreet, you have insufficient knowledge to assume it is anything like as grave as you suggest. It is probably merely misplaced."

Pitt smiled and put his hands in his pockets. "A member of the Foreign Office visited me in person," he replied, "on the instructions of Lord Salisbury, and officially requested me to look into the matter. The information which we are speaking of has turned up in the German Embassy, which is how they know of the matter. It is not a few pieces of paper that no one can put his hand on."

Farnsworth was aghast, but Pitt did not allow him to speak.

"The Germans are aware of some of our negotiating positions with reference to possessions in East Africa, Zambezia, and the possibilities of a British corridor from Cairo to the Cape," he went on. "However, Lady Warburton's diamonds . . ."

"To hell with Lady Warburton and her diamonds," Farnsworth exploded. "Tellman can deal with that." A look of spite crossed his well-formed features. "I only said my best man, I did not name him. And that is not necessarily the most senior, by any means. You go to the Colonial Office immediately. Concentrate on it, Pitt. Leave everything else until you have that solved. Do you understand me? And for God's sake, man, be discreet!"

Pitt smiled. "Yes, Mr. Farnsworth. That is what I intended, before the matter of Lady Warburton came up."

Farnsworth glared at him, but said nothing further.

Pitt opened the door. Farnsworth went out. Pitt followed him, calling the desk sergeant to send for Inspector Tellman.

2

P*ITT WALKED DOWN* Bow Street to the Strand, where he found a hansom and gave the driver instructions to take him to the Colonial Office on the corner of Whitehall and Downing Street. The driver looked at him with slight surprise, but after only a moment's hesitation, urged the horse forward and joined the stream of traffic moving west.

Pitt spent the journey going over in his mind what Matthew had said, and formulating the way in which he would approach the subject when he reached Whitehall. He had read Matthew's letter of authority, and the brief instructions and details with it, but it gave him little feeling for the nature or degree of difficulty he would face in obtaining cooperation.

The cab progressed slowly, stopping for every tangle of coaches, carriages, drays and omnibuses from the Strand and Wellington Street where Pitt had hired it. They inched past Northampton Street, Bedford Street, King William Street, and Duncannon Street right to Charing Cross. Everyone was in a hurry and determined to have the right-of-way. Drivers were shouting at each other. A brougham and a hearse had apparently got their wheels locked and were causing a major obstruction. Two youths with a dray were calling out advice, and a costermonger was having a quarrel with a pie seller.

It was fifteen minutes before Pitt's cab finally turned left into Whitehall and made its way towards Downing Street, and when it stopped, the duty constable approached to see what they wanted.

"Superintendent Pitt, going to the Colonial Office," Pitt told him, producing his card.

The cabdriver opened his eyes with interest.

"Yes sir." The constable saluted smartly and stood rather more to attention. "Didn't recognize you, sir."

Pitt paid the driver and turned to go up the steps, aware that he was a good deal less than smart, and certainly not attired like one of the officials and diplomats. In their cutaway coats, winged collars and striped trousers, they passed him on either side, carrying their furled umbrellas, although it was a fine May Day morning.

"Yes sir?" a young man enquired of him almost as soon as he came inside the building. "May I help you, sir?"

Pitt produced his card again as verification of his rank, which he admitted his appearance lacked. As always his hair was too long and curled untidily over his collar and from under his hat. His jacket was actually quite well cut, but his habit of poking all manner of things into the pockets had pushed it out of shape, and certainly his collar was not stiff, nor was it winged. His tie was something of an afterthought, and looked it.

"Yes, please," he replied immediately. "I have a confidential matter to discuss with the most senior official available."

"I'll make an appointment for you, sir," the young man replied smoothly. "Would the day after tomorrow be suitable to you? Mr. Aylmer should be available then, and I'm sure he will be happy to see you. He is Mr. Chancellor's immediate junior, and a very knowledgeable person."

Pitt knew the name of Linus Chancellor, Secretary of State for Colonial Affairs, as did every other man in London. He was one of the most brilliant of rising politicians, and it was held by many that one day he would lead the government.

31

"No, it would not," he said levelly, meeting the young man's eyes, and seeing a look of startled affront in them. "The matter is extremely urgent and must be attended to at the earliest moment possible. It is also confidential, so I cannot detail it to you. I have come at the request of the Foreign Office. If you wish to check with Lord Salisbury, you may do so. I shall wait for Mr. Chancellor."

The young man swallowed, uncertain now what he should do. He looked at Pitt with dislike.

"Yes sir, I shall inform Mr. Chancellor's office, and bring you his reply." He looked back at Pitt's card again, then disappeared upstairs.

It was nearly a quarter of an hour before he returned, and Pitt was beginning to find the waiting onerous.

"If you care to come this way, sir," the young man said coolly. He turned on his heel, leading the way back up again, knocking at the mahogany door and then standing aside to allow Pitt through.

Linus Chancellor was in his early forties, a dynamic man with a high forehead and dark hair which swept off his brow, showing a strong, jutting nose, wide mouth full of humor, volatility and a powerful will. He was a man to whom charm came easily, almost without conscious effort, and his natural fluency enabled him to say what other men struggled for and often missed. He was slender, of a good height and immaculately dressed.

"Good morning, Superintendent Pitt." He rose from his seat behind a magnificent desk and offered his hand. When Pitt took it, his grip was firm and strong. "I am informed that your errand is both urgent and confidential." He waved to the chair opposite and resumed his own seat. "You had better explain it to me. I have some ten minutes before I have to be at my next appointment. I'm afraid I can spare you no longer than that. I am due at Number Ten."

That needed no explanation. If he were to see the Prime Minister, which was his implication, it was not something which could be delayed, whatever Pitt had to say. It was also a very forthright statement of the importance of his own time and position. He did not intend Pitt to underestimate him.

Pitt sat down in the large, carved and leather-padded seat indicated and began immediately.

"I have been informed this morning by Matthew Desmond of the Foreign Office that certain information regarding the Colonial Office's dealings with our current exploration and trading negotiations in Africa, specifically Zambezia, have fallen into the hands of the German Embassy. . . ."

He did not need to go any further. He had Chancellor's total attention.

"So far as I know, only Mr. Desmond, his immediate senior, and Lord Salisbury himself are aware of the loss," Pitt continued. "I require your permission, sir, in order to investigate from this office. . . ."

"Yes, of course. Immediately. This is extremely serious." The polite affectation of interest was gone, and in its place an earnestness which was unmistakable. "Can you tell me what manner of information you are speaking of? Did Mr. Desmond tell you, or indeed does he know?"

"Not in detail," Pitt replied. "I gather it is largely to do with mineral rights and treaties with local chieftains."

Chancellor looked very grave, his mouth pinched at the corners.

"That could be extremely serious. A great deal rests on it for the future settlement of Africa. I assume Mr. Desmond told you as much? Yes, naturally. Will you please keep me informed, Mr. Pitt? Personally. I imagine you have already investigated the possibility that whatever information it is could not simply have reached the Germans through their own people?" There was no real hope in his face; he asked as a matter of form. "They have a great many explorers, adventurers and soldiers in East Africa, particularly along the coast of Zanzibar. I will not bore you with the details of their treaties with the Sultan of Zanzibar, and the settlement uprisings and violence. Accept, for this matter, that they have a considerable presence in the area."

"I have not looked into it myself, but that was the first question I asked Mr. Desmond," Pitt replied. "He assured me it could not be so, because of the detail of the information and the fact that it corresponded precisely with our own version of events which are open to many interpretations."

"Yes—" Chancellor nodded. "You are supposing treason in our midst, Mr. Pitt. Probably of a very high order. Tell me what you propose to do about it."

"All I can do, sir, is investigate everyone who has access to all the information that has been passed on. I assume that will be a limited number of people?"

"Certainly. Mr. Thorne has charge of our African affairs. Begin with him. Now if you will excuse me, Superintendent, I shall call Fairbrass and have him take you through. I have a short space of time free at quarter past four this afternoon. I will be obliged if you will report to me then whatever progress you have made, impressions you have gained."

"Yes sir." Pitt stood up and Chancellor rose also. A young man, presumably Fairbrass, appeared in the doorway and after brief instructions from Chancellor, conducted Pitt through a number of handsome corridors to a further, spacious, well-furnished office not unlike the first. The plate on the door read JEREMIAH THORNE, and Fairbrass was apparently so in awe of Mr. Thorne he considered Pitt would need no information as to who he was. He knocked tentatively, and upon receiving an answer, turned the handle and put his head around.

"Mr. Thorne, sir, I have a Superintendent Pitt here, from Bow Street, I think. Mr. Chancellor asked me to bring him along." He stopped abruptly, realizing he knew no more. He withdrew and pushed the door wider for Pitt to go in.

Jeremiah Thorne was superficially not unlike his political master. There was a difference in his bearing which was immediate, but equally it was indefinable. He was seated behind his desk but he appeared also to be of a good height. He had widely spaced eyes, dark hair, thick and smooth, and a broad, generous mouth. But he was a civil servant, not a politician. The difference was too subtle to name. The assurance with which he bore himself was based on generations of certainty, of being the unseen power behind those who campaign for office, and whose position depends upon the good opinion of others.

"How do you do, Superintendent," he said with a lift of interest in his voice. "Come in. What may I do for you? Some colonial crime in which the metropolitan police is interested?" He smiled. "In Africa, I imagine, or you would not have been directed to me."

"No, Mr. Thorne." Pitt came into the room and sat down in the chair indicated. He waited until the door was closed and Fairbrass had had time to retrace his steps along the passage. "I am afraid the crime almost certainly began here in the Colonial Office," he answered the question. "If indeed there is a crime. Mr. Chancellor has given me authority to enquire into it. I need to ask you several questions, sir. I apologize for taking up your time, but it is essential."

Thorne sat back in his chair and folded his hands.

"Then you had better proceed, Superintendent. Can you tell me what this crime is?"

Pitt did not answer directly. Jeremiah Thorne was privy to most of the information in the Colonial Office. He was almost certainly in a position to be the traitor, however unlikely it was that so senior a person would do such a thing. The other possibility was that he might inadvertently either warn the traitor simply because he did not believe the person capable of such duplicity, or that he might do it through sheer inexperience in suspecting one of his own colleagues.

And yet if the man were naive enough not to understand

the purpose of the questions, he was hardly competent to hold the position he did.

"I would prefer not to mention it until I am certain there has been a crime," Pitt hedged. "Would you tell me something about your principal staff, sir."

Thorne looked puzzled, but there was considerable humor in his dark eyes, masking any anxiety, if indeed he felt it.

"I report immediately regarding African affairs to Garston Aylmer, Mr. Chancellor's assistant," he said quietly. "He is an excellent man, very fine mind. A First at Cambridge, but I imagine it is not his academic qualifications you are interested in." He lifted one shoulder infinitesimally. "No, I thought not. He came straight to the Colonial Office from university. That would be some fourteen or fifteen years ago."

"Then he is close to forty?" Pitt interrupted.

"About thirty-six, I believe. He really is outstanding, Superintendent. He obtained his degree at twenty-three." He appeared about to add something else and then changed his mind. He waited patiently for Pitt to continue.

"What was his subject, sir?"

"Oh—classics."

"I see."

"I doubt you do." The smile was back in Thorne's eyes, bright like a hidden laughter. "He is an excellent all-round scholar, and a man with a profound knowledge of history. He lives in Newington, in a small house which he owns."

"Is he married?"

"No, he is not."

Then Newington was a curious place for him to live. It was south of the river, across the Westminster Bridge to the east of Lambeth. It was not far from Whitehall, but hardly fashionable for a man of such excellent position, and presumable ambition. Pitt would have expected him to have had rooms in Mayfair or Belgravia, or possibly Chelsea.

"What are his future prospects, Mr. Thorne?" he asked. "Can he look forward to further promotion?" Now there was a lift in Thomas's voice, but it was impossible to read his thoughts.

"I imagine so. He may in time take my position, or equally possibly he could head any of the other departments in the Colonial Office. I believe he has an interest in Indian affairs and the Far East. Superintendent, what has this to do with any possible crime that concerns you? Aylmer is an honorable man, about whom I have never heard the slightest suggestion of impropriety, let alone dishonesty. I don't believe the man even drinks."

There were many further questions, either of financial means or personal reputation, which Pitt could ask, but not of Thorne. This was going to be every bit as difficult as he had expected, and he had no liking for it at all. But Matthew Desmond would not have made the charge were he less than certain of it. Someone in the African section of the Colonial Office was passing information to the German Embassy.

"Who else, Mr. Thorne?" he asked aloud.

"Who else? Peter Arundell. He specializes in matters concerning Egypt and the Sudan," Thorne replied. He went on to describe him in some detail, and Pitt allowed him to finish. He did not yet wish to narrow down the area to Zambezia. He would like to have trusted Thorne, but he could not afford to.

"Yes," he prompted when Thorne hesitated.

Thorne frowned, but continued describing several other men with responsibility for other areas in the African continent, including Ian Hathaway, who was concerned with Mashonaland and Matabeleland, known together as Zambezia.

"He is one of our most experienced men, although very modest," Thorne said quietly, still sitting in the same easy position in his chair and regarding Pitt steadily. "He is perhaps fifty. And has been a widower for as long as I have known him. I believe his wife died quite young, and he has never remarried. He has one son who is in the Colonial Service, in the Sudan, and another who works in the missionary field, I am afraid I have forgotten where. Hathaway's father held quite a senior position in the church . . . an archdeacon, or something of the sort. He was from the West Country, Somerset or Dorset, I think. Hathaway himself lives in South Lambeth, just over the Vauxhall Bridge. I confess, I know nothing about his means. He is a very private person, very unassuming, but well liked, always a courteous word for everyone."

"I see. Thank you." It was not a promising beginning, but something decisive would have been too much to hope for at this stage. He hesitated, uncertain whether to ask Thorne now if he might trace the passage of information within the building, or if he should leave him unaware of the nature of the crime as yet, and pursue the personal lives of Aylmer, Hathaway and Thorne himself first, in hope of finding some weakness or deceit which might lead him eventually to his conclusion.

"That is all, Superintendent," Thorne cut across the silence. "Other than those I have mentioned, there are only clerks, messengers and assistants of junior rank. If you do not tell me what offense you are investigating, or at least its general nature, I do not know what further I can do to assist you." It was not a complaint, simply an observation, and there was still the mild, wry humor in Thorne's face as he made it.

Pitt equivocated. "Some information has found its way into the wrong hands. It is possible it has come from this office."

"I see." Thorne did not look horrified, as Chancellor had done. In fact he did not seem particularly surprised at all. "I presume it is financial information you are concerned with, or that which could be turned to financial advantage? I am afraid it is always a risk where great opportunities occur, such as those now in Africa. The Dark Continent"—his

38

mouth curled at the corners at the expression—"has attracted its share of opportunists as well as those who wish to settle, to colonize, to explore, to hunt big game or to save the souls of the natives and spread Christianity over the face of the benighted lands and impose British law and civilization on the heathen races."

The assumption was wrong, but it suited Pitt very well to allow it to remain.

"Nevertheless, it must be stopped," he said seriously.

"Of course," Thorne agreed. "You are welcome to any assistance I can give you, but I am afraid I have no idea where to begin. It would be exceedingly hard to believe that any of the men I have mentioned would stoop to such a level, but they may be able to tell you something which will point to who is at fault. I shall instruct them accordingly." He sat forward in the chair again. "Thank you for coming to me first, Superintendent, it was most civil of you."

"Not at all," Pitt said easily. "I think I shall begin by tracing the course of the information in general, rather than specifically financial, and see exactly who is privy to what."

"Excellent." Thorne stood up, an indication that the interview was at an end. "Would you care to have someone conduct you through the convolutions of the system, or would you rather make your own way? I am afraid I have no knowledge of police procedure."

"If you could spare someone, it might save me a great deal of time."

"Certainly." He reached out and pulled the very handsome embroidered bell cord beside his desk and a moment later a young man appeared from the adjoining office. "Oh, Wainwright," Thorne said almost casually. "This is Superintendent Pitt from the Bow Street police, who has some enquiries to make. The matter is highly confidential at this point. Will you please take him everywhere he requires to go, and show him the passage of information we receive from Africa itself, and regarding Africa from any other source. There appears to have been an irregularity." He used the word delicately, and without further explanation. "So it would be much better at this point if you did not allow anyone else to be aware of exactly what you are doing, or who Mr. Pitt is."

"Yes sir." Wainwright sounded a trifle surprised, but like the good civil servant he aspired to be, he did not even suggest a comment in his expression, much less make a remark. He turned to Pitt. "How do you do, sir. If you care to come with me, I will show you the various types of communications we receive, and precisely what happens to each from its point of arrival onwards."

Pitt thanked Thorne again and then followed Wainwright. He spent the rest of the day learning precisely how all the information was received from its various sources, by whom, where it was stored, how passed on, and who was privy to it. By half past three he had satisfied himself that the specific details Matthew Desmond had given him could individually have been known to a number of people, but all of them together passed through the hands of only a few: Garston Aylmer, Ian Hathaway, Peter Arundell, a man named Robert Leicester, and Thorne himself.

However he did not report that to Chancellor when he went back to his office at quarter past four, and found him free as he had promised. He merely said that he had been given every assistance and had been able to rule out several possibilities.

"And what is there remaining?" Chancellor said quickly, his eyes keen, his face grave. "You still have no doubt that we have a traitor who is passing information to the Kaiser?"

"That is the Foreign Office's conclusion," Pitt replied. "But it does seem the only one to answer the facts."

"Extremely unpleasant." Chancellor looked beyond Pitt into the distance, his mouth pinched and his brows drawn

40

down. "I don't mind what enemy I encounter face-to-face, but to be betrayed by one's own is the worst experience a man can endure. I hate a traitor more than anything else on earth." He looked at Pitt quickly, his blue eyes penetrating. "Are you a classicist, Mr. Pitt?"

It was an absurd question, but Pitt took it as a compliment that Chancellor obviously had no idea of his background. He could have been speaking to Micah Drummond, or even Farnsworth. It was a compliment to Arthur Desmond that he had helped his gamekeeper's son to the degree that such an error was possible.

"No sir. I am acquainted with Shakespeare, and the major poets, but not the Greeks," Pitt answered with a sober face.

"I was thinking more of Dante," Chancellor said. "He grades all the sins in his picture of the descent into Hell. He places traitors in the lowest circle of all, far beneath those who are guilty of violence, theft, lust or any other depravity of mind or body. He holds it the worst sin which mankind can conceive, uniquely an abuse of our God-given gifts of reason and conscience. He places the betrayers eternally alone, held fast in everlasting ice. A very terrible punishment, Mr. Pitt, do you not think? But meet for the offense."

Pitt felt a moment of chill, and then a clarity that was almost uplifting

"Yes . . ." he said. "Yes, perhaps it is the worst offense, the breaking of trust, and I suppose the eternal isolation is not so much a punishment as a natural conclusion which would be bound to follow such a nature. It is a self-chosen Hell, if you like."

"I see we have much in common, Mr. Pitt." Chancellor's smile was dazzling, a gesture of both warmth and intense, almost luminous, candor. "Perhaps there is nothing more important than that. We must get this abysmal affair dealt with. It darkens everything until we do." He bit his lip and shook his head fractionally. "The worst of it is that until it is exposed it poisons every other relationship. One quite unjustifiably suspects those who are perfectly innocent. Many a friendship has been broken for less. I admit, I should not look on a man the same if he had found it possible to suspect me of such treachery." He gazed at Pitt. "And yet since it is my duty, I cannot place any man beyond my suspicion. I dare not. What a filthy crime!" For a moment there was a bitter smile on his face. "You see what damage it has done already, by the mere fact of its existence?"

He leaned forward across the desk earnestly. "Look, Pitt, we can afford no niceties. I wish it were otherwise, but I know this office well enough to be perfectly aware, tragically, that it must be someone in considerable authority, which means probably Aylmer, Hathaway, Arundell, Leicester, or even, God forbid, Thorne himself. You will not be able to find which by chasing pieces of paper around here." Unconsciously he was drumming his fingers on the desk, almost without sound. "He will be cleverer than that. You will have to get to know the man himself, see a pattern, a flaw, and however small, a weakness. For that you need to know him in his personal life." He stopped, regarding Pitt with exasperation. "Come, man, don't show such surprise. I am not a fool!"

Pitt felt the color burn up his cheeks. He had not perceived Chancellor as a fool, or anything like it, but he had not expected such forthrightness either, nor such perception of what his investigation would entail.

Chancellor smiled quickly. "Forgive me. That was too frank. But nevertheless, what I say is true. You must meet them all socially. Can you come to the reception at the Duchess of Marlborough's this evening? I can obtain an invitation for you without any trouble at all."

Pitt hesitated only a moment.

"I realize it is absurdly short notice," Chancellor went

on. "But history waits for no man, and our treaty with Germany is on the doorstep."

"Of course," Pitt accepted. What Chancellor had said was true. It would be an ideal situation in which to make some judgment of the men in a more personal capacity. "It is an excellent idea. Thank you for your assistance, sir."

"Yourself and your wife? You are married, I presume?"

"Yes indeed."

"Excellent. I shall have my footman deliver them by six. Your address?"

Pitt gave it, with pleasure that it was the new house, and after a moment or two, took his leave. If he were to attend a reception at Marlborough House in a few hours, he had a very great deal to attend to. And Charlotte would have even more. Her sister, Emily, from whom she usually borrowed gowns for the better social occasions, was currently abroad in Italy again. Her husband, Jack, was very newly a member of Parliament, and since Parliament was in recess for the summer, they had taken the opportunity to travel. Borrowing from her would not be possible. She would have to try Lady Vespasia Cumming-Gould, Emily's great-aunt by her first marriage, to Lord Ashworth.

"What?" Charlotte said in disbelief. "Tonight? That's impossible! It's nearly five o'clock now!" She was standing in the kitchen with plates in her hand.

"I do realize it is not much time. . . ." Pitt began. It was only now beginning to dawn upon him what an enormity he had committed.

"Not much time!" Her voice rose in something close to a squeal and she put the plates down with a clatter. "To prepare for something like this would take a week. Thomas, you do know who the Duchess of Marlborough is, I suppose? There could be royalty present! There could be everybody who is anyone at all—there almost certainly will be." Suddenly the outrage vanished from her face and was replaced by an overwhelming curiosity. "How in Heaven's name did you get an invitation to the Duchess of Marlborough's reception? There are people in London who would commit crimes to get such a thing." Amusement tugged at the corners of her mouth. "Don't tell me someone has?"

He felt laughter at the absurdity of it well up inside him too. It was such a wild contrast with the truth. Perhaps he ought not to mention it to her. It was a highly confidential matter, but he had always trusted her in the past, although of course no previous case had involved matters of state.

She saw his hesitation. "They have!" Her eyes were wide, and she was uncertain whether to laugh or not.

"No—no," he said hastily. "The matter is very much more serious than that."

"Are you not working on Sir Arthur's death?" she said quickly. "That can't have anything to do with the Duchess of Marlborough. And even if it had, you wouldn't just get an invitation because you wanted one. I don't think even Aunt Vespasia could do that." That was the height of social power.

Vespasia had been the foremost beauty of her day, not only for her classic features and exquisite coloring, but for her grace, wit and extraordinary panache. Now in her eighties, she was still beautiful. Her wit had sharpened because she was assured in her position, and no longer cared in the slightest what anyone thought of her, as long as she rested easily in her own conscience. She espoused causes few others dared to, liked and disliked whom and what she pleased, and enjoyed pastimes of which many a younger and more cautious woman would have been afraid. But she still could not command an invitation to the Duchess of Marlborough's receptions at short notice, and for someone else.

"Yes, I am working on Sir Arthur's death," Pitt answered with some stretching of the truth. He followed her as she whirled into sudden activity, turning to go into the passage and up the stairs.

"But I am also working on another matter Matthew left with me this morning, and it is in connection with that," Pitt said from behind her, "that we are going to the Duchess of Marlborough's this evening. The invitations came through Mr. Linus Chancellor, of the Colonial Office."

She stopped on the landing. "Linus Chancellor. I've heard of him. He's very charming, and extremely clever, so they say. He may even be Prime Minister one day."

He smiled, and then hid it almost immediately as he followed her into the bedroom. Charlotte no longer moved in the social circles where people discussed serious politicians, as she had done before she had shocked her friends by marrying a policeman, a dramatic reduction of both her financial and social circumstances.

Her face fell. "Is that mistaken? Is he not charming at all?"

"Yes, he is most charming, and I should judge also very clever. Who told you about him?"

"Emily," she answered, throwing open the wardrobe door. "Jack has met him several times. But also Mama." She realized what he had meant. "All right, only two people. You actually met him today? Why?"

He was undecided for only a moment.

"It is highly confidential. It is a matter of state. I am not revealing the whole business even to those I question. Certain information is being passed from the Colonial Office to other people who should not know it."

She swung around to stare at him. "You mean there is a traitor in the Colonial Office? That's terrible! Why couldn't you just say that, instead of hemming and hawing? Thomas, you are becoming pompous."

"Well—I . . ." He was horrified. He loathed pomposity. He swallowed. "Can you find something to wear and get ready, or not?"

"Yes of course I can," she said instantly, eyes wide, as if the answer were the only one possible.

"How?"

She shut the wardrobe door. "I don't know yet. Give me a moment to think. Emily is away, but Aunt Vespasia is not. She has a telephone. Perhaps I can reach her and ask her advice. Yes. I'll do that immediately." And without waiting for comment from him, she brushed past him and went across the landing and down the stairs to the hallway where the new telephone was situated. She picked up the receiver. She was extremely unfamiliar with the instrument, and it took her several minutes before she was successful. She was naturally answered by the maid, and was obliged to wait for several moments.

"Aunt Vespasia." Her voice was unusually breathless when she heard Vespasia at last. "Thomas has just been put onto a most important case, which I cannot discuss, because I know very little about it, except that he has been invited immediately, this evening, to attend the reception at the Duchess of Marlborough's."

There was a very slight hesitation of surprise at the other end of the line, but Vespasia was too well bred to allow herself anything more.

"Indeed? It must be of the utmost gravity for Her Grace of Marlborough to allow the slightest alteration to her plans. How may I be of assistance, my dear? I imagine that is why you have called?"

"Yes." From anyone else such candor would have been disconcerting, but Vespasia had never been anything but frank with Charlotte, nor Charlotte with her. "I am not quite sure what to wear to such a function," Charlotte confessed. "I have never been to anything quite so—so very formal. And of course I do not own such a thing anyway."

Vespasia was thinner than Charlotte, but of a similar height, and it would not be the first occasion for which she had lent her a gown. Policemen of Pitt's previous rank did not earn the kind of salary to afford their wives attire for the London Season, and indeed none of them would have been invited.

"I shall find something suitable and have my footman bring it over," Vespasia said generously. "And don't worry about the time. It is not done to arrive early. About half past ten would be excellent. They will serve supper at around midnight. One should be there between thirty and ninety minutes of the hour mentioned on the invitation, which, if I recollect, is eleven o'clock. It is a formal occasion." She did not add that more intimate receptions might well begin an hour earlier. She expected Charlotte to know that.

"Thank you very much," Charlotte said with real gratitude. It was only after she had put the receiver back on its hook that she realized if Vespasia knew the time on the invitation, she must have one herself.

The dress, when it arrived, was quite the loveliest she had ever seen. It was of a deep blue-green shade, cut high at the front, and with a sheer sleeve, and decorated with a delicate beading at throat and shoulder. The bustle was narrow and heavily draped, caught up in a bow of gold and a shade of the gown itself, but so dark as to appear almost black. Included with it was a most elegant pair of slippers to match. The whole effect made her think of deep water, exotic seas and wild dawns over the sand. If she looked even half as wonderful as she felt, she would be the envy of every woman in the place.

Actually as she sailed down the stairs, several minutes later than she had said she would (having mislaid a packet of hairpins which were vital to the whole effect), Gracie was awestruck. Her eyes were enormous, and both children crouched, wide-eyed, on the landing. Even Pitt was a little startled. He had been pacing the hall with impatience, and when he had heard her step, he swung around, then saw her.

"Oh," he said, uncharacteristically lost for words. He had forgotten what a very handsome woman she was with her rich dark auburn hair and warm, honey skin. Tonight the

47

excitement had given her a color and a brilliance to her eyes that made her close to truly beautiful. "That . . ." Then he became self-conscious, and changed his mind. This was not the time to indulge in compliments, however merited. "It becomes you very well," he finished. It was immeasurably less than he meant. Actually it awoke in him an awareness of her physical presence, and a strangeness, a frisson of excitement as if she had been someone he had newly met.

She looked at him a trifle uncertainly, and said nothing.

He had hired a carriage for the evening. It was not an event for which one could arrive in a hansom cab. For one thing, its cramped space would have crushed Charlotte's dress, or more accurately Vespasia's dress, and for another, and more importantly, it would mark him out as different, and inferior.

There was a considerable jostle of carriages in the driveway, and indeed in the street beyond, as dozens of people arrived at what Vespasia had said would be the optimum time. They were almost swept along up the stairs and into the great foyer and the hall beyond. On all sides they were surrounded by swirling skirts, nervous laughter, just a little loud, and voices high-pitched, too obviously intent upon immediate companions and affecting to ignore everyone else. The lights of the chandeliers were thrown back in tiaras, brooches, necklaces, earrings, bracelets and rings. The men were girded by scarlet and purple sashes of orders of merit, and chests gleamed with medals against the sober black and stark white of formal dress.

Up the great staircase and into the reception rooms they were announced by a majordomo whose face remained entirely expressionless, regardless of the name or rank of the personage he introduced. If he had never heard of Mr. and Mrs. Thomas Pitt, there was nothing in his features to register it, not a flicker of his eyes or intonation of his voice.

Pitt was far more nervous than Charlotte. She was bred

to conduct herself at social events of this nature, even if not of this status. Pitt felt suddenly as if his stiff collar were cutting into his chin and he hardly dared turn his head. Charlotte had insisted on cutting his hair, and he was self-consciously aware now that he had not seen a respectable barber in years. His evening boots were excellent, a gift from Jack, but his black suit was of nothing like the quality of those around him, and he was certain they would be as aware of it as he was the first time they looked closely enough at him to conduct any sort of a conversation.

For the first fifteen minutes they drifted from one group to another, making the most superficial remarks, and feeling increasingly ridiculous and as if they were wasting time which could easily be better spent, even if only in bed asleep, ready for the next day and its duties.

Then at last Pitt saw Linus Chancellor, and beside him a uniquely striking woman. She was unusually tall, very nearly of a height with Chancellor himself. She was slender but well proportioned with handsome shoulders and arms, and awareness of her height had not made her stoop or try to hide it. She stood with head high and back straight. Her gown was palest oyster shading to pink and it flattered her dusky coloring and rather long, wide-eyed face.

"Who is she?" Charlotte whispered quickly. "Isn't she interesting, quite unlike most of the women here. There is nothing predictable about her at all!"

"I don't know, but perhaps she is Chancellor's wife," he replied under his breath, conscious of those close to him and possibly overhearing.

"Oh! Is that Linus Chancellor beside her? He's rather handsome, isn't he!"

Pitt looked at her with interest. He had not considered whether Chancellor was handsome or not, or indeed whether his looks might be appealing to women. He had only seen the strength and the imagination in his face, the unusual angle of nose and jaw and the power of will it sug-

49

gested, the fine eyes and the total confidence of his bearing. He had seen him as a politician, and tried to estimate his skill and his ability to judge men.

"Yes, I suppose he is," he said with growing conviction.

Charlotte looked at the woman again, and at that moment saw her place her hand on Chancellor's arm, not obtrusively—it was not a statement of ownership—but discreetly, a gesture of pride and affection. She was moving herself closer to him, not drawing him to her.

"If he is married, then she must be his wife," Charlotte said with absolute certainty. "She would never do that in public were she not now, or about to become so."

"Do what?"

Charlotte smiled and did exactly the same, slipping her hand through Pitt's arm and moving half a step closer.

"She is still in love with him," she said a little above a whisper.

Pitt knew he had missed something, but also that it had been in some way a compliment.

Further discussion of the subject was circumvented by the approach of one of the most homely men Charlotte had ever seen. The most charitable description of him possible could only have said there was no malice in his face, and no ill temper. He was barely Charlotte's height, although she was admittedly rather tall for a woman. He was very heavily set, with plump arms and shoulders and a massive series of chins which gave his face a most odd shape, as if it were dominated by the excellent hair and brown eyes under inadequate brows, and then it all faded away into his shoulders. Nevertheless, it was not in the least displeasing, and when he spoke his voice was beautiful and quite individual.

"Good evening, Mr. Pitt. How pleasant to see you at such a gathering." He waited politely to be introduced to Charlotte.

"Good evening, Mr. Aylmer," Pitt responded, and turned

to Charlotte. "May I present Mr. Garston Aylmer, of the Colonial Office?" He completed the introduction.

"How do you do, Mrs. Pitt." Aylmer bowed very slightly, an elegant gesture which seemed to come to him quite naturally. He regarded her with interest. "I hope you will enjoy yourself, although these functions can become tedious if one remains too long. Everybody says the same thing each time, and seldom means it anyway." He smiled suddenly and it illuminated his face. "But since we have not met before, perhaps we shall have something new and quite different to say, and be enthralled."

"I should love to be enthralled," Charlotte answered instantly "I am not in the slightest interested in the weather, or in gossip as to who has dined with whom, or been seen in whose company."

"Nor I," Aylmer agreed. "It will all be different next week anyway, and then no doubt back to the same the week after. What shall we discuss?"

Pitt was more than happy to be ignored. He took a step backwards, excusing himself inaudibly, and drifted towards Linus Chancellor and the woman at his side.

Charlotte thought hastily. It was an opportunity too precious to miss.

"Something I know nothing about," she said with a smile. "Then you can tell me whatever you please, and I shall not find fault with any of it, because I shall have no idea if you are right or wrong."

"What an original and superb idea," he agreed, entering the spirit of it with enthusiasm. "What do you know nothing about, Mrs. Pitt?" He offered her his arm.

"Oh, countless things," she said, taking it. "But many of them are of no interest anyway, which is why I have not bothered with them. But some must be engrossing," she added as they walked up towards the steps to the terrace. "What about Africa? If you are in the Colonial Office, you must know immeasurably more than I do about it."

"Oh certainly," he agreed with a broad smile. "Although

51

I warn you, a great deal of it is either violent or tragic, or of course both."

"But everything that people fight over is worth something," she reasoned. "Or they wouldn't be fighting. I expect it is terribly different from England, isn't it? I have seen pictures, engravings and so on, of jungles, and endless plains with every kind of animal imaginable. And curious trees that look as if they have all been sawn off at the top, sort of . . . level."

"Acacias," he replied. "Yes, undoubtedly it is different from England. I hate to confess it, Mrs. Pitt, because probably it robs me instantly of all real interest, but I have never been there. I know an enormous amount of facts about it, but I have them all secondhand. Isn't it a shame?"

She looked at him for only an instant before being perfectly certain he had no sense of loss whatever, and was still enjoying the conversation. It would be an overstatement to say he was flirting, but he was quite at ease with women, and obviously found their company pleasing.

"Perhaps there isn't any appreciable difference between secondhand and thirdhand," she responded as they made their way past a group of men in earnest conversation. "And it will be only a matter of description to me, because I shall never know if you are right or not. So please tell me, and make it very vivid, even if you have to invent it. And full of facts, of course," she plunged on. "Tell me about Zambezia, and gold and diamonds, and Doctor Livingstone and Mr. Stanley, and the Germans."

"Good heavens," he said in much alarm. "All of them?"

"As many as you can," she returned.

A footman offered them a silver tray with glasses of champagne.

"Well to begin with, the diamonds we know about are all in South Africa," Aylmer answered, taking a glass and giving it to her, then one for himself. "But there is a possibility of enormous amounts of gold in Zambezia. There are massive ruins of a civilization, a city called Zimbabwe, and we are only beginning to estimate the fortune that could be there. Which, quite naturally, is also what the Germans are interested in. And possibly everyone else as well." He was watching her face with wide brown eyes, and she had no idea how serious he was, or whether it was at least partially invention, to amuse her.

"Does Britain own it now?" she asked, taking a sip from her glass.

"No," Aylmer replied, moving a step away from the footman. "Not yet."

"But we will?"

"Ah—that is a very important question, to which I do not have the answer." He led the way on up the steps.

"And if you did, no doubt it would be highly secret," she added.

"But of course." He smiled and went on to tell her about Cecil Rhodes and his adventures and exploits in South Africa, the Rand and Johannesburg, and the discovery of the Kimberley diamond mine, until they were interrupted by a young man with a long nose and a hearty manner who swept Aylmer away with apologies, and obviously to his annoyance. Charlotte was left momentarily alone.

She looked around her to see whom she might recognize from photographs in the *London Illustrated News*. She saw a most imposing man with lush side-whiskers and curling beard, the light of the chandeliers gleaming on the bald dome of his head, his sad, bloodhound eyes gazing around the room. She thought he might be Lord Salisbury, the Foreign Secretary, but she was not certain. A photograph with only shades of gray was not like a living person.

Linus Chancellor was talking to a man superficially not unlike himself, but without the ambition in his face, or the mercurial temperament. They were deep in conversation, almost as if oblivious of the whirl of silks and glitter of lights, or the buzz of chatter all around them. Beside the second man, but facing the other way, apparently waiting for him, was a most unusual woman. She was of arresting

53

appearance because of her supreme confidence and the intelligence which seemed to radiate from her. But she was also quite unusually plain. Her nose was so high at the bridge, in profile it was almost a continuation of the line of her forehead. Her chin was a little too short, and her eyes were wide set, tilted down at the corners, and too large. It was an extraordinary face, compelling and even a trifle frightening. She was dressed extremely well, but one was so startled by her countenance it was of no importance whatever.

Charlotte exchanged a few polite and meaningless words with a couple who made it their duty to speak to everyone. A man with light auburn hair addressed her with effusive admiration, then once again she found herself alone. She did not mind in the least. She knew Pitt was here to pursue a specific case.

A delicately pale woman of about her own age was standing a few yards away, her fair hair elaborately coiffed, her pastel gown stitched with pearls and beads. She glanced discreetly at Charlotte over her fan and turned to the good-looking young man next to her.

"She must be from the country, poor creature."

"Must she?" the young man said with surprise. "Do you know her?" He made a move as if to approach Charlotte, his face alight with anticipation.

The woman's eyes widened dramatically. "Of course not. Really, Gerald! How would I know such a person? I merely remarked that she must have come up from the country because of her unfortunate coloring." She grasped Gerald's arm firmly, restraining him.

"I thought it was rather pleasing." He stopped short. "Sort of like well-polished mahogany."

"Not her hair. Her complexion. Obviously she cannot be a milkmaid, or she would not be here, but she looks as if she could have been. I daresay it is riding to hounds, or some such thing." She wrinkled her nose very slightly.

54

"She looks positively robust. Most unbecoming. But I daresay she is unaware of it, poor creature. Just as well."

Gerald pulled his mouth down at the corner. "How typical of you to feel such compassion for her, my dear. That is one of your most charming traits, your sensitivity to the feelings of others."

She glanced at him very quickly, some inkling in the back of her mind that there was an element in him she had missed, then chose to ignore it and swept forward to speak to a viscountess she knew.

Gerald shot a look of undisguised admiration at Charlotte, then followed obediently.

Charlotte smiled to herself and went to look for Pitt.

She glimpsed Great-Aunt Vespasia across the room, looking quite magnificent in a gown of steel-gray satin, her heavy-lidded silver eyes brilliant, her white hair a more gracious ornament to her head than many of the tiaras glistening around her.

As Charlotte looked at her, Vespasia quite slowly and deliberately winked, then resumed her conversation.

It took Charlotte several minutes to find Pitt. He had moved from the main reception room with its blazing chandeliers up a shallow flight of steps into a quieter room where he was deep in conversation with the man who resembled Linus Chancellor, and the extraordinary woman who was with him.

Charlotte hesitated, uncertain whether if she approached, she might be interrupting, but the woman glanced up and their eyes met with a jolt of interest that was almost a familiarity.

The man followed her line of sight, and Pitt also turned.

Charlotte went forward and was introduced.

"Mr. Jeremiah Thorne of the Colonial Office," Pitt said quietly. "And Mrs. Thorne. May I present my wife."

"How do you do, Mrs. Pitt," Mrs. Thorne said immediately. "Are you interested in Africa? I do hope not. I am bored to weeping with it. Please come and talk to me about something else. Almost anything would do, except India, which from this distance is much the same."

"Christabel . . ." Thorne said with alarm, but Charlotte could see that it was largely assumed, and he was possibly quite used to her manner, and in no way truly disturbed.

"Yes my dear," she said absently. "I am going to speak with Mrs. Pitt. We shall find something to entertain us, either something profoundly serious and worthy, like saving souls or bodies; or else totally trivial, like criticizing the fashions of everyone else we can see, and speculating on which respectable lady of uncertain years is seeking which wretched young man to marry her daughter."

Thorne smiled and groaned at the same time, but there was quite obviously profound affection in it; then he turned back to Pitt.

Charlotte followed Christabel Thorne with considerable interest; the conversation promised to be different and lively.

"If you come to these sort of things as often as I do, you must find them desperately tedious by now," Christabel said with a smile. Her large eyes were very penetrating, and Charlotte could imagine she would paralyze many a timid soul into silence, or stuttering and incoherent sentences.

"I have never been to one before." Charlotte decided to be just as frank. It was the only defense against pretentiousness, and being caught at it. "Since my marriage I have been out socially only on certain specific occasions that have called for . . ." She stopped. To have admitted they were when she was involving herself in Pitt's investigations was perhaps a little too candid even for this occasion.

Christabel's high eyebrows rose even higher, her face full of interest. "Yes?"

Charlotte still hesitated.

"You were going to say?" Christabel prompted. There was nothing unfriendly in her stare, simply a consuming interest.

Charlotte gave up. She knew already Christabel would

not forgive a lie, or even half of one, and naturally since Thorne knew Pitt's profession, she assumed Christabel did too. "A little meddling in my husband's cases," she finished with a slight smile. "There are sometimes places which as a member of the police—"

"How perfectly marvelous!" Christabel interrupted her. "But of course. You have no need to explain, my dear. It is all quite clear, and completely justified. This time you are here because he has been invited on this wretched business of African information going missing." A look of contempt crossed her face. "Greed can make people do the grubbiest of things . . . at least some people." She caught sight of Charlotte's face. "Don't look so upset, my dear. I overheard my husband speaking about it just now. One was always aware of the possibility. Wherever there is a fortune to be made, there will be those who cheat to get advantage. It is simply unusual that they have had the courage and openness to bring in the police. I applaud it. But you will still find this evening growing dull, because very few people say anything they really mean."

A footman stopped by them with another tray of champagne glasses. Christabel declined with a wave of her hand, and Charlotte followed suit.

"If you wish to meet someone interesting," Christabel went on, "and I cannot think what she is doing here, of all places—come and meet Nobby Gunne." She turned as if to lead the way, assuming assent. "She's a marvelous woman. Been up the Congo River in a canoe, or something equally unlikely. Maybe it was the Niger, or the Limpopo. Somewhere in Africa where nobody had ever been before."

"Did you say Nobby Gunne?" Charlotte asked with surprise.

"Yes—extraordinary name, isn't it? I believe it is actually short for Zenobia . . . which is even more odd."

"I know her!" Charlotte said quickly. "She's about fifty or so, isn't she? Dark hair and a most unusual face, not at

57

all conventionally pretty, but full of character, and not in the least displeasing."

A group of young women passed them, giggling and looking over their fans.

"Yes, that's right! What a generous description of her." Christabel's face was filled with amusement. "You must have liked her."

"I did."

"If it is not an impertinent question, how did a policeman's wife come to meet an African explorer like Nobby Gunne?"

"She is a friend of my sister's great-aunt by marriage," Charlotte began, then was obliged to smile at the convolution of it. "I am also very fond indeed of Great-Aunt Vespasia, and see her whenever I am able."

They were at the foot of the stair and brushed by an urn filled with flowers. Christabel whisked her skirt out of the way absentmindedly.

"Vespasia?" she said with interest. "Now there is another remarkable name. Your aunt could not by any chance be Lady Vespasia Cumming-Gould?"

"Yes, she is. You know her also?"

"Only by repute, unfortunately. But that has been sufficient for me to form a great respect for her." The banter and air of mockery drained out of her face. "She has been concerned in some very fine work to bring about social reform, most particularly the poor laws, and those regarding education."

"Yes, I remember. My sister did what she could to assist. We tried our hardest."

"Don't tell me you gave up!" It was more of a challenge than a question.

"We gave up on that approach." Charlotte met her gaze squarely. "Now Emily's husband has just become a member of Parliament. I am concerned with my husband's cases which fight injustice of various sorts, which I am not at liberty to discuss." She knew enough not to mention the Inner

58

Circle, no matter how she might be drawn to anyone. "And Aunt Vespasia is still fighting one thing and another, but I do not know precisely what at the moment."

"I didn't mean to insult you," Christabel apologized warmly.

Charlotte smiled. "Yes you did. You thought I might simply have been playing at it, to give myself something to do, and to feel good about, and then given it up at the first failure."

"You're right, of course." Christabel smiled dazzlingly. "Jeremiah tells me I am far too obsessed with causes, and that I lose all sense of proportion. Would you care to meet Zenobia Gunne again? I see her just at the top of the stairs."

"I should indeed," Charlotte accepted, and followed Christabel's glance to where a very dark woman in green stood staring across the room from the balcony, her eyes wandering from one person to another, her face only mildly interested. Charlotte recognized her with a jolt of memory. They had met during the murders on Westminster Bridge, when Florence Ivory was fighting so hard for women to have the right to vote. Of course there was no conceivable chance of her succeeding, but Charlotte could understand the cause well enough, more particularly when she had seen the results of some of the worst inequities under present law. "We were concerned for women's franchise," she added as she followed Christabel up the stairs.

"Good heavens!" Christabel stopped and turned; her face was full of curiosity. "How very forward thinking of you!" she said with admiration. "And completely unrealistic."

"And what are you concerned with?" Charlotte challenged.

Christabel laughed, but there was intense emotion in her face. "Oh, something equally unrealistic," she answered quickly. "Do you know what an 'odd woman' is, in modern parlance?"

"Not 'peculiar'?" Charlotte had not heard the term.

59

"Not in the least, and becoming more common all the time . . ." Christabel ignored the fact that they were on the stairs and people were obliged to brush past them. "She is a woman who is not paired up with some man, and therefore surplus, in a sense, unprovided for, without her accepted role of caring for a man. I would like to see 'odd women' able to educate themselves and take up professions, just as men do, provide for themselves, and have a place of honor and fulfillment in society."

"Good heavens." Charlotte was genuinely amazed at her courage. But it was a wonderful idea. "You are right."

A flash of temper darkened Christabel's face. "The average man is not a whit cleverer or stronger than the average woman, and certainly no braver." A look of total disgust filled her. "You are not going to quote that belief that women cannot use both their brains and their wombs, are you? That is an idea put about by men who are afraid that we may challenge them in their jobs, and sometimes win. It is a total canard. Rubbish! Nonsense!"

Charlotte was half amused, half awed, and certainly the idea was exciting.

"And how are you going to do it?" she asked, squeezing sideways a trifle to allow a large lady to pass.

"Education," Christabel replied, and there was a note of defiance underneath the assurance Charlotte felt was paper thin. In that instant she admired her courage intensely, and felt fiercely protective of the vulnerability and the hopeless cause she saw behind it. "For women, so they have the skills and the belief in themselves," Christabel went on. "And for men, to give them the opportunity to use them. That is the hardest part."

"That must need a lot of money. . . ." Charlotte said.

She was prevented from replying by the fact that they were almost level with Zenobia Gunne, and she had seen their approach. Her face lit with pleasure as she recognized Christabel Thorne, and then after only a moment's hesitation, she remembered Charlotte also. Then quite comically she also remembered that Charlotte was not always strictly honest about her identity. In the past, for purposes of assisting Pitt, she had affected to have nothing to do with the police, even assuming her maiden name.

Nobby turned to Christabel.

"How very nice to see you, Mrs. Thorne. I am sure I know your companion, but it is some little while since we met, and I am embarrassed to say I do not recollect her name. I do apologize."

Charlotte smiled, both with genuine friendship—she had liked Nobby Gunne greatly—and with amusement at her tact.

"Charlotte Pitt," she replied graciously. "How do you do, Miss Gunne. You seem in excellent health."

"I am indeed," Nobby answered, and she looked happier, and not a day older, than when Charlotte had seen her several years earlier.

They chatted for a few moments about various subjects, touching on the political and social events of interest. They were interrupted when a tall, lithe man with a heavily tanned complexion accidentally backed into Nobby in his effort to avoid a giggling young woman. He turned to apologize for his clumsiness. He had an unusual face, far from handsome: his nose was crooked, his mouth a little large and his fair hair was receding very considerably, and yet his presence was commanding, his intelligence apparent.

"I am sorry, ma'am," he said stiffly, the color spreading up his bony cheeks. "I hope I have not hurt you?"

"Not in the least," Nobby said with mild amusement. "And considering the encounter you were avoiding, your haste is understandable."

The color in his cheeks became even deeper. "Oh . . . was I so obvious?"

"Only to one who would have done the same," she replied, meeting his eyes squarely.

"Then we have something in common," he acknowl-

61

edged, but with no indication in his voice that he wished to continue further or to make her acquaintance.

"I am Zenobia Gunne," she introduced herself.

His eyes widened; his attention became suddenly real. "Not Nobby Gunne?"

"My friends call me Nobby." Her tone of voice made it apparent he was not yet included in that number.

"Peter Kreisler." He stood very upright, as if it were a military announcement. "I also have spent much time in Africa and learned to love it."

Now her interest was quickened also. She introduced Charlotte and Christabel only as a matter of form, then continued the conversation. "Have you? In what part of Africa?"

"Zanzibar, Mashonaland, Matabeleland," he answered.

"I was in the west," she responded. "Mostly up the Congo and that region. Although I did also travel up the Niger."

"Then you will have dealt with King Leopold of the Belgians." His face was expressionless.

Nobby schooled her features just as carefully. "Only in the very slightest," she replied. "He does not regard me in the same light as he would were I a man; for example, Mr. Stanley."

Even Charlotte had heard of Henry Mirton Stanley's triumphant progress through London only a week or so since, when on April 26 he had ridden from Charing Cross Station to Piccadilly Circus. The crowds had cheered him to the echo. He was the most admired explorer of the age, a double gold medalist of the Royal Geographical Society, a friend of the Prince of Wales and a guest of the Queen herself.

"There is some good fortune in that," Kreisler said with a bitter smile. "At least he will not ask you to lead an army of twenty thousand Congolese cannibals up to defeat the 'Mad Mahdi' and conquer the Sudan for Belgium!"

Nobby was incredulous. Her face was comical with disbelief.

Christabel looked shocked. Charlotte for once was speechless.

"You cannot be serious!" Nobby cried, her voice rising to a squeak.

"Oh, I am not." Kreisler's mouth was touched with humor. "But apparently Leopold was. He had heard that the Congo cannibals are excellent warriors. He wanted to do something to make the whole world sit up and take notice."

"Well that would certainly achieve it," Nobby agreed. "I can scarcely imagine what a war that would be! Twenty thousand cannibals against the hordes of the 'Mad Mahdi.' Oh, my God—poor Africa." Her face was touched with genuine pity beneath the wry amusement and the bantering tone. One could not mistake that she was conscious of the human misery it would involve.

Beyond their introduction, Kreisler had so far practically ignored both Christabel and Charlotte. He glanced at them to avoid rudeness, but all his interest was with Nobby, and the sense of her emotion had quickened it further.

"That is not Africa's real tragedy," he said with bitterness. "Leopold is a visionary, and frankly something of a lunatic. He poses very little real danger. For a start he is extremely unlikely to persuade any cannibals at all into leaving their own jungles. And for another, I would not be surprised if Stanley remains here in Europe anyway."

"Stanley not go back to Africa?" Nobby was amazed. "I know he has been there for the last three years, and then in Cairo for about three weeks, I hear. But surely after a rest he will return? Africa is his life! And I believe King Leopold treated him like a brother when he went back to Brussels this time. Is that not so?"

"Oh yes," Kreisler said quickly. "It is almost an understatement. Originally the king was lukewarm, and treated Stanley very offhandedly, but now he is the hero of the hour, studded with medals like a porcupine with quills, and feted like visiting royalty. Everyone is buzzing with excitement over news from Central Africa, and Stanley has but to turn up and he is cheered till people are hoarse. The king enjoys the reflected glory." There was light in Kreisler's blue eyes, laughter and pain at the same time.

Nobby asked the necessary question.

"Then why would he not return to Africa? He has left Belgium, so it cannot be that which is holding him."

"Not at all," Kreisler agreed. "He has fallen in love with Dolly Tennant."

"Dolly Tennant! Did you say Dolly Tennant?" Nobby could scarcely believe her ears. "The society hostess? The painter?"

"The same." Kreisler nodded. "And there has been a great change in her. She no longer laughs at him. It even seems she returns at least a good part of his regard. Times and fortunes have altered."

"My goodness, haven't they indeed," she agreed.

That particular speculation continued no further because they were joined by Linus Chancellor and the tall woman Charlotte had remarked upon earlier. Closer to, she was even more unusual. Her face was curiously vulnerable and full of emotion, which did not detract in the slightest from the strength in it. It was not a weakness, but an ability to feel pain with more intensity than was common. It was the face of a person who would launch herself wholeheartedly into whatever she undertook. There was no caution in it, no withholding for the sake of safety.

Introductions were performed for everyone, and she was indeed Chancellor's wife, as Charlotte had supposed.

Chancellor and Kreisler appeared to know each other, at least by repute.

"Recently back from Africa?" Chancellor asked politely.

"Two months ago," Kreisler replied. "More recently than that, from Brussels and Antwerp."

"Oh." Chancellor's face relaxed in a smile. "In the wake of the good Mr. Stanley?"

"By accident, yes."

Chancellor was obviously amused. Probably he had also

64

heard of King Leopold's plans to conquer the Sudan. No doubt he had his sources of information every bit as immediate as Kreisler's. Perhaps it was Kreisler himself. It occurred to Charlotte that it was more than likely.

Christabel Thorne took up the subject, looking first at Kreisler, then at Chancellor.

"Mr. Kreisler tells us he is more acquainted with the east of Africa and the new lands of Zambezia. He was about to tell us that the real tragedy of Africa does not lie in the west, nor in the Sudan, but he was prevented from elaborating by some turn of the conversation. I think to do with Mr. Stanley's personal hopes."

"For Africa?" Susannah Chancellor asked quickly. "I thought the king of the Belgians was building a railway."

"I daresay he is," Christabel returned. "But we were referring to his amorous intentions."

"Oh! Dolly Tennant!"

"So we hear."

"Hardly a tragedy for Africa," Chancellor murmured. "Possibly even a relief."

Charlotte was now quite sure he knew about Leopold and the cannibals.

But Susannah was genuinely interested. She looked at Kreisler seriously.

"What do you believe is Africa's tragedy, Mr. Kreisler? You have not told us. If your regard is as deep as Miss Gunne indicates, you must care about it very much."

"I do, Mrs. Chancellor," he agreed. "But unfortunately that does not give me any power to affect it. It will happen regardless of anything I can do."

"What will happen?" she persisted.

"Cecil Rhodes and his wagons of settlers will press further up from the Cape into Zambezia," he answered, looking at her with intensity. "And one by one the native princes will make treaties they don't understand and don't intend to keep. We will settle the land, kill those who rebel, and there will be slaughter and subjection of God knows

65

how many people. Unless, of course, the Germans beat us to it, driving westward from Zanzibar, in which case they will do the same, only worse—if past history is anything to judge from."

"Rubbish!" Chancellor said with good humor. "If we settle Mashonaland and Matabeleland we can develop the natural resources there for everyone's good, African and white alike. We can bring them proper medicine, education, trade, civilized laws and a code of society which protects the weak as well as the strong. Far from being Africa's tragedy, it would be the making of it."

Kreisler's eyes were hard and bright, but he looked only momentarily at Chancellor, then turned to Susannah. She had been listening to him with rapt attention, not with agreement, but rather with growing anxiety.

"That's not what you used to say." She looked at Chancellor with a crease between her brows.

His smile had only the barest shadow behind the obvious affection. "Perceptions change, my dear. One becomes wiser." He shrugged very slightly. "I now know a great deal that I did not two or three years ago. The rest of Europe is going to colonize Africa, whether we do or not. France, Belgium, Germany at least. And the Sultan of Turkey is nominally overlord of the Khedive of Egypt, with all that means to the Nile, and thus to the Sudan and Equatoria."

"It means nothing at all," Kreisler said abruptly. "The Nile flows northward. I'd be surprised if anyone in Equatoria had even heard of Egypt."

"I am thinking of the future, Mr. Kreisler, not the past." Chancellor was not in the least perturbed. "When the great rivers of Africa are among the world's highways of trade. The time will come when we will ship the gold and diamonds, exotic woods, ivory and skins of Africa along those great waterways as easily as we now ship coal and grain along the Manchester ship canal."

"Or the Rhine," Susannah said thoughtfully.

"If you like," Chancellor agreed. "Or the Danube, or any other great river you can think of."

"But Europe is so often at war," Susannah went on. "Over land, or religion, or any of a dozen other things."

He looked at her, smiling. "My dear, so is Africa. The tribal chieftains are always fighting one another. That is one of the reasons why all our attempts to wipe out slavery kept on failing. Really, the benefits are immense, and the costs relatively minor."

"To us, possibly," Kreisler said sourly. "What about to the Africans?"

"To the Africans as well," Chancellor answered him. "We shall bring them out of the pages of history and into the nineteenth century."

"That is exactly what I was thinking." Susannah was not convinced. "Transitions as sudden as that are not made without a terrible wrench. Maybe they don't want our ways? We are forcing them upon a whole nation without taking their opinions into account at all."

A spark of intense interest, even excitement, lit for a moment in Kreisler's eyes, and then as quickly was masked, as if deliberately.

"Since they cannot conceive what we are talking about," Chancellor said wryly, "they can hardly have an opinion!"

"Then we are deciding for them," she pointed out.

"Naturally."

"I am not certain we have the right to do that."

Chancellor looked surprised, and somewhat derisive, but he held his tongue tactfully. Apparently no matter how eccentric his wife's opinions, he did not wish to embarrass her publicly.

Beneath the surface argument he seemed to feel a confidence in her that overrode such things.

Nobby Gunne was looking at Kreisler. Christabel Thorne was watching everyone, each in turn.

"I was listening to Sir Arthur Desmond the other day," Susannah continued with a slight shake of her head.

67

Charlotte grasped her empty champagne glass so tightly it nearly shot out of her fingers.

"Desmond?" Chancellor frowned.

"From the Foreign Office," Susannah elaborated. "At least he used to be. I am not sure if he is there anymore. But he was most concerned about the subject of exploitation of Africa. He did not believe we would do it honorably at all. . . ."

Chancellor put his hand over hers very gently.

"My dear, I am grieved to have to tell you, but Sir Arthur Desmond died about two days ago, apparently by his own hand. He is not a source to be quoted with any authority." He looked suitably sad.

"No he didn't kill himself!" Charlotte burst out before thinking whether it was in the least wise, or would serve her purposes. All she could think of was Matthew's weary face and his distress, and Pitt's love for a man who had befriended him. "It was an accident!" she added in defense.

"I apologize," Chancellor said quickly. "I meant that he brought about the situation himself, whether by carelessness or design. Unfortunately it seems he was losing the clarity of mind he used to have." He turned back to his wife. "Thinking of Africans as noble savages, and wishing that they should remain so, is a sentimentality history does not allow. Sir Arthur was a fine man, but naive. Africa is going to be opened up by us or by others. Best for Britain and for Africa that it should be us."

"Would it not be better for Africa if we made treaties to protect them and keep Africa as it is?" Kreisler asked with apparent innocence which was belied by both his expression and the hard, thin edge to his voice.

"For adventurers and hunters like yourself?" Chancellor asked with raised eyebrows. "A sort of endless playground for explorers, with no civilized law to dictate anything at all."

"I am not a hunter, Mr. Chancellor, nor am I a scout for others," Kreisler rejoined. "An explorer, I accept. And I leave both the land and the people as I found them. Mrs. Chancellor has an excellent moral point. Have we the right to make decisions for other people?"

"Not only the right, Mr. Kreisler," Chancellor replied with absolute conviction. "Also the obligation when the others concerned have neither the knowledge nor the power to do it for themselves."

Kreisler said nothing. He had already registered his feelings. He looked instead at Susannah, his face thoughtful.

"I don't know about anyone else, but I am ready for supper," Christabel said in the momentary silence which followed. She turned to Kreisler. "Mr. Kreisler, since we outnumber you two to one, I am obliged to ask you to offer us an arm each to conduct us down the stairs. Miss Gunne, do you mind sharing Mr. Kreisler with me?"

There was only one possible answer, and Nobby gave it with a charming smile.

"Of course not. I shall be only too pleased. Mr. Kreisler?"

Kreisler offered his arms, and escorted Christabel and Nobby to supper.

Linus Chancellor did the same for Charlotte and Susannah, and together they swept down the great staircase, where at the bottom Charlotte recognized Pitt, who had been speaking to a very quiet, self-possessed man, quite bald, whom she judged to be nearer fifty than forty. He had round, pale blue eyes, a rather long nose, and a sense of calm about him, as if he knew some inner secret which was infinitely satisfying.

Pitt introduced him as Ian Hathaway, also of the Colonial Office, and when he spoke, Hathaway had the kind of voice, and perfect diction, that she felt she must have known him before, or at least met him.

She thanked Linus Chancellor and Susannah, and then found herself accompanied by two men as she approached the supper table, which held every kind of cold delicacy: pies, cold meats, fish, game, preserves in aspic, pastries of all sorts, and a multitude of ices, sherberts, jellies and creams amid crystal, flowers, candles and silver. The conversation at once became more sporadic, and largely meaningless.

Vespasia woke late the following morning, but with a considerable feeling of pleasure. She had enjoyed the reception more than usual. It had been a very grand affair and its splendor had brought back pleasant memories of her prime when she had commanded the admiration of every man who saw her, when she had danced the nights away and still risen early to ride in Rotten Row and return home with the blood pounding in her veins and ready to face a day of involvement in a dozen causes and intrigues.

She was still sitting in bed lazily eating her breakfast, smiling to herself, when her ladies' maid came to say that Mr. Eustace March had called to see her.

"Good gracious! What time is it?" she asked.

"Quarter past ten, m'lady."

"Whatever brings Eustace here at this time of the morning? Has he lost his pocket watch?"

Eustace March was her son-in-law, the widower of her late daughter, Olivia, who had borne him a large number of children and died comparatively young. Her marriage had been her own choice, but one Vespasia had never understood; nor had she found it easy to like Eustace. He was in every way her opposite. But it was Olivia who had married him, and as far as it was possible to judge from exteriors, he had made her happy.

"Shall I tell him to wait, m'lady? Or should I say you are unavailable today and he should come back another time?"

"Oh no. If he can wait, tell him I shall be down in half an hour."

"Yes m'lady." She withdrew obediently to deliver the message to the parlormaid to give to Eustace.

Vespasia finished her tea and set the tray aside. It would

take her half an hour at least to prepare for the day satisfactorily. Her maid had returned and was waiting to assist her, and she rose and began with a wash in hot water and scented soap.

She entered the cool, classically spacious withdrawing room and saw Eustace standing by the window looking into the garden. He was a very solid man, very robust. He believed intensely in good health as a fundamental Christian virtue, to be coupled with sanity of mind, and thus a proper balance in all things. He approved of plenty of long walks in fresh air, open windows regardless of the weather, a fine appetite, cold baths and good sportsmanship as an ideal of manhood.

He turned around with a smile as he heard Vespasia come in. His rather grizzled hair was grayer than last time she had seen him, and definitely receding a little at the front, but as always he had a good color and a clear eye.

"Good morning, Mama-in-law, how are you? Well, I hope?" He seemed in particularly fine spirits, and obviously had something he wished to say to her. His enthusiasm was bursting from him and she was afraid he was going to grip her hand and wring it.

"Good morning, Eustace. Yes, I am very well, thank you."

"You are quite sure? You are up a little late. Early is best, you know. Good for the circulation. A good walk would make you feel fit for anything."

"For my bed again," she said dryly. "I did not get home until three in the morning. I attended the reception at the Duchess of Marlborough's. It was most enjoyable." She sat down in her favorite chair. "To what do I owe the pleasure of your visit, Eustace? You have not come simply to enquire after my health. You could have done that with a letter. Please do sit down. You look so restless standing there, bristling with energy; as if you were about to leave even as you tell me what is on your mind."

71

Eustace obeyed, but perched on the edge of his chair, as if relaxing would put a strain on him more than he could bear.

"I have not been to call on you for some time, Mama-in-law. I came principally to rectify that omission and to see how you are. I am delighted to find you so well."

"Rubbish," she said with a smile. "You have something to tell me. It is on the tip of your tongue. What is it?"

"Nothing specific, I assure you," he reiterated. "Are you still engaged in fighting for social reforms?" He leaned back in the chair at last and crossed his hands over his stomach.

She found his manner irritating, but perhaps that was more due to memory than anything in the present. It had been his intolerable bullying and insensitivity which had at least in part precipitated the tragedy which had overtaken the whole family in Cardington Crescent. Only afterwards had he been even touched with the slightest perception of his own part in it. For a brief period he had been bewildered and ashamed. It had passed rapidly, and now he was fully back to his original ebullience and the total conviction that he was right in all his major beliefs and opinions. Like many people of intense physical energy and good health, he had an ability to forget the past and proceed with the present.

Nevertheless, she found his attitude patronizing, like that of a benevolent schoolmaster.

"Now and then," she replied coolly. "I have also entertained myself with renewing some old acquaintances." She did not tell him that the principal among these was Thelonius Quade, a high court judge some twenty years her junior, who had in the past been an ardent admirer, deeply in love with her. The friendship, reawoken, was increasingly precious to her. That was something she did not wish to share with Eustace. "And also there are Thomas Pitt's cases," she added truthfully, although she knew Eustace would not like it. Apart from its being socially unacceptable to involve oneself with the police, it would far more piquantly bring back his own memories, griefs, and probably even guilt.

"I think that is rather unsuitable, Mama-in-law," he said with a frown. "Especially when there is so much that is worthy to be done. I have never minded your eccentricities now and then, but . . ." He stopped. Vespasia's eyes froze him and the rest of his sentence died on his lips.

"How generous of you," she said icily.

"What I mean is—"

"I know what you mean, Eustace. This whole conversation is unnecessary. I know what you wish to say, and you know what my reply will be. You do not approve of my friendship with Thomas and Charlotte, still less of my assisting them now and again. I have every intention of continuing, and do not consider it to be any of your concern." She smiled at him very slightly. "Shall we proceed from there? Do you have some particular worthy cause in mind in which you think I should be involved?"

"Now that you mention it . . ." He recovered his composure almost immediately. It was a quality in him she both admired and found intensely irritating. He was like one of those toys with a round, weighted base which one cannot knock over because automatically it rights itself the moment you let go of it.

"Yes?"

His face lit with enthusiasm again. "I have recently been permitted to join a most exclusive organization," he said eagerly. "I say 'permitted' because members are accepted only when proposed by another member and closely examined by a selection committee. It is entirely charitable of course, with the highest possible aims."

She waited, trying to keep her mind open to hear all he said. There were, after all, a legion of societies in London, most of them excellent in their purposes.

He crossed his legs, his face supremely satisfied. He had

rather round, hazel-gray eyes, and they were shining with enthusiasm.

"Because all the members are men of means and in many cases considerable power in the community, in the world of finance or government, a great deal can be accomplished. Even laws changed, if it is desirable." His voice rose with the vigor of his feelings. "Enormous amounts of money can be raised to aid the poor, the disadvantaged, those suffering from injustices, disease or other misfortune. It is really very exciting, Mama-in-law. I feel highly privileged to be a member."

"Congratulations."

"Thank you."

"It sounds most praiseworthy. Perhaps I should join? Could you propose me?"

She watched his face with amusement. His mouth fell open, and his eyes reflected utter confusion. He was not even sure whether she was indulging in some distasteful joke. He had never been entirely certain of her sense of humor.

She waited, regarding him without a flicker.

"Mama-in-law, no serious society I know of accepts women! You must surely be aware of that?"

"Why not?" she asked. "I have money, no husband I am obliged to obey, and I am as capable of doing good as anyone else."

"That is not the point!" he protested.

"Oh. What is the point?"

"I beg your pardon?"

"What is the point?" she repeated.

Eustace was saved from justifying what to him was an assumption about the nature of the universe which was as beyond questioning as it was beyond explanation. The parlormaid came in to say that Mrs. Pitt had arrived.

"Oh, good gracious. Thank you, Effie," Vespasia said, acknowledging her. "I had not realized it was so late. Please ask her to come in." She turned back to Eustace. "Charlotte

74

will accompany me while we take our cards to the Duchess of Marlborough."

"Charlotte will?" Eustace was dumbfounded. "To the Duchess of Marlborough? Really, this is preposterous, Mama-in-law! She is utterly unsuitable. Heaven knows what she might say or do. Surely you're not serious."

"I am perfectly serious. Thomas has been promoted since you last saw him. He is now a superintendent."

"I don't care if he is commissioner of Scotland Yard!" Eustace said. "You still cannot have Charlotte call upon the Duchess of Marlborough!"

"We are not going to call upon her," Vespasia said patiently. "We are simply going to leave our cards, which, as you know as well as I do, is customary after attending a function. It is the accepted way of expressing our appreciation."

" 'Our appreciation'! Charlotte was there?" He was still completely nonplussed.

"She was."

The door opened and Charlotte was shown in. As soon as she saw Eustace March her face registered a conflicting mixture of emotions—surprise, anger, self-consciousness—all overridden by curiosity.

Eustace's feelings were much plainer. There was nothing in his face but a pure and simple embarrassment. He rose to his feet, his cheeks flaming.

"What a pleasure to see you again, Mrs. Pitt, how are you?"

"Good afternoon, Mr. March." She swallowed hard and came forward.

Vespasia could guess what manner of event she was remembering, most probably the ridiculous episode under the bed. No doubt, from the scarlet in Eustace's cheeks, so was he.

"I am in excellent health, thank you," she added. "I am sure that you are also." That may have been a memory of his ever open windows in Cardington Crescent, even on

75

cloudy mornings when the wind blew the breakfast room to almost intolerable temperatures, and everyone except Eustace was shivering over the porridge.

"Always, Mrs. Pitt," Eustace said briskly. "I am blessed in that manner."

"Eustace has been telling me about an excellent society he has been privileged to join," Vespasia said, indicating a chair for Charlotte.

"Ah—yes," Eustace agreed. "Dedicated to works of charity, and to influencing society for good."

"Congratulations," Charlotte said wholeheartedly. "You must feel a great sense of achievement. It is certainly sorely needed."

"Oh indeed." He resumed his own seat, sounding far more relaxed. He was back to discussing a subject which obviously pleased him enormously. "Indeed, Mrs. Pitt. It is most gratifying to feel that one can join with other men of like mind and dedication to the same purposes, and together we can be a real force in the land."

"What is the name of this society?" Charlotte asked innocently.

"Ah, you must not ask further, my dear lady." He shook his head a fraction, smiling as he did so. "Our aims and purposes are public and open to everyone, but our society itself is anonymous."

"You mean secret?" Charlotte asked boldly.

"Ah well." He looked taken aback. "I would not have chosen that word; it has a ring about it which gives quite the wrong idea, but it is anonymous. After all, is that not the way Our Lord commanded us we should do good?" His smile returned. " 'Let not your left hand know what your right hand doeth'?"

"Do you think a secret society was what He had in mind?" Charlotte asked with absolute seriousness, staring at him as she awaited his answer.

Eustace stared back at her as if he had been stung. His brain knew she was tactless, but he had almost forgotten

76

the manner and the reality of it. It was ill-mannered to embarrass anyone, and she consistently embarrassed him; he thought, deliberately. No woman could be quite as unintelligent as she sometimes appeared.

"Perhaps 'discreet' would be a better word," he said finally. "I see nothing questionable in men helping each other to meet the needs of the less fortunate. In fact it seems like excellent sense. The Lord never extolled inefficiency, Mrs. Pitt."

Charlotte smiled suddenly and disarmingly. "I am sure you are right, Mr. March. And to claim public admiration for every act of charity is to rob it of any virtue at all. It is possibly even a fine thing that you yourselves will know only a few other members, simply those of your own ring. Then it is doubly discreet, is it not?"

"Ring?" All color had gone from his face now, leaving it oddly pale under the sun and windburn of his complexion, assiduously earned in good outdoor exercise.

"Is that not an appropriate term?" Charlotte asked, wide-eyed.

"I—well . . ."

"Never mind." Charlotte waved it away. She had no need to press it; the answer was obvious. Eustace had joined the Inner Circle, in innocence, even naïveté, as had so many before him—Micah Drummond and Sir Arthur Desmond, to name only two. Micah Drummond had broken from it and survived, at least so far. Arthur Desmond had not been so fortunate.

She turned to look at Vespasia.

Vespasia was very grave. She held out her hand to him. "I hope you will be a powerful influence for good, Eustace," she said without pretense. "Thank you for coming to tell us your news. Would you care to stay to luncheon? Charlotte and I will not be long."

"Thank you, Mama-in-law, but I have other calls to make," he declined rapidly, rising to his feet and bowing very slightly, then similarly to Charlotte. "Charming to

meet with you again, Mrs. Pitt. Good day to you both."
And without waiting for anything further he left the room.
Charlotte looked at Vespasia and neither of them spoke.

3

THE INQUEST on Arthur Desmond was held in London since that was where he had died. Sitting in the gallery of the court, Pitt was grimly sure that it was also so that members of the Inner Circle could keep a greater command of the proceedings. Had it been in Brackley, where he and his family had been known and revered for three centuries, the personal regard in which he was held might have overridden even their power.

As it was he sat beside Matthew, who this morning looked almost haggard, and together they waited while the formal opening of the inquest took place amid a hush of anticipation. The room was full. People bumped and jostled each other making their way through the narrow doorway and under the beamed arch into the main area. The buzz of noise died away as people took their seats, facing the single bench at the front, the table to one side where an official in a black gown took notes, his pen at the ready, and the other side, where there was a stand for witnesses.

Pitt felt a strange sense of unreality. He was too filled with emotion to allow his mind to function with the clarity it usually had on such occasions. He had lost count of the number of inquests he had attended before this.

He looked towards the front. He could see at least fifteen or twenty men of sober bearing, dressed in full or half mourning, sitting shoulder to shoulder ready to give testi-

79

mony as they were called. Most of them had the solid, confident look of wealth and assured position. He assumed they were either professional experts of some sort or else the members of the club who had been present on the afternoon of Sir Arthur's death. A nervous man, a few years younger, dressed less expensively, was probably one of the club stewards who had served the brandy.

The coroner was ill-suited by appearance for his task. Anyone more robust and full of the vigor of life would be hard to imagine. He was large with red-gold hair and a highly florid complexion, features broad and full of enthusiasm.

"Well now," he said heartily, as soon as the preliminaries were completed. "Wretched business. Very sorry. Let us get it over with as soon as we may, with diligence and dispatch. Diligence and dispatch, best way to deal with the trappings of loss. Condolences to the family." He looked around the room and saw Matthew. Pitt wondered whether he had already met him, or if he were simply skilled enough to recognize bereavement at a glance. "Shall we proceed? Good, good. Let us hear the first witness to this sorry event. Mr. Usher, send for him, if you please."

The usher obediently called for the club steward, who was, as Pitt had surmised, the man with the less expensive coat, and whose general embarrassment was now acute. He was overwhelmed, afraid of making a mistake. His manners were self-conscious, as were his clothes and his voice. He was awed by all the majesty of the law, even at this level, and by the finality of death. He mounted the witness stand with his eyes wide and his face pale.

"No need to be afraid, my man," the coroner said benignly. "No need at all. You didn't do anything wrong, did you? Didn't kill the poor creature?" He smiled.

The steward was appalled. For half a second, a blood-chilling second, he thought the coroner was serious.

"N-no sir!"

"Good," the coroner said with satisfaction. "Then com-

80

pose yourself, tell us the truth, and all will be well. Who are you and what do you do? What have you to tell us about all this. Speak up!"

"M-my name is Horace Guyler, my lord. I am a steward at the Morton Club for Gentlemen. It was me as found poor Sir Arthur. I mean, o'course we all knew where 'e was, but . . ."

"I take your meaning perfectly," the coroner encouraged. "It was you who discovered he was dead. And I am not a 'my lord.' That is for the judges. I am merely a coroner. 'Sir' will do very well when you address me. Proceed. Perhaps you had better begin with Sir Arthur's arrival at the club. What time was that? When did you first see him? What was his appearance, his manner? Answer one at a time."

Horace Guyler was confused. He had already forgotten the first question, and the second.

"Sir Arthur's arrival," the coroner prompted.

"Ah. Yes sir. Well, 'e came in just after luncheon, which would be about quarter past three, sir, or thereabouts. 'E looked perfectly well to me at the time, which of course I realize now, but 'e must a' bin awful poorly. I mean, awful distressed in 'isself, about summink."

"You must not tell us what you realize now, Mr. Guyler, only what you observed at the time. What did Sir Arthur say to you? What did he do? What was his manner? Can you recall? It is only five days ago."

"As far as I remember, sir, 'e simply wished me a good day, same as always. 'E were always a very courteous gentleman. Not like some. And then he went through to the green room, sat down and read a newspaper to 'isself. *The Times,* I think it were."

There was a vague stirring in the room, murmurs of approval.

"Did he order anything to drink, Mr. Guyler?"

"Not straightaway, sir. About 'alf an hour later 'e ordered a large brandy. Best Napoleon brandy, 'e wanted."

"So you took it to him?"

"Oh yes sir, o' course I did," Guyler admitted unhappily. "O' course, I didn't know that then 'e was real upset and not 'isself. 'E seemed perfectly 'isself to me. Didn't seem upset at all. Just sat there reading 'is paper and muttering to 'isself now and then at pieces as 'e didn't agree with."

"Was he angry or depressed about it?"

"No sir." Guyler shook his head. "Just reading, like a lot o' gentlemen. 'E took it serious, o' course. But then gentlemen does. The more important the gentleman, the more serious 'e takes it. And Sir Arthur used to be in the Foreign Office."

The coroner looked grave. "Any subject in particular that you are aware of?"

"No sir. I weren't that close to 'im. I had a lot of other gentlemen to serve, sir."

"Naturally. And Sir Arthur had only the one brandy?"

Guyler looked unhappy. "No sir. I'm afraid 'e had a considerable number. I can't recall ezzac'ly 'ow many, but at least six or seven. Best part of one o' them 'alf bottles. I didn't know 'e weren't 'isself, or I'd never 'ave sent them!" He looked wretched, as if it really were somehow his responsibility, even though he was a club employee and might well have jeopardized his position had he refused to serve a member as he wished.

"And Sir Arthur remained in his usual spirits the whole time?" the coroner asked with a tiny frown.

"Yes sir, far as I could tell."

"Indeed. And what time did you serve the last brandy, do you recall?"

" 'Alf past six, sir."

"You are very precise."

"Yes sir. On account of a gentleman that asked me to call 'im to remind 'im of a dinner engagement 'e 'ad, so I knew ezzact."

There was no sound in the room.

"And the next time you saw Sir Arthur?"

"Well, I passed by 'im a few times, on me other errands like, but I took no notice 'cause 'e looked like 'e were asleep. O' course I wish now I'd a' done summink. . . ." He looked wretched, eyes downcast, face flushed.

"You are not responsible," the coroner said gently, the bonhomie gone from his expression. "Even had you known he was unwell and called a doctor, by the time anyone arrived there was probably little he could have done to save him."

This time there was a stirring in the room. Beside Pitt, Matthew shifted in his seat.

The steward looked at the coroner with a lift of hope.

" 'E were one of the nicest gentlemen," he said dolefully.

"I'm sure." The coroner was noncommittal. "What time was it when you spoke to Sir Arthur, Mr. Guyler, and realized that he was dead?"

Guyler drew a deep breath. "Well first I passed him an' thought 'e were asleep, like I said. Gentlemen who 'as drunk a lot o' brandy of an afternoon does fall asleep sometimes, an' is quite 'ard to rouse."

"I'm sure. What time, Mr. Guyler?"

"About 'alf past seven. I thought as if 'e wanted dinner it were time I booked a place for 'im."

"And what did you do?"

For a quarter of an hour no one in the court had moved or made any but the slightest of noises, merely a squeak of benches as the weight altered, or a creak and rustle of skirts from one of the two or three women present. Now there was a slow sighing of breath.

"I spoke to 'im, and 'e didn't answer," Guyler replied, staring straight ahead, painfully conscious of all eyes upon him. The court official at the table was taking rapid notes of everything he said. "So I spoke again, louder. 'E still didn't move, and I realized . . ." He took a deep breath and let it out slowly. He looked very nervous as the memory of death became sharper to him. He was frightened of it. It was something he chose never to think of in the normal course of things.

The coroner waited patiently. He had watched emotions like Guyler's chase across thousands of faces.

Pitt watched with a continuing sense of remoteness. Grief boiled up inside him; grief, a sudden overwhelming isolation as if he had been cut adrift from a safety he had been familiar with all his life. It was Arthur Desmond they were discussing so dispassionately. It was ridiculous to feel that they should have cared, should have spoken in hushed or tearful voices as if they understood the love, and yet he did feel it, even while his mind knew the absurdity.

He did not dare look at Matthew. He wanted to be done, to walk as quickly as he could, with the clear wind in his face, and the rain. The elements would keep him company as people could not.

But he must remain. Both duty and compassion required it.

"In the end I shook 'im." Guyler lifted his chin. "Just gentle like. 'E looked a terrible color, and I couldn't 'ear 'im at all. Gentlemen who is fallen asleep after the brandy very often breathe 'ard and deep. . . ."

"You mean they snore?"

"Well—yes sir."

There was a titter of laughter somewhere on the public benches, immediately suppressed.

"Why doesn't he get to what matters?" Matthew said fiercely beside Pitt.

"He will do," Pitt answered in a whisper.

"It was then I knew something was wrong," Guyler went on. He stared around the courtroom, not out of vanity but to remind himself where he was and dispel any memory of the club drawing room and what had happened there.

"You realized he was either ill or dead?" the coroner pressed.

"Yes sir. I sent for the manager, sir, and he sent for the doctor."

"Thank you, Mr. Guyler. That's all. Thank you for coming."

Guyler departed with relief, and the club manager took his place. He was a large, solid man with an agreeable face and a walleye which was most disconcerting. It was never possible to be certain whether he was looking at one or not. He testified to having been called by the steward and finding that Sir Arthur was indeed dead. He had sent for the doctor who was usually called upon if any of the gentlemen were taken unwell, which regrettably did happen from time to time. The average age of the membership was at least fifty-five, and many were a great deal older. The doctor had confirmed death without hesitation.

The coroner thanked the manager and permitted him to depart.

"This is pointless!" Matthew said between his teeth. He leaned forward and put his head in his hands. "It's all perfectly predictable and meaningless. They're going to get away with it, Thomas! Death by accidental overdose of an old man who didn't know what he was doing or saying!"

"Did you expect anything different here?" Pitt asked as quietly as he could.

"No." There was defeat in Matthew's voice.

Pitt had known it would hurt, but he was unprepared for how hard he found it to watch Matthew's distress. He wanted to comfort him, but there was nothing he could say.

The next witness was the doctor, who was professional and matter-of-fact. Possibly it was his way of dealing with the shock and finality of death. Pitt saw the dislike on Matthew's face, but it was born of emotion rather than reason, and this was not the time for an explanation which was irrelevant. It had nothing to do with what he was feeling.

The coroner thanked the doctor, dismissed him and then called the first of the members of the club who had been in the room during that afternoon. He was an elderly man with enormous white side-whiskers and a polished dome of a head.

"General Anstruther," the coroner said earnestly, "would you be good enough, sir, to tell us what you observed on that particular occasion, and if you consider it relevant, anything that you were aware of regarding Sir Arthur's health and state of mind."

Matthew looked up sharply. The coroner glanced at him. Matthew's face tightened but he said nothing.

General Anstruther cleared his throat loudly and began. "Decent chap, Arthur Desmond. Always thought so. Getting older, of course, like the rest of us. Forgetting things. Happens."

"That afternoon, General," the coroner prompted. "How was his demeanor? Was he . . ." He hesitated. "Distrait?"

"Ah . . ." Anstruther hesitated, looking deeply uncomfortable.

Matthew sat rigid, his eyes unwaveringly on Anstruther's face.

"Is this really necessary?" Anstruther demanded, glaring at the coroner. "The fellow's dead, damn it! What more do we need? Bury him and remember him kindly. He was a good man."

"No doubt, sir," the coroner said quietly. "That is not in any sense in question. But we do need to ascertain exactly how he died. The law requires that of us. The circumstances are unusual. The Morton Club wishes to clear its name of any question of carelessness or impropriety."

"Good God!" Anstruther blew through his nose. "Who's suggesting such a thing? Absolute nonsense. Poor Desmond was not well and a trifle confused. He took too much laudanum along with brandy. Simple accident. No more to be said."

Matthew jerked up. "He was not confused!" he said aloud.

Everyone in the room turned towards him, surprised and more than a little embarrassed. One did not show emotion of such a sort, especially not here. It was not done.

"We sympathize with you, Sir Matthew," the coroner

86

said clearly. "But please contain yourself, sir. I shall not allow any statements to pass without requiring they be substantiated." He turned back to the witness stand. "Now, General Anstruther, what causes you to say that Sir Arthur was confused? Please be specific."

Anstruther pursed his lips and looked annoyed. He was obviously very loath to accede. He glanced once at the front bench. "He . . . er . . . he forgot what he had said," he replied. "Repeated himself, don't you know? Got his facts muddled now and then. Talked a lot of nonsense about Africa. Didn't seem to understand."

Matthew rose to his feet before Pitt could restrain him. "You mean he disagreed with you?" he challenged.

"Sir Matthew!" the coroner warned. "I will not tolerate repeated interruption, sir. We are aware of your very natural grief, but there are limits to our patience. This inquest will be conducted in proper order and decorum, with respect both for the truth and for the dignity of the occasion. I am sure you would wish that as much as anyone."

Matthew drew in his breath, possibly to apologize, but the coroner held up his hand to silence him.

Matthew sat back down again, to Pitt's relief.

"General, please be good enough to elaborate upon what you mean." The coroner turned to General Anstruther. "Did Sir Arthur merely disagree with you upon some matters? What precisely causes you to believe his reasoning was confused?"

The dark color washed up Anstruther's cheeks, making his white whiskers seem even more pronounced.

"Talked a lot of nonsense about secret combinations of people plotting together to conquer Equatoria, or some such thing." He glanced again at the front row, and then away. "Made a lot of wild accusations. Absolute nonsense of course. Contradicted himself half the time, poor devil. Terrible thing, to start losing your sense of . . . of . . . God knows, all your old loyalties, where your trust and decency lie, who your own people are, and what the values are you believed all your life."

"You mean Sir Arthur had substantially changed from the man he had been in the recent past?"

"I wish you wouldn't force me to say this!" Anstruther persisted angrily. "Let us bury him in peace, and his latter misfortunes with him. Let us forget this nonsense and remember him as he was a year or so ago."

Matthew groaned so audibly that not only did Pitt hear him, the man on the far side of him heard as well. He looked around sharply, then flushed with discomfort at Matthew's obvious emotion, and looked away again.

"Thank you, General," the coroner said quietly. "I think you have told us enough for us to have some idea. You are excused."

Anstruther took out a white handkerchief and blew his nose savagely, then left, looking to neither side of him.

The Honorable William Osborne was called next, who said much the same as Anstruther had, adding one or two instances of Arthur Desmond's strange and irrational opinions, but he did not mention Africa. He was altogether a smoother and more assured man, and while he expressed regret in words, his manner did not suggest any emotion at all, except a slight impatience.

Matthew stared at him with implacable dislike, a growing bewilderment in his pain. It was more than possible that both Anstruther and Osborne were members of the Inner Circle. Pitt loathed to admit it, but it was also possible that Arthur Desmond had been somewhat irrational in his opinions, and that they were born more of emotion than a knowledge of fact. He had always been highly individual, even eccentric. It was possible that in old age he had become detached from reality.

Another regular club member was called, a thin man with a sallow face and a gold watch with which his fingers were constantly fiddling as if it gave him some kind of comfort. He repeated what Osborne had said, occasionally

88

using the same phrases to describe what he apparently viewed as the disintegration of Arthur Desmond's faculties of reason and judgment.

The coroner listened without interruption, and then adjourned the sitting until after luncheon. They had not begun until ten o'clock, and it was already well past midday.

Pitt and Matthew walked out into the brilliant sunlight side by side. Matthew was silent for several yards along the pavement, sunk in gloom. A passerby jostled him, and he seemed almost unaware of it.

"I suppose I should have expected this," he said at last as they turned the corner. He was about to walk on and Pitt caught him by the arm. "What?" he asked.

"Opposite." Pitt indicated a public house sign for the Bull Inn.

"I'm not hungry," Matthew said impatiently.

"Eat anyway," Pitt instructed, stepping off the curb and avoiding a pile of horse droppings. Matthew trod in it and swore.

At another time Pitt might have laughed at the sight of Matthew's face, but he knew this was not the occasion. They hurried to the far side, and Matthew scraped his feet angrily against the curb. "Don't they have any crossing sweepers anymore?" he demanded. "I can't go inside like this."

"Yes you can. They'll have a proper boot scraper at the door. Come on."

Reluctantly Matthew followed Pitt to the entrance, used the iron scraper meticulously, as if the state of his boots were of the utmost importance, and then they went in side by side. Pitt ordered for both of them and they sat down in the crowded, noisy room. Tankards gleamed on pegs above the bar, polished wood shone darkly, there was sawdust on the floor and the smell of ale, heat and bodies.

"What can we do?" Matthew said finally when their meal was served: thick bread with sharp crusts, butter, crumbling cheese, dark aromatic pickles and fresh cider.

Pitt made his sandwich and bit into it.

"Did you ever mean that we could achieve anything?" Matthew went on, his plate untouched. "Or were you just trying to comfort me?"

"Of course I meant it," Pitt replied with his mouth full. He was also angry and distressed, but he knew the importance of keeping up their strength if they were to fight. "But we cannot prove them liars until we know what they've said."

"And then?" Matthew asked with disbelief in his voice.

"And then we try," Pitt finished.

Matthew smiled. "How very literal of you. Absolutely exact. You haven't changed, have you, Thomas?"

Pitt thought of apologizing, and then realized there was no need.

Matthew appeared to be on the point of asking him something further, but decided against it and bit into his own sandwich. He ate it with surprising appetite, and did not speak again until it was time to leave.

The first witness of the afternoon was the medical examiner, who gave his evidence in detail, but he was very practiced at this unhappy task and avoided scientific terms. Quite simply, Arthur Desmond had died of an overdose of laudanum, administered within the hour. It was sufficiently large to have killed anyone, but there was a certain amount of brandy in his stomach, and that might well have masked the flavor. Personally he thought the laudanum would have tainted the brandy. He favored a very good cognac himself, but that was a matter of taste.

"Did you find any other signs of illness or deterioration?" the coroner asked.

The medical examiner pulled a long face. "Of course there was deterioration. The man was seventy! But that taken into account, he was in excellent health. I'll be happy to be as fit if I reach that age. And no, there was no other sign of illness whatever."

"Thank you, Doctor. That is all."

The medical examiner gave a little grunt and left the stand.

Pitt would have wagered that he was not a member of the Inner Circle. Not that he could think how that fact would be of any use.

The next witness was also a doctor, but an utterly different man. He was serious, attentive, polite, but he knew himself to be of great importance. He acknowledged his name and his qualifications and addressed himself to the matter in hand.

"Dr. Murray," the coroner began, "I believe you were Sir Arthur's physician; is that correct?"

"I was indeed."

"For some time."

"The last fourteen years, sir."

"Then you were very familiar with the state of his health, both in mind and body?"

Beside Pitt, Matthew was sitting forward, his hands clenched, his face tense. Pitt found himself also straining to hear.

"Naturally," Murray agreed. "Although I must confess I had no idea the deterioration had gone so far, or I should not have prescribed laudanum for him. I am speaking of the deterioration in his mood, his frame of mind."

"Perhaps you would explain further, Dr. Murray. What precisely are you referring to? Was Sir Arthur depressed, worried over some matter, or anxious?"

Now there was a breathless silence in the room. Journalists sat with pencils poised.

"Not in the sense you mean, sir," Murray replied with confidence. "He had bad dreams, nightmares, if you will. At least that is what he told me when he came to see me. Quite appalling dreams, you understand? I do not mean simply the usual unpleasant imaginings we all suffer from after a heavy meal, or some disagreeable experience." He shifted his position slightly. "He seemed to be increasingly disoriented in his manner, and had developed suspicions of

91

people he had trusted all his life. I admit, I assume that he was suffering some senile decay of his faculties. Regrettably, it can happen to even the most worthy people."

"Very sad indeed," the coroner said gravely.

Matthew could bear it no longer. He shot to his feet.

"That's absolute nonsense! He was as lucid and in command of his mind as any man I know!"

A flash of anger crossed Murray's face. He was not accustomed to being contradicted.

The coroner spoke quite quietly, but his voice carried across the entire room, and everyone turned to stare.

"Sir Matthew, we all understand your grief and the very natural distress you feel at the loss of your father, and especially at the manner of it, but I will not tolerate your interruptions. I will question Dr. Murray as to his evidence." He turned to look at Murray again. "Can you give any instance of this behavior, Doctor? Were it as strange as you suggest, I am surprised you gave him laudanum in sufficient quantities to allow the event which brings us here."

Murray did not seem in the least contrite, and certainly not guilty. His words, like Osborne's, were full of apology, but his face remained perfectly composed. There were the marks of neither pain nor humor in it.

"I regret this profoundly, sir," he said smoothly, and without looking towards Matthew. "It is a sad thing to have to make public the frailties of a good man, especially when we are met to ascertain the causes of his death. But I understand the necessity, and the reason for your pressing the point. Actually I was not aware of all these things myself at the time I prescribed the laudanum, otherwise, as you say, it would have been a questionable act."

He smiled very faintly. One of the men in the front now nodded.

"Sir Arthur told me of his nightmares and his difficulty in sleeping," Murray resumed. "The dreams concerned wild animals, jungles, cannibals and similar frightening images. He seemed to have an inner fear of being overwhelmed by such things. I was quite unaware of his obsession with Africa at that time." He shook his head. "I prescribed laudanum for him, believing that if he would sleep more easily, and deeply, these thoughts would trouble him less. I only learned afterwards from some of his friends how far his rational thoughts and memory had left him."

"He's lying!" Matthew hissed, not looking at Pitt, but the words were directed to him. "The swine is lying to protect himself! The coroner caught him out so he twisted immediately to excuse himself."

"Yes, I think he is," Pitt said under his breath. "But keep your counsel. You'll never prove it here."

"They murdered him! Look at them! Sitting together, come to blacken his name and try to make everyone believe he was a senile old man who had so lost his wits he accidentally killed himself." Matthew's voice was cracking with the bitterness which overwhelmed him.

The man on the far side of him looked uncomfortable. Pitt had the distinct impression he would have moved away were it not that it would have drawn such attention to him.

"You won't succeed by attacking him face-to-face," Pitt said harshly between his teeth, aware—with a chill in his stomach—of a new fear: that they had no way of knowing who was involved, who was friend and who enemy. "Keep your powder dry!"

"What?" Matthew swung around, incomprehension in his eyes. Then he understood the words, if not the weight of all that was behind them. "Oh. Yes, I'm sorry. I suppose that's exactly what they'd expect, isn't it? Me to get so angry I lose my sense of tactics."

"Yes," Pitt said bluntly.

Matthew lapsed into silence.

Dr. Murray had been excused and the coroner had called a man named Danforth who was a neighbor of Arthur Desmond's in the country, and he was saying, with some sadness, that indeed Sir Arthur had been extraordinarily

93

absentminded lately, quite unlike his old self. Yes, unfortunately, he seemed to have lost his grasp on matters.

"Could you be more specific, sir?" the coroner suggested.

Danforth looked straight ahead of him, studiously avoiding the public benches where he might have met Matthew's eyes. "Well sir, an instance that comes to mind was approximately three months ago," he replied quietly. "Sir Arthur's best bitch had whelped, and he had promised me the pick of the litter. I had been over to look at them, and fine animals they were, excellent. I chose the two I wanted and he agreed, approved of it in fact." He bit his lip doubtfully for a moment before continuing, his eyes downcast. "We shook hands on it. Then when they were weaned I went over to collect them, only to find Arthur had gone up to London on some errand. I said I'd come back in a week, which I did, and he was off somewhere else, and all the pups had been sold to Major Bridges over in Highfield. I was very put out." He looked at the coroner, frowning. There was a slight movement in the room, a shifting of position.

"When Sir Arthur finally came back I tackled him on the matter." The umbrage was still apparent in his voice and in the set of his shoulders as he gripped the edge of the box. "I'd set my heart on those pups," he went on. "But Arthur looked completely confused and told me some cock-and-bull story about having heard from me that I didn't want them anymore, which was the exact opposite of the case. And then he went on with a lot of nonsense about Africa." He shook his head and his lips tightened. "The terrible thing was, he obviously believed what he was saying. I'm afraid he had what I can only call an obsession. He imagined he was being persecuted by some secret society. Look, I say, sir . . . this is all very embarrassing."

Danforth shifted awkwardly, clearing his throat. Two or three men in the front now nodded sympathetically.

"Arthur Desmond was a damn decent man," Danforth

said loudly. "Do we have to rake up all this unfortunate business? The poor devil accidentally took his sleeping medicine twice over, and I daresay his heart was not as strong as he thought. Can't we call an end to this?"

The coroner hesitated only a moment, then acquiesced.

"Yes, I believe we can, Mr. Danforth. Thank you for your evidence, sir, in what must have been a painful matter for you. Indeed, for all of us." He looked around the room as Danforth left the stand. "Are there any more witnesses? Anyone who has anything relevant to say in this matter?"

A short, broad man stood up in the front row.

"Sir, if you please, so this tragedy can be laid to rest, I and my colleagues"—he indicated the men on either side of him—"the full extent of the front row were in the Morton Club on the afternoon of Sir Arthur's death. We can confirm everything that the steward has said, indeed everything that we have heard here today. We would like to take this opportunity to extend our deepest sympathies to Sir Matthew Desmond." He glanced around in the general direction of the bench where Matthew sat hunched forward, his face white. "And to everyone else who held Sir Arthur in esteem, as we did ourselves. Thank you, sir." He sat down amid murmurs of agreement. The man immediately to his right touched him on the shoulder in a gesture of approval. The one on the left nodded vigorously.

"Very well." The coroner folded his hands. "I have heard sufficient evidence to make my verdict sad, but not in doubt. This court finds that Sir Arthur Desmond died as the result of an overdose of laudanum, administered by himself in a moment of absentmindedness. Possibly he took the laudanum in mistake for a headache powder, or a remedy for indigestion. We shall never know. Death by misadventure." He looked up at Matthew very steadily, something of a warning in his expression.

The court erupted in excitement. Newspaper reporters made a dash for the doors. People in the public benches

turned to one another, bursting with comment and speculation; several rose to their feet as a relief from sitting.

Matthew's face was ashen, his lips parted as if he were
about to speak.

"Be quiet!" Pitt whispered fiercely.

"It is not a misadventure!" Matthew retorted between his
teeth. "It was cold-blooded murder! Do you believe
those—"

"No I don't! But on the evidence, we are damned lucky
they didn't bring in a verdict of suicide."

The last traces of color drained out of Matthew's face.
He turned to look at Pitt. They both knew what suicide
meant: it was not merely dishonor, it was a crime against
both the church and the state. He would not be given a
Christian burial. He would die a criminal.

The coroner adjourned the court. The people rose and
filed out into the sunshine, still talking busily, full of
doubts, theories, explanations.

Matthew walked beside Pitt in the dusty street, and it
was several minutes before he spoke again. When he did
his voice was husky, almost paralyzed in the savaging of
his pain and confusion.

"I've never felt like this in my life. I didn't think it was
possible to hate anyone so much."

Pitt said nothing. He did not trust his own emotions.

Vespasia spent the afternoon in what had once been a
very usual pursuit but was now one she practiced less and
less often. She sent for her carriage at five minutes before
three o'clock, and dressed in ecru-colored lace and a highly
fashionable hat with a turned-up brim and trimmed with a
huge white cabbage rose. And then, carrying an ivory-
handled parasol, she came down the front steps and was assisted up into her carriage.

She instructed the coachman to take her first to Lady
Brabazon's house in Park Lane, where she stayed for exactly fifteen minutes, which was the appropriate duration

for an afternoon call. Less would have been too brief for courtesy, more would risk outstaying one's welcome. It was even more important to know when to leave than it was to know when to arrive.

Next she drove to Mrs. Kitchener's in Grosvenor Square, arriving a little before half past three, still well within the hour allotted for ceremonious calls. From four until five was for those less formal. From five until six was for those with whom one was on terms of friendship. Vespasia adhered to the convention. There were rules of society one might disobey, and there were those where it would be pointless and unacceptable. The timing of afternoon calls was among the latter.

What she was hoping to learn was a little more about the various members of the Colonial Office from a social point of view. For this it was necessary she begin to circulate again, in order that she might hear the appropriate gossip.

From Mrs. Kitchener's she proceeded north to Portman Square, and then to George Street, and Mrs. Dolly Wentworth's house, where she presented her card and was immediately invited in. It was now just past four o'clock, and an hour when tea might be offered and a call might last a little over the usual fifteen minutes.

"How charming of you to visit, Lady Cumming-Gould," Dolly Wentworth said with a smile. There were already two other ladies sitting perched on the edges of their chairs, backs ruler straight, parasols propped beside them. One was elderly with a handsome nose and imperious manner, the other at least twenty-five years younger, and from the resemblance in brow and coloring, presumably her daughter. Dolly Wentworth had a son, as yet unmarried. Vespasia drew her own conclusions as to their purpose, and was very soon proved correct. They were introduced as the Honorable Mrs. Reginald Saxby and Miss Violet Saxby.

Mrs. Saxby rose to her feet. It was customary for one party to leave as another arrived, and in no way a discourtesy. Miss Violet Saxby followed suit reluctantly.

"So unfortunate George should have been at his club," Mrs. Saxby said critically.

"I am sure he will be devastated to have missed you," Dolly murmured. "I often wonder why men go to their clubs so very often. It seems to me that some of them spend every afternoon there, or else at the races, or cricket, or some such thing."

"I don't know why they have clubs at all," Violet said petulantly. "There are hundreds of clubs for men, and barely half a dozen for women."

"The reason for that is perfectly obvious," her mother retorted. "Men have clubs in which to meet each other, talk a lot of nonsense about politics and sport and the like, and occasionally a little gossip, or business. It is where their social life is largely conducted."

"Then why not for women?" Violet persisted.

"Don't be absurd, child. Women have withdrawing rooms for such things."

"Then why do they have clubs for women at all?"

"For those who don't have their own withdrawing rooms, of course," Mrs. Saxby said impatiently.

"I don't know any ladies who don't have their own withdrawing rooms."

"Of course you don't. Any lady who does not have her own withdrawing room is not fit to be in Society, and consequently, she is not," Mrs. Saxby rejoined.

And with that Miss Saxby had to be content.

"Oh dear," Dolly said when they were gone. "Poor George is finding being single something of a trial." Further explanation was unnecessary.

"I think it is being so very eligible that is the trial," Vespasia said with a smile.

"Of course you are perfectly right. Please do sit down." Dolly waved vaguely at one of the pale blue chairs. "It seems like simply ages since I have seen you anywhere where it was possible to have a sensible conversation."

"That is because I have been to far too few such places."

Vespasia accepted the invitation. "Although I did enjoy the Duchess of Marlborough's reception this week. I saw you in the distance, but of course one can never reach people at these affairs, except by accident. I did meet Susannah Chancellor. What an interesting creature. She reminded me of Beatrice Darnay. She isn't one of the Worcestershire Darnays, is she?"

"No! Not at all. I don't know where her family comes from originally, but her father was William Dowling, of Coutts Bank."

"Indeed. I don't think I know him."

"Oh, you wouldn't, my dear. He's been gone several years now. Left a very considerable fortune. Susannah and Maude inherited it all, equally, I believe. No sons. Now Maude is dead, poor child, and her husband inherited it, along with the principal interest in the family banking business. Francis Standish. Do you know him?"

"I believe I have met him," Vespasia replied. "A distinguished-looking man, if I recall correctly. Very fine hair."

"That's right. Merchant banker. That sort of power always gives men an air of confidence, which has its own attractions." She settled a little more comfortably in her seat. "Of course his mother was related to the Salisburys, but I don't know how, precisely."

"And a woman of the most unusual appearance, named Christabel Thorne . . ." Vespasia continued.

"Ah, my dear!" Dolly laughed. "I think she is what is known as a 'new woman'! Quite outrageous, of course, but most entertaining. I don't approve. How could I? How could anyone with the least sense? It is really rather frightening."

"A new woman?" Vespasia said with interest. "Do you think so?"

Dolly's eyebrows rose. "Don't you? If women start wanting to leave their homes and families, and carve out a totally new role for themselves, whatever is going to happen to society in general? No one can simply please themselves all the time. It is completely irresponsible. Did you see that fearful play of Mr. Ibsen's? *A Doll's House*, or some such thing. The woman simply walked out, leaving her husband and children, for no reason at all."

"I think she felt she had reason." Vespasia was too old to care about being contentious. "He was excessively patronizing and treated her as a child, with no power or right to make her own decisions."

Dolly laughed.

"For heaven's sake, my dear, most men are like that. One simply finds one's own way 'round it. A little flattery, a little charm, and a great deal of tact to his face, and disobedience once his attention is elsewhere and most things can be achieved."

"She did not want to have to work for what she felt was every woman's right."

"You are sounding like a 'new woman' yourself!"

"Certainly not. I am a very old woman." Vespasia changed the subject. "What does this Christabel Thorne do that is so radical? She has not left her home, I'm sure."

"Far worse than that." Now there was real disapproval in Dolly's face; the laughter had gone entirely. "She has some sort of an establishment which prints and distributes the most detailed literature encouraging women to educate themselves and attempt to enter the professions. I ask you! Who on earth is going to employ a woman lawyer, or architect, or judge, or a woman physician? And it is all quite pointless. Men will never tolerate it anyway. But of course she will not listen."

"Extraordinary," Vespasia said with as little expression in her voice as she could manage. "Quite extraordinary."

They got no further with the subject because another caller arrived, and although it was well past four o'clock, it was apparent that Vespasia should take her leave.

The last person she visited was Nobby Gunne. She found her in her garden staring at the flag irises, a distracted expression on her face. Curiously, she looked anxious and yet inwardly she had a kind of happiness which lent her skin a glow.

"How nice to see you," she said, turning from the iris bed and coming forward. "I am sure it must be teatime. May I send for some for you? You will stay?"

"Of course," Vespasia accepted.

They walked side by side across the wide sunny sweep of the lawn, the occasional longer spikes of the uncut edges catching their skirts. A bumblebee flew lazily from one early pink rose to another.

"There is something about an English summer garden," Nobby said quietly. "And yet I find myself thinking more and more often of Africa."

"Surely you don't wish to go back there now, do you?" Vespasia was surprised. Nobby was past the age when such an enterprise would be either easy to arrange or comfortable in execution. What was an adventure at thirty could be an ordeal at fifty-five.

"Oh no! Not in the slightest." Nobby smiled. "Except in the occasional daydream. Memory can be misleadingly sweet. No, I worry about it, most particularly after the conversation we had the other evening. There is so much money involved in it now, so much profit to be made from settlement and trade. The days of exploration to discover a place, simply because no white man had seen it before, are all past. Now it is a matter of treaties, mineral rights and soldiers. There's been so much blood already." She looked sad, gazing at the honeysuckle spilling over the low wall they were passing.

"Nobody talks about missionaries anymore. I haven't heard anyone even mention Moffatt or Livingstone in a couple of years. It is all Stanley and Cecil Rhodes now, and money." She stared up at the elm trees shining and whispering in the sun, and below them the climbing white roses beginning to open. It was all intensely English. Africa with its burning heat and sun and dust seemed like a fairy story not real enough to matter.

But looking at Nobby's face, Vespasia could see the depth of her emotion, and how deeply she still cared.

"Times do change," she said aloud. "I am afraid that after the idealists come the realists, the practical profiteers. It has always been so. Perhaps it is inevitable." She walked quietly beside Nobby and stopped in front of a massive lupine whose dozen spikes were already showing pink. "Be grateful that you were privileged to see the best days and be part of them."

"If that were all"—Nobby frowned—"if it were only a matter of personal regret, I would let it go. But it really does matter, Vespasia." She looked around, her eyes dark. "If settlement of Africa is done badly, if we sow the wind, we will reap the whirlwind for centuries to come, I promise you." Her face was so grim, so full of undisguised fear, that Vespasia felt a chill in the summer garden and the cascades of blossoms seemed bright and far away, and even the warmth on her skin lacked a sense of reality.

"What exactly is it you think will happen?" she asked.

Nobby stared into the distance. She was not marshaling her thoughts; that had obviously already happened. She was seeing some inner vision, and the sight appalled her.

"If some of Linus Chancellor's plans go forward, and the men he is allied with, who are putting up enormous sums of money to colonize the interior . . . I'm speaking about Mashonaland, Matabeleland, the shores of Lake Nyasa, or on towards Equatoria . . . as they plan to, because they believe there is unlimited gold there," she replied, "then hordes of people will follow who are not in the least interested in Africa or its peoples, or in developing the land for themselves, or their children, but simply to rape it of its minerals." A butterfly drifted past them and settled on an open flower.

"There'll be profiteers of every kind, swindlers and cheats will be the least of them; there'll be violent men with their own private armies, and one by one they will draw in the native tribal chiefs. The internal wars are bad enough now, but they are only armed with spears. Think of it when some have guns and others don't."

She turned to face Vespasia. "And don't underestimate the Germans. They have a very powerful presence in Zanzibar, and are keen to press inland. There's been fearful bloodshed there already. And that may not be the worst of it. The Arab slavers will protect their interests by force, if they can. They have risen against the Germans once already."

"Surely the government is aware of all this?" Vespasia asked dubiously.

Nobby turned back to the garden, shrugging her shoulders very slightly. "I don't know if they believe it. It all seems different when you talk about it in England, so many names on paper, secondhand accounts, and all very far away. It's different when you've been there, and loved it, when you've known the people. They are not all noble savages with clear eyes and simple hearts."

They were walking again very slowly over the soft grass. She laughed jerkily. "They can be as devious and exploitative as any white man, and just as despotic. They can sell their enemies into slavery to any Arab who will buy them. It is the customary way to deal with prisoners of war. I don't think it's the morality that's the difference; it's the degree of power." She blinked hard. "It's our modern inventions, gunpowder, steel, our massive organization . . . we can do so much more evil, or good, with it. And I am so afraid with the greed for profit, the hunger for empire, it will be mostly evil we do."

"Is there anything to be done to prevent it?" Vespasia asked her. "Or at least to moderate it?"

"That is what troubles me," Nobby replied, starting to walk away from the border back across the lawn towards the shade of the cedar tree. They both sat down on the white bench.

103

"I am uncertain, and confused at present, but I feel that there is. I have spoken a little lately to Mr. Kreisler. He is very recently returned, and I respect his opinions." There was a very faint trace of color in her cheeks, and she did not look at Vespasia. "He was familiar with Abushiri, the leader of the rebellion against the Germans in Zanzibar. I gather it was principally a group of ivory and slave traders, who were beginning to feel restricted in their activities, but it was put down very messily. I confess, I know very little. Mr. Kreisler only mentioned it in passing, but it left me with an increasing anxiety."

Vespasia felt it too, but for different reasons. She was aware of the fall of Otto von Bismarck, the brilliant chancellor of Germany, the virtual creator of the new unified country. His nominal master, the old Kaiser, had been ill at the time, and died very shortly afterwards, of cancer of the throat. Now the sole ruler of the young and enormously vigorous state was the youthful, headstrong, supremely confident Kaiser Wilhelm the Second. German ambitions would know no cautious or restraining hand.

"I remember Livingstone's early years," Nobby said with a self-conscious smile. "That makes me sound old, doesn't it? How excited everyone was then. Nobody said anything about gold or ivory. It was all a matter of discovering people, finding new and wonderful sights, great cataracts like the Victoria Falls." She stared up through the dark green boughs of the cedar at the brilliance of the sky. "I met someone who had seen it once, just a few months earlier. I was standing outside in the evening. It was still hot, really hot. England is never close to the skin like that, touching, breathing heat.

"All the acacia trees were flat-topped against a sky burning with stars, and I could smell the dust and the dry grass. It was full of insects singing, and half a mile away at the water hole, I heard a lioness roar. It was so still, I felt as if I could have reached out and touched her."

There was a sadness close to tears in Nobby's face. Vespasia did not interrupt her.

"The man was an explorer who had set out with a party. A white man," Nobby went on quietly, almost as if to herself. "He was ill with a fever when he reached us. He staggered into our camp so exhausted he could barely stand. He was wasted until he was skin and bone, but his face lit up when he spoke and his eyes were like a child's. He had seen it some three months before . . . the greatest cataract in the world, he said . . . as if the ocean itself poured off the cliffs of the sky in an endless torrent, leaping and roaring into a chasm of which one could not see the bottom for the white spume flying and the endless rainbows. The river had a dozen arms, and every one of them flung itself into that gorge and the jungle clung to the sides and leaned over the brink in a hundred different places." She fell silent.

"What happened to him?" Vespasia asked.

Somewhere above them a bird was singing in the cedar tree.

"He died of fever two years later," Nobby answered. "But please God the falls will be there till the end of time." She stood up again and began to walk back across the grass towards the house, Vespasia behind her. "I'm sure tea must be ready. Would you care for some now?"

"Yes please." Vespasia caught up with her.

"Mr. Kreisler hunted with Selous, you know," Nobby continued.

"Who is Selous?"

"Oh! Frederick Courtney Selous, a marvelous hunter and scout," Nobby replied. "Mr. Kreisler told me Mr. Selous is the one leading the Rhodes column north to settle Zambezia." The shadow was back in her face, and yet there was a lift in her voice, a subtle alteration when she spoke Kreisler's name. "I know Mr. Chancellor is backing Rhodes. And of course Francis Standish's bank."

"And Mr. Kreisler disapproves," Vespasia said. It was not really a question.

"I fear he has reason," Nobby answered, looking across at Vespasia suddenly. "I think he loves Africa genuinely, not for what he hopes to gain, but for itself, because it is wild and strange, beautiful and terrible and very, very old." There was no need to say how much she admired him for it; it shone in her face and whispered in the gentleness of her voice.

Vespasia smiled and said nothing. They continued side by side across the lawn, their skirts brushing the grass, and went up the steps and in through the French window to take tea.

There was a charity bazaar the day after which Vespasia had promised to attend. It was being conducted by an old friend, and in spite of disliking such events, she felt obliged in kindness to support her efforts, although she would far rather simply have donated the money. However she thought Charlotte might find it entertaining, so she dispatched her carriage to fetch her if she wished.

As it turned out, it was not at all as she had expected, and the moment she and Charlotte had arrived, she knew it would at least be entertaining, at best possibly informative. Her friend, Mrs. Penelope Kennard, had omitted to tell her that it was a Shakespearean bazaar, where everyone who had any official part in the proceedings dressed as a character from a Shakespearean play. As a result they were greeted at the garden gate by a very handsome Henry V, who bade them welcome in ringing tones. And almost immediately after they left him, they were assaulted by a villainous Shylock demanding money or a pound of flesh.

Startled only for a moment, Vespasia good-naturedly handed him a handsome entry fee for herself and Charlotte.

"Good gracious, whatever next?" she murmured as they passed out of earshot and towards a stall where a young society matron was attired as Titania, Queen of the Fairies from *A Midsummer Night's Dream*, and looking very fetching indeed. A great deal more of her was visible than even

106

the most daring evening gown would have displayed. Lengths of gauze were swathed around her, leaving arms, shoulders and waist bare, and much more could be guessed at beneath its diaphanous folds. There were two young gentlemen bickering over the price of a lavender pomander, and several more waited eagerly to take their turn.

"Effective!" Charlotte said with reluctant admiration.

"Oh very," Vespasia agreed, smiling to herself. "The last time Penelope did one of these bazaars it was all characters from Mr. Dickens, and not nearly so much fun. They all looked rather alike to me. Look! There! Do you see Cleopatra selling pincushions?"

Charlotte followed Vespasia's indication and saw a remarkably handsome young woman with dark hair and eyes, a rather Grecian nose, perhaps a trifle high at the bridge for beauty, and a willful, highly individual mouth. It was a countenance that could indeed have belonged to a woman used to power and an extraordinary mixture of self-discipline and self-indulgence. She was at that moment offering a small, embroidered, lace-edged pincushion to a gentleman in an immaculate frock coat and striped trousers. He looked like a city banker or a dealer in stocks and securities.

A bishop in traditional gaiters walked by slowly, smiling in the sun and nodding first to one side then the other. His eyes lingered for several moments upon Cleopatra, and he very nearly stopped and bought a pincushion, before judicious caution prevailed and he continued on his way towards Titania, still smiling.

Vespasia glanced at Charlotte; words were unnecessary.

They walked gently on between the stalls where imaginatively dressed young women were selling sweetmeats, flowers, ornaments, ribbons, cakes and pictures, and yet others were offering games to play for various prizes. She saw one booth decked out in curtains of shadowy material with silver stars pinned to them, and letters proclaiming that for a sixpence the witches of *Macbeth* would tell your fortune and recite to you all the great achievements which lay in your future. There was a queue of giggling girls waiting their turn to go in, and even a couple of young men, pretending they were there simply to accompany them, and yet with a spark of interest in their faces.

Just past them Charlotte saw the sturdy figure of Eustace March, standing very upright, talking intently to a broad man with flowing white hair and a booming voice. They both laughed heartily, and Eustace bade him farewell and turned towards Charlotte. He saw her with a look of alarm, but it was too late for him to pretend he had not. He straightened his shoulders and came forward.

"Good afternoon, Mrs. Pitt. How pleasant to see you. Supporting a worthy cause, I see!" He laughed jerkily. "Excellent." Vespasia had stopped to speak to an acquaintance, and he had not seen her. He hesitated, searching for something to say, undecided whether he had satisfied good manners sufficiently to leave yet. "Lovely day. A joy to be out in it. Fine garden, don't you think?"

"Delightful," Charlotte agreed. "Most kind of Mrs. Kennard to lend it for the bazaar. I think there will be a great deal to clear up after all these people."

He winced very slightly at her candor in mentioning such a thing.

"All in a good cause, my dear lady. These small sacrifices are necessary if we are to be of service. Nothing without effort, you know!" He smiled, showing his teeth.

"Of course," she agreed. "I imagine you know a great many of the people here?"

"Oh no, hardly any. I have little time to mix in Society as I used to. There are too many important things to be done." He looked poised to depart and set about them immediately.

"You interest me greatly, Mr. March," she said, meeting his eyes.

He was horrified. It was the last thing he had intended.

She always made him uncomfortable. The conversation so seldom went as he had wished.

"Well, my dear lady, I assure you . . . I . . ." He stopped.

"How modest of you, Mr. March." She smiled winningly.

He blushed. It was not modesty but an urgent desire to escape.

"But I have thought a great deal about what you said only yesterday concerning organizing together to do good," she said eagerly. "I am sure in many ways you are right. When we cooperate, we can achieve so much more. Knowledge is power, is it not? How can we be effective if we do not know where the greatest need lies? We might even end up doing more harm, don't you think?"

"Yes, I imagine that is true," he said reluctantly. "I am so glad you have realized that hasty judgment is very often mistaken. I assure you, the organization to which I belong is most worthy. Most worthy."

"And modest," she added with a perfectly straight face. "It must have been so distressing for you that Sir Arthur Desmond was saying such disagreeable things about it, before the poor man died."

Eustace looked pale, and acutely uncomfortable.

"Er . . . most," he agreed. "Poor man. Senile, of course. Very sad." He shook his head. "Brandy," he added, pushing out his lower lip. "Everything in moderation, I always say. A healthy mind in a healthy body. Makes for both virtue and happiness." He took a deep breath. "Of course I don't hold with laudanum and the like at all. Fresh air, cold baths, brisk exercise and an easy conscience. No reason why a man shouldn't sleep every night of his life. Never think of powders and potions." He lifted his chin a little and smiled again

A menacing Richard III walked crabwise past them, and two young women laughed happily. He shook a fist and they entered into the spirit of it by pretending to be frightened.

"An easy conscience requires a life of extraordinary

virtue, frequent and profound repentance, or absolute insensitivity," Charlotte said with a slight edge to her voice, and only turning to look at Eustace at the last moment.

He blushed very pink, and said nothing.

"Unfortunately I did not know Sir Arthur," she went on. "But I have heard he was one of the kindest and most honorable of men. Perhaps he had pain, and that was what caused him to be wakeful? Or anxieties? If one is responsible for others, it can cause a great deal of worry."

"Yes—yes, of course," Eustace said unhappily. She knew memory was awakening in him, with all its discomforts. If he slept well every night, she felt he had no right to.

"Did you know him?" she pressed.

"Uh—Desmond? Oh ... well ... yes, I met him a few times. Not to say I knew him, you understand?" He did not look at her.

She wondered if he and Sir Arthur could conceivably have been in the same ring of the Inner Circle, but she had no idea even how many people were in a ring. She thought she recalled from something Pitt had said that it was no more than half a dozen or so, but she was unclear. For it to be effective, the groups would surely have to be larger than that in some way? Perhaps each ring had a leader, and they knew the others, and so on.

"You mean socially?" she asked with as much naïveté as she could manage. She found it was not very much. "At hunt balls and so on? Or to do with his work?"

Eustace looked somewhere over his left shoulder, his cheeks pink. "His work?" he said with alarm. "I ... I am not sure what you mean. Certainly not."

It was sufficient. He had taken her to be referring to the Inner Circle. Had it been a social acquaintance he would have admitted it without embarrassment, but she had been almost sure Eustace March did not move in the higher regions of old society, landed gentry, the true aristocracy where Arthur Desmond lived because he was born to it.

"I meant the Foreign Office." She smiled sweetly. "But of course I knew it was unlikely."

"Quite. Quite so." His answering smile was sickly. "Now, my dear lady, if you will excuse me, I must be about my duty. There is so much to do. One must show one's presence, you know? Buy a little here and there, give encouragement and set the example." And without allowing her a chance to argue he hastened away, nodding to either side as he saw acquaintances present or wished for.

Charlotte stood thoughtfully for a few moments, then turned and went back the way Vespasia had gone. Within a few moments she was near Cleopatra's pincushions again, and found herself interested to observe the interplay of an elderly matron, torn between envy and disapproval, and a young lady fast approaching an unmarriageable age, unless she were an heiress. With them was a gentleman Charlotte's practiced eye recognized as having had his collars and cuffs turned, to make them wear another six months or so. She had turned enough of Pitt's to know them when she saw them.

It was after a few moments she realized she had heard Cleopatra addressed as Miss Soames. Could she be Harriet Soames, to whom Matthew Desmond was betrothed?

When the purchase was made and the three people moved away, Charlotte went up to the counter of the stall.

"Excuse me?"

Cleopatra looked at her helpfully, but without interest. Closer to she was even more unusual. Her dark eyes were very level, her mouth not voluptuous, her upper lip unfashionably straight, and yet her face was full of deep inner emotion.

"May I show you something?" she asked. "Is it for yourself, or a gift?"

"Actually I overheard the previous purchaser address you as Miss Soames. Are you by any chance Miss Harriet Soames?"

111

She looked puzzled. "Yes. I am. But I am afraid I cannot recall our having met."

It was a polite and predictable reply from a well-bred young woman who did not wish to be rushed into an acquaintance with a person she knew nothing about, and to whom she had not been introduced.

"My name is Charlotte Pitt." Charlotte smiled. "My husband has been a lifelong friend of Sir Matthew Desmond. May I offer you my felicitations on your betrothal, and my sympathies for the death of Sir Arthur. My husband feels his loss so deeply, I know he must have been a most unusual man."

"Oh—" Having received a satisfactory explanation, Harriet Soames was perfectly prepared to be friendly. Her face softened into a charming smile. "How kind of you, Mrs. Pitt. Yes indeed, Sir Arthur was one of the nicest people I ever knew. I expected to be in awe of him, as one usually is of a prospective father-in-law, but from the moment I met him, I felt completely at ease." Memory in her face was touched at once with pleasure and pain.

Charlotte wished even more sharply that she had met Sir Arthur. She would have felt his death more keenly herself, but she would have been better able to share Pitt's emotion. She knew that his grief bit very deep and was mixed with guilt, and at the moment she was outside it. It was beyond either of them to alter that.

"Sir Matthew came to visit us the other evening," Charlotte continued, largely for something to say. "I had not met him before, but I found I liked him immediately. I do wish you every happiness."

"Thank you, that is most kind." Harriet seemed about to add something further, but was prevented by the arrival of a young woman whose face grew more and more appealing the longer one looked at it. At a glance one would have said she was ordinarily pretty with regular features and typically pleasing English fair coloring, not flaxen, but the warm deep tone of honey, and her complexion was unfashionably glowing with natural color. But with further regard there was an intelligence and humor in her face which made her anything but ordinary.

Not realizing Charlotte and Harriet were speaking as friends, rather than vendor and purchaser, she did not hesitate to interrupt, and then hastily apologized when Harriet introduced them. The newcomer's name was Miss Amanda Pennecuick.

"Oh, I am so sorry," Amanda said quickly. "How appallingly rude of me. Forgive me, Mrs. Pitt. I have nothing of the least importance to say."

"Nor I," Charlotte confessed. "I was merely introducing myself, since my husband is a very old friend of Sir Matthew Desmond's." She assumed Amanda knew of Harriet's betrothal, and her face made it immediately plain that she did.

"I am so cross," Amanda confided. "Gwendoline Otway is doing those fearful astrology readings again, and she promised she wouldn't. You know there are times when I feel I could slap her! And she has dressed herself as Anne Boleyn."

"With or without her head?" Harriet asked with a sudden giggle.

"With it . . . for the moment," Amanda replied grimly.

"I didn't know Anne Boleyn was Shakespearean." Harriet screwed up her brow.

"Farewell. . . . 'A long farewell to all my greatness,' " a beautifully modulated masculine voice said from just behind Amanda's shoulder, and they turned to see the bright, homely face of Garston Aylmer. "Cardinal Wolsey," he said cheerfully, looking at Amanda. "*Henry the Eighth*," he added.

"Oh, yes of course. Good afternoon, Mr. Aylmer," she replied, regarding him levelly, and almost without expression in her face, which was difficult because it was a countenance naturally given to emotion.

"Why does it displease you so much that she should

pretend a little astrology?" Charlotte asked. "Is it not a fairly harmless way of entertaining people and raising money for the bazaar?"

"Amanda disapproves of astrology," Harriet said with a smile. "Even as a game."

"The stars are not in the least magical," Amanda said quickly. "At least not in that sense. The truth of them is far more wonderful than a lot of silly names and ideas about classical heroes and imaginary beasts. If you had any idea of the real magnitude . . ." She stopped, aware that Garston Aylmer was staring at her with intensity, and an admiration in his face so plain no one watching him could have been unaware of it.

"Forgive me," she said to Charlotte. "I really should not allow myself to get so upset over something so silly. No doubt she is amusing people who would never look through a telescope even if you placed one into their hands." She laughed self-consciously. "Perhaps I had better buy a pincushion. Please let me see that one with the white lace on it."

Harriet passed it across.

"Perhaps you would allow me to escort you to tea, Miss Pennecuick? And you, Mrs. Pitt?" Aylmer offered.

Charlotte knew well enough when not to intrude. She had no idea what Amanda felt, but Aylmer's feelings were apparent, and she rather liked him.

"Thank you, but I have come with my great-aunt, and I should find her again before too long," she declined.

Amanda hesitated, apparently considering the matter, then coolly accepted, excusing herself to both Charlotte and Harriet. She made her purchase and left, walking beside Aylmer, but not taking his proffered arm. They looked unsuited together; she was so slender and elegant, and he was quite unusually plain, short legged, and definitely too plump.

"You should have gone," Harriet said under her breath. "Poor Amanda."

"I really did come with my great-aunt," Charlotte replied with a wide smile. "Honestly."

"Oh!" Harriet blushed. "I'm so sorry! I thought you were . . ." She started to laugh, and a moment later Charlotte joined in.

Fifteen minutes later she found Vespasia and together they went to the tent where afternoon tea was being served. They saw Aylmer and Amanda Pennecuick just leaving, apparently still in conversation.

"An unexpected couple," Vespasia observed.

"His design, not hers," Charlotte replied.

"Indeed." Vespasia looked at the young girl who had come to offer them sandwiches and little cakes decorated and iced in a variety of designs. They made their choice, and Vespasia poured the tea. It was still too hot to sip when Charlotte noticed Susannah Chancellor at the next table, which was rather more behind them so it was half hidden by a samovar on a stand and a large potted plant with a price ticket poking out of it. However, when for a moment neither she nor Vespasia were speaking, Susannah's voice was just audible. It sounded polite and curious, but there were the beginnings of anxiety in it.

"I think you are leaping to conclusions without knowing all the facts, Mr. Kreisler. The plans have been very thoroughly thought through, and a great many people consulted who have traveled in Africa and know the natives."

"Such as Mr. Rhodes?" Kreisler's voice was still on the borders of courtesy, but he was not concealing his disbelief, nor the dislike he felt for Cecil Rhodes and his works.

"Of course he is one of them," Susannah agreed. "But certainly not the only one. Mr. MacKinnon—"

"Is an honorable man," he finished for her. His voice was still light, almost bantering in tone, but there was an intensity beneath which was unmistakable to the ear. Charlotte could not see him, but she could imagine the unwavering look in his eyes, even if he were pretending to smile.

115

"But he has to make a profit. That is his business, and his honor depends upon it, even his survival."

"Mr. Rhodes has a great deal of his own money invested in this venture," Susannah went on. "Neither my husband nor my brother-in-law would have backed him as they have were he simply an adventurer with no stake in it himself."

"He is an adventurer with a very great stake in it himself," Kreisler said with a slight laugh. "He is an empire builder of the highest order!"

"You sound as if you disapprove of that, Mr. Kreisler. Why? If we do not, then others will, and we shall have lost Africa, perhaps to Germany. You can't approve of that, can you? Or of the slavery that goes on now?"

"No, of course not, Mrs. Chancellor. But the evil there now is centuries old, and part of their way of life. The changes we will bring about will not necessarily get rid of them, only produce war with the Arabs, who are the largest slavers, with the ivory traders and with the Portuguese, and undoubtedly with the Germans and the Sultan of Zanzibar. And most of all, it will set up our own empire in Equatoria, which will eventually overtake Emin Pasha, Lobengula, and the Kabaka of Buganda and everyone else. White settlers with guns will drive out the old ways, and in half a century the Africans will be a subject people in their own land. . . ."

"You're exaggerating!" There was laughter and disbelief on the surface of her voice, but underneath a beginning of worry, a sharp note of doubt. "There are millions of Africans, and only a handful of us . . . a few hundred."

"Today," he said harshly. "And tomorrow, when there's gold—and land? When the wars have been fought and there is adventure and profit to offer all the younger sons with no lands here? For those who've made a mess in Europe, or whose families won't support them or protect them anymore?"

"It won't be like that," she said urgently. "It will be like India. There will be a proper standing army, and a civil ser-

116

vice to administer it and keep the law and . . ." She stopped.

"Is that what you believe?" he said so softly Charlotte had to strain to catch his words.

"Well . . ." Susannah hesitated. "Not exactly, of course. It will take time. But yes, eventually it will."

"India is a culture and a civilization thousands of years older than ours. They were reading and writing, building cities and painting great art, dreaming philosophy, when we were running around painting ourselves blue and wearing animal skins!" he said with his contempt barely hidden.

"We still brought them the benefits of our laws," she said. "We settled their internal quarrels and united them as a great country. We may be upstarts in some ways, but we brought them peace. We'll do it in Africa too."

Kreisler said nothing. It was impossible to imagine what expression was in his face. Neither Charlotte nor Vespasia had said a word since they had both recognized Susannah Chancellor's voice. Their eyes had met a dozen times with thoughts that needed no speech.

"Did you know Sir Arthur Desmond?" Susannah said after a moment or two.

"No. Why?"

"No reason, except that he would have agreed with you. He seemed to be worried about Africa too."

"Then I should like to know him."

"I am afraid that is not possible. He died last week."

Kreisler said nothing, and a moment later they were apparently joined by Christabel Thorne, and the conversation became quite general, and to do with the bazaar.

"A man of great passions, Mr. Kreisler," Vespasia said, sipping the last of her tea. "An interesting man, but I fear a dangerous one."

"Do you think he is right . . . about Africa?" Charlotte asked.

"I have no idea. Perhaps, at least in part, he is. But I am

117

quite sure he has no doubts at all. I wish Nobby were not so fond of him. Come, my dear, we have done our duty now. We may feel free to leave."

4

CHARLOTTE AND PITT ARRIVED early at the village of Brackley for the funeral of Arthur Desmond. They alighted from the train into brilliant sunshine; the small station had only a single platform stretching a hundred yards or so with the building in the center containing the waiting room, ticket office and stationmaster's house. The rest bordered on fields already deep in corn, and the heavy trees beyond were towering vivid green with new leaf. Wild roses in bud were hanging sprays out of the hedgerows and the may blossom, with its sweet perfume, was starting to open.

Pitt had not been back to Brackley for fifteen years, and now suddenly it enveloped him in familiarity as if he had left only last night. Everything was exactly the same, the angle of the station roof against the sky, the curve of the lines as the track swerved away towards Tolworth, the huge coal bunkers for refueling. He even found he stepped automatically to avoid the bad patch of platform where it had become worn immediately before the doorway. Only it all looked just a little smaller than he had recalled, and perhaps a little shabbier.

The stationmaster's hair had turned gray. Last time he had seen him it had been brown. And he wore a black band of mourning on his arm.

He was about to speak some automatic word of greeting, then he stopped and looked again. "Young Thomas? It is young Thomas, isn't it? 'Course it is! I told old Abe as you'd come. A sad day for Brackley, an' no mistake."

"Good morning, Mr. Wilkie," Pitt replied. He added the "Mr." intentionally. He was a superintendent of police in London, but this was his home; here he was the gamekeeper's son from the Hall. The stationmaster was his equal. "Yes, very sad." He wanted to add something else about why he had not been back in so long, but excuses were empty, and today no one would care. Their hearts were full; they had no room left for anything but the sense of loss which united them. He introduced Charlotte and Wilkie's face lit up. Clearly it was a courtesy he had not fully expected, but one that pleased him greatly.

They were no farther than the door onto the road when another three people came in from the platform. Apparently they had been farther along in the train. They were all gentlemen of middle or later years and, to judge from their dress, of substantial means. With a cold jolt of memory Pitt recognized at least one of them from the inquest, and felt a rush of hatred so powerful he stood motionless on the step in the sunlight and Charlotte went on without him. Had it not been so ridiculous, he would have liked to have gone back and accused the man. There was nothing remotely useful he could say, simply relieve himself of some of the anger and pain he felt, and the outrage that the man could say such things publicly, regardless of what he may have suspected in private. It was a kind of betrayal of whatever friendship he and Arthur Desmond had shared.

Perhaps it was the sheer indignity of it which stopped him, and the knowledge that it would embarrass Charlotte—although she would understand—and even more, Wilkie, the stationmaster. But it was also his own sense of guilt. Had he been back here more often he would have been in a position to deny the slanders from knowledge, not merely memory and love.

"Thomas?"

Charlotte's voice cut across his thoughts and he turned

and followed her out onto the bright road, and they set out the half mile or so to the village street, and the church beyond.

"Who were they?" she asked.

"They came to the inquest." He did not add in what capacity and she did not ask. Almost certainly his tone of voice had told her.

It was a short walk and they did not speak again. There was no sound but that of their feet on the roadway and the faint whisper of breeze now and then in the hedges and trees, and birds calling. Far away a sheep bleated and a lamb replied, sharper, higher pitched, and a dog barked.

The village too was unusually silent. The grocer, the ironmonger and the baker were all closed for business, blinds drawn, and wreaths or black ribbons on the doors. Even the smithy's forge was cold and tidy, and deserted. A small child, perhaps four or five years old, stood in the doorway of one of the houses, its face solemn, wide-eyed. No one was playing outside. Even the ducks on the pond drifted idly.

Pitt glanced at Charlotte and saw the awe in her face, and the soft sadness, for a community in mourning, and for a man she had never known.

At the farther end of the main street there were half a dozen villagers dressed in black, and as Charlotte and Pitt approached them they turned. At first all they saw was Charlotte's black gown and Pitt's black armband and black tie, and they felt an immediate fellowship; then after a second look one of them spoke.

"Young Tom, is that you?"

"Zack, you didn't ought to speak like that!" his wife whispered quickly. "He's a gentleman now, look at him! I'm sorry, young Thomas, sir. He didn't mean no disrespect."

Pitt scrambled through memory to place the man whose dark hair was streaked with gray and whose face was burned by weather and lined with screwing it up against the wind.

"That's all right, Mrs. Burns. 'Young Tom' is fine. How are you?"

"Oh, I be fine, sir, an' Mary and Lizzie too. Married and got children, they 'ave. O' course you knew as our Dick joined the army?"

"Yes, I heard." The lie was on Pitt's tongue before he had time to think. He did not wish her to know how completely he had lost touch. "It's a fine career," he added. He dared not say any more. Dick might have been maimed or even killed.

"Glad ye've come back for Sir Arthur," Zack said with a long sniff. "I s'ppose it's time we went. Bell's started."

And indeed the sound of the tolling of the church bell was carrying over the fields in a sonorous, mournful knell that must have reached the next village in the still air.

Farther back along the street a door closed and a figure in black emerged and started towards them. The smith came out of his house, a huge-chested, bowlegged man. He wore a rough jacket which barely fastened, but his black armband was new and neat and very plain to see.

Pitt offered Charlotte his arm, and they began to walk slowly away from the village along the road towards the church, which was still some quarter of a mile away. They were joined by more and more people: villagers, tenants and laborers from the local farms, the grocer and his wife, the baker and his two sisters, the ironmonger and his son and daughter-in-law, the cooper, the wheelwright, even the innkeeper had closed for the day and turned out in solemn black with his wife and daughters beside him.

From the other direction came the hearse drawn by four black horses with black plumes over head and shoulders, and a driver with black cloak and top hat. Behind it Matthew walked bareheaded, his hat in his hand, his face pale, Harriet Soames by his side. After them were at least eighty or ninety people, all the servants from the Hall both indoor

122

and outdoor, all the tenant farmers from the estate with their families, and after them the neighboring landowners from half a dozen miles around.

They filed into the church and those who could not find a seat stood at the back, heads bowed.

Matthew had saved a place in the family pew for Pitt and Charlotte, as if Pitt were a second son. Pitt found himself overcome with emotion, gratitude, guilt, a warmth of belonging that brought tears to his eyes and prevented him from speaking. He dared not look down in case they spilled over. And then as the bell ceased and the minister stepped forward it became purely grief and a profound sense of having lost something irretrievable.

The service itself was simple, all the old, familiar words which were both soothing and deeply moving as the mind repeated them over in silent poetry, the terms of brevity of life like a flower in its season. The season was over, and it was gathered into eternity.

What was special about this particular funeral was the number of people who were met, not because it was required of them, but because they wished to be there. The gentry, the men from London, Pitt ignored; it was the villagers and tenant farmers who held the meaning for him.

When it was over they went to the burial in the Desmond family vault, at the far side of the churchyard under the yew trees. It was silent in the shade, even though there were above a hundred people still there. Not one of them moved or spoke as the coffin was placed inside and the door closed again. One could hear the birds singing in the elms on the far side, in the sun.

Next came the long ritual of thanking people, the expressions of sorrow and condolences.

Pitt glanced at Matthew where he stood on the path back towards the lych-gate on the road. He looked very pale, the sun catching the fair streak across his hair. Harriet Soames was beside him, very close, her hand on his arm. She looked somber, as befitted the occasion, but there was also

123

a gentleness in her when she looked up at Matthew, as if she had more than an ordinary understanding of his anger as well as his grief.

"Are you going to stand with him?" Charlotte whispered.

He had been undecided, but in that moment he knew. "No. Sir Arthur was a father to me, but I was not his son. This is Matthew's time. For me to go there would be intrusive and presumptuous."

Charlotte said nothing. He was afraid she knew that he also felt he had forfeited his right to do that by his long absence. It was not Matthew's resentment he feared but that of the villagers. And they would be right to resent him now. He had been gone too long.

He waited a little while, watching Matthew's face as he spoke to them with great familiarity, accepting halting and deeply felt words. Harriet stood beside him smiling and nodding.

One or two neighbors paid their respects, and Pitt recognized Danforth, who had given evidence so reluctantly. There was a strange play of emotions over Matthew's face: resentment, caution, embarrassment, pain, and resentment again. It was not possible from where Pitt stood to hear what each of them said before Danforth shook his head and walked away towards the lych-gate.

Others followed, and then the men from London. They looked oddly out of place. The difference was subtle, an unease in the wide spaces with the view of fields beyond the churchyard and giant trees in the sun, the sense of the seasons and the heavy physical labor of turning the earth, plowing and reaping, the comfortable familiarity with animals. It was nothing so obvious as a difference in clothes, but perhaps a more closely barbered head, thinner soles to the boots, a glance as if the road winding away towards the trees and boundaries of the Hall were an enemy and not a friend, a distance one was not happy to walk when one was more accustomed to carriages.

Matthew spoke to them with an effort. It would not have

been apparent to any one of them, only to Pitt, who had known him from childhood and could see the boy in the man.

When the last of them had said what was expected, and Matthew had managed to reply, Pitt went over to him. The carriages had been dismissed. Together they walked the bright road back up towards the Hall, Matthew and Pitt in front, Charlotte and Harriet behind.

For the first hundred yards or so it was in agreeable silence, during which Charlotte gained the impression that Harriet would like to say something but could not find the words to broach the subject.

"I think it is the greatest tribute that all the village should come," Charlotte said as they passed the crossroads and turned into the narrower lane. She had never been here before, and had no idea how far it would be, but she could see huge stone gateposts about a quarter of a mile away, obviously the entrance to an estate of size. Presumably there would be a surrounding parkland, and also a drive of some length.

"He was deeply loved," Harriet replied. "He was the most charming man, and quite sincere. Anyone less hypocritical I could not imagine." She stopped, and Charlotte had the distinct impression she would have added "but," except that sensitivity prevented her.

"I never knew him," Charlotte answered. "But my husband loved him dearly. Of course it is some time since he saw him, and people do change in some ways. . . ."

"Oh, he was still as honest and generous as ever," Harriet said quickly.

Charlotte looked at her, and she colored and turned away. They were almost at the gates.

"But absentminded?" Charlotte said it for her.

Harriet bit her lip. "Yes, I think so. Matthew won't have it, and I can understand that. I do sympathize, really . . . my mother died when I was quite young, and so I have grown very close to my father also. Neither Matthew nor I have siblings. That is one of the things that draw us together, an understanding of the loneliness, and the special closeness to a parent. I could not bear anyone to speak ill of my father. . . ."

They turned in at the gates and Charlotte saw with a gasp of pleasure the long curve of the drive between an avenue of elm trees, and another quarter of a mile away the great house standing on a slight rise. Long lawns fell away to the banks of a stream to the right, and to the left more trees, and the roofs of the coach houses and stables beyond. There was a grace in the proportions which was immensely pleasing to the eye. It sat naturally on the land, rising out of it amid the trees, nothing alien or awkward, nothing jarring the simplicity of it.

Harriet took no notice. Presumably she had been here before, and although she was soon to be mistress of it, at this moment such thoughts were far from her mind.

"I would protect him as fiercely as if he were my child, and I his parent," she said with a rueful smile. "That's absurd, I know, but emotions don't always have reasons we can see. I do understand how Matthew feels."

They walked several paces in silence. The great elms had closed over their heads and they were in a dappled shadow. "I am afraid that Matthew will be hurt in this crusade to prove that Sir Arthur was murdered. Of course he does not want to believe that his father could have been so . . . so disturbed in his mind as to have had the thoughts he did about secret societies persecuting him, and to have taken an overdose by accident."

She stopped and faced Charlotte. "If he pursues this, he may very well have the truth forced upon him, and have to face it in the end, and it will be even harder than it is now. Added to which, he will make enemies. People will have some sympathy at first, but it will not last, not if he starts to make accusations as he is doing. Could you persuade your husband to speak to him? Prevail upon him to stop searching for something which really is . . . I mean, will

126

only hurt him more, and make him enemies no one can afford? Patience will turn into laughter, and then anger. That is the last thing Sir Arthur would have wanted."

Charlotte did not know immediately what to say. She should not have been surprised that Harriet did not know anything of the Inner Circle or imagine that such a society could exist. Had she not known of it herself, the suggestion would have seemed absurd to her too, the delusion of someone whose fancy had become warped, and who imagined conspiracies where there were none.

What was harder to accept, and hurt the emotions as well as the reason, was that Harriet thought Sir Arthur had become senile, and had indeed been responsible for his own death. Of course it was good that her concern was born of her love for Matthew, but that would be of only marginal comfort to him if he realized what was in her mind. At the moment his grief for his father was much too raw to accept it.

"Don't speak of this to Matthew," she said urgently, taking Harriet's arm and beginning to walk forwards again in case their hesitation should be questioned. "I am afraid at this point he may feel your disbelief as another wound, if you like, another betrayal."

Harriet looked startled, then slowly realization came into her face.

They were still moving very slowly and Pitt and Matthew were drawing ahead of them, not noticing their absence.

Harriet increased her pace to keep their distance from those coming after them. She did not wish to be overheard, still less for Matthew to turn around and come back to them, fearing something amiss.

"Yes. Yes, perhaps you are right. It is not really sensible, but I think I might take a great deal of time to come to accept that my father was no longer the man I had known, no longer so . . . so fine, so strong, so . . . wise," she went on. "Perhaps we all tend to idealize those we love, and when

127

we are forced to see them in truth, we hate those who have shown us. I could not bear Matthew to feel like that about me. And perhaps I am asking equally as much of your husband, if I am to request him to tell Matthew what he so much does not wish to hear."

"There is no point in asking Thomas," Charlotte said honestly, keeping pace beside her. "He thinks just as Matthew does."

"That Sir Arthur was murdered?" Harriet was amazed. "Really? But he is a policeman! How could he seriously believe . . . are you sure?"

"Yes. You see, there are such societies. . . ."

"Oh, I know there are criminals. Everyone who is not totally sheltered from reality knows that," Harriet protested.

Charlotte remembered with a jolt that when she had been Harriet's age, before she met Pitt, she had been just as innocent about the world. Not only the criminal aspect of it was unknown to her, but perhaps more seriously, she had not had the least idea of what poverty meant, or ignorance, endemic disease, or the undernourishment which produced rickets, tuberculosis, scurvy and such things. She had imagined that crime was the province of those who were violent, deceitful and innately wicked. The world had been very black and white. She should not expect of Harriet Soames an understanding of the shades of gray which only experience could teach, or a knowledge outside the scope of her life and its confines. It was unfair.

"But you didn't hear what Sir Arthur was saying," Harriet went on. "Who it was he was accusing!"

"If it is quite untrue," Charlotte said carefully, choosing her words, "then Thomas will tell Matthew, however it hurts. But he will want to look into it himself first. And that way, I think Matthew will accept it, because there will be no alternative. Also, he will know that Thomas wants Sir Arthur to have been right, and sane, just as much as he does himself. I think it would be best if we said nothing, don't you?"

"Yes. Yes, you are right," Harriet said with relief. They were fast approaching the last section of the driveway to the house. The elms had fallen away behind them and they were in the open sunlight. There were several carriages standing on the gravel before the front doors, and the gentlemen ahead were going into the Hall for the funeral meats. It was time they joined them.

It was when he was almost ready to leave that Pitt was given the opportunity to speak to Danforth and ask him further about the episode of the dogs. Sir Arthur had always cared deeply about his animals. If he took the matter of finding homes for his favorite bitch's pups lightly, then he had changed almost beyond recognition. It was not as if he had forgotten the matter entirely; according to Danforth he had sold them to someone else.

He found Danforth in the hallway taking his leave. He still looked uncomfortable, not quite sure if he should be here or not. It must be his testimony at the inquest weighing on his mind. He had been a close neighbor and agreeable friend for years. There had never been bad blood between the estates, although Danforth's was much smaller.

"Good afternoon, Mr. Danforth." Pitt approached him as if by chance. "Good to see you looking so well, sir."

"Er—good afternoon," Danforth replied, squinting a little in an effort to place Pitt. He must have looked as if he came from London, and yet there was an air about him as if he belonged, and a vague familiarity.

"Thomas Pitt," Pitt assisted him.

"Pitt? Pitt—oh yes. Gamekeeper's son, I recall." A shadow crossed his face, and quite suddenly the past flooded back and Pitt could recall the disgrace, the fear, the shame of his father's being accused of poaching, as if it were yesterday. It had not been Danforth's estate, but that was irrelevant now. The man who had pressed the charge and seen him sent to prison, where he had died, had been one of Danforth's social class and background, one who owned land as he did; and poachers were a common enemy.

Pitt felt his face burn and all the old humiliation come back, the resentment and the feeling of being inferior, foolish, of not knowing the rules. It was absurd. He was a policeman now, a very senior policeman. He had arrested better men than Danforth, wiser, richer, and more powerful men, men of better blood and lineage.

"Superintendent Pitt, of Bow Street," Pitt said coldly, but the words fumbled on his tongue.

Danforth looked surprised.

"Good God! Not a police matter, for heaven's sake. Poor man died of . . ." He let out his breath with a sigh. "They don't send superintendents for—suicide. And you'll never prove it. Certainly not through me!" Now his face was equally cold, and there was a bitter affront in his eyes.

"I came to pay my respects to a man I loved deeply," Pitt said with a clenched jaw. "And to whom I owe almost all I have. My occupation has no more to do with my presence here than does yours."

"Then dammit, sir, why did you say you were from the police?" Danforth demanded. He had been made to look a fool, and he resented it.

Pitt had done it to show that he was no longer merely a gamekeeper's son, but he could hardly admit that.

"I was at the inquest." He evaded the subject. "I know what you said about the pups. Sir Arthur always cared very much about his dogs."

"And his horses," Danforth agreed with a frown. "That's how I know the poor fellow was really losing a grip on things. He not only promised me the pick of the litter, he actually came with me to choose. Then, dammit, he went and sold them to Bridges." He shook his head. "I could understand simple forgetfulness. We all forget the odd thing now and again as we get older. But he was convinced I'd said I didn't want them. Swore blind to it. That's what was so unlike the man. Terribly sad. Fearful way to go. But glad you came to pay your respects, Mr. er—Superintendent."

"Good day, sir," Pitt acknowledged him, and then without giving it conscious thought, turned and went back through the baize door into the kitchens. He knew precisely where he was going. The paneled walls were so familiar he could recognize every variation in the wood, every place worn smoother and darker by countless touches of the hand, or brushes of fabric from the shoulders of footmen and butlers, and skirts of maids, housekeepers and cooks for generations past. He had added to the patina of it himself when his mother had worked here. In the history of the Hall, that must seem like only yesterday. He and Matthew had crept down here to beg biscuits and milk from the cook, and odd titbits of pastry. Matthew had teased the maids, and put a frog in the housekeeper's sitting room. Mrs. Thayer had hated frogs. Matthew and Pitt had laughed themselves nearly sick when they heard her scream. Tapioca pudding for a week had been a small price to pay for the savoring of such a delight.

The smell of furniture polish and heavy curtains and un carpeted floors was indefinable, and yet so sharp he would hardly have been surprised to face the mirror and see himself reflected a twelve-year-old boy with lanky limbs, steady gray eyes and a shock of hair.

When he turned into the kitchen, the cook, still in her black bombazine with her apron over it, looked up sharply. She was new since Pitt's time, and to her he was a stranger. She was flustered as it was, with the loss of her master, being allowed to attend the service herself, while still being in charge of the funeral meats.

"You lost, sir? The reception rooms are back that way."

She pointed to the door through which he had come. " 'Ere, Lizzie, you show the gentleman—"

"Thank you, Cook, but I am looking for the gamekeeper. Is Mr. Sturges about? I need to speak to him about Sir Arthur's dogs."

"Well I don't know about that, sir. It isn't 'ardly the day for it. . . ."

"I'm Thomas Pitt. I used to live here."

"Oh! Young Tom. I mean . . ." She colored quickly. "I didn't mean no . . ."

"That's all right." He brushed it aside. "I'd still like to speak to Mr. Sturges. It's a matter Sir Matthew wished me to look into, and I need Sturges's help."

"Oh. Well 'e was 'ere about 'alf an 'our ago, an' 'e went out to the stables. Land needs to be cared for, funeral or no funeral. You might find 'im out there."

"Thank you." He walked past her, barely glancing at the rows of copper pans and kettles, or the great black cast-iron range still emanating heat, even with all its oven doors closed and its lids down. The dressers were filled with china, the larder door closed, the wooden bins for flour, sugar, oatmeal and lentils were tight. All the vegetables would be in racks outside in the scullery, and the meat, poultry and game would be hung in the cold house. The laundry and still room were along the corridor to the right.

He went out of the back door, down the steps and turned left without conscious thought. He would have known his way even in the dark.

He found Sturges just outside the door to the apple room, the ventilated place with shelf after shelf of wooden slats where all the apples were placed in the autumn, and as long as they did not touch each other, usually kept all through the winter and well into the late spring.

" 'Allo, young Tom," he said without surprise. "Glad as you made it for the funeral." He looked Pitt directly in the eye.

It was a difficult relationship and it had taken many years to reach this stage. Sturges had replaced Pitt's father, and to begin with Pitt had been unable to forgive him for that. He and his mother had had to leave the gamekeeper's cottage and all their furnishings which had gone with it, the things they had grown accustomed to: the kitchen table and dresser, the hearth, the comfortable chair, the tin bath. Pitt had had his own room with a small dormer window next to the apple tree. They had moved up into the servants' quarters in the Hall, but it was nothing like the same. What was a room, when you had had a house, with your own doorway and your own kitchen fire?

Of course he knew with his head how lucky they were that Sir Arthur either had believed Pitt's father innocent or had not cared, and had given his wife and child shelter and made them welcome. Many a man would not have, and there were those in the county who thought him a fool for it, and said so. But that did not stop Pitt from hating Sturges and his wife for moving into the gamekeeper's cottage and being warm and comfortable there.

And Sturges had then walked the fields and woods that had been Pitt's father's work and his pleasure. He had changed a few things, and that also was a fault not easily forgiven, especially if in one or two instances it was for the worse. Where it was for the better, that was an even greater offense.

But gradually memory had softened at least a little, and Sturges was a quiet, patient man. He knew the habits and the rules of the country. He had not been above poaching on the odd occasion as a youth, and he also knew it was by the grace of God, and a landowner willing to look the other way, that he had never been caught himself. He made no judgment as to whether Pitt's father had been guilty or innocent, except to remark that if he were guilty, he was more of a fool than most men.

And he loved animals. At first tentatively, then as a matter of course, he had allowed young Thomas to help him. They had begun in suspicious silence, then as cooperation necessitated speed they had broken the ice between them. It had melted completely one early morning, about half past six when the light was spreading across the fields still heavy with dew. It had been spring and the wildflowers were thick in the hedges and under the trees, the new leaves opening on the chestnuts, and the later beeches and elms thick with bud. They had found a wounded owl, and Sturges had taken it home. Together they had cared for it

133

until it mended and flew away. Several times all summer they had seen its silent form, broad winged and graceful, swooping in flight around the barn, diving on mice, crossing the lantern's ray like a ghost, and then gone again. From that year on there had been an understanding between them, but never any blunting of criticism.

"Of course I came," Pitt answered him, breathing in deeply. The apple room smelled sweet and dry, a little musty, full of memories. "I know I should have come earlier. I'll say it before you do."

"Aye, well, so long as you know," Sturges said without taking his eyes off Pitt's face. "Look well, you do. And very fancy in your city clothes. Superintendent now, eh? Arresting folk, no doubt."

"Murder and treason," Pitt replied. "You'd want them arrested, wouldn't you?"

"Oh aye. No time for murdering people, at least not most people. Done well for yourself then?"

"Yes."

Sturges pursed his lips.

"Got a wife? Or too busy bettering yourself to go a-courting?"

"Yes, I have a wife and two children: a son and a daughter." He could not keep the lift of pride out of his voice.

"Have you indeed?" Sturges looked him straight in the eye. He tried to keep his dour manner, but the pleasure shone out of him in spite of it. "Where are they then? Up London way?"

"No, Charlotte is here with me. I'll bring her to meet you."

"You do that, if you want." Sturges was damned if he was going to appear as if he cared. He turned away and began absentmindedly tidying some of the old straw.

"Before I do, can you tell me what happened about the dogs and Mr. Danforth?" Pitt asked.

"No I can't, Tom, and that's a fact. Never took to

134

Danforth a lot, myself, but he was always fair, far as I knowed. And bright enough, considering."

"He came over and chose two pups?"

"Aye, he did that." He heaped the straw in a pile. "Then a couple o' weeks later sent a note by one o' his men to say he didn't want 'em anymore. And a couple o' weeks after that, came back to collect 'em and was as put out as all hell that we hadn't still got them. Said a few unkind things about Sir Arthur. I'd have liked to 'ave given 'im a piece of my mind, but Sir Arthur wouldn't 'ave wanted me to."

"Did you see the note, or did Sir Arthur just tell you about it?"

He stared at Pitt, abandoning the straw.

" 'Course I saw the note! Were writ to me, me being the one as cares for the dogs, and Sir Arthur himself up in London at the time anyway."

"Very strange," Pitt agreed, thoughts racing in his head. "You are quite right. Someone is playing very odd games, and not in any good spirit, I think."

"Games? You mean it weren't Mr. Danforth going a bit gaga?"

"Not necessarily, although it does look like it. Do you still have the note?"

"Whatever for? Why should I keep a thing like that? No use to anyone."

"Just to prove it was Mr. Danforth who was in the wrong, not Sir Arthur," Pitt replied.

"And who needs proof o' that?" Sturges pulled a face. "Nobody else as knows Sir Arthur thought it was 'im!"

Pitt felt a sudden lift of happiness, and found himself smiling in spite of the occasion. Sturges was a loyal man, but he moderated the truth for no one.

"Sturges, do you know anything about the accident Sir Arthur had when the runaway horse came down the street and the rider caught him with his whip?"

"Some." Sturges looked unhappy, his face drawn into

lines of doubt. He leaned against the apple racks. "Why are you asking, Tom? Who told you about it anyway? Mr. Matthew?" He had not as yet adjusted to the idea that Matthew was now the master, and heir of the title.

Somewhere outside a horse whinnied, and Pitt heard the familiar sound of hooves on the cobbled stableyard.

"Yes. He seemed to think it was not an accident." He did not want to put words into Sturges's mouth by saying it had been devised as a threat.

"Not an accident?" Sturges looked puzzled but not dismissive of the idea. "Well, in a manner o' speaking, o' course, it wasn't. Fool came down the road like Jehu. Man like that should never 'ave bin on a horse in the first place. I look on an accident as something as couldn't be helped, 'cept by the Almighty. Two ha'pence worth o' sense 'd helped this. Came galloping down the street like a clergyman, by all accounts, whip flyin' all over the place. It was a mercy no one else was hurt but Sir Arthur, and the animal he was ridin' at the time. Caught the poor beast a fair lashin' 'round the head and shoulders. Took us weeks to get 'im right again. Still scared o' the whip, it is. Probably always will be."

"Who was the rider?"

"God knows," Sturges said with disgust. "Some idiot from the far side of the country, seems like. No one 'round here knew him."

"Did anybody know who he was? Do you know now?" Pitt pressed.

The sunlight was warm through the apple room door. A yellow-haired retriever poked its head in and wagged its tail hopefully.

" 'Course I don't know," Sturges answered angrily. "If I knew who he was I'd have had him on a charge." It was a brave statement, more wish than actuality, but Pitt was quite sure he would have tried.

"Who else saw it happen?" Pitt asked him.

The dog came in and Sturges patted it automatically.

"Nobody, far as I know. Wheelwright saw the man go past. So did the smith, but didn't see him hit Sir Arthur. Why? What are you saying? That it was Sir Arthur's fault? He got in the way?"

"No." Pitt did not resent his anger, or the defensiveness in his face. "No, I'm saying it may not have been an accident in any sense. The man may have spurred his horse to a gallop intentionally, meaning to catch Sir Arthur with the whip. . . ."

Sturges's face was full of amazement and disbelief.

"Why would anybody want to do that? It don't make sense. Sir Arthur had no enemies."

Pitt was not sure how far he should go in telling Sturges the truth. Perhaps the Inner Circle would be straining his belief a little far.

"Who would it be then?"

"Sir Arthur had no enemies. Not around here." Sturges was watching him closely.

"Is that what he thought?"

Sturges stared at Pitt. "What have you heard, Tom? What are you trying to say?"

"That Sir Arthur was a danger to a certain group he had joined, and about whom he had discovered some very unpleasant truths, and was bent on exposing them. They caused this accident as a warning to him to keep his covenants of silence," Pitt answered him.

"Oh aye, this Circle he spoke about." Sturges blinked. "Pretty dangerous to go that far though. Could have killed him!"

"You know about the Circle?" Pitt said with surprise.

"Oh yes, he talked about it. Evil men, from what he said, but from up London." He hesitated, searching Pitt's face. "You mean what I think you mean, Tom?"

"Well, was he wandering in his mind, imagining things?"

"No he was not! Upset, maybe, pretty angry about some of the things he said was going to happen abroad, but as sane as you or me." There was no pretense in his voice, no effort to convince himself of something that in his heart he had doubted. It was the quality of his tone as much as any words that drove away Pitt's last reservations. He was filled with a sudden and intense gratitude, almost a kind of happiness. He found himself smiling at Sturges.

"Then, yes," he replied firmly, "I mean what you think I do. It was a warning, which he was too angry and too honest to heed, and so they murdered him. I don't know how it was done yet, or if there is any way I can prove it, but I shan't stop trying until I do."

"I'm glad of that, Tom. I'm right glad of that," Sturges said quietly, leaning a little to scratch the dog's head. "It grieves me sore that those who didn't know him should think what they do of him. I'm not a vicious man. There's too many die as shouldn't as it is, but whoever did that to him, I'd dearly like to see them hanged. The whole of Brackley will be grateful to you if you do that, an' I can speak for all." He did not add that he would even be forgiven for not having come back, but it was in his face. He would have held it crass to put such a delicate thing into words.

"I'll do everything I can," Pitt replied. To have made a promise he did not know if he could keep would be a second betrayal. Sturges was not a child to be given words of comfort instead of the truth.

"Aye. Well, if there's aught I can do, or anyone here, you know where we are. Now you'd best be getting back to the baked meats, or you'll be missed."

"I'll find Charlotte and bring her to meet you."

"Aye. You said you'd do that, so be about it then."

In the morning Pitt was back in his office at Bow Street. He was barely through the door when Inspector Tellman came in, his lantern face dour and resentful as always. He had been forced to respect Pitt, both superficially in his manner, and genuinely because of his ability. However he still felt affronted that Pitt, whom he viewed as socially little better than himself, and professionally no better at all, should have been promoted to the senior position when Micah Drummond resigned. Drummond had been a gentleman, and that made all the difference. He expected gentlemen to be given superior posts; it was no reflection of their ability. For Pitt to have been given it he took personally.

"Good morning, Mr. Pitt," he said sharply. "Missed you yesterday, sir. Quite a few things to report." He made it sound as if he had been waiting there all night.

"Good morning, Tellman. I was at a family funeral in Hampshire. What have you got?"

Tellman pursed his lips, but made no reference to the bereavement. That happened to everyone. It stirred emotions in him, but he was certainly not going to allow Pitt to know about them.

"Those people you had the men check up on," he replied. "Bit difficult when we don't know what we are looking for, or why. They're all very respectable seeming gentlemen. What are they supposed to have done?"

"That is what I need to find out," Pitt replied tersely. He disliked not being able to tell the man as much truth as he knew. His instinct was to trust Tellman, but he dare not take the chance. The Circle could be anywhere.

"Blackmail," Tellman said darkly. "Makes it hard. You can blackmail a man for dozens of different things, but I suppose mostly it's cheating, theft or fornicating with someone he shouldn't." His expression did not change, but his contempt seemed to fill the room. "Although with gentlemen, it's not easy for the likes of us to know who he shouldn't, and who doesn't matter a damn," he added. "Some gentlemen swap wives and mistresses around like lending a good book. It's all right, so long as nobody actually catches you reading it. Doesn't even matter if they know you got it. Everyone knows what the Prince of Wales does, and who cares?"

"You could keep a particular eye for debt," Pitt suggested, ignoring the social comment. He was already well familiar with Tellman's views. "Anyone with a style of living that his income doesn't seem to support."

"Embezzlement?" Tellman said with surprise. "What can you embezzle from the Colonial Office?" His voice became heavily sarcastic. "Sorry, Tailor, old boy, can't pay me bill the usual way this month, but have a couple of telegrams from Africa, that should see you right." Then quite suddenly his face changed and his eyes lit with knowledge. "Geez! That's it, isn't it? There's information gone missing! You're after a traitor! That's why you are not saying anything. . . ."

"I'm still not saying anything," Pitt said, masking his surprise at Tellman's acuity and facing him with a long, level stare. "You must suppose what you will, and keep it to yourself. The assistant commissioner would be very angry if he thought we mentioned such a possibility, and I think the Prime Minister would be even angrier."

"Did you get called to see the Prime Minister?" Tellman was impressed, in spite of himself.

"No. I have never met the Prime Minister, and the only place I have been to in Downing Street is the Colonial Office. You still haven't told me what you have found out."

Tellman looked sour. "Nothing that seems of any relevance. Jeremiah Thorne is as virtuous as is possible. Seems to be devoted to his wife, who is exceedingly plain, and spends a lot of money on some teaching foundation to do with women. It is highly disapproved of, except by the very moderns, but that might be scandalous at the worst. It isn't illegal and she doesn't do it secretly. In fact she is quite brazen about it. No one could blackmail her over it; she'd probably thank them for the notoriety."

Pitt already knew that to be true.

"What else?"

"Mr. Hathaway seems to be a very proper gentleman who lives quietly, alone, taking his pleasures rather seriously. Reads a lot, goes to the theater now and then, takes

140

long walks in the fine weather." Tellman recited it dryly, as if the man were as boring as the details. "He knows a lot of people, but does not seem to have more than a passing acquaintance with them. Dines out once a week at his club. He is a widower with two grown sons, also eminently respectable, one in the Colonial Service and the other in the church." Tellman's mouth curled down at the corners. "His tastes are good, he likes quality, but not excessively expensive. He seems to live well within his salary. No one has an ill word to say about him."

Pitt drew in a deep breath. "And Aylmer? Is he a paragon of virtue as well?"

"Not quite." There was a shadow of humor at the back of Tellman's bleak expression. "Face like a burst boot, but fancies the ladies all the same. Quite a charmer in a harmless sort of way." He shrugged. "At least it is harmless from all I have been able to find out so far. I'm still looking into Mr. Aylmer. Spends quite a lot of money—more than I can see the source of so far."

"More than his Colonial Office salary?" Pitt asked with a quickening interest, and at the same time a pang of regret.

"Looks like it," Tellman replied. "Of course he could have been saving up, or he might even have private means. Don't know yet."

"Any ladies in particular?"

"A Miss Amanda Pennecuick. Very nice-looking young lady indeed, and very well bred."

"Does she return his interest?"

"Apparently not. Although that has not yet deterred him." He looked at Pitt with amusement. "If you are thinking she is pursuing Mr. Aylmer in order to get information out of him, she's very clever at it. From all I could see, she is trying to avoid him, and not succeeding."

"She wouldn't wish actually to succeed, only to appear to try," Pitt pointed out, "if she were doing as you suggest. Find out about Miss Pennecuick. See who else her friends are, her other admirers, her background, any connection she

141

might have with . . ." He stopped. Should he mention Germany?

Tellman waited. He was far too quick to be deceived. He knew the reason for Pitt's hesitation, and the resentment of it was plain in his eyes.

"Africa, Belgium or Germany," Pitt finished. "Or anything else that's unusual, for that matter."

Tellman put his hands in his pockets. It was not intended insolence as much as instinctive lack of respect.

"You missed out Peter Arundell and Robert Leicester," Pitt prompted.

"Nothing interesting," Tellman replied. "Arundell is a clever young man from a good family. Younger son. Oldest got the title, next one bought a commission in the army, third one went into the Colonial Office, that's him, youngest one got the family living somewhere in Wiltshire."

"Family living?" Pitt was momentarily confused.

"Church," Tellman said with satisfaction that he had left Pitt behind. "Well-to-do families often own the living and can give it to whoever they like. Bring in quite a lot, some of those country parishes. Lot of tithes. Where I grew up the priest had three livings, and hired a vicar or a curate for each one. Himself, he lived in Italy on the proceeds. They don't do that anymore, but they used to."

It was on the edge of Pitt's tongue to say he knew that, but he refrained. Tellman would probably not believe him anyway.

"What about Arundell?" he asked. "What sort of a man is he?" It did not matter. He had no access to the information on Zambezia.

"Just what you'd expect," Tellman replied. "Rooms in Belgravia, attends a lot of Society functions, dresses well, dines well, but a good deal of it at other people's expense. He is a bachelor and highly eligible. All the mothers with unmarried daughters are chasing after him, except those with something higher in their sights. He'll no doubt marry well in the next few years." Tellman finished with a slight downturn of his mouth. He despised what he knew of Society and never lost an opportunity to say so.

"And Leicester."

Tellman grunted. "Much the same."

"Then you'd better get on with Amanda Pennecuick," Pitt instructed. "And Tellman . . ."

"Yes sir?" It was still sarcasm underlying his voice, not respect, and his eyes were too direct.

"Be discreet." He met Tellman's look with equal candor and challenge. No further explanation was necessary. They were utterly different in background and values. Pitt was from the country with the innate respect, even love, for the landed gentry who had made and preserved his world, and who had personally given him so much. Tellman was from the city, surrounded by poverty, and hated those born to wealth, most of whom he considered idlers. They had created nothing, and now only consumed without returning. All he and Pitt had in common was a dedication to police work, but that was sufficient for a complete understanding, at least on that level.

"Yes, Mr. Pitt," he said with something close to a smile, and turned on his heel and left.

Just under half an hour later Assistant Commissioner Farnsworth sent for Pitt to come to his office. The note was written in such terms there was no question about obeying, and Pitt went from Bow Street and caught a hansom along the embankment to Scotland Yard to report.

"Ah." Farnsworth looked up from his desk when Pitt was shown in. He waited until Pitt had closed the door before he continued. "This matter at the Colonial Office. What have you found?"

Pitt was reluctant to tell him how very little it was.

"They are all outwardly without fault," he replied. "Except possibly Garston Aylmer." He saw Farnsworth's face quicken with interest, but took no notice. "He has something of a weakness in his regard for a Miss Amanda

143

Pennecuick, which is apparently not returned. He is a remarkably plain man, and she is unusually handsome."

"Not an uncommon occurrence," Farnsworth said with obvious disappointment. "That's hardly suspicious, Pitt, simply one of life's many disappointments. Being plain, or even downright ugly, has never stopped anyone from falling in love with the beautiful. Very painful sometimes, but a tragedy, not a crime."

"A great deal of crime springs from tragedy," Pitt answered him. "People react differently to pain, especially the pain of wanting something out of reach."

Farnsworth looked at him with a mixture of impatience and contempt. "You can steal anything from a meat pie to a diamond necklace, Pitt, but you cannot steal a woman's affection. And we are not talking about a man who would descend to thieving."

"Of course you cannot steal it." Pitt was equally derisive. "But it is sometimes possible to buy it, or to buy a very good semblance of it. He wouldn't be the first plain man to do that."

Farnsworth disliked agreeing with him, but he was forced to do so. He had too much knowledge of life to argue the issue.

"Selling information to the Germans for money to get her gifts, or whatever she wants?" he said reluctantly. "All right. Look into it. But for God's sake be discreet, Pitt. He's probably a perfectly decent man simply in love with the wrong woman."

"I was thinking also of the possibility that Miss Pennecuick may have an interest in Germany, and rather than Aylmer selling information for money, she might be drawing it from him as the price of her favor. Unlikely, but we have nothing better yet."

Farnsworth chewed on his lower lip. "Find out all you can about her," he ordered. "Who she is, where she comes from, who else she associates with."

"I have Tellman on it."

"Never mind Tellman, get on it yourself." Farnsworth frowned. "Where were you yesterday, Pitt? No one saw you all day."

"I went to Hampshire to a family funeral."

"I thought your parents died a long time ago?" There was challenge in Farnsworth's voice as well as question.

"They did; this was a man who treated me like a son." Farnsworth's eyes were very hard, clear blue.

"Indeed?" He did not ask who that man was, and Pitt could not read his face.

"I believe you went to the inquest on Sir Arthur Desmond," he went on. "Is that true?"

"Yes."

"Why?" Farnsworth's eyebrows rose. "There's no case there. Tragedy that a man of his standing should end that way, but illness and age are no respecters of persons. Leave it alone now, Pitt, or you'll only make it worse."

Pitt stared at him.

Farnsworth misunderstood his surprise and anger for incomprehension.

"The least that is said about it, the least will have to be known." He was irritated by Pitt's slow-wittedness. "Don't let the whole sorry matter drag out before his friends and associates, never mind the general public. Let it all be forgotten, then we can remember him as the man he used to be, before all this obsession began."

"Obsession?" Pitt said thinly. He knew he would achieve nothing by pursuing it with Farnsworth, and yet he could not help himself.

"With Africa," Farnsworth said impatiently. "Saying there were conspiracies and secret plots and so on. He thought he was being persecuted. It's quite a well-known delusion, but very distressing, very sad. For heaven's sake, Pitt, if you had any regard for him at all, don't make it public. For his family's sake, if nothing else, let it be buried with him."

Pitt met his eyes squarely and did not look away.

145

"Sir Matthew does not believe his father was mad, or so forgetful or careless as to have taken laudanum in the middle of the afternoon, and in such a quantity as to kill himself."

"Not unnatural," Farnsworth dismissed it with a slight movement of his well-manicured hand. "It is always hard to accept that those we love are mentally deranged. Wouldn't have cared to think it of my father. I have every sympathy with him, but it has nothing to do with the facts."

"He may be right," Pitt said stubbornly.

Farnsworth's lips thinned. "He's not right, Pitt. I know more about it than you do."

It was on the edge of Pitt's tongue to argue with him, then he realized that over the last ten years his knowledge of Sir Arthur was sporadic at best, although Farnsworth could not know that. Still, it left him in a fragile position to argue.

His thoughts would not have shown in his face, but something of his emotions must have. Farnsworth was watching him with growing certainty, and something like a bitter amusement.

"Just what is your personal knowledge of Sir Arthur, Pitt?"

"Very little . . . lately."

"Then believe me, I have seen him frequently and he was unquestionably suffering from delusions. He saw conspiracies and persecutions all over the place, even among men who had been his friends for years. He is a man for whom I had a high regard, but feelings, however deep or honorable, do not change the truth. For friendship's sake, Pitt, let him rest in peace, and his memory be as little damaged as possible. In kindness you must do that."

Still Pitt wanted to argue. Sturges's weather-beaten face came sharply to his mind. Or was his judgment just loyalty, an inability to believe that his master could have lost touch with reality?

"Right," Farnsworth said briskly. "Now get on with the

job in hand. Find out who is passing information from the Colonial Office. Give it your entire attention, Pitt, until it is finished. Do you understand me?"

"Yes, of course I understand," Pitt said, while still in his head determining not to leave the death of Arthur Desmond as it was, a quietly closed matter.

5

"WHAT IT AFFECTS MOSTLY is treaties," Matthew said with a frown, regarding Pitt over his desk at the Foreign Office. He looked a little less harrowed than at the funeral in Brackley, but the shadow was still there at the back of his eyes and in the pallor of his skin. There was a tension in his body which Pitt knew too well to ignore or misread. The past was still intimate, for all that had happened since, and the experiences which separated them.

If anyone had asked him for dates, he could not have given them, nor even the events that one might have considered important. But the memories of emotion were as powerful as if they had happened yesterday: surprise, understanding, the desire to protect, the confusion and the learning of pain. He could recall vividly the death of a beloved animal, the first magic and surprise of love, the first disillusionment, the fear of change in people and places that framed one's life. These things he and Matthew had faced together, in some things at least, he a year the sooner, so when Matthew's turn came, he had already experienced them, and shared his emotions with an acuteness no one else could.

He knew now that Matthew was still just as deeply hurt over his father's death; only his outward command of himself was better, as the sense of shock wore away. They were sitting in his wide office with its polished oak furniture,

148

pale green carpet, and deep windows overlooking St. James's Park.

"You mentioned the treaty with the Germans," he answered. "What I really need is to know what the information is, as far as you can tell me. That is the only way I am going to have a chance to trace where it came from, and through whose hands it passed."

Matthew's frown deepened. "It isn't quite as cut and dried as that. But I'll do what I can."

Pitt waited. Outside somewhere in the street a horse whinnied and a man shouted. The sun made bright patterns through the window and onto the floor.

"One of the things that stands out most is the agreement made with King Lobengula, late in the year before last," Matthew began thoughtfully. " 'Eighty-eight. In September Rhodes's delegation, led by a man called Charles Rudd, rode into the king's camp in Bulowayo—that's in Zambezia. They are the Ndebele tribe." His fingers drummed on the desk softly as he spoke. "Rudd was an expert in mining claims, and apparently quite ignorant about African rulers and their customs. For that purpose he had along a fellow called Thompson, who spoke some language understood by the king. The third member of the party was called Rochfort Maguire, a legal man from All Souls' College in Oxford."

Pitt listened patiently. So far this was of no help to him at all. He tried to imagine the heat of the African plains, the courage of these men and the greed that drew them.

"Of course there were other people seeking mineral concessions as well," Matthew went on. "We very nearly lost them."

"We?" Pitt interrupted.

Matthew grimaced. "As far as one can call Cecil Rhodes 'we.' He was—is— acting with the blessing of Her Majesty's government. We had a standing agreement, the Moffatt Treaty, made with Lobengula in February of the same year,

149

that he would not give away any of his territories, I quote, 'without the previous knowledge and sanction' of the British government."

"You say we nearly lost them," Pitt brought the conversation back to the point. "Because of information going to the Germans?"

Matthew's eyes widened very slightly. "That's curious. The German Embassy certainly, but it began to look as if the Belgians might have known about it too. All of Central and East Africa is swarming with adventurers, hunters, mining prospectors and people hoping to be middlemen in all sorts of ventures." He leaned a little further forward across the desk. "Rudd was successful because of the advent of Sir Sidney Shippard, deputy commissioner for Bechuanaland. He is a great supporter of Cecil Rhodes, and believes in what he is trying to do. So does Sir Hercules Robinson at the Cape."

"What do you know that without question has passed from the Colonial Office to the German Embassy?" Pitt pressed. "For the time being, exclude suspicions. Tell me the information, and I'll find out how it came in, by word of mouth, letter, telegram, who received it and where it went after that."

Matthew reached out his hand and touched a pile of papers beside him.

"I have several things here for you. But there are other things also, which have very little to do with the Foreign Office, matters of money. A great deal of this rests on money." He looked at Pitt to see if he understood.

"Money?" Pitt did not know what he meant. "Surely money would be useless in buying land from native kings? And the government would equip explorers and scouts going to claim land for Britain?"

"No! That's the point," Matthew said urgently. "Cecil Rhodes is equipping his own force. They are well on their way even now. He put up the finance himself."

150

"One man?" Pitt was incredulous. He could not conceive of such wealth.

Matthew smiled. "You don't understand Africa, Thomas. No, actually he's not putting up all of it, but a great deal. There are banks involved, some in Scotland, and particularly Francis Standish. Now perhaps you begin to see the sort of treasures we are speaking of: more diamonds than anywhere else in the world, more gold, and a continent of land owned by people who live in the dark ages as far as weapons are concerned."

Pitt stared at him, ideas uncertain in his mind, cloudy images, remembered words of Sir Arthur's about exploitation, and the Inner Circle.

"When men like Livingstone went in, it was completely different," Matthew continued, his face bleak. "They wanted to take medicine and Christianity, get rid of ignorance, disease and slavery. They may have gained a certain immortality out of it, but they didn't look for anything for themselves. Even Stanley wanted glory more than any kind of material reward.

"But Cecil Rhodes wants land, money, power, and more power. We need men like him for this stage in the development of Africa."

His face shadowed over even more. "At least I think we do. Father and I argued about it. He thought the government should have taken a larger part in it and sent over our own men, openly, and to the devil with what the Kaiser or King Leopold thought. But of course Lord Salisbury never really wanted anything to do with it right from the beginning. He would have left Africa alone, if he could, but circumstances and history would not allow."

"You mean Britain is doing it through Cecil Rhodes?" Pitt still could not believe what Matthew seemed to be saying.

"More or less," Matthew agreed. "Of course there is quite a lot of other money as well, from London and Edinburgh. It is that information which has reached the German Embassy, at least some of it."

They heard footsteps in the corridor outside, but whoever it was did not stop.

"I see."

"Only part of it, Thomas. There are a lot of other factors as well: alliances, quarrels, old wars and new ones. There are the Boers to consider. Paul Kruger is not a man ever to overlook with impunity. There is all the heritage of the Zulu Wars. There is Emin Pasha in Equatoria, and the Belgians in the Congo, the Sultan of Zanzibar in the east, and most of all there is Carl Peters and the German East Africa Company." He touched the pile of papers at his elbow again. "Read these, Thomas. I cannot allow you to take them with you, but it will show you what you are looking for."

"Thank you." Pitt reached his hand for them, but Matthew did not pass them across.

"Thomas . . ."

"Yes."

"What about Father? You said you would look into the accident." He was embarrassed, as if he were criticizing, and hated it, but was compelled by conviction to do it. "The longer you leave it, the harder it will be. People forget, they become afraid when they have time to realize that there are those who . . ." He took a deep breath and his eyes met Pitt's. They were bright hazel, full of pain and confusion.

"I have already started," Pitt said quietly. "I spoke to Sturges when I was in Brackley. He is convinced the business with the pups was Danforth's mistake. Danforth sent a letter saying he didn't want them, he'd changed his mind. At least it purported to come from Danforth, whether it did or not, but Sturges saw it, it was addressed to him. It had nothing to do with Sir Arthur."

"That's something." Matthew grasped onto it, but the

anxiety did not leave his face. "But the accident? Was it deliberate? It was a warning, wasn't it?"

"I don't know. No one else saw it, as far as Sturges knows, though both the smith and the wheelwright saw the horseman careering up the street at a breakneck gallop, apparently completely out of control. But even a bolting horse won't usually charge into another it can clearly see, or go close enough for the rider to catch someone else with his whip. I think it was deliberate, but I don't know any way of proving it. The man was a stranger. No one knows who he was."

Matthew's face tightened. "And I suppose the same will be true of the underground railway. We'll never prove that either. From everything we can learn, no one he knew was with him." He looked down. "Clever. They know how to do it so if you say anything, tell anyone, it sounds absurd, like the ramblings of someone who has been eating opium, or lives permanently in his cups," He looked up suddenly, panic in his eyes. "It begins to make me feel helpless. I'm not consumed with hatred anymore. It has turned into something a lot more like fear, and a terrible weariness, as if it is all pointless. If it was anyone but Father, I might not even try."

Pitt understood the fear. He had felt it himself in the past, and now its cause was real. He also understood the enveloping exhaustion, now that the first shock of grief was over. Anger is a very depleting emotion; it burns up all the strength of the mind and the body. Matthew was tired, but in a while he would be renewed, and the anger would return, the sense of outrage, the passionate desire to protect, to prove the lie and restore some semblance of justice. He hoped profoundly that Harriet Soames was wise enough and generous enough to be gentle with him, to wait with patience for him to work his way through the tiredness and the confusion of feelings, that she would not just at that moment seek anything from him for herself beyond trust and the knowledge that he was willing to share all he was able to.

"Don't do anything alone," Pitt said very seriously.

Matthew's eyes widened a fraction, surprise and question in them, then after a moment, even a shadow of humor.

"Do you think I'm incompetent, Thomas? I've been fifteen years in the Foreign Office since we knew each other. I do know how to be diplomatic."

It had been a clumsiness of words rather than thought, and a desire to protect him which still lingered from youth.

"I'm sorry," Pitt apologized. "I meant that we could duplicate our efforts, and not only waste time but cause suspicion by it."

Matthew's face relaxed into a smile. "Sorry, Thomas. I am oversensitive. This has hit me harder than I could have foreseen." He gave Pitt the papers at last. "Look at these in the room next door, then give them back to me when you have finished."

Pitt rose and took them. "Thank you."

The room provided him was high ceilinged and full of sun from the long window, also facing the park. He sat in one of the three chairs and began. He made no notes but committed to memory the essence of what he needed. It took him to the middle of the day to be certain he knew precisely where to look to trace the information he could be quite certain had reached the German Embassy. Then he rose and returned the papers to Matthew.

"Is that all you require?" Matthew asked, looking up from his desk.

"For the moment."

Matthew smiled. "How about luncheon? There is an excellent public house just 'round the corner, and an even better one a couple of hundred yards along the street."

"Let's go to the even better one," Pitt agreed with an attempt at enthusiasm.

Matthew followed him to the door and along the corridor to the wide stairs down and into the bright busy street.

They walked side by side, occasionally jostled by pass-ersby, men in frock coats with top hats, now and then a woman, highly fashionable, carrying a parasol and smiling and nodding to acquaintances. The street itself was teeming with traffic. Coaches, carriages, hansoms, broughams and open landaus passed by every few minutes, moving at a brisk trot, horses' hooves rapping smartly, harnesses jin-gling.

"I love the city on a fine day," Matthew said almost apologetically. "There is such life here, such a sense of pur-pose and excitement." He glanced sideways at Pitt. "I need Brackley for its peace, and the feel of permanence it has. I find I always remember it so clearly, as if I had only just closed my eyes from seeing it, smelling the sharp coldness of winter air, the snow on the fields, or the crackle of frost under my feet. I can breathe in and re-create the perfume of the summer wind from the hay, the dazzle of sunlight and the sting of heat on my skin, the taste of apple cider."

A handsome woman in pink and gray passed by and smiled at him, not as an acquaintance, but out of interest, but he barely noticed her.

"And the glancing light and sudden rain of spring," he went on. "In the city it's just wet or dry. There's no burst-ing of growth to see, no green haze over the fields, no strong, dark furrows of earth, no awareness at once of the turning seasons, and the timelessness of it all because it has happened since the creation, and presumably always will."

A coach rumbled by, close to the curb, and Matthew on the outside stepped in hastily to avoid being hit by the jut-ting lamps.

"Fool!" he muttered under his breath.

They were a dozen yards from the crossing.

"My favorite time was always autumn," Pitt said, smiling with recollection. "The shortening days, golden at the end where the long light falls across the stubble fields, the piled stooks against the sky, clear evenings where the clouds fall away towards the west, scarlet berries in the hedgerows, wild rose hips, the smell of wood smoke and leaf mold, the blazing colors of the trees." They came to the curb and stopped. "I loved the bursting life of spring, the flowers, but there was always something about autumn when everything is touched with gold, there is a fullness, a completion. . . ."

Matthew looked at him with a sudden, intense affection. They could have been twenty years younger, standing together at Brackley, gazing across the fields or the woods, instead of at Parliament Street, waiting for the traffic to allow them to cross.

A hansom went by at a brisk clip and there was a space. They set out smartly, side by side. Then out of nowhere, swinging around the corner, a coach and four came careering over the curb edge, horses wild-eyed, frightened and squealing. Pitt leaped aside, pushing Matthew as hard as he could. Even so Matthew was caught by the near side front wheel and sent sprawling across the road to fetch up with his head barely a foot from the gutter and the curb edge.

Pitt scrambled to his feet, whirling around to catch sight of the coach, but all that was visible was the back of it as it disappeared around the corner of St. Margaret Street heading towards the Old Palace Yard.

Matthew lay motionless.

Pitt went over to him. His own leg hurt and he was going to be bruised all down his left side, but he was hardly aware of it.

"Matthew!" He could hear the panic rising in his voice and there was a sick terror in his stomach. "Matthew!" There was no blood. Matthew's neck was straight, no twisting, no awkward angle, but his eyes were closed and his face white.

A woman was standing on the pavement sobbing, her hands up to her mouth as if to stifle the sound.

Another woman, elderly, came forward and knelt down beside Matthew.

156

"May I help?" she said calmly. "My husband is a doctor, and I have assisted him many times." She did not look at Pitt, but at Matthew. She ignored the permission she had not yet received, and touched Matthew's cheek lightly, taking her gloves off, then put her finger to his neck.

Pitt waited in an agony of suspense.

She looked up at him after a moment, her face quite calm.

"His pulse is very strong," she said with a smile. "I expect he will have a most unpleasant headache, and I daresay several bruises which will no doubt be painful, but he is very much alive, I assure you."

Pitt was overwhelmed with relief. It was almost as if he could feel the blood surge back into his own body and life into his mind and his heart.

"You should have a stiff brandy yourself," the woman said gently. "And I would recommend a hot bath, and rub your bruises with ointment of arnica. It will help, I promise you."

"Thank you. Thank you very much." He felt momentarily as if she had saved their lives.

"I suppose you have no idea who the driver was?" she went on, still kneeling at the roadside by Matthew. "He should be prosecuted. That sort of thing is criminal. It was only by the grace of God your friend avoided the curbstone, or he would have cracked his head open and might very well have been killed."

"I know." Pitt swallowed hard, realizing with force how true that was. Now that he knew Matthew was alive, he could see it more sharply, and begin to understand all that it meant.

She looked at him curiously, her brow puckered, sensing there was much more to it than the accident she had seen.

Other people were beginning to gather around. A stout man with splendid side-whiskers came forward, elbowing his way.

"Now then, what's happened here?" he demanded. "Need a doctor? Should we call the police? Has anyone called the police?"

"I am the police." Pitt looked up at him. "And yes, we need a doctor. I'd be obliged if anybody would send for one."

The man looked doubtful. "Are you indeed?"

Pitt went to fish in his pocket and produce his card, and to his disgust found that his hands were shaking. He pulled out the card with difficulty and passed it to the man without bothering to see his reaction.

Matthew stirred, made a little choking sound which turned into a groan, then opened his eyes.

"Matthew!" Pitt said stiffly, leaning forward, peering at him.

"Bloody fool!" Matthew said furiously. He shut his eyes in pain.

"You should lie still, young man," the elderly lady advised him firmly. "We are sending for a doctor, and you should receive his counsel before you make any attempt to rise."

"Thomas?"

"Yes . . . I'm here."

Matthew opened his eyes again and focused them on Pitt's face. He made as if to speak, then changed his mind.

"Yes, exactly what you are thinking," Pitt said quietly.

Matthew took a very deep breath and let it out in a shudder. "I shouldn't have taken offense when you told me to be careful. I was childish, and as it turns out, quite mistaken."

Pitt did not reply.

The elderly lady looked around at the man with the whiskers. "May we take it that someone has been dispatched for a doctor, sir?" she enquired in much the manner a good governess might have used towards an indifferent butler.

"You may, madam," he replied stiffly, and moved away, Pitt was certain, in order to perform that task.

"I am sure that with a little help I could stand up," Matthew said. "I am causing something of an obstruction here, and making a spectacle of myself." He began to struggle to climb to his feet and Pitt was not able to prevent him, only to give him his arm and then catch him as he swayed and lost his balance. He clung on for several seconds before his head cleared and he was able, with concentration, to regain himself and stand, not unaided, but at least upright.

"I think we had better call you a hansom to take you home, and then send for our own physician as soon as possible," Pitt said decisively.

"Oh, I don't think that is necessary," Matthew argued, but was still swaying a trifle.

"You would be exceedingly unwise to ignore that advice," the elderly lady said severely. Now that Pitt and Matthew were both standing, she was considerably beneath their height, and obliged to look up at them, but her assurance was such that it made not the slightest difference. Pitt at least still felt as if he were in the schoolroom.

Matthew must have felt similarly, because he offered no argument, and when Pitt hailed a cab and it drew in, he thanked the lady profusely. They both took their leave and climbed in.

Pitt accompanied Matthew to his rooms and saw that the doctor was sent for, then went into the small sitting room to consider what he had read from the papers in the Foreign Office until the doctor should have been and delivered his opinion. Matthew was happy to relax and lie on his bed.

"A very ugly accident," the doctor said, some fifty minutes later. "But fortunately I think you have suffered no more than a slight concussion and some unpleasant bruising. Did you report the matter to the police?"

He was standing in Matthew's bedroom. Matthew was lying on the bed looking pale and still very shocked and Pitt was standing beside the door.

159

"Mr. Pitt is a policeman," Matthew explained. "He was beside me when it happened. He was knocked over as well."

"Were you? You said nothing." The doctor looked at him with raised eyebrows. "Do you need any attention, sir?"

"No thank you, just a few bruises," Pitt dismissed it. "But I'm obliged for your concern."

"Then I presume you will be reporting the matter to your superiors. To drive like that, to injure two men and simply keep on going, is a criminal offense," the doctor said sternly.

"Since neither of us knows who it was, nor do any of the other people in the street, there is very little that can be done," Pitt pointed out.

Matthew smiled wanly. "And Superintendent Pitt has no superiors, except the assistant commissioner. Do you, Thomas?"

The doctor looked surprised, and shook his head.

"Pity. People like that should be prosecuted. Like to see the man made to walk everywhere from now on. Still, there are a lot of things I'd like to see, and won't." He turned to Matthew. "Take a day or two's rest, and call on me again if the headache gets any worse, if your vision is affected, or if you are sick."

"Thank you."

"Good day, Sir Matthew."

Pitt conducted him out and returned to Matthew's room.

"Thank you, Thomas," Matthew said grimly. "If you hadn't pushed me I'd have been mangled to bits under those hooves. Do I presume it was the Inner Circle, warning me?"

"Or both of us," Pitt replied. "Or someone with a great deal of money at stake in Africa. Although I think that's less likely. Or it may have been simply an accident, and quite impersonal."

"Do you believe that?"

160

"No."

"Neither do I." Matthew made an attempt to smile. His long face with its hazel eyes was very pale indeed, and he made no effort to hide the fact that he was frightened.

"Leave it for a day or two," Pitt said quietly. "We can't accomplish anything by getting hurt or killed ourselves. Stay here. We'll think what our next move should be. We must make it count. This is not a battle where we can afford blows that do no damage."

"Not a lot I can do . . . just yet." Matthew winced. "But I'm damned well going to think of nothing else."

Pitt smiled and took his leave. He could do no more now, and Matthew needed to sleep. He left with his mind still whirling and full of dark thoughts and fears.

It was nearly four o'clock when he walked across Downing Street and up the steps of the Colonial Office. He asked to see Linus Chancellor, and was told that if he was prepared to wait, that would be possible.

As it turned out, he waited only half an hour, and then was shown into Chancellor's office. He was sitting at his desk, his broad brow puckered with interest and anxiety, his eyes keen.

"Afternoon, Pitt," he said without standing. He waved to the chair near the desk and Pitt took it. "I presume you have come to report your findings so far? Is it too soon to look for a suspect? Yes, I can see by your face that it is. What have you?" His eyes narrowed. "You look awkward, man. Very stiff. Are you hurt?"

Pitt smiled ruefully. In truth he was beginning to hurt very much. He had almost ignored his own injuries in his fear for Matthew. Now they were too sharp to be forgotten.

"I was hit by a coach a few hours ago, but I very much doubt it had anything to do with this."

Chancellor's face reflected real concern and a degree of shock. "Good God! You don't mean there is a possibility

161

that someone deliberately tried to kill you?" Then his face tightened and a bleak, almost venomous look came into his eyes. "Although I don't know why I should be surprised. If a man will sell out his country, why should he balk at killing someone who looked like exposing him at it? I think my scale of values needs a little adjusting."

He leaned back in his chair, his face taut with emotion. "Perhaps violence offends our sensibility so profoundly we tend to think of it as worse than the unseen corruption of betrayal, which in some very essence is immeasurably worse. It is murder behind the smiling face, the thrust in the back"—his fist clenched as if he were dealing the blow himself—"when you are turned elsewhere, and then the sudden realization that all trust may be misplaced.

"It is robbery of everything that makes life worthwhile, the belief in good, the love of friends, honor itself. Why would I think he would not indulge in a simple push in a crowd? A man falls off the curb under the wheels of a carriage?" He looked at Pitt with concern on the surface over a passionate anger beneath. "Have you seen a physician? Should you be up and walking around? Are you sure there is no serious injury?"

Pitt smiled in spite of himself. "Yes, I have seen a doctor, thank you." He was stretching the truth. "I was with a friend who was considerably more hurt than I, and we shall both be well enough in a few days. But I appreciate your concern. I saw Sir Matthew Desmond this morning and he gave me details of the information which reached the Germans. I read it in the Foreign Office and left it there, but I can recall the essence of it, and I would be obliged if you could tell me if there is any common source or link, or at least anyone who would be excluded from possibility because they could not have known."

"Of course. Relate it to me." Chancellor leaned back in his seat and folded his hands, waiting.

With concentration Pitt recalled all the information he

had gleaned from Matthew's papers, set it in an orderly fashion, progressing from one category to the next.

When he had finished Chancellor looked at him with puzzlement and renewed anxiety.

"What is it?" Pitt asked.

"Some of that is information I did not know myself," Chancellor replied slowly. "It doesn't pass through the Colonial Office." He let the words fall on silence, and stared at Pitt to see if he grasped the full implication of what he had said.

"Then our traitor has help, witting or unwitting," Pitt concluded reluctantly. Then a new thought came to him. "Of course that may be his weakness. . . ."

Chancellor saw what he meant instantly. The spark of hope leaped in his eyes and his body tensed. "Indeed it may! It gives you somewhere to start, to search for proofs, communications, perhaps even payments, or blackmail. The possibilities are considerable."

"Where do I begin?"

"What?" Chancellor was startled.

"Where else may the other information have come from?" Pitt elaborated. "What precisely is it that does not pass through this office?"

"Oh. Yes, I see. Financial matters. You have included details here of the various loans and guarantees given MacKinnon and Rhodes, among others. And backing from the City of London and from bankers in Edinburgh. The generalities any diligent person with a knowledge of finance might learn for himself, but the times, conditions, precise amounts could only have come from the Treasury."

His lips tightened. "This is very ugly indeed, Pitt. It seems there is a traitor in the Treasury as well. We shall owe you a great deal if you uncover this for us, and manage to do it discreetly." He searched Pitt's eyes. "Do I need to warn you how damaging this could be to the entire government, not only to British interests in Africa, if it becomes public that we are riddled with treason?"

"No," Pitt said simply, rising to his feet. "I shall do everything in my power to deal with it discreetly, even secretly if possible."

"Good. Good." Chancellor sat back and looked up at Pitt, his handsome, volatile face released of some of its tension at last. "Keep me aware of your progress. I can always make a few minutes in the day to see you, or in the evening if necessary. I don't imagine you keep exact hours any more than I do?"

"No, sir. I shall see you are acquainted with my progress. Good day, Mr. Chancellor."

Pitt went immediately to the Treasury, but it was nearly five o'clock, and Mr. Ransley Soames, the man he needed to see, had already left for the day. Pitt was tired and aching profoundly. He was not sorry to be thwarted in his diligence, and able to stop a hansom in Whitehall and return home.

He had debated whether or not to tell Charlotte the full extent of the incident with the coach. It would be useless trying not to mention it at all. She would be aware that he was hurt the instant she saw him, but it would not be necessary to mention the gravity of it, or that Matthew had been injured even more. He decided it would only worry her to no purpose.

"What happened?" she pressed him the moment he had finished telling her the barest outline. They were sitting in the parlor with a hot cup of tea. Both children were upstairs, having had their meal. Jemima was doing homework. There were only four more years to go before the examinations which would decide her educational future. Daniel, two years younger, was still excused such rigorous study. At five and a half he could read quite tolerably, and was learning multiplication tables by heart, and a great deal more spelling than he desired. But at this time in the early evening he was permitted simply to play. Jemima was endeavoring to master a list of all the Kings of England from Edward the Confessor in 1066 to the present Queen in 1890, which was a formidable task. But when it was time for her examinations she would be required to know not only their names and order of succession, but their dates and the outstanding events of their reigns as well.

"What happened?" Charlotte repeated, watching him closely.

"A coach had apparently run out of control, and brushed me when it came 'round the corner at close to a gallop. I was knocked over, but not hurt more than a few bruises." He smiled. "It is really nothing serious. I wouldn't have told you at all, except I don't want you to fear I am crippled with old age just yet!"

There was no answering smile in her face.

"Thomas, you look dreadful. You should see a doctor, just to make sure. . . ."

"It is not necessary."

She made as if to stand up. "I think it is!"

"No, it isn't!" He heard the edge to his voice, and was unable to curb it. He sounded sharp, frightened.

She stopped, looking at him with a pucker between her brows.

"I'm sorry," he apologized. "I have already seen a doctor." He told her the same stretching of the truth he had told Chancellor. "There is nothing at all except a few bruises, and a sense of shock and anger."

"It is not all. Why did you go to a doctor?" she asked, looking at him narrowly.

It was too complicated to lie, and he was too tired. It was only to protect her that he had evaded it. He wanted to tell her.

"Matthew was with me," he replied. "He was more seriously hurt. The doctor came for him. But he will be all right," he added quickly. "It was simply that he was insensible for a few moments."

She looked at him closely, her eyes clouded with worry. "Was it an accident, Thomas? You don't think the Inner Circle came after Matthew as well, do you?"

"I don't know. I doubt it, because dearly as I would like to think he is a danger to them, I don't."

She looked at him doubtfully, but said no more on the matter. Instead she went to run him a hot bath and find some ointment of arnica.

"Good morning, Superintendent." Ransley Soames made it a question, although the wording was not such. He was a good-looking man with regular features and thick, wavy, fair hair brushed back off his brow. His nose was rather high at the bridge and his mouth had a hint of softness in it. Without self-discipline he might have been indulgent. As it was he had a considerable presence and he looked at Pitt steadily and with gracious interest. "What may I do for you?"

"Good morning, Mr. Soames," Pitt answered, closing the office door behind him and accepting the seat offered. Soames was sitting behind a high and very finely carved desk, a red box to one side, closed and with its ribbons tied. "I apologize for troubling you, sir, but I am enquiring, at the request of the Foreign Office, into certain information which has been very seriously misdirected. It is necessary that we know the source of the information, and all who may have been privy to it, in order to rectify the error."

Soames frowned at him. "Your language is very diplomatic, Superintendent, one might even say obscure. What sort of information are you referring to, and where has it gone that it should not?"

"Financial information regarding Africa, and I should prefer at this point not to say where it has gone. Mr. Linus Chancellor has asked that I be as discreet as possible. I expect you understand the necessity for that."

"Of course." But Soames did not look as if he thought

166

well of being included in the proscription. "You will also understand, Superintendent, if I require some confirmation of what you say ... simply as a formality?"

Pitt smiled. "Naturally." He produced a letter of authority Matthew had given him, with the Foreign Secretary's countersignature.

Soames glanced at it, recognized Lord Salisbury's hand, and sat up a little straighter. Pitt noticed a certain tension in him. Perhaps he was becoming aware of the gravity of the matter.

"Yes, Superintendent. Precisely what is it you wish to learn from me? An enormous amount of financial information passes across my desk, as you may appreciate. More than a little of it is to do with African matters."

"That which concerns me is to do with the funding of Mr. Cecil Rhodes's expedition into Matabeleland, which is presently taking place, among other things."

"Indeed? Are you not aware, Superintendent, that the greatest part of that has been funded by Mr. Rhodes himself, and his South Africa Company?"

"Yes sir, I am. But it was not always so. It would help me greatly if you could give me something of the history of the finances of the expedition."

Soames's eyes widened.

"Good gracious! Going back how far?"

The window was open, and amidst the faint rumble of traffic came the sound of a hurdy-gurdy, then it was gone again.

"Let us say, the last ten years," Pitt replied.

"What do you wish to know? I cannot possibly recount to you the entire matter. I shall be here all day." Soames looked both surprised and irritated, as if he found the request unreasonable.

"I only need to know who dealt with the information."

Soames sighed. "You are still asking the impossible. Mr. Rhodes first tried to secure Bechuanaland from the Cape. Back in August of 'eighty-three he addressed the Cape Parliament on that issue." He sat back farther in his chair, folding his hands across his waistcoat. "It was the gateway to the enormous fertile northern plains of Matabeleland and Mashonaland. But he found Scanlen, the prime minister, to be quite uninterested. The Cape Parliament was in debt to an immense degree with a railway obligation of some fourteen million pounds, and having just suffered a war with Basutoland which had been a crippling additional expense. It was at that time that Rhodes first turned to London for finances . . . unwillingly, I may say. Of course that was during Mr. Gladstone's Liberal government. Lord Derby was Foreign Secretary then. But he was no more interested than had been Scanlen of the Cape." Soames regarded Pitt narrowly. "Are you familiar with all this, Superintendent?"

"No sir. Is it necessary that I should be?"

"If you are to understand the history of the financing of this expedition." Soames smiled belatedly, and continued. "After our fearful losses at Majuba, Lord Derby wanted nothing to do with it. However, the following year there was a complete turn in events, largely brought about by fear of the Transvaal pushing northwards and eclipsing our efforts, our very necessary efforts for the safety of the Empire, the sea lanes 'round the Cape, and so on. We could not afford to allow the Cape ports to fall solely into the hands of the Afrikaners. Are you following me?"

"Yes."

"Kruger and the other Transvaal delegates sailed to London the following year, 'eighty-four, to renegotiate the Pretoria Convention. Part of this agreement—I won't bore you with the details—included Kruger letting go of Bechuanaland. Boer freebooters were moving northward." He was watching Pitt closely to see if he understood. "Kruger double-crossed Rhodes and annexed Goshen to the Transvaal, and Germany entered the scene. It became increasingly complicated. Do you begin to see how much information there is, and how difficult to ascertain who knew what?"

"I do," Pitt conceded. "But surely there are usual channels through which information passes which concerns Zambezia and Equatoria?"

"Certainly. What about the Cape, Bechuanaland, the Congo and Zanzibar?"

The sounds from the open window seemed far away, like another world.

"Exclude them for the time being," Pitt directed.

"Very well. That makes it easier." Soames did not look any less concerned or irritated. His brow was furrowed and there was a tension in his body. "There are only myself, Thompson, Chetwynd, MacGregor, Cranbourne and Alderley who are aware of all of the areas you mention. I find it hard to think that any of them have been careless, or allowed information to pass to anyone unauthorized, but I suppose it is possible."

"Thank you."

Soames frowned. "What do you intend to do?"

"Pursue the matter," Pitt replied with a noncommittal smile. He would have Tellman deal with it, see if there were any connections between one of these men and Miss Amanda Pennecuick, among other things.

Soames was regarding Pitt steadily. "Superintendent, I presume the information has been used inappropriately, for personal gain, speculation of some sort? I trust it in no way jeopardizes our position in Africa? I am aware of how serious it is," He leaned forward. "Indeed it is imperative that we obtain Zambezia and the entire Cape-to-Cairo route. If it falls to the wrong powers, God alone knows what harm may be done. All the work, the profound influence of men like Livingstone and Moffatt, will be overtaken by a tide of violence and religious barbarism. Africa may be bathed in blood. Christianity could be lost in the continent." His face looked bleak and sad. It was obviously something he believed in profoundly and without question.

Pitt felt a sudden wave of sympathy for the man. It was so far from the opportunism and the exploitation Sir Arthur

169

had feared. Ransley Soames at least had no part in the Inner Circle and its manipulation. Pitt could like him for that alone. It was an overwhelming relief. After all, he was to be Matthew's father-in-law.

"I'm sorry. I wish I could say that it were," he answered gravely. "But it has been passed to the German Embassy."

The color drained from Soames's face and he stared at Pitt in horror. "Information . . . accurate information? Are you sure?"

"It may not yet have done any irreparable harm," Pitt strove to reassure him.

"But . . . who would do such a . . . a thing?" Soames looked almost desperate. "Will the Germans press in from Zanzibar with armies? They do have men, weapons, even gunboats there, you know? There has already been rebellion, suppression and bloodshed!"

"That may be enough to prevent them pressing inland just yet," Pitt said hopefully. "In the meantime, Mr. Soames, thank you for this information. I shall take this with me." He rose to his feet and was at the door before he took a sudden chance. After all, Harriet Soames was a young woman of fashion and society. "Sir, are you by any chance familiar with the name of Miss Amanda Pennecuick?"

"Yes." Soames looked startled. "Whatever makes you ask such a question? She can have nothing to do with this. She is a friend of my daughter's. Why do you ask, Superintendent?"

"Is she acquainted with any of the gentlemen on this list?"

"Yes, yes I believe so. Alderley has met her in social circumstances in my house, that I am aware of. He seems very taken with her. Not unnaturally. She is an unusually charming young woman. What has that to do with the financial information on Africa, Superintendent?"

"Possibly nothing." Pitt smiled quickly and opened the door. "Thank you very much, sir. Good morning."

* * *

The following day was Sunday, and for Nobby Gunne it was the happiest day she could remember. Peter Kreisler had invited her to go down the river with him, and had hired a small pleasure boat for the afternoon. They were to return by carriage through the long, late spring evening after supper.

Now she sat in the small craft on the bright water, the sun in her face, the breeze just cool enough to be pleasant, and the sounds of laughter and excited voices drifted across the river as women in pale muslin dresses, men in shirtsleeves, and excited children leaned over the rails of excursion boats, or looked down from bridges or across from either bank.

"All London seems to be out today," she said happily as their boatman steered dexterously between a moored barge and a fishing trawler. They had boarded at Westminster Bridge under the shadow of the Houses of Parliament, and were now well down the outgoing tide beyond Blackfriars, almost to the Southwark Bridge, with London Bridge ahead of them.

Kreisler smiled. "A perfect May day, why not? I suppose the virtuous are still in church?" They had earlier heard the sound of bells drifting across the water, and he had already pointed out one or two elegant Wren spires in the distance.

"I can be just as virtuous here," she replied with questionable truth. "And certainly a great deal better tempered."

This time he made no effort to hide his amusement. "If you are going to try to convince me you are a conventional woman, you are far too late. Conventional women do not paddle up the Congo in canoes."

"Of course not!" she answered happily. "They sit in pleasure boats on the Thames, and allow gentlemen of their acquaintance to take them up to Richmond or Kew, or down to Greenwich for the afternoon. . . ."

"Would you rather have gone up to Kew? I hear the botanical gardens are among the wonders of the world."

"Not in the least. I am perfectly happy going to Greenwich. Besides, on a day like this, I fear all the world and his aunt will be at Kew."

He settled a little more comfortably in his seat, relaxing back in the sun and watching the myriad other craft maneuvering the busy waterway, and the carriages and omnibuses on the banks, the stalls selling peppermint drinks, pies, sandwiches and cockles, or balloons, hoops, penny flutes and whistles, and other toys. A girl in a frilly dress was chasing a little boy in a striped suit. A black-and-white dog barked and jumped up and down in excitement. A hurdy-gurdy played a familiar tune. A pleasure boat passed by, its decks lined with people, all waving towards the shore. One man had a red bandanna tied around his head, a bright splash of color in a sea of faces.

Nobby and Kreisler glanced at each other. Speech was not necessary; the same amusement was in both their faces, the same wry enjoyment of humanity.

They had passed under the Southward Bridge. The old Swan Pier was to the left, London Bridge ahead, and then Custom House Quay.

"Do you suppose the Congo will ever become one of the great waterways of the world?" she said thoughtfully. "In my mind's eye I can only see it as a vast brown sliding stream hemmed in by a jungle so immense it covers nations, and just isolated canoes paddling a few miles from village to village." She trailed her hand gently in the water. The breeze was warm on her face. "Man seems so small, so ineffectual against the primeval strength of Africa. Here we seem to have conquered everything and bent it to our will."

"We won't ever conquer the Congo," he said without hesitation. "The climate won't let us. That is one of the few things we cannot tame or subdue. But no doubt we will build cities, take steamboats there and export the timber, copper and everything else we think we can sell. There is already a railway. In time I expect they will build another from Zambezia to the Cape, to take out gold, ivory and whatever else, more efficiently."

"And you hate the idea," she said with gravity, all the laughter vanished.

He looked at her steadily. "I hate the greed and the exploitation. I hate the duplicity with which we cheat the Africans. They've cheated and duped Lobengula, the king of the Ndebele in Mashonaland. He's illiterate, of course, but a wily old devil, I think perhaps even intelligent enough to understand some of his own tragedy."

The ebbing tide had them well in its grip and they passed under London Bridge. A girl in a large hat was staring down at them, smiling. Nobby waved to her and she waved back.

Custom House Quay was to their left, and beyond it Tower Hill and the Great Tower of London with its crested battlements and flags flying. Down at the water's edge was the slipway of Traitors Gate, where the condemned had been delivered by boat to their execution in days past.

"I wonder what he was like," Kreisler said quietly, almost as if to himself.

"Who?" Nobby asked, for once not following his thoughts.

"William of Normandy," he answered. "The last conqueror to subdue these lands and subjugate its people, set up his fortresses across the hills, and with armed soldiers to keep order and take profit from the land. The Tower was his." They were sliding past it as he spoke, on the swift ebbing water; the boatman had little to do to keep their speed.

She knew what Kreisler was thinking. It had nothing to do with William of Normandy or an invasion over eight centuries ago. It was Africa again, and European rifles and cannons against the assegais of the Zulu impis, or the Ndebele, British formations across the African plains, black men ruled by white as the Saxons had been by the Nor-

173

mans. Only the Normans were blood cousins, allied by race and faith, different only in tongue.

She looked at him and held his gaze steadily. They were passing St. Catherine's Dock and heading towards the Pool of London. On either side of the river there were docks, wharves, and stairs going to the water's edge. Barges were moored, others moved out slowly into the stream and went up towards further docks, or down towards the estuary and the sea. Pleasure boats were fewer now; this was the commercial shore. Here was trade with all the world.

As if having taken her thoughts, he smiled. "Cargoes of silk from China, spices from Burma and India, teak and ivory and jade," he said, lying back a little farther. The sun on his brown face caught the pale color of his hair where it was already bleached by a far fiercer light than that of this gentle English afternoon with its dappled water. "I suppose it should be cedars of Lebanon and gold from Ophir! It won't be long before it's gold from Zimbabwe and mahogany and skins from Equatoria, ivory from Zanzibar and minerals from the Congo. And they will be traded for cotton from Manchester, and guns and men from half Europe. Some will come home again, many won't."

"Have you ever met Lobengula?" she asked curiously.

He laughed, looking up quickly. "Yes . . . I have. He's an enormous man, nearly twenty-two stones in weight, and over six feet tall. He wears nothing except a Zulu ring 'round his head and a small loincloth."

"Good heavens! Really? So big?" She regarded him closely to see if he was joking, although she knew almost certainly he was not.

His smile was steady, but his eyes were full of laughter. "The Ndebele are not a building people like the Shona, who created the city of Zimbabwe. They live by cattle raising and raiding, and making only villages of grass huts covered with dung. . . ."

"I know the sort," she said quickly, and memory returned so she could almost smell the dry heat in spite of the rush-

174

ing and slapping of water all around her and the bright reflections dancing in her eyes.

"Of course you do," he apologized. "Forgive me. It is so rare a treat for me to be able to speak with someone who needs no explanation or word pictures to imagine what I'm describing. Lobengula holds a very formal court. Anyone seeking audience with him has to approach him crawling on hands and knees—and remain so throughout." He pulled a face. "It can be a very hot and exhausting experience, and not necessarily with any pleasure or profit at the end. He can neither read nor write, but he has a prodigious memory . . . for all the good that will do him dealing with Europe, poor devil."

She waited in silence. Kreisler was lost in thoughts of his own and she was content to allow it. She had no sense of being excluded; it was perfectly companionable. The light, the sound of the water, the wharves and warehouses of the Pool of London slipped by, and the shared dreams of the past in another land, the shared fears for its future as a different kind of darkness loomed over it.

"They duped him, of course," he said after a while. "They promised they would bring no more than ten white men to work in his country."

She sat upright suddenly, her eyes wide with disbelief.

"Yes." He looked at her through his lashes. "Unbelievable to you or me, but he accepted it. They also said they would dig nowhere near towns, and that they and their people would abide by the laws of the Ndebele, and behave generally as Lobengula's subjects." The bitterness crept in only at the end.

"And the price?" she asked quietly.

"A hundred pounds a month, a thousand Martini-Henry breech-locking rifles and a hundred thousand rounds of ammunition, and a gunboat on the Zambezi."

She said nothing. They were passing Wapping Old Stairs on their left as they sped downriver. The Pool of London was teeming with boats, barges, steamers, tugs, trawlers and here and there the odd pleasure boat. Would the brown, jungle-crusted Congo ever be like this, teeming with civilization and the goods of the world to be bought and sold, and consumed by men and women who had never left their own counties or shires?

"Rudd set off at a gallop to take the news to Rhodes in Kimberley," Kreisler went on, "before the king realized he had been cheated. The fool almost died of thirst in his eagerness to carry the news." There was disgust in his voice, but the only emotion registered in his face was a deep and acutely personal pain. His lips were stiff with the intensity of it as if it resided with him all the time, and yet for all his leanness of body and the strength she knew was there, he looked vulnerable.

But it was a private pain. She was perhaps the only person with whom he had or could share the full nature of it and expect any degree of understanding, yet she knew not to intrude into intimacy. Part of the sharing was the delicacy of the silence between them.

They were past the Pool and the London Docks and leaving Limehouse. Still the wharves and stairs lined either side, massive warehouses with painted names above them. The West India Docks were ahead, and then Limehouse Reach and the Isle of Dogs. They had already passed the old pier stakes sticking above the receding water, where in the past pirates had been lashed till the incoming tide drowned them. They had both seen them, glanced at each other, and said nothing.

It was very comfortable not to have to search for speech. It was a luxury she was not used to. Almost everyone else she knew would have found the silence a lack. They would have been impelled to say something to break it. Kreisler was perfectly happy just to catch her eye now and then, and know that she too was busy with the wind, the smell of salt, the noise and bustle around them, and yet the feeling of being detached from it by the small space of water that separated them from everyone else. They passed through it with impunity, seeing and yet uninvolved.

Greenwich was beautiful, the long green swell of ground rising from the river, the full leaf of the trees and the park beyond, the classical elegance of Vanburgh's architecture in the hospital and the Royal Naval Schools behind.

They went ashore, rode in an open trap up to the park and then walked slowly side by side through the lawns and flowers and stood under the great trees listening to the wind moving gently in the branches. A huge magnolia was in full bloom, its tulip flowers a foam of white against the blue sky. Children chased each other and played with hoops and spinning tops and kites. Nursemaids in crisp uniforms walked, heads high, perambulators in front of them. Soldiers in scarlet tunics lounged around, watching the nursemaids. Lovers, young and less young, walked arm in arm. Girls flirted, swinging parasols and laughing. A dog capered around with a stick in its mouth. Somewhere a barrel organ was playing a musical tune.

They had afternoon tea, and talked of frivolous things, knowing that darker matters were always there, but understood; nothing needed explaining. The sadness and the fear had all been shared and for this warm, familiar afternoon it could be left beneath the surface of the mind.

In the sunset, with the moth-filled air cooling and the smell of earth and leaves rising from the pathway, they found the carriage which was to take them on the long ride back westwards. He handed her in, and they drove home with only an occasional word as the dusk deepened. The light flared in apricot and amber and turquoise over the river, making it look for a brief moment as if it could have been as magical as the lagoons of Venice, or the seaway of the Bosphorus, the meeting of Europe and Asia, instead of London, and the heart of the greatest empire since Caesar's Rome.

Then the color faded to silver, the stars appeared to the

south, away from the stir and lamps of the city, and they moved a little closer together as the chill of darkness set in. She could not remember a sweeter day.

6

THE MONDAY AFTERWARDS Nobby spent largely in her own garden. Of all the things she liked about England—and when she thought about it, there were really quite a few—its gardens gave her the greatest pleasure. There were frequent occasions when she loathed the climate, when the long, gray days of January and February depressed her and she ached for the African sun. The sleet seemed to creep between the folds of every conceivable garment designed against it. Icy water trickled down one's neck, onto one's wrists between glove and sleeve, no boots kept it all off the feet, skirt hems became sodden and filthy. Did the designers of gowns have the faintest idea what it was like to walk around carrying a dozen yards of wet fabric wrapped around one's torso?

And there were days, sometimes even weeks, when fog obliterated the world, clinging, blinding fog which caught in the throat, muffled and distorted sounds, held the smoke and fumes of a hundred thousand chimneys in a shroud like a cold, wet cloth across the face.

There were disappointing days in the summer when one longed for warmth and brilliance, and yet it persistently rained, and the chill east wind came in off the sea, raising goose pimples on the flesh.

But there were also the days of glory when the sun shone in a perfect sky, great trees a hundred, two hundred feet high soared into the air in a million rustling leaves, elms, whispering poplars, silver-stemmed birches and the great beeches she loved most of all.

The land was always green; the depth of summer or the bleakest winter did not parch or freeze it. And the abundance of flowers must surely be unique. She could have named a hundred varieties without having to resort to a book. Now as she stood in the afternoon sunlight looking down her long, shaven velvet lawn to the cedar, and the elms beyond, an Albertine rose in a wild profusion of sprays was spilling over the old stone wall, uncountable buds ready to open into a foam of coral and pink blossom. The spires of delphiniums rose in front of it, ready to bloom in royal and indigo, and bloodred peonies were fattening to flower. The may blossom perfumed the air, as did pink and purple lilac.

On a day like this the empire builders were welcome to Africa, India, the Pacific or the Spice Islands, or even the Indies.

"Excuse me, ma'am?"

She turned, startled out of her reverie. Her maid was standing looking at her with a surprised expression.

"Yes, Martha?"

"Please ma'am, there's a Mrs. Chancellor 'as called to see you. A Mrs. Linus Chancellor. She's very ..."

"Yes?"

"Oh, I think you'd better come, ma'am. Shall I say as you'll receive her?"

Nobby contained her amusement, and not inconsiderable surprise. What on earth was Susannah Chancellor doing paying an afternoon call here? Nobby was hardly in her social or her political sphere.

"Certainly tell her so," she replied. "And show her out onto the terrace."

Martha bobbed something like half a curtsy and hurried with insufficient dignity back across the grass and up the steps to discharge her errand.

A moment later Susannah emerged from the French doors, by which time Nobby was coming up the shallow stone steps from the lawn, her skirt brushing against the urns with scarlet and vermilion nasturtiums spilling out of them, almost luminous in their brilliance.

Susannah was dressed very formally in white, trimmed with pale pink and a thread of carmine-shaded ribbon. White lace foamed at her throat and wrists and her parasol was trimmed with ribbon and a blush pink rose. She looked exquisite, and unhappy.

"Good afternoon, Mrs. Chancellor," Nobby said formally. This was an extremely formal time of the afternoon to call. "How very pleasant of you to come."

"Good afternoon, Miss Gunne," Susannah replied with less than her usual assurance. She looked beyond Nobby to the garden as if seeking someone else. "Have I interrupted you with . . . with other visitors?" She forced a smile.

"No, I am quite alone," Nobby replied, wondering what so troubled the younger woman. "I was simply enjoying the perfect weather and thinking what a delight it is to have a garden."

"Yes, isn't it," Susannah agreed, stepping farther across the terrace and starting down the steps to the lawn. "Yours is particularly beautiful. Would you think me discourteous to ask if you would show me 'round it? It is too much to take in at a glance. And it looks as if there is more of it yet, beyond that stone wall and the archway. Is that so?"

"Yes, I am very fortunate in its size," Nobby agreed. "Of course I should be delighted to show you." It was far too early to offer refreshment, and anyway that was not customary during the first hour of time appropriate for receiving. Although, of course, some fifteen minutes was all one stayed; it was also not done to walk around the garden, which would take half an hour at the very least.

Nobby was now quite concerned as to why Susannah had come. It was impossible to imagine it was a simple call for the usual social purposes. Leaving her card would have been quite adequate, in fact the proper thing, since they were not in any real sense acquainted.

They walked very gently, Susannah stopping every few yards to admire something or other. Often she appeared not to know its name, simply to like its color, form, or its position complementing something else. They passed the gardener weeding around the antirrhinums and pulling a few long spears of grass from the mass of the blue salvia.

"Of course, as close to Westminster as we live," Susannah went on, "we do not have room for a garden such as this. It is one of the things I most miss. We do go down to the country when my husband can arrange it, but that is not so very often. His position is most demanding."

"I can imagine that it would be," Nobby murmured.

A brief smile touched Susannah's face and immediately vanished again. A curious expression followed, a softness in her eyes, at once pleasure and pain, yet her lips were pulled tight with some underlying anxiety which would not let her relax. She said the words "my husband" with the pride of a woman in love. Yet her hands fiddled incessantly with the ribbons on her parasol, her fingers stiff, as if she did not care if she broke the threads.

There was nothing Nobby could do but wait.

Susannah turned and began walking towards the great cedar and the white garden seat under its shade. The grass was thin where the needles had shed on it until the ground became bare altogether near the trunk, the roots having taken all the nourishment from the earth.

"You must have seen a great many wonderful things, Miss Gunne." Susannah did not look at her but through the stone archway beneath the roses. "Sometimes I envy you your travels. Then of course there are other times—most of them, I admit—when I am too fond of the comforts of England." She looked at Nobby beside her. "Would it bore you to tell me something of your adventures?"

"Not at all, if that is really what you wish? But I assure you, you have no need of it in order to be polite."

182

"Polite?" Susannah was surprised, this time stopping to face Nobby. "Is that what you think?"

"A great many have thought it was the proper thing to do," Nobby replied with amusement and a flood of memory, much of it painful at the time, but merely absurd now.

"Oh, not at all," Susannah assured her. They were still in the shade of the cedar, and considerably cooler. "I find Africa fascinating. My husband has a great deal to do with it, you know?"

"Yes, yes I know who he is." Nobby was not sure what else to say. The more she knew of Linus Chancellor's backing of Cecil Rhodes, the less happy she was about it. The whole question of the settlement of Zambezia had troubled her ever since she had met Peter Kreisler. The thought of him brought a smile to her lips, in spite of the questions and the anxiety.

Susannah caught the intonation; at least it seemed as if she did. She looked around quickly, and was about to say something, then changed her mind and turned back to the garden again. She had been there ten minutes already. For a strictly formal call, she should now be taking her leave.

"I suppose you know Africa quite well—the people, I mean?" she said thoughtfully.

"I am familiar with them in certain areas," Nobby replied honestly. "But it is an inconceivably enormous country, in fact an entire continent of distances we Europeans can scarcely imagine. It would be ridiculous to say I know more than a fraction. Of course, if you are interested, there are people in London who know far more than I do and who have been there more recently. I believe you have already met Mr. Kreisler, for example?" She found herself oddly self-conscious as she spoke his name. That was foolish. She was not forcing him into the conversation, as a young woman does when in love, introducing a man's name into every possible subject. This was most natural; in fact it would have been unnatural not to have spoken of him.

"Yes." Susannah looked away from the arch and the roses and back down the lawn towards the house. "Yes, I have met him. A most interesting man, with vigorous views. What is your opinion of him, Miss Gunne?" She swiveled back again, her face earnest. "Do you mind my asking you? I don't know who else's opinion would be of the least worth, compared with yours."

"I think perhaps you overrate me." Nobby felt herself blushing, which made it even worse. "But of course what little I know you are most welcome to hear."

Susannah seemed to be most relieved, as if this were the real purpose of her visit.

"Thank you. I feared for a moment you were going to decline."

"What is it you are concerned about?" The conversation was becoming very stilted. Susannah was still highly nervous, and Nobby felt more and more self-conscious as time passed. The garden was so quiet behind the walls she could hear the wind in the tops of the trees like water breaking on a shore, gently as a tide on shingle. A bee drifted lazily from one open flower to another. The warmth of the afternoon was considerable, even under the shade of the cedar, and the air was heavy with the odor of crushed grass, damp leaves under the weight of foliage by the hedges, and the sweet pervasive blossom of lilacs and the may.

"His opinion of Mr. Rhodes is very poor," Susannah said at last. "I am not entirely sure why. Do you think it may be personal?"

Nobby thought she heard a lift of hope in her voice. Since Linus Chancellor had vested so much confidence in him, that would not be surprising. But what had Kreisler said to her which had caused her to doubt, and come seeking Nobby's opinion, and not her husband's? That in itself was extraordinary. A woman automatically shared her husband's status in life, his religious views, and if she had political opinions at all, they were also his.

"I am not sure whether he has even met Mr. Rhodes,"

Nobby replied slowly, hiding her surprise and feeling for words to convey the facts she knew, without the coloring of her own mistrust of the motives for African settlement and the fears she had of the exploitation of its people. "Of course he, like me, is a little in love with the mystery of Africa as it is," she went on with an apologetic smile. "We are apprehensive of change, in case something of that is lost. When you feel you were the first to see something, and you are excited and overwhelmed and deeply moved by it, you do feel as if no one else will treat it with the same reverence you do. And it causes one to fear, perhaps unjustly. Certainly Mr. Kreisler does not share Mr. Rhodes's dreams of colonization and settlement."

A smile flashed across Susannah's face and vanished.

"That is something of an understatement, Miss Gunne. If what he says is true, he fears it will be the ruination of Zambezia. I have heard some of his arguments, and I wondered if you would share with me your view of them."

"Oh " Nobby was taken aback. It was too frank a question for her to answer without considerable thought, and a censorship of the emotions that came to her mind before she permitted them to anybody else, particularly Susannah Chancellor. There were many aspects to weigh. She must not, even accidentally, betray a confidence Kreisler might have placed in her by allowing her to share emotions and fears which he might not have been willing to show others. The boat trip down the Thames had been an unguarded afternoon, not intended to be repeated to anyone else. She certainly would have felt deeply let down had he spoken of it freely, describing her words or experiences to friends, whatever the cause.

It was not that she thought for a moment that he was ashamed of any of his views. On the contrary. But one does not repeat what a friend says in a moment of candor, or on an occasion which is held in trust.

And yet she was painfully aware of a vulnerability in the woman who stood beside her gazing at the massed bloom of the lupines in colors of pinks and apricots, purples, blues and creams. Their perfume was almost overwhelming. Susannah was full of doubts so deep she had been unable to endure them in silence. Were they born of fear for the husband she loved, for the money invested by her mother-in-law, or by something in her own conscience?

And for Nobby, above even those considerations, was honesty, being true to her own vision of Africa and what she knew of it so deeply it had been part of her fiber, interwoven with her understanding of all things. To betray that, even for the sake of pity, would be the ultimate destruction.

Susannah was waiting, watching her face.

"You are unwilling to answer?" she said slowly. "Does that mean you believe he is right, and my husband is wrong in backing Cecil Rhodes as he does? Or is it that you know something to Mr. Kreisler's discredit, but you are unwilling to say it to another?"

"No," Nobby said firmly. "Nothing at all. It simply means that the question is too serious to be answered without thought. It is not something I should say lightly. I believe Mr. Kreisler holds his opinions with great depth, and that he is well acquainted with the subject. He is afraid that the native kings have been duped—"

"I know they have," Susannah interrupted. "Even Linus would not argue that. He says it is for a far greater good in the future, a decade from now. Africa will be settled, you know? It is impossible to turn back time and pretend that it has not been discovered. Europe knows there is gold there, and diamonds, and ivory. The question is simply who will do it. Will it be Britain, Belgium or Germany? Or far worse than that, possibly one of the Arab countries, who still practice slavery?"

"Then what is it in Mr. Kreisler's view that disturbs you?" Nobby asked with cutting frankness. "Naturally we would wish it to be Britain, not only for our benefit, quite selfishly, but more altruistically, because we believe we will do it better, instill better values, more honorable forms of government in place of what is there now, and certainly better than the slavery you mentioned."

Susannah stared at her, her eyes troubled.

"Mr. Kreisler says that we will make the Africans subject peoples in their own land. We have backed Mr. Rhodes and let him put in most of the money, and all of the effort and risk. If he succeeds, and he probably will, we shall have no control over him. We will have made him into an emperor in the middle of Africa, with our blessing. Can he be right? Does he really know so much and see so clearly?"

"I think so," Nobby said with a sad smile. "I think you have put it rather well."

"And perhaps those thoughts should frighten anyone."

Susannah twisted the handle of her parasol around and around between her fingers.

"Actually it was Sir Arthur Desmond who put it like that. Did you know him? He died about two weeks ago. He was one of the nicest men I ever knew. He used to work in the Foreign Office."

"No, I didn't know him. I'm very sorry."

Susannah stared at the lupines. A bumblebee drifted from one colored spire to another. The gardener passed across the far end of the lawn with a barrow full of weeds and disappeared towards the kitchen garden.

"It is absurd to mourn someone I only saw half a dozen times a year," Susannah went on with a sigh. "But I'm afraid that I do. I have an awful sadness come over me when I think that I shall not see him again. He was one of those people who always left one feeling better." She looked at Nobby to see if she understood. "It was not exactly a cheerfulness, more a sense that he was ultimately sane, in a world which is so often cheap in its values, shallow in its judgment, too quick to be crushed, laughs at all the wrong things, and is never quite optimistic enough."

"He was obviously a most remarkable man," Nobby said gently. "I am not surprised you grieve for him, even if you

saw him seldom. It is not the time you spend with someone, it is what happens in that time. I have known people
for years, and yet never met the real person inside, if there
is one. Others I have spoken with for only an hour or two,
and yet what was said had meaning and honesty that will
last forever." She had not consciously thought of anyone in
particular when she began to speak, and yet it was
Kreisler's face in the sunlight on the river that filled her
mind.

"It was . . . very sudden." Susannah touched one of the
early roses with her fingertips. "Things can change so
quickly, can't they. . . ."

"Indeed." The same thought was filling Nobby's mind;
not only circumstances but also emotions. Yesterday had
been cloudless; now she was unable to prevent the flickers
of doubt that entered her mind. Susannah was obviously
deeply troubled, torn in her loyalties between her husband's
plans and the questions that Kreisler had raised in her. She
did not want to think he was right, and yet the fear was in
her face, the angle of her body, the hand tight on the parasol, holding it as if it were a weapon, not an ornament.

Exactly what had he said to her, and perhaps more urgently than that, why? He was not naive, to have spoken
carelessly. He knew who she was, and he knew Linus
Chancellor's part in raising the additional financing and the
government backing for Cecil Rhodes. He knew Susannah's
relationship to Francis Standish and her own inheritance in
the banking business. She had to have been familiar with at
least some of the details. Was he seeking information from
her? Or was he planting in her mind the seeds of disinfor-
mation, lies and half truths for her to take back to Linus
Chancellor and the Colonial Office, ultimately the Prime
Minister himself? Kreisler was a German name. Perhaps for
all his outward Englishness, it was not Britain's interests in
Africa he had at heart, but Germany's?

Maybe he was using them both, Susannah and Nobby?

She was surprised how profoundly that thought hurt, like a gouging wound inside.

Susannah was watching her, her wide eyes full of uncertainty, and the beginnings of just as deep a pain. There was a spirit between them of perfect understanding. For an instant Nobby knew that Susannah also was facing a disillusion so bitter the fear of it filled her mind with darkness. Then as quickly it was gone again, and a new thought took its place. Surely Susannah could not also be in love with Peter Kreisler? Could she?

Also? What on earth was she saying to herself? She was attracted ... that was all. She barely knew the man ... memories in common, a dream that had found them both in youth, enough to take them separately upon the same great adventure into a dark continent in which they had found a light and a brilliance, a land to love, and had come home with its fever and magic forever within them. And now they both feared for it.

One afternoon on the river when understanding had been too complete to need words, only a few hours out of a lifetime—enough to call enchantment, not love. Love was less ephemeral, less full of magic.

"Miss Gunne?"

She jerked herself back to the garden and Susannah.

"Yes?"

"Do you think Mr. Rhodes is just using us? That he will build his own empire in Central Africa, turn Zambezia into Cecil Rhodes land, and then cock a snook at us all? He would have the wealth to do it. No one can imagine the gold and the diamonds there, quite apart from the land, the ivory, timber and whatever else there is. It is teeming with beasts, so they say, creatures of every kind imaginable."

"I don't know." Nobby shivered involuntarily, as if the garden had suddenly become cold. "But it is certainly not impossible." There was no other answer she could give. Susannah did not deserve a lie, nor would she be likely to believe one.

"You say that very carefully." The ghost of a smile crossed Susannah's face.

"It is a very large thought, and one too dangerous to treat with less than care. But if you look back even a little way through history, many of our greatest conquests, and most successful, have been largely at the hands of one man," Nobby answered. "Clive in India is perhaps the best example."

"Yes, of course you are right." Susannah turned and looked up the long lawn towards the house. "And I have been here the better part of an hour. Thank you for being so . . . generous." But she did not say that she felt better or clearer in her mind, and Nobby was sure that it was not so.

She walked back towards the French doors to the house with her, not because she was expecting further callers, thank goodness—she was in no mood for them—but out of a sense of friendship, even a futile desire to protect someone she believed desperately vulnerable.

To those making the very most of the London Season, a night at the theater or the opera was positively a rest after the hectic round of riding in the park before breakfast, shopping, writing letters, seeing one's dressmaker or milliner in the morning, luncheon parties, making and receiving calls in the afternoon, or visiting dog shows, exhibitions or galleries, garden parties, afternoon teas, dinners, *conversaziones*, soirees or balls. To be able to sit in one place without having to make conversation, even to drift off into a gentle doze if so inclined, while at the same time be seen to be present, was a luxury not to be overlooked. Without it one might have collapsed from the sheer strain of it all.

However, since Vespasia had long since given up such a frantic pattern of behavior, she visited the theater purely for the pleasure of seeing whatever drama was presented. This particular May the offerings included Lillie Langtry in a new play titled *Esther Sandraz*. She had no desire to see Mrs. Langtry in anything. Gilbert and Sullivan's *The Gon-*

doliers was naturally at the Savoy. She was not in the mood for it. She would have seen Henry Irving in a work called *The Bells*, or Pinero's farce *The Cabinet Minister*. Her opinion of cabinet ministers inclined her towards that. It looked more promising than the season of French plays, in French, currently at Her Majesty's, except that Sarah Bernhardt was doing *Joan of Arc*. That was tempting.

The operas were *Carmen*, *Lohengrin* or *Faust*. She had a love for Italian opera and was not fond of Wagner's, for all its current and surprising popularity. No one had expected it to be so. Had Simon Boccanegra been playing, or Nabucco, she would have gone even if she had to stand.

As it was she settled for *She Stoops to Conquer*, and found a remarkable number of her acquaintances had made the same decision. Although it was in many ways restful, the theater was still a place for which one dressed formally, at least for the three months of the Season, from May to July. At other times it was permissible to be rather more casual.

Theater outings were frequently organized in groups. Society seldom cared to do things in ones or twos. Dozens, or even scores, suited them better.

On this occasion Vespasia had invited Charlotte for pleasure, and Eustace as a matter of duty. He had been present when she made the decision to attend, and had shown so obvious an interest it would have been pointed not to include him, and for all the intense irritation he awoke in her from time to time, he was still part of her family.

She had invited Thomas also, of course, but he had been unable to come because of the pressure of work. He would not be able to leave Bow Street sufficiently early, and to enter one's box when the play was in progress was not acceptable.

Thus it was that, long before the curtain went up, she, Charlotte and Eustace were seated in her box indulging in the highly entertaining pastime of watching the other members of the audience arrive.

"Ah!" Eustace leaned forward slightly, indicating a gray-haired man of distinguished appearance entering a box to their left. "Sir Henry Rattray. A quite excellent man. A paragon of courtesy and honor."

"A paragon?" Vespasia said with slight surprise.

"Indeed." Eustace settled back and turned towards her, smiling with intense satisfaction. In fact he looked so well pleased with himself his chest had expanded and his face seemed to glow. "He embodies those knightly virtues of courage before the foe, clemency in victory, honesty, chastity, gentleness with the fair sex, protection of the weak, which are at the foundation of all we hold dear. That is what a knight was in times past, and an English gentleman is now—the best of them, of course!" There was absolute certainty in his voice. He was making a statement.

"You must know him very well to be so adamant," Charlotte said with wonder.

"Well you certainly know much of him that I do not," Vespasia said ambiguously.

Eustace held up one finger. "Ah, my dear Mama-in-law, that is precisely the point. I do indeed know much of him that is not known to the public. He does his greatest good by stealth, as a true Christian gentleman should."

Charlotte opened her mouth to make some remark about stealing, and bit it off just in time. She looked at Eustace's serene face and felt a chill of fear. He was so supremely confident, so certain he understood exactly what he was dealing with, who they were and that they believed the same misty, idealistic picture he did. He even thought in Arthurian language. Perhaps they held their meetings at round tables—with an empty seat for the "siege perilous" in case some wandering Galahad should arrive for the ultimate quest. The cleverness of it was frightening.

"A very perfect knight," Charlotte said aloud.

"Indeed!" Eustace agreed with enthusiasm. "My dear lady, you have it exactly!"

"That was said of Lancelot," Charlotte pointed out.

"Of course." Eustace nodded, smiling. "Arthur's closest friend, his right hand and ally."

"And the man who betrayed him," Charlotte added.

"What?" Eustace swung to face her, dismay in every feature.

"With Guinevere," Charlotte explained. "Had you forgotten that? In every way it was the beginning of the end."

Eustace obviously had forgotten it. The color spread up his cheeks, both with embarrassment at the indelicacy of the subject and confusion at having been caught in such an inappropriate analogy.

To her surprise Charlotte felt sorry for him, but she could not say anything which would be interpreted as praise for the Inner Circle, which was what the whole conversation was about. Eustace was so naive, sometimes she felt as if he were a child, an innocent.

"But the ideals of the Round Table were still the finest," she said gently. "And Galahad was without sin, or he would never have seen the Holy Grail. The thing is, one may find the good and the bad together, professing the same beliefs; all of us have weaknesses, vulnerabilities, and most of us have a tendency to see what we want to in others, most especially others we admire."

Eustace hesitated.

She looked at his face, his eyes, and saw for a moment his struggle to understand what she really meant, then he abandoned it and settled for the simple answer.

"Of course, dear lady, that is undoubtedly true." He turned to Vespasia, who had been listening without comment. "Who is that remarkable woman in the box next to Lord Riverdale? I have never seen such unusual eyes. They should be handsome, they are so large, and yet they are not, I declare."

Vespasia followed his gaze, and saw Christabel Thorne, sitting beside Jeremiah and talking to him with animation. He was listening with his gaze never wavering from her face, and with not only affection but very apparent interest.

193

Vespasia told Eustace who they were. Then she pointed out Harriet Soames in company with her father, and also displaying a most open affection and pride.

It was only a few moments after that when there was something of a stir in the audience. Several heads turned and there was a cessation of general whispering, but also a sudden swift commenting one to another.

"The Prince of Wales?" Eustace wondered with a touch of excitement in his voice. As a strict moralist he would have disapproved unequivocally of the Prince of Wales's behavior in anyone else. But princes were different. One did not judge them by the standards of ordinary men. At least Eustace did not.

"No," Vespasia said rather tartly. She applied the same standards to all; princes were not exempt, and she was also fond of the Princess. "The Secretary of State of Colonial Affairs, Mr. Linus Chancellor, and his wife, and I believe her brother-in-law, Mr. Francis Standish."

"Oh." Eustace was not sure whether he was interested or not.

Charlotte had no such doubts. Ever since she and Pitt had seen Susannah Chancellor at the Duchess of Marlborough's reception, she had found her of great interest, and over-hearing her discussion with Kreisler at the Shakespearean bazaar had naturally added to it. She watched them take their seats, Chancellor attentive, courteous, but with the ease of one who is utterly comfortable in a marriage while still finding it of intense pleasure. Charlotte found herself smiling as she watched, and knowing precisely what Susannah felt with her turning of the head to accept his re-arranging of the shawl across her chair, the smile on his lips, the momentary meeting of the eyes.

The lights dimmed and the music of the national anthem began. There was no more time for wandering attention.

When the applause died down and the first interval commenced it was a different matter.

Eustace turned to Charlotte. "And how is your family?"

he enquired, but out of politeness, and to preempt any return to the subject of King Arthur, or any other society, past or present.

"They are all well, thank you," she replied.

"Emily?" he pressed.

"Abroad. Parliament is in recess."

"Indeed. And your mama?"

"Traveling also." She did not add that it was on honeymoon. That would be altogether too much for Eustace to cope with. She saw a twitch of laughter in Vespasia's mouth, and looked away. "Grandmama has moved into Ashworth House with Emily," she continued hastily. "Although of course she has no one there but the servants at present. She does not care for it at all."

"Quite." Eustace had the feeling that something had passed him by, but he preferred not to investigate it. "Would you care for some refreshment?" he offered gallantly.

Vespasia accepted, then Charlotte felt free to do so too. Obediently Eustace rose and took his leave to obtain it for them.

Charlotte and Vespasia glanced at each other, then both turned and looked, as discreetly as possible, at Linus and Susannah Chancellor. Francis Standish had gone, but there was nevertheless a third person in the box, and from the outline, quite obviously a man, tall, slender, of a very upright and military bearing.

"Kreisler," Charlotte whispered.

"I think so," Vespasia agreed.

A moment later as he half turned to speak to Susannah, they were proved right.

They could not possibly overhear the conversation, yet watching the expressions in their faces it was possible to draw very many conclusions.

Kreisler was naturally civil to Chancellor, but there was a pronounced coolness in both men, presumably due to their acknowledged political differences. Chancellor stood close to his wife, as though automatically including her in the opinions or arguments he expressed. Kreisler was not quite opposite them, a little to one side, so his face was invisible to Charlotte and Vespasia. He addressed Susannah with a sharpness of attention far more than mere good manners required, and seemed to direct his reasoning towards her rather than Chancellor, even though it was almost always Chancellor who answered.

Once or twice Charlotte noticed Susannah begin to speak, and Chancellor cut in with a reply, including her with a quick look or a gesture of the hand.

Again Kreisler would retort, always as much to her as to him.

Neither Charlotte nor Vespasia said anything, but Charlotte's mind was full of conjecture when Eustace returned. She thanked him almost absently, and sat with her drink, deep in thought, until the lights dimmed and the drama onstage recommenced.

During the second interval they left the box and went out into the foyer, where Vespasia was instantly greeted by several acquaintances, one in particular, an elderly marchioness in vivid green, with whom she spoke for some time.

Charlotte was very happy to spend her time merely watching, again finding a most absorbing subject in Linus and Susannah Chancellor and Mr. Francis Standish. She was most interested when she observed Chancellor's attention distracted for several minutes, and Standish alone with Susannah seeming to be arguing with her. From the expression on her face, she stood her ground, and he glanced angrily more than once in the direction of the far side of the foyer where Peter Kreisler was standing.

Once he took Susannah by the arm, and she shook him off impatiently. However when Chancellor returned Standish seemed to be quite satisfied that he had won, and led the way back towards their box. Chancellor smiled at Susannah with amusement and affection, and offered her his arm. She took it, moving closer to him, but there seemed to be a distress in her, some shadow across her face which haunted Charlotte so deeply she was unable to rid herself of it and enter into the rest of the play.

The next day was gusty but fine, and a little after midmorning Vespasia ordered her carriage to take her to Hyde Park. It was not necessary to stipulate that it must be near the corner by the Albert Memorial. There was only the choice between that and Marble Arch if one were to meet the members of Society who customarily took their morning rides or walks in the park. In the walk between the Albert and Grosvenor Gate one could meet everyone in Society who had elected to take the air.

Vespasia would have been perfectly happy anywhere, but she had come specifically to find Bertie Canning, an admirer. At the theater last evening her friend the marchioness had mentioned that he had a vast knowledge of people, especially those whose fame or notoriety rested on exploits in the greater part of the Empire, rather than in the confines of England. If anyone could tell her what she now quite urgently desired to know about Peter Kreisler, it was he.

She did not wish to ride: she could too easily miss Canning, and it offered no opportunity for conversation. She alighted and walked slowly and with the utmost elegance towards one of the many seats along the north side of the Row. Naturally, it was the fashionable side, where she would be able to watch in reasonable comfort as the world passed by. It was an entertainment she would enjoy at any time, even were there no purpose to it, but her observations last night, coupled with what she had overheard at the bazaar, had woken in her an anxiety she wished to satisfy as soon as possible.

She was dressed in her favorite silver-gray with touches of slate blue, and a hat of the very latest fashion. It was not unlike a riding hat, with a high crown and very slightly curled brim, and it was swathed with silk. It was extraordinarily becoming. She noticed with satisfaction that she drew the interest of several of those passing by in the lighter carriages customary at this hour, uncertain who she was, or if they should bow to her.

The Spanish ambassador and his wife were walking in the opposite direction. He touched his hat and smiled, sure he must know her, or if he did not, then he ought to.

She smiled back, amused.

Other vehicles passed by, tilburies, pony chaises, four-in-hands; small, light and elegant. Every one was exquisitely turned out, leather cleaned and polished, brasses gleaming, horses groomed to perfection. And of course the passengers and drivers were immaculate, servants in full livery, if indeed there were servants present. Many gentlemen cared to drive themselves, taking great pride in their handling of the "ribbons." Several she knew, in one way or another. But then Society was so small almost everyone had some degree of acquaintance.

She saw a European prince she had known rather better some thirty years ago, and as he strolled past they exchanged glances. He hesitated, a flash of memory in his eyes, a momentary laughter and warmth. But he was with the princess, and her peremptory hand on his arm prevailed. And perhaps the past was better left in its own cocoon of happiness, undisturbed by present realities. He passed on his way, leaving Vespasia smiling to herself, the sunlight gentle on her face.

It was nearly three quarters of an hour, spent agreeably enough, but not usefully, before she at last saw Bertie Canning. He was strolling alone, not unusually, since his wife did not care to leave the house except by carriage and he still preferred to walk. Or at least that was what he claimed. He said it was necessary for his health. Vespasia knew perfectly well he treasured the freedom it gave him, and he would still have done so had he needed two sticks to prop himself up.

She thought she might be obliged to approach him, and if so she would have done it with grace, but fortunately it was not necessary. When he saw her she smiled with more than the civility good manners required, and he seized the opportunity and came over to where she was sitting. He was a handsome man in a smooth, hearty way, and she had been fond of him in the past. It was no difficulty to appear pleased to see him.

"Good morning, Bertie. You look very well."

He was in fact nearly ten years younger than she, but time had been less generous to him. Ho was undeniably growing portly, and his face was ruddier than it had been in his prime.

"My dear Vospasia. How delightful to see you! You haven't changed in the least. How your contemporaries must loathe you! If there is anything a beautiful woman cannot abide, it is another beautiful woman who bears her years far better."

"As always, you know how to wrap a compliment a little differently," she said with a smile, at the same time moving a trifle to one side in the smallest of invitations for him to join her.

He accepted it instantly, not only for her company, but very possibly also to rest his feet. They spoke of trivia and mutual acquaintances for a few moments. She enjoyed it quite genuinely. For that little time the passage of years had no meaning. It could have been thirty years ago. The dresses were wrong—the skirts too narrow, no crinolines, no hoops; there were far too many fashionable demimondaines about, too many women altogether—but the mood was the same, the bustle, the beauty of the horses, the excitement, the May sunshine, the scent of the earth and the great trees overhead. London Society was parading and admiring itself with self-absorbed delight.

But Nobby Gunne was not twenty-five and paddling up the Congo River in a canoe; she was fifty-five, and here in London, far too vulnerable, and falling in love with a man about whom Vespasia knew very little, and feared too much.

"Bertie . . ."

"Yes, my dear?"

"You know everyone who has anything to do with Africa. . . ."

"I used to. But there are so remarkably many people now." He shrugged. "They appear out of nowhere, all kinds of people, a great many of them I would rather not know. Adventurers of the least attractive kind. Why? Have you someone in mind?"

She did not prevaricate. There was no time, and he would not expect it.

"Peter Kreisler."

A middle-aged financial magnate drove past in a four-in-hand, his wife and daughters beside him. Neither Vespasia nor Bertie Canning took any notice. An ambitious young man on a bay horse doffed his hat and received a smile of encouragement.

A young man and woman rode by together.

"Engaged at last," Bertie muttered.

Vespasia knew what he meant. The girl would not have ridden out with him were they not.

"Peter Kreisler?" she jogged his memory.

"Ah, yes. His mother was one of the Aberdeenshire Calders, I believe. Odd girl, very odd. Married a German, as I recall, and went to live there for a while. Came back eventually, I think. Then died, poor soul."

Vespasia felt a jar of sudden coldness. In other circumstances to be half German would be irrelevant. The royal family was more than half German. But with the present concern over East Africa high on her mind, and acutely relevant to the issue, it was a different matter.

"I see. What did his father do?"

A popular actor rode by, handsome profile lifted high. Vespasia thought very briefly of Charlotte's mother, Caroline, and her recent marriage to an actor seventeen years her junior. He was less handsome than this man, and a great deal more attractive. It was a scandalous thing to have done, and Vespasia heartily wished her happiness.

"No idea," Bertie confessed. "But he was a personal friend of the old chancellor, I know that."

"Bismarck?" Vespasia said with surprise and increasing unhappiness.

Bertie looked at her sideways. "Of course, Bismarck! Why are you concerned, Vespasia? You cannot know the fellow. He spends all his time in Africa. Although I suppose he could have come home. He's quarreled with Cecil Rhodes—not hard to do—and with the missionaries, who tried to put trousers on everybody and make Christians out of them . . . much more difficult."

"The trousers or the Christianity?"

"The quarrel."

"I should find it very easy to quarrel with someone who wants to put trousers on people," Vespasia replied. "Or make Christians out of them if they don't want it."

"Then you will undoubtedly like Kreisler." Bertie pulled a face.

A radical member of Parliament passed them, in deep conversation with a successful author.

"Ass," Bertie said contemptuously. "Fellow should stick to his last."

"I beg your pardon?"

"Politician who wants to write a book and a writer who wants to sit in Parliament," Bertie replied.

"Have you read his book?" Vespasia asked.

Bertie's eyebrows rose. "No. Why?"

"Terrible. And John Dacre would do less harm if he gave up his seat and wrote novels. Altogether I think it would be an excellent idea. Don't discourage them."

He stared at her with concern for a moment, then started to laugh.

"He quarreled with MacKinnon as well," he said after a moment or two.

"Dacre?" she asked.

"No, no, your fellow Kreisler. MacKinnon the money fellow. Quarreled over East Africa, of course, and what should be done there. Hasn't quarreled with Standish yet, but that's probably due to his relationship with Chancellor." Bertie frowned thoughtfully. "Not that there isn't something in what he says, dammit! Bit questionable, this chap Rhodes. Smooth tongue, but a shifty eye. Too much appetite for power, for my taste. All done in a hurry. Too fast. Too fast, altogether. Did you know Arthur Desmond, poor devil? Sound fellow. Decent. Sorry he's gone."

"And Kreisler?" She rose to her feet as she said it. It was growing a little chilly and she preferred to walk a space.

He stood and offered her his arm.

"Not sure, I'm afraid. Bit of a question mark in my mind. Not certain of his motives, if you understand?"

Vespasia understood very well.

A famous portrait artist passed by and tipped his hat to her. She smiled in acknowledgment. Someone muttered that the Prince of Wales and the Duke of Clarence were coming and there was a rustle of interest, but since they rode here fairly often, it was no more than a ripple.

An elderly man with a sallow face approached and spoke to Bertie. He was introduced, and since he obviously intended staying, Vespasia thanked Bertie Canning and excused herself. She wished to be alone with her thoughts. The little she had learned of Peter Kreisler was no comfort at all.

What were his motives in pursuing Susannah Chancellor? Why did he argue his point so persistently? He could not be so naive as to think he could influence Chancellor. He was already publicly committed to Cecil Rhodes.

Where were Kreisler's own commitments? To Africa and the self-determination he spoke of, or to German interests? Was he trying to provoke an indiscretion from which he could learn something, or to let slip his own version of facts, and mislead?

And why did he court Nobby Gunne?

* * *

Vespasia would have been a great deal unhappier had she been in the Lyric music hall and seen Nobby and Kreisler together in the stalls laughing at the comedian, watching the juggler with bated breath as he tossed plate after plate into the air, groaning at the extraordinary feats of the yellow-clad contortionist, tapping their feet with the dancing girls.

It was definitely slumming, and they were enjoying it enormously. Every few moments they exchanged glances as some joke delighted or appalled them. The political jokes were both vicious and ribald.

The last act, top of the bill, was an Irish soprano with a full, rich voice who held the audience in her hands, singing "Silver Threads Among the Gold," "Bedouin Love Song," Sullivan's "The Lost Chord," and then, to both smiles and tears, Tosti's "Good-bye."

The audience cheered her to the echo, and then when at last the curtain came down, rose from their seats and made their way outside into the warm, busy street where gas lamps flared, hooves clattered on the cobbles, people called out to passing cabs and the night air was balmy on the face and damp with the promise of rain.

Neither Nobby nor Kreisler spoke. Everything was already understood.

7

"NOTHING," TELLMAN SAID, pushing out his lip. "At least nothing that helps." He was talking about his investigation into Ian Hathaway of the Colonial Office. "Just a quiet, sober, rather bookish sort of man of middle years. Doesn't do anything much out of the ordinary." He sat down in the chair opposite Pitt without being asked. "Not so ordinary as to be without character," he went on. "He has his oddities, his tastes. He has a fancy for expensive cheeses, for example. Spends as much on a cheese as I would on a joint of beef. He hates fish. Won't eat it at any price."

Pitt frowned, sitting at his desk with the sun on his back.

"Buys plain shirts," Tellman went on. "Won't spend a farthing extra on them. Argues the toss with his shirtmaker, always very politely. But he can insist!" Tellman's face showed some surprise. "At first I thought he was a bit of a mouse, one of the quiet little men with nothing to say for themselves." His eyes widened. "But I discovered that Mr. Hathaway is a person of enough resolve when he wants to be. Always very quiet, very polite, never raises his voice to anyone. But there must be something inside him, something in his look, because the tailor didn't argue with him above a minute or two, then took a good stare at him, and all of a sudden backed down sharply, and it was all 'yes sir, Mr. Hathaway; no sir, of course not; whatever you wish, sir.' "

"He does hold a fairly senior position in the Colonial Office," Pitt pointed out.

Tellman gave a little snort, fully expressive of his derision. "I've seen more important men than him pushed around by their tailors! No sir, there's a bit more steel to our Mr. Hathaway than first looks show."

Pitt did not reply. It was more Tellman's impression than any evidence. It depended how ineffectual Tellman had originally thought him.

"Buys very nice socks and nightshirts," Tellman went on. "Very nice indeed. And more than one silk cravat."

"Extravagant?" Pitt asked.

Tellman shook his head regretfully. "Not the way you mean. Certainly doesn't live beyond his income; beneath it if anything. Takes his pleasures quietly, just the occasional dinner at his club or with friends. A stroll on the green of an evening."

"Any lady friends?"

Tellman's expression conveyed the answer without the need for words.

"What about his sons? Has he any other family, brothers or sisters?"

"Sons are just as respectable as he is, from all I can tell. Anyway, they both live abroad, but nobody says a word against them. No other family as far as I know. Certainly he doesn't call on them or write."

Pitt leaned backwards farther into the sun. "These friends with whom he dines once a week or so, who are they? Have they any connection with Africa or Germany? Or with finance?"

"Not that I can find." Tellman looked both triumphant and disgusted. It gave him some satisfaction to present Pitt with a further problem, and yet he resented his own failure. His dilemma amused Pitt.

"And your own opinion of him?" Pitt asked with the shadow of a smile.

Tellman looked surprised. It was a question he apparently had not foreseen. He was obliged to think hastily.

"I'd like to say he's a deep one with a lot hidden under the surface." His face was sour. "But I think he's just a very ordinary, bald little man with an ordinary, open and very tedious life; just like ten thousand others in London. I couldn't find any reason to think he's a spy, or anything else but what he looks."

Pitt respected Tellman's opinion. He was bigoted, full of resentments both personal and rooted in his general social status, but his judgment of crime, and a man's potential for it, was acute, and seldom mistaken.

"Thank you," he said with a sincerity that caught Tellman off guard. "I expect you are right."

Nevertheless he contrived an occasion to go to the Colonial Office and meet Hathaway for himself, simply to form an impression because he did not have one. Not to have spoken with him again would have been an omission, and with as little certainty in the case as he had, he could not afford omissions, however slight.

Hathaway's office was smaller than Chancellor's or Jeremiah Thorne's, but nevertheless it had dignity and considerable comfort. At a glance it looked as if nothing in it were new; everything had a gentle patina of age and quality. The wood shone from generations of polishing, the leather gleamed, the carpet was gently worn in a track from door to desk. The books on the single shelf were morocco bound and gold lettered.

Hathaway sat behind the desk looking benign and courteous. He was almost completely bald, with merely a fringe of short, white hair above his ears, and he was clean-shaven. His nose was pronounced and his eyes a clear, round blue. Only when one had looked at him more closely did their clarity and intelligence become apparent.

"Good morning, Superintendent," he said quietly. His

voice was excellent and his diction perfect. "How may I be of assistance to you? Please, do sit down."

"Good morning, Mr. Hathaway." Pitt accepted the offer and sat in the chair opposite the desk. It was remarkably comfortable; it seemed to envelop him as soon as he relaxed into it, and yet it was firm in all the right places. But for all the apparent ease, Hathaway was a government servant of considerable seniority. He would have no time to waste. "It is regarding this miserable business of information going astray," Pitt continued. There was no point in being evasive. Hathaway was far too clever not to have understood the import of the investigations.

There was no change whatever in Hathaway's face.

"I have given it some thought, Superintendent, but unfortunately to no avail." The shadow of a smile touched his mouth. "It is not the sort of news one can ever forget. You made fairly light of it when you spoke to me before, but I am aware that it is anything but a light matter. I do not know precisely what the material is, nor to whom it has been passed, but the principle is the same. Next time it could be something vital to British interests or well-being. And of course we do not always know who our enemies are. We may believe them friends today . . . and yet tomorrow . . ."

It was a chilling thought. The bright, comfortable room only seemed to add to the reality of it. Pitt did not know whether Hathaway was speaking in the narrow sense of Britain's enemies, or in the more general breadth of enemies in general. Arthur Desmond's face came sharply to his mind. How many of his enemies had he guessed at? How surprised would he have been had he heard the evidence at his own inquest? What faces there would have startled him, what testimony?

It was the worst of a secret society, the everyday masks behind which were hidden such different faces. There were executioners in the Inner Circle, although *murderers* would be a more honest word. They were men set apart to exact

207

the punishment the society had deemed in its best interests. Sometimes it was merely personal or financial ruin, but on rare occasions, like that of Arthur Desmond, it was death.

But who were the executioners? Even the members of his own ring almost certainly did not know. That would be necessary, both for the executioner's protection and for the efficiency of his work. He could face the victim with a smile and a handshake, and at the same time deal him a death blow. And the rest of the Inner Circle would be sworn on covenant of blood to assist him, protect him, keep silence as commanded.

Hathaway was staring at him, waiting patiently. Pitt forced his mind back to the African information.

"Of course, you are quite right," he said hastily. "It is one of the bitterest of realities. We have traced a great deal from its arrival in the Colonial Office until it is stored permanently. I believe I know everyone who has access to it. . . ."

Hathaway smiled sourly. "But of course it is more than one person. I presume I am suspect?"

"You are one of those who is privy to the information," Pitt conceded guardedly. "I have no more cause to consider you than that. I believe you have a son in Central Africa?"

"Yes, my son Robert is in the mission field." There was very little expression in Hathaway's face. It was impossible to tell if he were proud of his son's vocation or not. The light in his eyes might have been pleasure, or love, or indulgence, or merely a reflection of the sunlight streaming through the window to his left. There was nothing in his gentle voice but good manners, and the slight anxiety the subject of Pitt's call required.

"Where?" Pitt asked.

This time a flicker crossed Hathaway's face. "The shores of Lake Nyasa."

Pitt had been studying the atlas. The coast of Africa was fairly well charted, with some few exceptions, but there were vast areas inland which were crossed by only a few tracks. Features were put in tentatively: tracks from east to west, the trails of the great explorers, a lake here, a range of mountains there. But most of it was borderless, regions no cartographer had seen or measured, perhaps no white man had trodden. He knew Lake Nyasa was close to the area which Cecil Rhodes would claim, and where Zimbabwe, the city of black gold, was fabled to be.

Hathaway was watching him closely, his round, pale eyes seeing everything.

"That is the area with which you are concerned." He made it a statement rather than a question. He did not move, nor did his face change appreciably, but there was a sudden deepening of his concentration. "Superintendent, let us stop playing games of words with each other. Unless you correct me, I shall assume that it is the German interest in Mashonaland and Matabeleland which concerns you. I am aware we are negotiating a new treaty on the zones of influence, that Heligoland is involved, that the fall of Chancellor Dismarck has affected matters substantially, and that Carl Peterson and the German presence in Zanzibar, the rebellion there and its swift and bloody repression, are features of great importance. So also must be Mr. Rhodes's expedition from the Cape, and his negotiations with Mr. Kruger and the Boers. We should be considerably disadvantaged in our position if all we know were also to be known to the Kaiser."

Pitt said nothing. There was no sound from beyond the windows, which overlooked not the street or the park but a more enclosed courtyard.

Hathaway smiled a little and settled farther back in his seat "This is not merely a matter of someone seeking a dishonest personal advantage in gold or diamond investments," he said gravely. "This is treason. All private considerations must be forgotten in an effort to find the man who would do this." His voice was no louder, no higher, yet there was a subtle change in its timbre, a passionate sincerity. He had not moved, but his physical presence was charged with energy.

It would have been pointless to deny the truth. Pitt would not have been believed; he would simply have insulted the man opposite him and driven a wedge of evasion between them.

"One of the problems with treason," Pitt replied slowly, choosing his words with care, "is that once we know it is there, it makes us distrust everyone. Sometimes the suspicion will do almost as much damage as the act itself. Our fears may cripple us as effectively as the truth."

Hathaway's eyes widened. "How perceptive of you, Superintendent. Indeed, that is so. But are you saying that you consider it possible there is no treason, simply a clever semblance of it, in order that we should so maim ourselves?" There was surprise in his voice, but also a slow realization that it could be the truth. "Then who has planted it?"

Footsteps passed by in the corridor, hesitated, then continued.

Pitt shook his head fractionally. "I meant only that we must not make it worse than it is, not do his work for him by causing suspicion where there are no grounds. Those with access to the information are few."

"But they are highly placed," Hathaway deduced immediately. "Thorne, myself, or Chancellor! Dear heaven, if it is Chancellor, we are in a desperate pass." There was humor in his face. "And I know it was not I."

"There are other possibilities," Pitt said quickly. "But few. Aylmer, for example. Or Arundell. Or Leicester."

"Aylmer. Ah yes, I had forgotten him. A young man, relatively speaking, and ambitious. He has not yet fulfilled all his family expects of him. That can be a powerful spur to a man." His eyes did not move from Pitt's face. "I am increasingly grateful as I grow older that my mother was a mild creature whose only dream for her sons was that they marry agreeable women, and I was fortunate to oblige her in that while still in my twenties." He smiled for a moment with recollection, but his unusual eyes met Pitt's again with total directness. "I don't doubt that you are here to speak to me in an effort to make some assessment of my character, but beyond that elementary exercise, is there some practical way in which I can assist you?"

Pitt had already made up his mind.

"Yes, Mr. Hathaway, if you would. I have ascertained that much of this information comes first to you, even before it reaches Mr. Chancellor."

"It does. I think I perceive what you have in mind: to change it in some way that will not cause great damage, and disseminate different versions of it to Chancellor, Aylmer, Thorne, Arundell and Leicester, and yet keep the original for Lord Salisbury, to prevent the possibility of a serious error." He pushed out his lip. "It will need some thought, I shall have to find just the right piece of information, but I can see it has to be done." He looked eager as he said it, almost relieved to have some part to play.

Pitt could not help smiling. "If it would be possible? And the sooner it is done, the sooner we may achieve a result."

"Indeed! Yes, it must be done with care, or it will be obvious." He sat forward in his chair again. "It must tally with all the information we already possess, or at least it must not contradict it. I shall keep you informed, Superintendent." He smiled with frankness and a kind of intense, energetic happiness brimming inside him.

Pitt thanked him again and rose to take his leave, still uncertain if he had been wise, but knowing of nothing better to precipitate matters. He had not yet told Matthew or Assistant Commissioner Farnsworth of his intention.

"You did what?" Farnsworth said, his face aghast. "Good God, man, do you realize what could happen as a result of this . . . this . . ."

"No," Pitt said brazenly. "What could happen?"

Farnsworth stared at him. "Well the very least of it is

211

that misinformation could be passed to ministers of Her Majesty's government! In fact it most certainly will be!"

"Only to Chancellor . . ."

"Only? Only Chancellor!" Farnsworth's face was deep pink. "Do you realize he is the senior minister responsible for colonial affairs? The British Empire covers a quarter of the face of the earth! Have you no sense of what that means? If Chancellor is misinformed, heaven knows what damage could follow."

"None at all," Pitt replied. "The information being changed is trivial. Hathaway knows the truth, and so will the Foreign Secretary. No decisions will be implemented without reference to one or the other of them, probably to both."

"Possibly," Farnsworth said reluctantly. "All the same, it was damned high-handed of you, Pitt. You should have consulted me before you did this. I doubt the Prime Minister will approve of it at all."

"If we don't provoke something of the sort," Pitt replied, "we are unlikely to find out who is passing information before the treaty has to be concluded."

"Not very satisfactory." Farnsworth bit his lip. "I had hoped you would have learned something definite by ordinary investigation." They were in Farnsworth's office. He had sent for Pitt to report on his progress so far. The weather had changed and sharp spring rain was beating against the windows. Pitt's trouser bottoms were damp from the splashing of passing carriages and cabs. He sat with his legs crossed, deliberately relaxed.

Farnsworth leaned over his desk, his brows drawn down. "You know, Pitt, you've made one or two foolish mistakes, but it is not too late to amend them."

"Too late?" For a moment Pitt did not understand him.

"You have had to do this alone, against a largely hostile and suspicious background," Farnsworth went on, watching Pitt's face earnestly. "You have gone in as an intruder, a policeman among diplomats and politicians, civil servants."

212

Pitt stared at him, not sure if he were leaping to absurd conclusions, a familiar darkness now at the edge of his mind.

"There are those who would have helped you!" Farnsworth's voice dropped, a more urgent note in it, deeper, wavering between harshness and hope. "Men who know more than you or I could expect to learn in a year of investigation with questions and deductions. I offered it to you before, Pitt. I'm offering it again."

The Inner Circle. Farnsworth was pressing him to join the Inner Circle, as he had almost as soon as Pitt had succeeded Micah Drummond. Pitt had refused then, and hoped the offer would not be repeated or referred to. Perhaps he should have known that was a willful blindness, a foolishness in which he should not have indulged. It was always there to be faced now or later.

"No," Pitt said quietly. "My reasons are still the same. The help would be at too high a price."

Farnsworth's face hardened. "You are very unwise, Pitt. Nothing would be asked of you that a decent, patriotic man would not willingly give. You are denying yourself success, and promotion when the time comes." He leaned forward a fraction farther. "With the right help, you know, there is no limit to where you could go. All manner of doors would eventually be opened to you! You would be able to succeed on merit. And you have merit! Otherwise the rules of Society will make it impossible for you. You must be aware of that! How can you not see the good in such a thing?" It was a demand for an answer, and his blue-gray eyes met Pitt's unflinchingly.

Pitt was aware not only of the strength of will behind the calm, almost bland countenance, but suddenly of an intelligence he had not previously suspected. He realized that until that moment he had had a certain contempt for Farnsworth, an unconscious assumption that he held office because of birth, not ability. Farnsworth's lack of understanding of certain issues, certain characteristics or turns of

213

phrase, he had taken for slowness of mind. It came to him with a jolt that it was far more probably a narrowness of experience. He was one of the vast numbers of people who cannot imagine themselves into the class or gender, least of all the emotions, of a different person. That is lack of vision or sensitivity, even compassion, but it is not stupidity.

"You are favoring one closed group which favors its own, over another doing just the same," he replied with a candor he had not shown Farnsworth before, and even as he said it he was aware he was treading on the edge of danger.

Farnsworth's impatience was weary and only peripherally annoyed. Perhaps he had expected little more. "I'm all for idealism, Pitt, but only to a point. When it becomes divorced from reality it ceases to be any use and becomes an encumbrance." He shook his head. "This is how the world works. If you don't know that, I confess I don't understand how you have succeeded as far as you have. You deal with crime every day of your life. You see the worst in humanity, the weakest and the ugliest. How is it you are so blind to higher motives, men who cooperate together to bring about a greater good, from which in the end we shall all benefit?"

Pitt would like to have said that he did not believe the motives of the leaders of the Inner Circle were anything of the sort. Originally, perhaps, they had had a vision of good, but it was now so interwoven with their own power to bring it about, and their own glory in its achievement, that too much of it was lost on the way. But he knew that saying as much would not sway Farnsworth, who had too much invested in believing as he did. It would only produce denial and conflict.

And yet for an instant there was understanding on the edge of his mind, a moment when some sympathy between them was possible. He should grasp it. There was a moral and a human imperative to try.

"It is not a question of the justice or honor of those goals," he replied slowly. "Either for themselves or for others. And I don't doubt that many people would benefit from much of what they bring about. . . ."

Farnsworth's face lit with eagerness. He almost interrupted, then disciplined himself to wait for Pitt to finish.

"It is that they decide what is good, without telling the rest of us," Pitt continued, choosing his words with great care. "And they bring it about by secret means. If it is good, we benefit, but if it is not, if it is not what we wanted, by the time we know, it is too late." He leaned forward unconsciously. "There is no stopping it, no redress, because we don't know who to blame or to whom we can appeal. It denies the majority of us, all of us outside the Circle, the right or the chance to choose for ourselves."

Farnsworth looked puzzled, a crease between his brows.

"But you can be in the Circle, man. That is what I'm offering you."

"And everyone else?" Pitt said. "What about their choices?"

Farnsworth's eyes widened. "Are you really suggesting that everyone else, the majority"—he raised his hand to indicate the mass of population beyond the office walls—"are able to understand the issues, let alone make a decision as to what is right, wise, profitable . . . or even possible?" He saw Pitt's face. "No, of course you aren't. What you're suggesting is anarchy. Every man for himself. And God knows, perhaps every woman and every child too?"

Until now Pitt had acted on a passionate instinct, not needing to rationalize what he thought; no one had required it of him.

"There is a difference between the open power of government and the secret power of a society whose members no one knows," he said with commitment. He saw the derision in Farnsworth's face. "Of course there can be oppression, corruption, incompetence, but if we know who holds the power, then they are to some degree accountable. We can at least fight against what we can see."

"Rebellion," Farnsworth said succinctly. "Or if we fight

against it secretly, then treason! Is that really what you prefer?"

"I don't want the overthrow of a government." Pitt would not be goaded into taking a more extreme position than he meant. "But I have no objection to its downfall, if that is what it merits."

Farnsworth's eyebrows rose.

"In whose judgment? Yours?"

"The majority of the people who are governed."

"And you think the majority is right?" Farnsworth's eyes were wide. "That it is informed, wise, benevolent and self-disciplined or, God damn it, even literate—"

"No, I don't," Pitt interrupted. "But it can't ever be if it is governed in secret by those who never ask and never explain. I think the majority have always been decent people, and have the right, as much right as you or anyone else, to know their own destiny and have as much control over it as is possible."

"Consistent with order"—Farnsworth sat back, his smile sardonic—"and the rights and privileges of others. Quite. We have no difference in aim, Pitt, only in how to achieve it. And you are hopelessly naive. You are an idealist, quite out of touch with the reality both of human nature and of economics and business. You would make a good politician on the hustings, telling the people all the things they want to hear, but you'd be hopeless in office." He crossed his hands, interlacing his fingers, and gazing at Pitt with something close to resignation. "Perhaps you are right not to accept the offer of membership in the Inner Circle. You haven't the stomach for it, or the vision. You'll always be a gamekeeper's son at heart."

Pitt was not certain whether that was intended as an insult or not; the words were, judging from Farnsworth's voice, and yet the tone was disappointed rather than deliberately offensive.

He stood up. "I expect you're right," he conceded, surprised that he minded so little. "But gamekeepers protect and preserve what is good." He smiled. "Is that not what you have been talking about?"

Farnsworth looked startled. He opened his mouth to dismiss the idea, then realized its truth and changed his mind.

"Good day, sir," Pitt said from the doorway.

There was only one thing Pitt could profitably do regarding the Colonial Office. The routine investigation of associates, personal habits, the search for weakness, could be accomplished as well by Tellman and his men as by Pitt himself. Not that he expected any of it to yield much of value. But quite apart from that, Arthur Desmond's death still filled his thoughts in every quiet moment and the underlying sadness was with him all the time. It grew gradually more compelling that he should resolve what he could, for Matthew's sake and for his own.

Charlotte had said little to him on the subject, but her unusual silence was more eloquent than speech. She had been gentle with him, more patient than was characteristic, as if she were sensitive not only to his loss but to his awareness of guilt. He was grateful for it. He would have found her criticism painful, because it would have been fair, and when one is most vulnerable, one is also the least able to bear the wound.

But he also longed to return to the frankness that was more natural to both of them.

He began with General Anstruther, and was obliged to pursue him from one of his clubs to a second, and ultimately find him in a quiet reading room of a third. Or it would be more accurate to say he was informed by the steward that General Anstruther was there. Pitt, not being a member, was not permitted into that very private and privileged sanctuary.

"Would you please ask General Anstruther if he can spare me a few moments of his time?" Pitt said politely, hating having to beg. He had no authority in this case, and could not use his office to insist. It galled him far more than he should have allowed it to.

"I will ask him, sir," the steward replied expressionlessly. "Who may I say is asking?"

"Superintendent Pitt, of Bow Street." Pitt handed him his card.

"Very well, sir. I shall enquire." And leaving Pitt standing in the large and extremely opulent hall, he retreated upstairs, carrying the card on a silver tray.

Pitt gazed around the walls at the marble busts of long-dead soldiers and saw Marlborough, Wellington, Moore, Wolfe, Hastings, Clive, Gordon, and two he did not recognize. It crossed his mind with amusement, but no surprise, that Cromwell was not there. Above the doors were the arms of Richard Coeur de Lion, and Henry V. On the farther wall was a somber and very fine painting of the burial of Moore after Corunna, and opposite, another of the charge of the Scots Greys at Waterloo. More recent battle honors hung from the high ceiling, from Inkermann, the Alma and Balaclava.

General Anstruther came down the stairs, white whiskers bristling, his face pink, his back stiff as a ramrod.

"Good day to you, sir. What can I do for you?" He made it almost a demand. "Must be damned urgent to seek a fellow out at his club, what?"

"It is not urgent, General Anstruther, but I think it is important," Pitt replied respectfully. "And I can get the information accurately from no one else, or I should not have troubled you."

"Indeed! Indeed. And what is it, Mr. . . . . Superintendent? Unless it is very brief, we can hardly stand around here like a couple of butlers, what. Come into the guests' room." He waved a heavy, florid hand towards one of the many oak doors off the hallway, and Pitt followed him obediently.

The room was filled with extremely comfortable armchairs, but the pictures and general decor were forbidding, perhaps to remind visitors of the military grandeur of the club's members and the utter inferiority of civilians permitted in on sufferance.

General Anstruther indicated one of the chairs, and as Pitt sat down, took the one opposite him and leaned back, crossing his legs.

"Well then, Superintendent, what is it that troubles you?"

Pitt had thought carefully what he should say.

"The matter of the death of the late Sir Arthur Desmond," he replied candidly. He saw Anstruther's face tighten, but continued speaking. "There have been certain questions asked, and I wish to be in possession of all the facts so that I can refute any unpleasant or unwarranted suggestions that may be made."

"By whom, sir? Suggestions of what?" Anstruther demanded. "Explain yourself, sir. This is most unfortunate."

"Indeed it is," Pitt agreed. "The suggestions are concerning his sanity, and the possibility of either suicide or—just as bad—murder."

"Good God!" Anstruther was genuinely shocked; there was nothing assumed in the horror in his face, the slackness of initial disbelief, and then the growing darkness in his eyes as all the implications came to him. "That's scandalous! Who has dared to say such a thing? I demand to know, sir!"

"At the moment it is no more than suggestion, General Anstruther," Pitt replied, somewhat mendaciously. "I wish to be in a position to refute it decisively if it should ever become more."

"That's preposterous! Why should anyone murder Desmond? Never knew a more decent chap in my life."

"I don't doubt that is true, until the last few months," Pitt said with more confidence than he felt. He had a growing fear in his mind that Anstruther's outrage might be so deep as to prompt him to complain in a manner which would reach Farnsworth's ears, and then Pitt would be in serious trouble. Perhaps he had overstated his case and brought about more harm than good?

It was too late to go back.

"Well ..." Anstruther said guardedly. "Ah—yes." He was obviously remembering what he had said at the inquest. "That is true—up to a point."

"That is what I am worried about." Pitt felt he had regained a little ground. "Just how erratic was his behavior, sir? You were naturally very discreet at the inquest, as becomes a friend speaking in a public place. But this is private, and for quite a different purpose."

"Well ... I hardly know what to say, sir." Anstruther looked confounded.

"You said earlier that Sir Arthur was forgetful and confused," Pitt prompted him. "Can you give me instances?"

"I ... er. One doesn't choose to remember such things, man! For heaven's sake, one overlooks the failings of one's friends. One does not commit them to memory!"

"You don't remember any instance?" Pitt felt a stirring of hope, too thin to rely on, too bright to ignore.

"Well ... er ... it is more of an impression than a catalog of events, don't you know, what?" Anstruther was now thoroughly unhappy.

Pitt had the sudden sharp impression that he was lying. He did not actually know anything at all. He had been repeating what he had been told by fellow members of the Inner Circle.

"When did you last see Sir Arthur?" he asked quite gently. Anstruther was embarrassed. There was no point in making an enemy of him; then he would learn nothing.

"Ah ..." Anstruther was pink-faced now. "Not certain. Events put it rather out of my mind. I do recall quite plainly dining with him about three weeks before he died, poor fellow." His voice gained in confidence. He was on firm ground now. "Seemed to me to have changed a lot. Rambling on about Africa."

"Rambling?" Pitt interrupted. "You mean he was incoherent, disconnected in his ideas?"

"Ah—that's a little steep, sir. Not at all. I mean simply

that he kept returning to the subject, even when the rest of us had clearly passed on to something else."

"He was a bore?"

Anstruther's eyes widened. "If you like, sir, yes. He didn't know when to leave the matter alone. Made a lot of accusations that were most unfortunate. Quite unfounded, of course."

"Were they?"

"Good heavens, of course they were." Anstruther was appalled. "Talked about secret plots to conquer Africa, and God knows what else. Quite mad—delusory."

"You are profoundly familiar with Africa, sir?" Pitt did his best to keep every shred of sarcasm out of his voice and thought he succeeded.

"What?" Anstruther was startled. "Africa? What makes you say that, Superintendent?"

"That you know that there are no conspiracies regarding the financial backing of settlement there. There is a great deal of money involved, and presumably fortunes to be made by those who obtain mineral rights."

"Ah . . . well . . ." Anstruther had been about to dismiss the idea in anger, then just in time realized that he had no grounds for it at all, however repugnant the idea was to him. Pitt watched the changing emotions in his face, and knew that his reactions to Sir Arthur's charges were from the heart rather than the head, a plain man's disbelief and horror of intrigue, complexities he did not understand and corruption he despised.

"I hope it is not true," Pitt said gently. "But the belief in it does not seem so farfetched to me that one might consider it madness. Boundless wealth usually draws adventurers and thieves as well as honest men. And the prospect of such power has corrupted people before. Sir Arthur, as a politician, would be familiar with some of the scandals of the past, and not unnaturally fear for the future."

Anstruther drew in his breath. His face was even pinker and he was obviously struggling between loyalties. Pitt did not know whether one of them was to the Inner Circle, but he believed it was. In all probability he saw it as Farnsworth had described it to Pitt: an organization of intelligent, enlightened men banded together to bring about the best good of the country, including the majority of blind and foolish men and women who could not decide for themselves, having neither the knowledge nor the wisdom. Honor and duty required that those who had these qualities should protect them for their own good. Anstruther would have given oaths of loyalty, and he was a man born and bred to unquestioning loyalties. A lifetime in the army had ingrained in his being obedience without question. Desertion was a capital offense, the last and most terrible sin of which a man was capable.

And yet now he was faced with truth he could not deny, and both his innate sense of honor and his general decency were at war with his sworn allegiances and his lifetime habit.

Pitt waited for him to find his resolution.

Outside in the street a hansom drew up and a short man in military uniform stepped out, paid the driver, and came up the stairs to the club. A four-in-hand drove by at a brisk trot.

"What you say, sir, is probably true," Anstruther conceded with great difficulty, the words forced out of him. "Perhaps it was not so much that poor Desmond was convinced of conspiracy that was ridiculous, as it was the men whom he charged. That, sir, was undoubtedly beyond the bounds of reason. Decent men, fine and honorable men I have known all my life." His face was suffused with color, and his voice rang with the absolute conviction that he was right. "Men who have served their fellows, their country, their queen, without recognition or gain, sir."

Only secret and unquestioned power, Pitt thought to himself, perhaps the headiest reward of all. But he did not say so.

"I can imagine that that was extremely offensive to you, General," he said instead.

"Extremely, sir," Anstruther agreed vehemently. "Most distressing. Liked Desmond for years. Most agreeable chap. Decent, what. Tragedy he should come to such an end. Damned tragedy." He was at last satisfied with his own resolution to the dilemma, and he faced Pitt squarely, allowing his emotion to fire his words. That at least was unquestioned and presented no problems at all. "Very sorry," he went on. "Sorry for the family, dammit. I hope you manage to keep this thing quiet, sir. Use your discretion. Nobody needs to know. Let it be buried. Best thing. Best thing altogether, for everyone. Nobody believed the nonsense he spoke in the end. No harm done, what!"

Pitt rose. "Thank you for your time, General Anstruther. You have been most frank, and I appreciate it, sir."

"Least I can do. Painful matter." Anstruther rose also and accompanied Pitt to the door and into the hallway. "Best set to rest. Good day to you, Superintendent."

"Good day, General Anstruther."

Outside in the street in the broad May sunshine Pitt had a strange feeling of light headedness. He barely noticed the carriages and horses passing by, or the fashionable woman who brushed his elbow as he strode along the footpath. He was just off Piccadilly, and there was a faint sound of music coming from Green Park.

He walked rapidly without realizing it, a spring in his step. Anstruther had said what he had most hoped. Sir Arthur was not irrational; simply startling, disturbing and profoundly unwelcome. Anstruther was a decent man caught in a situation he could not handle. He was not used to complex loyalties which vied with each other. He was incapable of rethinking his values, his friendships and his trust without a wrench to his mind he would do everything in his power to avoid.

There was no proof in what he had learned, except in his

own mind, and perhaps his emotions would be more at rest. Sir Arthur was vindicated . . . at least so far.

Next he found the Honorable William Osborne. He was an entirely different manner of man. It was late afternoon before he would receive Pitt, and then it was at his own house in Chelsea. It was opulent, close to the banks of the Thames and in a lushly shaded garden along a quiet tree-lined street. He greeted Pitt with impatience. Obviously he had an engagement for the evening and resented the interruption.

"I have no idea what I can do for you, Mr. Pitt." He was standing in his oak-paneled library, into which Pitt had been shown, and he did not sit down himself nor offer a seat. There was no mistaking that he did not intend the interview to be long enough to require one. "I said all I know about this unfortunate affair at the inquest, which is a matter of public record. I know nothing else, nor would I be inclined to discuss it if I did."

"You testified that Sir Arthur had recently expressed some irrational opinions," Pitt said with an effort to keep his temper.

"As I have just said, Mr. Pitt, that is a matter of public record." He was standing in the middle of the blue Turkish carpet, rocking very slightly on the balls of his feet. He reminded Pitt vaguely of a more ill-tempered Eustace March.

"Can you tell me what these opinions were, sir?" Pitt asked, looking directly at him but keeping his voice light and his tone courteous.

"I don't wish to repeat them," Osborne replied. "They were ludicrous, and to no one's credit."

"It is important that I know," Pitt insisted.

"Why?" Osborne's rather thin eyebrows rose. "The man is dead. How could it matter now what nonsense he said in his last few months?"

"Since he is dead," Pitt said quietly and very firmly, "he cannot now withdraw them." He made a rash decision. He smiled very slightly. "There are men of goodwill, honorable men who prefer to remain anonymous, whose names he has slandered, by implication if not directly. I know that you understand what I am saying, sir. Mr. Farnsworth . . ."—he pronounced the name carefully—"is concerned that no taint should linger. . . ." He let the suggestion speak for itself.

Osborne stared at him, his dark gray eyes hard and level.

"Then why the devil didn't you say so, sir? There's no need to be so coy."

Pitt felt his stomach lurch. Osborne had understood him and believed the lie. He thought he was speaking to a fellow member of the Inner Circle.

"I am used to being careful," Pitt replied with a modicum of truth. "It is a habit hard to forget."

"Has its uses," Osborne conceded. "Very bad business. Of course the wretched fellow was making all sorts of rash accusations. Had hold of the wrong end of the stick altogether." His face was tight, his lips a thin line. "No vision. No vision at all. Decent enough chap, but bourgeois at heart. Totally impractical. A well-intentioned fool can do more real harm than a wagonload of villains who know what they are about!" He looked at Pitt dourly. There was still a suspicion in him. In his judgment Pitt was not Inner Circle material. He was neither a gentleman nor a loyal servant.

On both points he had made, he was correct. Pitt had no desire to argue the first. The second was another matter.

"I agree with you, sir," he said honestly. "A well-intentioned fool can be extremely dangerous, if given power, and frequently brings about the downfall of many others, although it may be the last of his intentions."

Osborne looked surprised. Apparently he had not expected Pitt to agree with him. He grunted. "Then you will take my point, sir." He stopped abruptly. "Precisely what is it you wish to know, and who is in danger of being slandered by all this wretched nonsense?"

"I should prefer not to give names," Pitt answered. "And

in truth, I do not know them all. In the interest of discretion, much of it was kept from me."

"Rightly so." Osborne nodded. After all, Pitt might be a member, but he was merely a person of use. "The charges Sir Arthur made were that certain gentlemen, our friends, were secretly organized together to fund a settlement expedition in Central Africa," he explained, "which would at once exploit both the native African tribal leaders and the British government's financial and moral backing in the venture. The suggestion was that when the settlement proved successful, and vast wealth was found, both real and potential, then they would profit unfairly, in terms of money and of political power in the new country to be established, nominally under British suzerainty, but in fact a law unto itself. And then they would prevent others from sharing in this fortune by excluding them, by means of these secret dealings and agreements." Osborne's face was bleak and angry, and he stared at Pitt, waiting for his response.

"That was a very foolish thing to have said," Pitt replied with honesty, even though he believed it was almost certainly true. "He had undoubtedly lost a grip upon reality."

"Absolutely," Osborne agreed fervently. "Totally absurd! And irresponsible, dammit. He might have been believed."

"I doubt it," Pitt said with a sudden rush of bitterness. "It is a truly appalling thought, and very few people believe what they do not wish to, particularly if it is nothing they have feared before, even in nightmare, and there is no evidence of it to prove it true."

Osborne looked at him narrowly, as if he suspected sarcasm, but Pitt's eyes were guileless. He felt no compunction at all in being as devious as he could, or in quite plainly lying.

Osborne cleared his throat.

"That is all I have to tell you, Pitt. I know of nothing else. Africa is not my field of expertise."

"That has been most helpful, thank you, sir," Pitt conceded. "I think it possible I may be able to establish the truth with a little more assistance from others. Thank you for your time, sir. Good day."

"Good day to you." Osborne drew breath as if to add something further, then changed his mind.

By the time Pitt had found Calvert, the third man who had given evidence at the inquest, it was late, and in spite of being mid-May, nearly dark. He heard a similar story from him, full of hearsay, confusion, accusations repeated with outrage, ignorance of Africa except that somehow it should be British by right, moral if not political.

Pitt was so weary his feet were sore and he found he had unconsciously clenched his shoulders and his jaw till his throat ached. It was all nebulous, a matter of impressions, assumptions springing from anger, and a sense of having been betrayed by someone they should have been able to trust. For all the words of pity, the blame was there all the time. Arthur Desmond had made public suggestions, true or false, that they were corrupt. Men who should have given them respect would now not do so. People who should not even have guessed at the existence of the Inner Circle would wonder and speculate about it. That had been the greatest sin in the man's view, the spreading before the general gaze of that which should have been private. No matter what the sin or the crime, one did not wash one's linen in public. It was not the act of a gentleman. If you could not rely upon a gentleman to behave like one, what was there left of worth?

Pitt did not know if the man was a member of the Inner Circle or not. What he had said could simply have been a class loyalty. So could what Osborne had said, for that matter, but he was almost certain of Osborne.

Who else? Hathaway, Chancellor, Thorne, Aylmer? Of Farnsworth there was no doubt, and he loathed Farnsworth. But he had loved Arthur Desmond all his life, and he had been a member. So had Micah Drummond, whom he had grown to like immensely and to trust without question. He should talk to him. He was probably the only person who could help. Even as he lengthened his stride along the footpath, his decision was made. He would go now!

Membership had now been offered to Pitt. It was not exclusive to gentlemen. Anyone might be a member, might even be the executioner. It could have been the steward of the club, or the manager. Or the doctor who was called.

He was walking briskly and the night was balmy. He should have been warm, but he was not. He was chilled inside, and his legs were so tired every step required an effort of will, but he was determined to see Drummond, and the sense of purpose lent him strength.

A hansom came around the corner too quickly and he was obliged to move sharply out of its way, knocking into a stout man who had not been looking where he was going.

"Have a care, sir!" he said furiously, facing Pitt with bulging eyes. He held a heavy carved walking stick in one hand, and he gripped it tightly as if he would have raised it to defend himself if necessary.

"Look where you are going, and I won't need to!" Pitt said.

"Why you ruffian!" The man lifted the end of the stick a foot off the ground in a threatening gesture. "How dare you speak to me like that. I'll call the police, sir! And I'll warn you, I know how to use this, if you force me."

"I am the police! And if you touch me with that thing, I'll arrest you and charge you with assault. As it is, keep a civil tongue in your head or I'll charge you with being a public nuisance."

The man was too startled to retaliate, but he kept his hand hard on his stick.

Had Pitt gone too far with Osborne? Perhaps Osborne was high enough in the Inner Circle to know perfectly well who were members and who were not. Pitt had damaged the Inner Circle before. It was naive to imagine they would not know him. They had killed Arthur Desmond—why not Pitt? An attack in the street, a quick push under the wheels of a vehicle. A most regrettable street accident. It had already happened once, with Matthew—hadn't it?

He turned on his heel and strode away, leaving the man gibbering with outrage.

This was absurd. He must control his imagination. He was seeing enemies everywhere, and there were above three million people in London. There were probably no more than three thousand of them members of the Inner Circle. But he could never know which three thousand.

Around the corner he took a cab, giving Micah Drummond's address, and sat back, trying to compose himself and master his flying thoughts. He would ask him if he had any idea how large the Circle was. He was frightened of the answer, yet it could be helpful to know. On thinking of it now, he was foolish not to have gone to him for help as soon as he knew of Sir Arthur's death. Drummond had been naive to begin with, and perhaps he still only half understood the evil even now, but he had been a member for many years. He might recall incidents, rituals, and see them in a different light with the wisdom of hindsight.

Even if he had no new insights, no concrete suggestions, Pitt would feel less alone simply to talk to him.

The cab pulled up and he alighted and paid the driver with something close to a sense of elation.

Then he saw that there were no lights in the house, at least not at the front. Drummond and Eleanor might be out for the evening, but the servants would have left on the outside lamps if that were so. They could not have retired this early. The only answer was that they must be away. Disappointment overwhelmed him, engulfing him like a cold tide.

"Was they expectin' you, sir?" the cabby said from behind him. He must have seen the darkness and reached his own conclusion. Possibly it was compassion which kept him, equally possibly the hope of another immediate fare. "Shall I take you somewhere else, then?"

Pitt gave him his home address, then climbed in and shut the door.

"Thomas, you look terrible," Charlotte said as soon as she saw him. She had heard his key in the lock and came into the hall to meet him. She was dressed in deep pink, and looked warm, almost glowing, and when he took her in his arms there was an air of may blossom about her. He could hear one of the children upstairs calling out to Gracie, and a moment later Jemima appeared on the landing in her nightgown.

"Papa!"

"What are you doing out of bed?" he called up.

"I want a drink of water," she answered with assurance.

"No you don't." Charlotte disengaged herself and turned around. "You had a drink before you went to bed. Go back to sleep."

Jemima tried another avenue. "My bed's all untidy. Will you come and make it straight for me, please, Mama?"

"You're big enough to make it straight for yourself," Charlotte said firmly. "I'm going to get some supper for Papa. Good night."

"But Mama . . ."

"Good night, Jemima!"

"Can I say good night to Papa?"

Pitt did not wait for Charlotte's answer to this, but strode up the stairs two at a time and picked up his daughter in his arms. She was so slight, so delicately boned she felt fragile as he held her, even though she clung to him with surprising strength. She smelled of clean cotton and soap, and the hair around her brow was still damp. Why on earth did he challenge the Inner Circle? Life was too precious, too sweet to endanger anything. He could not destroy them, only bruise himself trying. Africa was half the earth away.

"Good night, Papa." Jemima made no move to be put down.

"Good night, sweetheart." He let her go gently, turned her around and gave her a little push on her way.

This time she knew she was beaten, and disappeared without further argument.

Pitt came downstairs too full of emotion to speak. Charlotte looked at his face, and was content to bide her time.

In the morning he slept in, then ignored Bow Street entirely and went directly to the Morton Club to look for Horace Guyler, the steward who had given evidence at the inquest. He was too early. The club was not yet open. Presumably there were maids and footmen cleaning the carpets, dusting and polishing. He should have thought of that. He was obliged to kick his heels for an hour, and then he was allowed in, and had to wait a further thirty minutes before Guyler was given the freedom to see him.

"Yes sir?" Guyler said with some apprehension. They were standing in the small steward's room, at present empty but for the two of them.

"Good morning, Mr. Guyler," Pitt replied casually. "I wonder if you would tell me a little more about the day Sir Arthur Desmond died here."

Guyler looked uncomfortable, but Pitt had a strong feeling it was not guilt so much as a deep-seated fear of death and everything to do with it.

"I don't know what else I can say, sir." He shifted from one foot to the other. "I already said all I know at the inquest."

If he were an Inner Circle member, he was a consummate actor. Or perhaps he was a cat's paw? Perhaps the executioner simply used him?

"You answered all you were asked." Pitt smiled, although no smile was going to put him at his ease. "I have a few questions the coroner did not think to ask you."

"Why, sir? Is something wrong?"

"I want to make sure that nothing becomes wrong," Pitt

said ambiguously. "You were serving gentlemen in the drawing room that day?"

"Yes, sir."

"Alone?"

"Beg pardon, sir?"

"Were you the only steward on duty?"

"Oh no, sir. There's always two or three of us at least."

"Always? What if someone is ill?"

"Then we hire in extra staff, sir. Happens quite often. Fact, I saw one that day."

"I see."

"But I was looking after that part o' the room, sir. I was the one what served Sir Arthur, at least most o' the time."

"But someone else did for part of it?" Pitt kept the rising urgency out of his voice as much as possible, but he still heard it there, as Guyler did. "One of these extra staff, perhaps?"

"I don't know for sure, sir."

"What do you mean?"

"Well ... I can't really see what other stewards are doing if I'm pouring drinks for someone, taking an order or an instruction, sir. People is every so often coming and going. Gentlemen go to the cloakroom, or to the billiard room, or to the library, or the writing room or the like."

"Did Sir Arthur move around?"

"Not as I recall, sir. But I don't rightly know. I wouldn't swear to nothing."

"I certainly wouldn't press you," Pitt tried to reassure him.

Guyler's anxious expression did not change in the slightest.

"You said that Sir Arthur drank a great deal of brandy that day," Pitt pursued.

"Yes, sir. At my judgment, I would say five or six glasses at any rate," Guyler replied with conviction.

"How many of those did you serve him?"

"About four, sir, clear as I can remember."

"So someone else served him one, perhaps two?"

Guyler heard the lift of hope, even excitement in Pitt's voice.

"I don't know that, sir. I'm just supposing," he said quickly, biting his lip, his hands clenched.

"I don't understand. . . ." Pitt was genuinely confused; he had no need to pretend.

"Well, sir, you see . . . I'm saying Sir Arthur had about five or six glasses o' brandy because that's what I counted from what people said—"

"From what people said?" Pitt broke in sharply. "What people? How many glasses did you serve him yourself, Guyler?"

"One, sir. One glass o' brandy a little before dinner. The last one . . ." He gulped. "I suppose. But I swear before God, sir, that I never put nothing in it but brandy out o' the best decanter, exactly as I'm supposed to!"

"I don't doubt that," Pitt said steadily, looking at Guyler's frightened face. "Now explain to me these other four or five brandies you say Sir Arthur had. If you did not serve them, and you don't know whether any of the other stewards did, what makes you assume they existed at all?"

"Well, sir . . ." Guyler's eyes met Pitt's with fear, but no evasion. "I remember Sir James Duncansby saying as Sir Arthur wanted another drink, and I poured one and gave it to him to take to Sir Arthur. Seeing as Sir James had one at the same time, and said as he'd take it back to Sir Arthur. It isn't done to argue with gentlemen, sir."

"No, of course it isn't. That accounts for one. What about the others?"

"Well, er . . . Mr. William Rodway came and ordered a second one from me, saying as the first, which he'd had from one of the other stewards, he'd given to Sir Arthur."

"That's two. Go on."

"Mr. Jenkinson said as he'd treat Sir Arthur, and 'e took two, one for himself like."

"Three. You want one or two more."

"I'm not really sure, sir." Guyler looked unhappy. "I just overheard Brigadier Allsop saying as he'd seen Sir Arthur ordering one from one of the other stewards. At least I think it was one, I'm not sure. It could have been two."

Pitt felt a curious sense of lightness. The steward had served Sir Arthur only one drink! All the rest were hearsay. They might never have reached him at all. Suddenly the confusion and nightmare were sorting into some kind of sense. Sanity was returning.

And with sanity were the darker, uglier, but so much less painful conclusions that if this were not the truth but a conspiracy, then Sir Arthur had been murdered, just as Matthew believed.

And perhaps if Pitt had been there, if he had been home to Brackley and Sir Arthur had been able to turn to him in the first place with his terrible suspicion of the Inner Circle, then maybe Pitt could have warned him, have advised him, and he would not now be dead.

He thanked Guyler and left him, anxious and more puzzled than when he had come in.

Dr. Murray was not a man to be so easily led or persuaded. Pitt had been obliged to make an appointment to see him in Wimpole Street and to pay for the privilege, and Murray was not amused when he discovered that the purpose for Pitt's presence in his surgery was to ask questions, rather than to seek aid for some complaint. The rooms were imposing, soberly furnished, exuding an air of well-being and confidence. It crossed Pitt's mind to wonder what had drawn Arthur Desmond to such a man, and how long he had consulted him.

"Your request was somewhat misleading, Mr. Pitt, at the outset, and that is the kindest I can say for it." Murray leaned back from his huge walnut desk and looked at Pitt with disfavor. "What authority have you for enquiring into the unfortunate death of Sir Arthur Desmond? The coroner has already given his judgment on the causes and closed the case. I fail to see what good can be done by further discussion of the matter."

Pitt had expected some difficulty, and even if Murray were a member of the Circle, as he suspected, he knew his trick with Osborne would not work a second time. Murray was far too confident to be duped. And he thought it likely he was also much more senior in the hierarchy which governed it, and might well know who Pitt was, his past enmity to the Circle and his very recent refusal to join. He forced from his mind the further possibilities that Murray himself was the executioner, though as he sat in the consulting room with the door closed behind him, and the windows with their thick, velvet curtains, he could see the bright street beyond and carriages passing to and fro in the sunlight. But the glass was so thick and so well fitted he could hear nothing of the rattle and bustle of life. He felt suddenly claustrophobic, almost imprisoned.

He thought of lying about the coroner's being dissatisfied, but then he dared not. The coroner might be an Inner Circle member as well. In fact almost anyone might be, even among his own men. He had always felt Tellman was too angry, too full of resentment to lend himself to anything so dedicated to the power of governing. But perhaps that was blind of him.

"I am a personal friend of Sir Matthew's," he said aloud. That at least was perfectly true. "He asked me to make a few further enquiries on his behalf. He is not well at the moment. He met with an accident in the street a few days ago, and was injured." He watched Murray's face intently, but saw not even a flicker in his eyes.

"I am so sorry," Murray sympathized. "How very unfortunate. I hope it was not serious?"

"It seems not, but it was very unpleasant. He could have been killed."

"I am afraid it happens all too often."

Was that a veiled threat? Or only an innocent and truthful observation?

"What is it you wish to know, Mr. Pitt?" Murray continued, folding his hands across his stomach and looking at Pitt gravely. "If you are indeed a friend of Sir Matthew's, you would do him the greatest service by persuading him that his father's death was in many ways a mercy, before he became sufficiently ill to damage his reputation beyond recall, and possibly to have suffered greatly in his more lucid moments. It is most unpleasant to face, but less damaging in time than to go on fighting against the truth, and possibly causing a great deal of unpleasantness along the way." A smile flickered across his face and disappeared. "Men of goodwill, of whom there are many, wish to remember Arthur as he was, but to rake the matter up over and over will not allow that to happen." His eyes did not waver from Pitt's.

One moment Pitt was sure it was a warning; the men of goodwill he referred to were members of the Circle, large in number, but immeasurably more powerful than number alone would suggest. They would retaliate if Matthew pressed them.

Then the next moment he knew there was no proof of that. Murray was simply a doctor stating the obvious. Pitt was developing a delusion about being persecuted himself, seeing plots everywhere, accusing innocent people.

"I shall be better able to convince him if I have some facts and details to tell him," he replied, not moving his gaze either. "For example, had you ever prescribed laudanum for Sir Arthur before? Or was this his first experience with it, as far as you were aware?"

"It was his first experience," Murray replied. "He told me that himself. But I did explain to him most carefully both its properties and its dangers, Mr. Pitt. I showed him precisely how and when to take it, and how much would produce a sleep of reasonably natural depth and duration."

"Of course," Pitt agreed. "But in his confused state . . . he was confused, was he not? Irrational and contradictory at times?"

"Not with me." Murray said what he had to, to protect himself, as Pitt had expected. "But I have subsequently learned from others that he had some strange obsessions, not altogether rational. I take your point, Mr. Pitt. He may have forgotten what I told him and taken a lethal dose, thinking it would merely give him an afternoon nap. We can't know what was in his mind at the time, poor man."

"How was the laudanum made up?"

"In powders, which is the usual way." He smiled very slightly. "Each dose separated and in a folded paper. It would be difficult to take more than one dose, Mr. Pitt, unless one had forgotten and taken a second in absentmindedness. I regret it could not more satisfactorily fill your theory. It is a precaution I usually take."

"I see." It did not affect Pitt's real belief. It would still have been perfectly possible for Murray to make up a dose that was lethal and put it in with the others. He kept the look of agreeable enquiry on his face. "When did Sir Arthur come to you, Dr. Murray?"

"He first consulted me in the autumn of 1887, over a congestion of the lungs. I was able to help him and he effected a complete cure. If you are referring to this last visit, that was . . . let me see." He looked through a calendar of appointments on his desk. "April twenty-seventh." He smiled. "At four-forty in the afternoon, to be precise. He was here some half hour or more. He was very troubled indeed, I regret to say. I did all I could to reassure him, but I am afraid he was beyond my ability to help this time. I don't think I flatter myself if I say he was past the help of any man of medicine."

"Did you make up the laudanum yourself, Dr. Murray?"

"No, no. I don't keep supplies of all the drugs I prescribe for my patients, Mr. Pitt. I gave him a prescription which

237

I presume he took to an apothecary. I recommended Mr. Porteous of Jermyn Street. He is an excellent man, both knowledgeable and extremely careful. I am most particular, for the very cause you mention, that the laudanum should be precisely measured and each dose separately wrapped. Sir Arthur had been to him on several previous occasions, and said that he would indeed use him."

"I see. Thank you very much, Dr. Murray. You have been most patient." Pitt rose to his feet. He had learned only little that was of use, but he could think of no more to ask without raising suspicion, if not actual certainty, that he was pursuing the Inner Circle again, and that he was convinced of murder. That would achieve nothing, and he was acutely aware of his own danger.

As it was, he was absurdly relieved to be outside in the bright air amid the rattle of hooves and hiss of carriage wheels and the vitality and movement of the street.

He went straight to Jermyn Street and found the apothecary's shop.

"Sir Arthur Desmond?" The old man behind the counter nodded benignly. "Such a nice gentleman. Sorry to hear about his death. Very sad. So unfortunate. What may I do for you, sir? I have just about everything a body can need to repair or ease whatever troubles you. Have you seen a physician, or may I advise you?"

"I don't need to purchase anything. I'm sorry for misleading you. It is your memory I need to consult." Pitt did feel guilty for offering no business, but there was nothing he needed. "When was Sir Arthur last in here?"

"Sir Arthur? Why do you wish to know that, young man?" He squinted at Pitt curiously but not unkindly.

"I—I am concerned about his death . . . the manner of it," Pitt answered a little awkwardly. The old man looked not unlike Sir Arthur, and it brought an odd twist of memory back, seeing him behind the counter of the dark shop.

"Oh. Well, so am I, and that's the pity of it. If he'd come

here with his writ from the doctor, as he usually did, I'd have given him the laudanum all wrapped separately, as I always do for all my customers, and then this dreadful accident would never have happened." The old man shook his head sorrowfully.

"He didn't come here?" Pitt said sharply. "You are sure?"

The old gentleman's eyebrows rose. "Of course I am sure, young man. Nobody serves behind this counter but myself, and I did not serve him. I haven't seen Sir Arthur since last winter. About January, it would be. He had a cold. I gave him some infusion of herbs to put in hot water, to clear his head. We talked about dogs. I recall it very well."

"Thank you. Thank you, Mr. Porteous. I am greatly obliged to you, sir. Good day."

"Good day, young man. I shouldn't run like that, sir, if I were you. No good for the digestion. You'll get overexcited. . . ."

But Pitt was out of the door and off down Jermyn Street at a flying pace.

He was halfway along Regent Street before he realized he did not know where he was going. Where had Sir Arthur obtained the laudanum? If not in Jermyn Street, then from some other apothecary. Or had Murray given it to him after all? Was there any way whatever of proving it?

Perhaps Matthew would know? Apothecary's papers frequently had their names on them. It was both a safeguard and a means of advertising. He retraced his steps and called a cab to take him to Matthew's apartments.

"What is it?" Matthew asked quickly. He was sitting up at his desk in the small room which served him as dining room and study. He was wearing a dressing robe, and still looked very pale. There were shadows around his eyes as if latent bruises were at last beginning to show.

"You look ill," Pitt said anxiously. "Should you be up?"

"I have nothing worse than a headache," Matthew dismissed it quickly. "What is it? What have you found?"

Pitt sat on one of the other chairs. "I've been to see several people. It seems all of Sir Arthur's irrational behavior is either hearsay or based on the fact he upset people's prejudices and desires. . . ."

"I told you!" Matthew said triumphantly, light and eagerness in his face for the first time since he had come to Pitt's house with the news of Sir Arthur's death. "He wasn't the least confused or senile. He knew only too well what he was saying. What else? What about the brandy, and the laudanum? Have you proved that wrong yet?" He smiled apologetically. "I'm sorry, I'm expecting miracles. You've done brilliantly, Thomas. I am grateful."

"The brandy is hearsay too. The steward only served him one glass; the rest were ordered by other people on his behalf . . . perhaps."

Matthew frowned. "Perhaps? What do you mean?"

Pitt recited what Guyler had told him.

"I see," Matthew said quietly, leaning back. "God, isn't it frightening. The Inner Circle is all over the place. But surely not everyone you've spoken to can be members, can they? Or can they?" His face looked pale again at the thought.

"I don't know," Pitt confessed. "I presume members can be summoned if they are needed. And this was something of an emergency for them. After all, Sir Arthur was breaking the covenant of secrecy and accusing them of conspiracy to commit fraud, and in some senses even treason."

Matthew sat silent, deep in thought.

"Matthew . . ."

He looked up.

"I went to see Dr. Murray as well. He says he recommended Sir Arthur to get the laudanum he prescribed at the usual apothecary in Jermyn Street, but Porteous is quite certain that Sir Arthur did not go to him. Have you any idea where else he might have got it?"

"Does it matter? Do you think it was wrong dosages or something? An apothecary who was the executioner of the Circle?" His face was pinched with revulsion. "What an appalling thought . . . but it makes excellent sense."

"Or the doctor himself," Pitt added. "Do you know?"

"No. But if we could find one of the papers it would probably tell us." He stood up. "There may be some left among his effects. I'll look. Come, we'll both go."

Pitt rose. "He only had them two or three days. It was April twenty-seventh he went to see Murray for the consultation."

Matthew stood and turned to face Pitt.

"The twenty-seventh. Are you sure?"

"Yes. Why?"

"He said nothing about it to me. He can't have got them that day, because we went to Brighton in the afternoon."

"What time?"

"To Brighton? About half past two. Why?"

"And what time did you get back?"

"We didn't. We dined with friends and came back the following morning."

"Murray said that was the day he saw Sir Arthur—at four-forty in the afternoon. Are you sure it was the twenty-seventh you went to Brighton, not the day before, or after?"

"Absolutely certain. It was Aunt Mary's birthday and we had a party. We always do on the twenty-seventh of April, every year."

"Then Murray lied. He never saw Sir Arthur!"

Matthew frowned. "Could he have misunderstood the date?"

"No. He looked it up in his book. I saw him."

"Then the whole consultation was a lie," Matthew said, curiously melancholy. "And if that is so, then where did the laudanum come from?"

"God knows!" Pitt whispered huskily. "Someone in that club room . . . someone who took him a brandy he didn't order."

Matthew swallowed hard and said nothing.

Pitt sat down again, feeling curiously weak and frightened, and looking across at Matthew's white face, he knew he felt just the same.

8

P*ITT WOKE UP SLOWLY,* the thumping in his head becoming more persistent till it dragged him to the surface of consciousness and forced him awake. He opened his eyes. The bedroom was barred with sunlight where the curtains did not quite meet. Charlotte was still asleep beside him, warm and hunched up, her hair in loose braids beginning to come undone.

The banging was still going on. There was no sound in the street outside, no carriages, no drays, no noise of footsteps or voices.

He turned over and looked at the clock beside the bed. It was ten minutes before five.

The banging was getting worse. It was downstairs at the front door.

He sat up reluctantly and pushed his fingers through his hair, then put his jacket on over his nightshirt and walked barefoot across the floor to open the window. Charlotte stirred but did not fully waken. He pushed up the sash and looked out.

The banging stopped and a foreshortened figure stepped back from the door and looked up. It was Tellman. His face was very white in the early morning light and he had come without his usual bowler hat. He looked disheveled and upset.

Pitt indicated that he would come down, and after closing the window again, he walked as quietly as he could back to the door to the landing and went down the stairs into the hall. He undid the lock and pulled the door open.

Tellman looked even worse closer to. His face was ashen and what little flesh there was seemed to be sunken away. He did not wait to be asked.

"Something terrible has happened," he said as soon as he saw Pitt. "You'd better come and deal with it yourself. I haven't told anybody yet, but Mr. Farnsworth's going to be in a right state when he hears."

"Come in," Pitt ordered, standing back. "What is it?" All sorts of fears whirled around in his head; presumably some terrible news had come from the German Embassy. Although how would Tellman know that? Had someone absconded, taking papers with them? "What is it?" he demanded more urgently.

Tellman remained on the step. He was so pale he looked as if he might collapse. That in itself alarmed Pitt. He would have thought Tellman inured to anything.

"Mrs. Chancellor," Tellman said, and coughed painfully, then gulped. "We've just found her body, sir."

Pitt was stunned. His breath caught in his throat and the words came out in a whisper. "Her body?"

"Yes sir. Washed up in the river at the Tower." He watched Pitt with hollow eyes.

"Suicide?" Pitt said slowly, unable to believe it.

"No." Tellman stood motionless except that he shivered very slightly although the morning was mild. "Murder. She'd been strangled, and then put in the water. Sometime last night by the looks of it. But you'll need the medical examiner to tell you for sure."

Pitt felt a sorrow so sharp it exploded in him in a kind of wild anger. She had been such a beautiful, vulnerable woman, so full of life, so highly individual. He remembered her vividly at the Duchess of Marlborough's reception. He could picture her face in his mind as Tellman was talking. It was so seldom he had known a victim in life, the sense of loss was personal, different from the pity that he usually felt.

"Why?" he said violently. "Why would anyone want to destroy a woman like that? It doesn't make any kind of sense." Without realizing it he had clenched his fists and his body was tight with rage under his jacket. He was not even aware of his bare feet on the step or the fact he had no trousers on.

"The treason at the Colonial Office . . ." Tellman said unhappily. "Maybe she knew something?"

Pitt thumped the door lintel with the heel of his clenched fist, and swore.

"You'd better get dressed, sir, and come," Tellman said quietly. "There's no one knows about it yet, except the boatman as found her and the constable who reported it to me, but we can't keep it that way for long. Don't matter what you say to 'em, discretion and all that, somebody'll talk to someone."

"They know who she is?" Pitt was startled.

"Yes sir. That's why I was called."

Pitt was irritated with himself; he should have thought of that before.

"How?" he demanded. "How could riverboat men know her?"

"The constables," Tellman explained patiently. "They were the ones who knew who she was. She was obviously someone of quality, any fool could see that, but she had a locket 'round her neck, little gold thing that opened up, with a picture in it." He sighed and there was a sadness for a moment in his eyes. "Linus Chancellor, it was, clear as you like. That's why they called us. Whoever she was, they knew that picture meant something that could only mean trouble."

"I see. Where is she now?" Pitt looked back at him.

"Still at the Tower, sir. I had 'em cover her up, and left her where she was, more or less, so as you could see."

"I'll be down," Pitt said, and left Tellman on the step. He

went back upstairs, taking off his jacket as he reached the landing and pulling off his nightshirt as soon as he was through the bedroom door.

Charlotte had drifted back to sleep and it seemed cruel to waken her, but he had to give her some account of where he had gone. He finished dressing first. There was no time to shave. A brisk splash of cold water in the basin and a rubdown with the towel would have to do.

He reached over and touched her gently.

There must have been some rigidity in him, or perhaps the coldness of his hands after the water, but she woke immediately.

"What is it? What's wrong?" She opened her eyes and saw him dressed. She struggled to sit up. "What's happened?"

He had no time to tell her gently. "Tellman's come to say they have found Susannah Chancellor's body washed up from the river."

She stared at him, unable for a moment to comprehend what he had said.

"I have to go." He bent to kiss her.

"She committed suicide?" she said, her eyes still fixed on his. "The poor creature . . . I . . ." Her face was wrenched with pity.

"No . . . no. She was murdered."

There was both shock and a kind of relief in her face.

"Why did you think she committed suicide?" he asked.

"I . . . I don't know. She seemed so troubled."

"Well there was no doubt about it, from what Tellman says."

"How was she killed?"

"I haven't been there yet," he answered, not wanting to tell her. He kissed her quickly on the cheek and stepped back.

"Thomas!"

He waited.

"You said 'from what Tellman said.' What did he say?"

246

He let out his breath slowly. "She was strangled. I'm sorry. He's waiting for me."

She sat still, her face full of grief. There was nothing he could do. He went out feeling sad and helpless.

Tellman was waiting in the hall and he turned and led the way out into the street as soon as Pitt appeared. Pitt closed the door and hastened to catch him up. At the corner they crossed into the main thoroughfare, and it was only a matter of minutes before they hailed a hansom and Tellman directed it to the Tower of London.

It was a long journey from Bloomsbury. They went south first to Oxford Street, and then east until it turned into High Holborn and then for nearly a mile before turning right farther towards the river down St. Andrews Street, Shoe Lane and St. Bride's to Ludgate Circus.

Tellman sat in silence. He was not a companionable man. Whatever his thoughts were he was disinclined to share them and he sat uncomfortably, staring straight ahead.

Several times it was on the edge of Pitt's tongue to ask him something, but he could think of nothing that would be useful. Tellman had already said all he knew for certain. The rest would be only speculation. Anyway, Pitt was not sure he wanted to hear Tellman's ideas on Susannah Chancellor. Her lovely, intelligent face with its capacity for pain was too sharp in his mind, and he knew what he was going to see when they got to the Tower.

They turned along Ludgate Hill and swung around St. Paul's churchyard with the giant mass of the cathedral above them. Its dome was dark against the pale, early sky, which was marked only by a few shreds of cloud like banners across its limpid blue. There were very few people about. Down the whole length of Canon Street they passed only half a dozen cabs, two drays and a dung cart. Canon Street turned into East Cheap and then into Great Tower Street.

Tellman leaned forward and suddenly banged sharply against the roof for the cabby's attention.

"Turn right!" he ordered. "Turn down Water Street to Lower Thames Street."

"Ain't nothing down there but Queen's Stairs and Traitors Bridge," the cabby replied. "If you want the Tower, like you said, you'd be better off in Trinity Square, which is up to the left."

"Just take us to Queen's Stairs and then go about your business," Tellman said curtly.

The cabby muttered something inaudible, but obeyed.

They glimpsed the Custom House to the west, already busy with men coming and going. Then they turned right facing the great medieval bastion of the Tower of London, a stone memory of a conquest that spanned back to the Dark Ages and a history recorded only in brief bursts by illuminated writing and quaint works of art and tales of bloody battles and exquisite, passionate islands of Christianity.

The hansom stopped at Queen's Stairs. Pitt paid the cabby and he turned and left, his horses moving into a brisk trot.

It was two minutes before six. The great silver sheet of the river was utterly calm. Even the cargo barges, dark against the bright surface, barely made a ripple. The air was fresh and slightly damp and smelled of salt from the tide.

Tellman led the way along the water's edge to the stairs, where a boatman was waiting for them. He looked up without a change of expression and deftly maneuvered the small craft around so they could get in.

Pitt looked questioningly at Tellman.

"Traitors Gate," he said succinctly, climbing in ahead of Pitt and sitting down. He disliked boats, and it showed in his face.

Pitt followed him easily and thanked the boatman as he pulled away.

"She was washed up at Traitors Gate?" he asked with a catch in his voice.

"Tide left her there," Tellman replied. It was only a few

yards down the river to the gate itself, the entrance to the Tower by which condemned people had been brought to their execution, and which opened directly onto the water.

Pitt could see the little knot of people already gathered around: a constable in uniform looking cold in spite of the mildness of the morning, a scarlet tunic of a Yeoman of the Guard, the traditional Beefeaters who man the Tower, and the other of the two boatmen who had first found her.

Pitt climbed ashore, only just avoiding getting his feet wet on the slipway. Susannah was lying on the waterline where the high tide had left her, only her feet below the surface, a long, slender form barely crumpled, turned over half onto her face. One white hand was visible protruding from the wet, dripping cloth of her gown. Her hair had come unraveled from its pins and lay like seaweed around her neck, spilling onto the stone.

The constable turned as Pitt came ashore, recognized him and stepped back from the body.

"Morning, sir." He looked very pale.

"Good morning, Constable," Pitt replied. He did not remember the man's name, if indeed he knew it. He looked down at Susannah. "When was she found?"

" 'Bout 'alf past three, sir. High tide'd be just before three, 'cording to the boatman 'ere. Reckon as they were the first past 'ere on this side o' the river after she were washed up, poor creature. Weren't no suicide, sir. Poor soul was strangled, no two ways about that." He looked sad and very solemn for his twenty-odd years. His beat was on the river's edge, and this was not the first body he had seen, nor the first woman, but she was perhaps the first he had seen with beautiful clothes and—when the hair was pulled back, as it was now—such a passionate, vulnerable face. Pitt knelt down to look at her more closely. He saw the unmistakable finger marks purple on her throat, but from the lack of swelling or bloating on her face, he thought perhaps she had actually died of a broken neck rather than suffocation. It was a tiny thing, very tiny, but the fact that she was not disfigured eased the hurt. Possibly she had suffered only very briefly. He would think that as long as he could.

"We didn't touch her, sir," one of the boatmen said nervously. " 'Cept to make sure as she was dead, and we couldn't 'elp 'er, poor creature." He knew enough of the circumstances which drive people to suicide to have no judgment over it. He would have put them all in consecrated ground and left the decision to God. But he was not a churchgoing man by choice. He went only to please his wife.

"Thank you," Pitt said absently, still looking at Susannah. "Where would she have been put in the water to be washed up here?"

"That depends, sir. Currents is funny. 'Specially in a river like this where it twists and turns, like. Most often bodies sink at first, then come up again right about where they went in. But if she was put in on the turn o' the tide, into the water, like, if she moved at all it could a' bin upriver from 'ere. That's if she were put in off a boat. But if she were put in off the shore, more like it were on the incoming tide, and she came upriver from below. And that would depend on when she were put in, as to where, if you follow me, guv?"

"So all we know for sure is that she was here when the tide turned?"

"Yer got it right," the boatman agreed. "Bodies stay in the water different sorts of times. Depends on what passes making a wake, or if they bump summink. Things get caught and pulled sometimes. There's eddies and currents you can't always account for. Maybe the doc can tell yer 'ow long she's been gone, poor thing. Then we can tell yer if she were put in then, like, just about where it would be."

"Thank you." Pitt looked up at Tellman. "Have you sent for the mortuary wagon?"

"Yes sir. It will be waiting up in Trinity Square. Didn't want a whole lot of talk going on," Tellman answered without glancing at the boatmen. If they didn't know who she was, so much the better. The news would spread fast enough. It would be an appalling way for Chancellor to learn, or anyone else who had cared for her.

Pitt straightened up with a sigh. He should tell Chancellor himself. He knew the man, and Tellman did not. Apart from that it was not a duty to delegate.

"Get them down here to take her to the medical examiner. I must report it as soon as possible."

"Yes sir, of course." Tellman glanced once more at Susannah, then turned on his heel and went back to the boat, his face twisted with distaste.

A few moments later Pitt left also, climbing up the Queen's Stairs and walking slowly around to Great Tower Hill. He was obliged to walk as far as East Cheap before he found another cab. The morning was beginning to cloud over from the north and now there were more people about. A newsboy shouted some government difficulty. A running patterer had an early breakfast at a pie stall while he studied the day's events, getting ready to compose his rhymes. Two men came out of a coffee shop, arguing animatedly with each other. They were looking for a cab, but Pitt reached it just before them, to their considerable annoyance.

"Berkeley Square, please," he directed the driver, and climbed in. The driver acknowledged him and set off. Pitt sat back and tried to compose in his mind what he would say. It was useless, as he had known it would be. There was no kind or reasonable way in which to break such news, no way to take the pain out of it, no way even to lessen it. It was always absolutely and unequivocally terrible.

He tried to think at least what questions to ask Chancellor, but it was of little use. Whatever he decided now, he would still have to think again when he saw Chancellor's state of mind, whether he was able to retain sufficient composure to answer anything at all. People were affected differently by grief. With some the shock was so deep it did not manifest itself to begin with. They might be calm for days before their grief overcame them. Others were hysterical, torn with helpless anger, or too racked with weeping to be coherent, or think of anything but their loss.

"What number, sir?" the cabby interrupted his thoughts.

"Seventeen," he replied. "I think."

"That'll be Mr. Chancellor, sir?"

"That's right."

The cabby seemed about to add something more, but changed his mind and closed the trapdoor.

A moment later Pitt alighted, paid him and stood on the doorstep, shivering in spite of the early morning sun. It was now after seven. All around the square maids were busy bringing out carpets to the areaways to be beaten and swept, and bootboys and footmen went in and out on errands. Even a few early delivery boys pushed carts, and news vendors handed over their papers for the maids to iron so they could be presented at breakfast before the masters of the houses left for the day's business in the city.

Pitt rang the doorbell.

It was answered almost immediately by a footman who looked surprised to see someone at the front door so very early.

"Yes sir?" he said politely.

"Good morning. My name is Pitt." He produced his card. "It is imperative I see Mr. Chancellor immediately. It is on a matter that cannot wait. Will you tell him so, please."

The footman had worked for a cabinet minister for some time and he was not unused to matters of dire emergency.

"Yes sir. If you will wait in the morning room, I will inform Mr. Chancellor that you are here."

Pitt hesitated.

"Yes sir?" the footman said politely.

"I am afraid I have some extremely unpleasant news. Perhaps you would send the butler to me first."

The footman paled.

"Yes sir, if you think that's necessary?"

"Has he been with Mr. Chancellor long?"

"Yes sir, some fifteen years."

"Then please send him."

"Yes sir."

The butler came within moments, looking anxious. He closed the morning room door behind him and faced Pitt with a frown.

"I'm Richards, sir, Mr. Chancellor's butler. I gather from Albert that something distressing has happened. Is it one of the gentlemen in the Colonial Office? Has there been a . . . an accident?"

"No, Richards, I am afraid it is far worse than that," Pitt said quietly, his voice rough at the edges. "I am afraid Mrs. Chancellor has met with . . . has met with a violent death." He got no further. The butler swayed on his feet as if he were about to faint. Every vestige of color fled from his skin.

Pitt lunged forward and grasped him, guiding him backwards towards one of the chairs.

"I'm . . . I'm sorry, sir," Richards gasped. "I don't know what came over me. I . . ." He looked up at Pitt beseechingly. "You are sure, sir? There could not be some error . . . some mistake as to identity?" Even as he said it his face reflected his knowledge that it could not be so. How many women were there in London who looked like Susannah Chancellor?

Pitt gave no answer. None was necessary.

"I think it would be wise if you were to make yourself available close at hand when I have to break the news to Mr. Chancellor," Pitt said gently. "Perhaps a decanter of brandy. And you might make sure that there are no callers and no messages until he feels able to deal with them."

"Yes. Yes, of course. Thank you, sir." And still looking very shaken and uncertain in his step, Richards rose and left the room.

Linus Chancellor came in a moment or two later, an eagerness in his step and a directness in his eyes that gave Pitt a bitter jolt. He realized Chancellor was expecting news

253

about the African information that was being passed. And with that keenness in his eyes, he also realized, if he had ever doubted it, that Chancellor was innocent of any involvement.

"I'm sorry, sir. I have very grave news," he said almost before Chancellor had closed the door. He could not bear the misapprehension.

"Is it one of my senior colleagues?" Chancellor asked. "It is good of you to come here to tell me in person. Who is it? Aylmer?"

Pitt felt cold in spite of the warmth of the room and the sun now bright outside.

"No, sir. I am afraid it is about Mrs. Chancellor I have come." He saw the surprise in Chancellor's face and did not wait. "I am profoundly sorry, sir, but I have to tell you that she is dead."

"Dead?" Chancellor repeated the word as though he did not know its meaning. "She was perfectly well last evening. She went out to . . ." He turned and went to the door. "Richards?"

The butler appeared immediately, the salver with brandy decanter and glass in his hands, his face ashen white.

Chancellor looked back at Pitt, then at the butler again.

"Have you seen Mrs. Chancellor this morning, Richards?"

Richards looked enquiringly at Pitt.

"Mr. Chancellor, there is no doubt," Pitt said gently. "She was found at the Tower of London."

"The Tower of London?" Chancellor said incredulously. His eyes were wide with disbelief, and there was a look on his face that seemed close to laughter, as if the sheer idea of it were too absurd to be true.

Pitt had seen hysteria before; it was not altogether unexpected.

"Please sit down, sir," he asked. "You are bound to feel unwell."

Richards set the tray down and offered a glass of brandy.

Chancellor took it and drank it all, then coughed severely for several seconds until he managed to regain control of himself.

"What happened?" he asked slowly, fumbling to get his tongue around the words. "What could she possibly have been doing at the Tower of London? She went out to visit Christabel Thorne. I know Christabel is eccentric . . . but the Tower of London? Where, for heaven's sake? She can surely not have been inside it at that time of night?"

"Could she and Mrs. Thorne have taken a trip on the river?" Pitt asked, although it seemed a strange thing for two ladies to do alone. Would they find Christabel's body also, on some further stretch of the riverbank?

"And what . . . a boating accident?" Chancellor said doubtfully. "Did Mrs. Thorne suggest such a thing?"

"We have not yet enquired of Mrs. Thorne. We did not know Mrs. Chancellor had been with her. But it was not an accident, sir. I am deeply sorry, but I am afraid it was murder. The only comfort I can offer is that it would have been very quick. It is unlikely she suffered."

Chancellor stared at him, his face white, then red. He seemed about to choke on his own breath.

Richards offered him another glass of brandy and he drank it. The blood left his face and he looked ill.

"And Christabel?" he whispered, staring at Pitt.

"So far we know nothing about her, but we will naturally make enquiries."

"Where . . . where was she found . . . my . . . wife?" Chancellor seemed to have difficulty saying the words.

"At Traitors Gate. It has a slipway down—"

"I know! I know, Superintendent. I have seen it many times, I know what it is." He swallowed again, gulping in air. "Thank you for coming to tell me yourself. It must be one of your most unpleasant tasks. I appreciate that you came in person. I imagine you will be in charge of the case? Now if you don't mind, I would prefer to be alone.

255

Richards, please inform the Colonial Office that I shall not be in this morning."

Pitt walked from Linus Chancellor's to the home of Jeremiah Thorne, across the square and along to the far end of Mount Street, and north to Upper Brook Street. It took him less than twenty minutes to reach the front door and ring the bell. His heart was pounding as if he had run twice the distance, his tongue dry in his mouth.

The bell was answered by a footman who enquired as to his business, and when presented with his card, showed him into the library and asked him to wait. He would enquire whether Mrs. Thorne was at home. At this time in the morning it was a ridiculous pretense. He could hardly fail to know if she were at home, but he had been trained to use the polite fiction before allowing any visitor in. If it were inconvenient, or his employer did not wish to see someone, he could hardly return and say so as bluntly.

Pitt waited with a tension so severe he was unable to sit down or even to stand in one spot. He paced back and forth, once catching his knuckles on the edge of a carved table as he turned, oblivious of his surroundings. He was aware of the pain, but only dimly. His ears strained to hear the sound of footsteps. Once when a maid passed he went to the door and was on the point of flinging it open, when he realized he was being absurd. Then he heard giggling and a male voice answering back. It was a simple piece of domestic flirtation.

He was still close to the door when Christabel came in. She was wearing a pale gray morning dress and looked in excellent health, but very questionable temper. Although curiosity was holding it in check, at least until she had ascertained the cause of his call at such a time.

"Good morning, Superintendent," she said coolly. "You alarmed my footman by your rather vehement insistence upon speaking to me. I hope your reason is adequate to justify it. This is a very uncivil time to call."

He was too shaken to respond sharply; the tragedy was

real. His mind's eye was still filled with Susannah's face as she lay in the silence of Traitors Gate, the water of the river lapping over her feet.

"I am extremely relieved to see you well, Mrs. Thorne."

Something in the gravity of his face frightened her. Quite suddenly her manner altered entirely, the anger evaporated.

"What is it, Mr. Pitt? Has something happened?"

"Yes, ma'am. I am very sorry indeed to have to tell you that Mrs. Chancellor met her death last night. Mr. Chancellor had believed she was with you, so I naturally came immediately to make sure you were not . . ."

"Susannah?" She looked stricken, staring at him with her enormous eyes, the arrogance fled out of her. "Susannah is dead?" She took a step backwards, then another until she found the chair behind her and sank into it. "How? If . . . if you feared for me also, then it was . . . violent?"

"Yes, Mrs. Thorne. I am afraid she was murdered."

"Oh, dear God!" She put her hands up to her face and sat quite motionless for several moments.

"May I call someone for you?" he offered.

She looked up. "What? Uh—no, no thank you. My poor Susannah. How did it happen? Where was she, for heaven's sake, that she could be . . . was she attacked? Robbed?"

"We don't yet know. She was found in the river, washed up on the shore."

"Drowned?"

"No, she was strangled, so violently that her neck may well be broken. It was probably very quick. I'm sorry, Mrs. Thorne, but since Mr. Chancellor had believed she was coming to visit you, I have to ask you if you saw her last evening."

"No. I dined at home, but Susannah did not come here. She must have been attacked before she . . ." She sighed and a shadow of a smile, small and very sad, touched her lips. "That is, if, of course, she intended to come here. Perhaps she went somewhere else. It would be unwise to suppose it had to be here she had in mind. Although I do not believe it would be an assignation. She was too much in love with Linus for that to be . . . likely."

"You don't say 'possible,' Mrs. Thorne?" he said instantly.

She rose to her feet and turned to look out of the window, her back to him. "No. There is not much that is impossible, Superintendent. That is something you learn as you get older. Associations are not always what you suppose, and even when you love one person, you may not necessarily behave in a manner other people would understand."

"Are you speaking in generalities, or do you have Mrs. Chancellor in mind?" Pitt asked quietly.

"I don't really know. But Linus is not an easy man. He is witty, charming, handsome, ambitious, and certainly extremely talented. But I have always wondered if he was capable of loving her as much as she loved him. Not that many marriages are composed of two people who love each other equally, except in fairy stories." She kept her back to him and her voice suggested she was indifferent whether he understood her or not. "Not everyone is able to give so much. There is usually one party who has to compromise, to accept what is given and not be bitter or lonely for the rest. That is especially true for women who are married to powerful and ambitious men. Susannah was clever enough to know that, and I think wise enough not to fight against it and lose what there was for her . . . which I believe was much."

"But you do not think it impossible she may have found some friendship or admiration elsewhere?"

"Not impossible, Superintendent, but unlikely." She turned back to face him. "I liked Susannah very much, Mr. Pitt. She was a woman of intelligence, courage, and great integrity. She loved her husband, but she was well able to speak and act for herself. She was not . . . dominated. She had spirit, passion and laughter. . . ." Suddenly her eyes filled with tears and they spilled down her cheeks. She stood quite still and wept without screwing up her face, simply lost in a deep and consuming grief.

"I am so sorry," Pitt said quietly, and went to the door. He found Jeremiah Thorne in the hall outside, looking surprised and a little anxious.

"What the devil are you doing here?" he demanded.

"Mrs. Chancellor has been murdered," Pitt replied without preamble. "I had reason to believe your wife might also have been harmed. I am delighted that she is not, but she is distressed and in need of comfort. Mr. Chancellor will not be in to the Colonial Office today."

Thorne stared at him for a moment, barely comprehending what he had heard.

"I'm sorry," Pitt said again.

"Susannah?" Thorne looked stricken; there was no mistaking the reality of his emotion. "Are you sure? I'm sorry, that's an absurd question. Of course you are, or you would hardly have come here. But how? Why? What happened? Why in God's name did you think Christabel was involved?" He searched Pitt's face as if he might have seen some answer in it more immediate than words.

"Mr. Chancellor had been under the impression that his wife was intending to visit Mrs. Thorne yesterday evening," Pitt replied. "But apparently she did not reach here."

"No! No . . . she was not expected."

"So Mrs. Thorne told me."

"Dear God, this is dreadful! Poor Susannah. She was one of the loveliest women I ever knew—lovely in the truest sense, Pitt. I am not thinking of her face, but of the spirit that lit her inside, the passion and the courage . . . the heart. Forgive me. Come back and ask anything you like later on, but now I must go to my wife. She was deeply fond of Susannah. . . ." And without adding anything further he turned and went towards the library, leaving Pitt to find his own way out.

It was far too soon to expect any information from the medical examiner. The body would barely have reached him. The physical evidence was slight. As the boatman had said, she could have been put into the water upstream after the tide had turned at about two-thirty and drifted down, or downstream on the flood tide, and have been carried up, and thus left when the ebb began. Or as likely as either of those, she could have gone in roughly where she was found. Below the Tower were only Wapping, Rotherhithe, Limehouse, the Surrey Docks, and the Isle of Dogs. Deptford and Greenwich were too far for the brief time before the change from flow to ebb. What on earth would Susannah Chancellor have been doing in any of those places?

Above were much more likely sites: London Bridge, Blackfriars, Waterloo; even Westminster was not so far. He was talking about miles. Although she was probably put in either from a bridge or from the north bank to have washed up on the north side as she was.

To have gone in where she was found, at the Tower of London, seemed impossible. What could she have been doing there? Nor could she have been in the immediate area. There was only Customs House Quay on one side and St. Catherine's Docks on the other.

The best thing would be to find out what time she left her home in Berkeley Square, and how. No one had mentioned if she took one of her own carriages; presumably they had at least one. Where had the coachman left her? Was it conceivable she had been killed by one of her own servants? He could not imagine it, but it had better be eliminated all the same.

He was already retracing his steps to Berkeley Square and it took him only another few minutes to reach number seventeen again. This time he went down to the areaway steps rather than disturb them at the front door.

It was opened by the bootboy looking white-faced and frightened.

"We ain't buyin' nuffink today," he said flatly. "Come back another time." He made as if to close the door.

"I am the police," Pitt told him quietly. "I need to come in. You know what has happened. I have to find out who did it, so I must discover all you know."

"I don't know nuffink!"

"Don't you know what time Mrs. Chancellor went out?"

"Who is it, Tommy?" a man's voice called from somewhere behind him.

"It's the rozzers, George."

The door opened wider and a servant with his right arm in a sling faced Pitt suspiciously.

Pitt handed him his card.

"You'd better come in," the man said reluctantly. "I don't know what we can tell you."

The bootboy stood aside to allow Pitt in. The scullery was full of vegetables, pots and pans, and a small maid with red eyes and her apron bunched up in one hand.

"Mr. Richards is busy," the man went on, leading Pitt through the kitchen and into the butler's pantry. "And the footmen are in the hall. The maids are all too upset to answer the door."

Pitt had assumed he was a footman, but apparently he was mistaken.

"Who are you?" he asked.

"Coachman, George Bragg."

Pitt looked at the arm. "When did you do that?"

"Last night." He smiled bitterly. "It's only a scald. It'll mend."

"Then you did not drive Mrs. Chancellor when she went out?"

"No sir. She took a hansom. Mr. Chancellor went with her to get one. She was going to be some time, and Mr. Chancellor himself was planning to go out later, in the carriage."

"They keep only one carriage?" Pitt was surprised. Carriages, horses and general harness and livery were marks of social standing. Most people kept as many and of as high a quality as they could, often running into debt to maintain them.

"Oh no sir," Bragg said hastily. "But Mrs. Chancellor hadn't been planning to go out, and so we hadn't got the big carriage harnessed up, and Mr. Chancellor was going to use the brougham himself, later. She was going only less than a mile away. I daresay she'd have walked it in daylight."

"So it was after dark when she left?"

"Oh yes sir. About half past nine, I would say. And looked like it could come on to rain. But Lily saw her go. She would tell you more exact. That is if she can pull herself together long enough. She was very fond of Mrs. Chancellor, and she's in a terrible state."

"If you can find her, please," Pitt requested.

George left Pitt alone to do as he asked, and was gone nearly a quarter of an hour before he returned with a red-faced, puffy-eyed girl of about eighteen, who was obviously extremely distressed.

"Good morning, Lily," Pitt said quietly. "Please sit down."

Lily was so unused to being asked to sit in the presence of superiors, she did not comprehend the order.

"Sit down, Lily." George pushed her with a gentle hand into the chair.

"George says you saw Mrs. Chancellor leave the house last night, Lily," Pitt began. "Is that so?"

"Yes sir." She sniffed.

"Do you know what time that was?"

"About half past nine, sir. I'm not sure exact."

"Tell me what happened."

"I were up on the landing, from turning down the beds, an' I saw the mistress going across the 'all to the front door." She gulped. "She were wearin' her blue cloak which she's so fond of. I saw her go out the front door. That's the truth. I swear it is." She started to cry again, quietly and with surprising dignity.

"And you usually turn the beds down at half past nine?"

"Yes, yes . . . sir . . ."

"Thank you. That's all I need to trouble you for. Oh— except, you saw Mrs. Chancellor. Did you see Mr. Chancellor as well?"

"No, sir. 'E must a' gone out already."

"I see. Thank you."

She stood up with a little assistance from George, and left the room, closing the door behind her.

"Is there anyone else you need to see, sir?" the coachman asked.

"You said Mr. Chancellor went out later?"

"Yes sir."

"But you didn't drive him?" Pitt looked at the arm in the sling.

"No, sir. I hurt my arm before he went out, in fact just before. Mr. Chancellor drove himself. He's quite good with a light vehicle. He could manage the brougham easily, and of course he'd called down before, so it was already harnessed."

"I see. Thank you. Do you know what time he came back?"

"No sir. But he's often late. Cabinet meetings and the like can go on half the night, if the government's got troubles . . . and when hasn't it?"

"Indeed. Thank you, I don't think there is anything else I need to ask here, at least for the moment. Unless you can tell me anything you think may be of use?"

"No sir. It's the most terrible thing I ever heard. I don't know what can have happened." He looked grieved and confused.

Pitt left, his mind full of doubts and ugly speculation. He walked back along Bruton Street deep in thought. Susannah had told her husband that she was going to see Christabel Thorne, but apparently that was untrue; unless she had been waylaid somewhere along Mount Street, within ten minutes of leaving home?

263

But why lie, unless it was something she did not wish him to know? Where could she be going, and with whom, that she felt compelled to keep it from him? Was it possible she knew who the traitor was in the Colonial Office? Or at least that she suspected? Was it even conceivable that it was she herself, stealing information from Chancellor without his knowledge? Did he take papers home with him, and she had somehow seen them? Or did he discuss such matters with her, since her family was so prominent in banking? Could she have been on the way, even then, to the German Embassy? Then who had stopped her? Who had found her between Berkeley Square and Upper Brook Street, and taken her to the riverbank and killed her? He must have been waiting for her, if that were true.

Or was it a far simpler, more ordinary explanation, one of an assignation with a lover? Christabel Thorne had doubted it, but she had not thought it impossible. Was that what lay between Susannah and Kreisler, and all the arguments about Africa were of only secondary importance, or even none at all? Was the emotion that racked her guilt?

And why had the hansom driver not come to the police? Surely he would do once the discovery of the body was broadcast throughout London when the newspapers reached the streets. That could only be a matter of hours. The early editions would have it now, and by lunchtime newsboys would be shouting it.

It was a bright day, people were smiling in the sun, women in frocks of muslin and lace, parasols spread, carriage harnesses shining, and yet he felt none of it as he walked, head down, towards Oxford Street.

Was it even imaginable that it was anything to do with the Inner Circle? She had known Sir Arthur, and apparently liked him profoundly. Could she possibly have known anything about his death? Was that the secret that troubled her, some dreadful suspicion which she had at last realized?

If so, who was it? Not Chancellor. Pitt would be prepared to swear Chancellor was not a member. What about

Thorne? Susannah was a close friend of Christabel. She would feel she was betraying a relationship that was dear to her, and yet she would feel equally unable to keep her silence in the face of murder. No wonder Charlotte had said she looked tormented.

Two young women passed him, laughing, their skirts brushing his feet. They seemed a world away.

Did Christabel know anything about it? Or was she speaking the truth when she said Susannah had not been there? Perhaps she had no idea that the husband she seemed so close to was capable of murdering her friend to prevent her from exposing the Circle. How would she bear it when she was forced to know?

Was Jeremiah Thorne, in his own way, another victim of the Inner Circle, destroyed by a covenant made in ignorance, if not innocence, a man who dared not be true to himself, for fear of losing . . . what? His position, his social standing, his financial credit, his life?

In Oxford Street he hailed a cab and gave the driver the address of the Bow Street station. The medical examiner might have made a preliminary report, at least, a guess as to the time of death, and apart from that, he should see Farnsworth.

He spent the journey considering what steps to take next. It would be difficult. One did not lightly investigate the wife of a cabinet minister, and one of the most popular at that. People would have their own ideas as to what had happened to her, fundamental beliefs they would not wish challenged. Emotions would be raw. He would present an easy target, someone to blame for the grief and the anger, and for the fear which would follow. If a cabinet minister's wife, in a hansom in Mayfair, could be murdered, who is safe?

By the time he alighted in Bow Street the late editions of the newspapers were on sale, and a boy was shouting in a clear, penetrating voice.

"Extra! Terrible murder! Minister's wife! Linus Chancellor's wife found dead at Tower o' London! Extra! Extra!" His voice dropped. " 'Ere, Mr. Pitt. You wanna copy? It's all 'ere!"

"No thank you," Pitt refused. "If I don't know it already, then it is a lie." And leaving the boy giggling, he walked up the steps and into the police station.

Farnsworth was already there, tight faced and less immaculate than usual. He was coming down the stairs as Pitt reached the bottom to go up.

"Ah, good," Farnsworth said immediately. "I've been waiting for you. Good God, this is awful!" He bit his lip. "Poor Chancellor. The most brilliant colonial secretary we've had in years, possibly even a future prime minister, and this had to happen to him. What have you learned?" He turned on the steps and started back up again towards Pitt's office.

Pitt followed him up, closing the door before replying.

"She left the house at half past nine yesterday evening, Chancellor with her, but he only went so far as to call her a hansom and put her in it. She said she was going to visit Christabel Thorne, in Upper Brook Street, about fifteen minutes away at the most. But Mrs. Thorne says she never reached there, nor was she expecting her."

"Is that all?" Farnsworth said grimly. He was standing with his back to the window, but even so his expression was unmistakable, a mixture of shock and despairing anxiety.

"So far," Pitt replied. "Oh, she was wearing a blue cloak when she left home, according to the maid who saw her go, but it wasn't on her when we found her. Possibly it's still in the river. If it is washed up somewhere else, it might provide an indication as to where she went in."

Farnsworth thought for a moment. He opened his mouth to say something, then possibly realized the answer, and merely grunted. "Suppose it could have been anywhere, depending on the tide?"

"Yes, although according to the river boatmen, more of-

266

ten than not they surface again more or less where they went in."

Farnsworth pulled a face of distaste.

"The time of death may help with that," Pitt went on. "If it is early enough it had to be well before the tide turned."

"When did it turn?"

"About half past two."

"What a damnable thing! I suppose you have no idea as to motive? Was she robbed . . . or . . ." His face crumpled and he refused to put words to the second thought.

Pitt had not even entertained that idea. His mind had been too full of treason, and knowledge of the murder of Arthur Desmond.

"I don't know, sir," he confessed. "The medical examiner will tell us that. I haven't a report from him yet. It is a little early."

"Robbery?" Farnsworth looked hopeful.

"I don't know that either. There was a locket 'round her neck when she was found. That was how they knew who she was. I didn't ask Chancellor if she were wearing anything else of value."

Farnsworth frowned. "No, perhaps not. Poor man. He must be devastated. This is terrible, Pitt! For every reason, we must clear this up as soon as possible." He came forward from the window. "You'd better leave the Colonial Office business to Tellman. You concentrate on this. It's dreadful . . . quite dreadful. I can't remember a case so . . . so shocking since . . ." He stopped.

Pitt would have said, The autumn of 'eighty-eight, and the Whitechapel murders, but there was no point. One did not compare horrors one with another.

"Unless they are connected," he said instead.

Farnsworth's head jerked up. "What?"

"Unless Mrs. Chancellor's death and the Colonial Office treason are connected," he elaborated.

Farnsworth looked at him as if he had spoken blasphemy.

"It is not impossible," Pitt said quietly, meeting his eyes.

"She may quite accidentally have discovered something, without any guilt on her part."

Farnsworth relaxed.

"Or she may very possibly be involved," Pitt added.

"I hope you have sufficient intelligence not to say that anywhere but here?" Farnsworth said slowly. "Not even hint that you have thought it?"

"Of course I have."

"I trust you to deal with this, Pitt." It was something of a question, and Farnsworth stared at him with entreaty in his face. "I don't always approve of your methods, or your judgments, but you've solved some of the worst cases in London, at one time or another. Do everything you can with this. Think of nothing else until it is finished . . . do you understand?"

"Yes, of course." He would not have done anything else regardless of what Farnsworth had said, and perhaps Farnsworth knew that.

Further discussion was preempted by a sharp knock on the door, and a constable poked his head around the moment Farnsworth answered.

"Yes?" Farnsworth said abruptly.

The constable looked embarrassed. "There's a lady to see Mr. Pitt, sir."

"Well tell her to wait!" Farnsworth snapped. "Pitt is busy."

"No, sir. I—I mean a real lady." The constable did not move. "I daren't tell 'er that, sir. You haven't seen 'er."

"For heaven's sake, man! Are you scared of a woman just because she thinks she's important?" Farnsworth barked. "Go and do as you're told!"

"But, sir, I . . ." He got no further. An imperious voice behind him interrupted his embarrassment.

"Thank you, Constable. If this is Mr. Pitt's office, I shall tell him myself that I am here." And the moment after the door swung wide and Vespasia fixed Farnsworth with a glittering eye. She looked magnificent in ecru lace and silk, and pearls worth a fortune across her bosom. "I don't believe I have your acquaintance, sir," she said coolly. "I am Lady Vespasia Cumming-Gould."

Farnsworth took a deep breath and gulped, swallowed the wrong way and relapsed into a fit of coughing.

Vespasia waited.

"Assistant Commissioner Farnsworth," Pitt said for him, hiding both his astonishment and his amusement with some difficulty.

"How do you do, Mr. Farnsworth." Vespasia swept past him into the office and sat down on the chair in front of Pitt's desk, resting her parasol, point down, on the carpet and waiting until Farnsworth should have recovered himself, or taken his leave, or preferably both.

"Have you come to see me, Aunt Vespasia?" Pitt asked her.

She looked at him coldly. "Of course I have. Why on earth else should I come to this unfortunate place? I do not frequent police stations for my amusement, Thomas."

Farnsworth was still in considerable difficulty, gasping for breath, tears running down his cheeks.

"How may I be of service?" Pitt asked Vespasia as he took his place behind his desk, Micah Drummond's very beautiful oak desk with the green leather inlay. Pitt was very proud to have inherited it.

"You may not," she replied, a slight melting in her silver eyes, "I have come in order to help you, or at least to give you further information, whether it helps or not."

Farnsworth was still unable to stop coughing. He stood with his handkerchief to his scarlet face.

"In relation to what?" Pitt enquired.

"For heaven's sake, assist that man before he chokes himself!" she ordered. "Haven't you brandy, or at least water to offer him?"

"There's a bottle of cider in the corner cupboard," Pitt suggested.

Farnsworth grimaced. Micah Drummond would have

kept brandy. Pitt could not afford it, and had no taste for it anyway.

"If . . . you will . . . excuse me . . ." Farnsworth managed to get out between gasps.

"I will." Vespasia inclined her head sympathetically, and as soon as Farnsworth was gone, she looked back at Pitt. "Regarding the murder of Susannah Chancellor. Can anything else be on your mind this morning?"

"No. I had not realized you would have heard of it already."

She did not bother to reply to that. "I saw her the evening before last," she said gravely. "I did not overhear her conversation, but I observed it, and I could not help but see that it aroused the profoundest emotions."

"With whom?"

She looked at him as if she knew exactly what he feared. There was profound sorrow in her face.

"Peter Kreisler," she replied.

"Where was this?"

"At Lady Rattray's house in Eaton Square. She was holding a musical evening. There were fifty or sixty people there, no more."

"And you saw Kreisler and Mrs. Chancellor?" he prompted, a sinking feeling of disappointment inside him. "Can you describe the encounter for me, as precisely as possible?"

A flicker of disapproval crossed her face and disappeared. "I do understand the importance of the issue, Thomas. I am not inclined to embroider it. I was some ten or twelve feet away, half listening to an extremely tedious acquaintance talking about her health. Such a tasteless thing to do. No one wishes to know the details of somebody else's ailments. I observed Mrs. Chancellor first. She was talking very earnestly to someone whose face was mostly hidden behind a very luxuriant potted palm. The wretched place was like a jungle. I was forever expecting insects to drop out of the trees down my neck. I did not envy the young women with deep décolletages!" She shrugged very slightly.

Pitt could picture it, but it was not the time to comment.

"Her face wore an expression of deep concern, almost anguish," Vespasia continued. "I could see that she was on the verge of a quarrel. I moved so as to learn who her companion was. He seemed to be pleading with her, but at the same time adamant that he would not change his own mind. The course of the argument altered, and it seemed she was the one entreating. There was an appearance of something close to desperation in her. But judging from her face, he could not be moved. After the course of some fifteen minutes or so, they parted. He looked well pleased with himself, as if he found the outcome quite acceptable. She was distraught."

"But you have no idea of the subject of this conversation?" he asked, though he already knew the answer.

"None at all, and I refuse to speculate."

"Was that the last time you saw Mrs. Chancellor?"

"Yes. And also the last time I saw Mr. Kreisler." She looked profoundly unhappy, and the depth of her sadness troubled him.

"What is it you fear?" he asked frankly. She was not someone with whom subtlety or evasion would be successful. She could read him far too well.

"I am afraid Mr. Kreisler's love for Africa, and what he sees as its good, far outweigh any other consideration with him, or any other loyalty," she replied. "It is not a quality which will leave Nobby Gunne unhurt. I have known several men during my life whose devotion to a cause would excuse in their minds any behavior towards a mere individual, in the firm belief that it is a nobler and greater ideal." She sighed and allowed her parasol to fall sideways against her skirt.

"They all had an intense vitality about them, a charm based upon the fire and bravado of their nature, and an ability to treat one, for a short time, as if all the ardor of their

271

spirit were somehow reachable to others, to love, if you like. Invariably I found there was a coldness at the core of them, an obsession which fed upon itself and which consumed sacrifices without return. That is what I am afraid of, Thomas—not for myself, but for Nobby. She is a fine person, and I am extremely fond of her."

There was nothing to say, no argument to make that was honest.

"I hope you are mistaken." He smiled at her gently. "But thank you very much for coming to tell me." He offered his hand, but she rose, disregarding it. She walked, stiff backed, head erect, to the door, which he opened for her, and then he conducted her downstairs and out into the street, where he handed her up into her waiting carriage.

"Before she went into the water, without doubt," the medical examiner said, pushing his lower lip out and taking a deep breath. He looked up at Pitt, waiting for criticism. He was a long-faced, dour man who took the tragedies of his calling seriously. "One thing to be said for the swine that did this, though, he was quick. Hit her a couple of times, very hard."

"I don't see it!" Pitt interrupted.

"You wouldn't. Side of the head, mostly hidden by her hair. Then he throttled her so violently he broke the bone"—he touched his own neck—"and killed her almost immediately. Doubt she felt more than the first blow, and then a moment's choking before it was all over. Wasn't strangled to death."

Pitt looked at him with a sense of chill. "Very violently?"

"Very. Either he meant to kill her, or he was in such a monumental fury he didn't realize his own strength. You're looking for a very dangerous man, Pitt. Either he's completely merciless and he kills to rob, even when there's no need—he could have silenced her perfectly well without doing this to her—or else he's someone with such a hatred

272

in him it erupts in something close to madness, if not actually into it."

"Was she . . . molested?"

"Good God, of course she was molested! What do you call that?" He jerked his head towards the body on the table, now covered with a sheet. "If you mean was she raped, don't be so damned lily-livered about it. God, I hate euphemisms! Call a crime by its ugly name, and be honest with the victim. No she wasn't."

Pitt let out a sigh of relief. He had cared about that more than he realized. He felt the knots in his shoulders easing a little and something of the pain inside him dulled.

"When did she die? Can you judge a time?" he asked.

"Not close enough to be of much use to you," the medical examiner replied with a snort. "Anything between eight and midnight, I should think. Being put into the river doesn't help. Cold, even at this time of the year. Makes a mess of rigor mortis. Makes a damned mess of everything! Actually, talking about a mess . . ." He frowned, looking across at Pitt with a puzzled expression. "Found some odd marks on her body, very slight, 'round her shoulders. Or to be more accurate, under her arms and across the back of her neck. She'd been dragged around in the water a lot. Could have been her clothes got caught up in something, pulled tight and caused it. When was she found?"

"About half past three."

"And when was the last time she was seen alive?"

"Half past nine."

"There you are then. You can work out for yourself almost as much as I can tell you. You've got a very dangerous man to look for, and good luck to you. You'll need it. Lovely woman. It's too bad." And without waiting for anything further he turned back to the body he was presently examining.

"Can you tell how long she was in the water?" Pitt asked.

"Not any closer than you can work out for yourself. I

should say more than thirty minutes, less than three hours. Sorry."

"Was she killed manually?"

"What? Oh yes. He killed her with his bare hands, no ligature, just fingers around the throat. As I already said, a very powerful man, or one driven by a passion the like of which I hope never to see. I don't envy you your job, Pitt."

"Nor I yours," Pitt said sincerely.

The medical examiner laughed with a short barklike sound. "It's all over when I get them, no more pain, no more violence or hatred left, just peace and a long silence. The rest is up to God . . . if He cares."

"I care," Pitt said between his teeth. "And God has got to be better than I am."

The medical examiner laughed again, and this time there was a softer tone to it. But he said nothing.

It was a surprisingly long time from half past nine in the evening until about midnight. Not many people could account for their whereabouts for those two and a half hours, beyond possible dispute. Pitt took two men from other cases, leaving Tellman on the matter of the Colonial Office, and also diverted his own time to questioning and checking, but he found no evidence that was conclusive of anything.

Linus Chancellor said that he had gone out, driving his own carriage owing to the accident to his coachman. He had gone to deliver a package of crucial importance to Garston Aylmer, who had apparently been out when he got there. He was most annoyed about it, but had left it with Aylmer's footman, who upon being asked, confirmed that Chancellor had indeed called at a little before eleven o'clock.

Chancellor's own servants had not heard him come in, but they had been instructed not to wait up for him.

Susannah's maid had sat up for her mistress, naturally, as was her duty, so that she might assist her to undress when

274

she returned, and hang up her clothes. She had fallen asleep in her chair about half past three, and only realized Susannah's failure to return in the morning. She refused to say anything about it, or to explain why she had not raised any alarm earlier.

It was apparent to Pitt that she had assumed her mistress had kept an assignation, and while she desperately disapproved of it, she was too loyal to betray it either. No pressure from Pitt, or the butler, would make her alter her account.

Pitt went to find Peter Kreisler and require him to account for his movements, but when he presented himself at Kreisler's rooms he was informed that Kreisler was out, and not expected home for several hours. He was obliged to wait for that answer.

Aylmer said he had been out looking at the stars. He was an enthusiastic astronomer. No one could confirm it. It was not an avocation shared by many, and could be conducted excellently alone. He had taken a small telescope on a tripod to Herne Hill, away from the city lights. He had driven himself in a gig which he kept for such purposes, and saw no one he knew. If his story were true, one would not have expected him to. There would not be many gentlemen from the Colonial or Foreign Offices wandering around Herne Hill in the small hours of the morning.

Jeremiah and Christabel Thorne had spent the evening at home. She had retired early. He had stayed up till past midnight reading official papers. The servants agreed that this was true. They also agreed that had either Mr. or Mrs. Thorne left the house by the garden door to the dining room, none of them would have been aware of it, having all retired beyond the baize door to their own quarters after dinner was cleared away. There were no fires to stoke, no visitors to show in or out, and Mr. Thorne had said he would draw the curtains himself and make sure the doors were fast.

Ian Hathaway had dined at his club and left at half past

eleven. He said he had gone straight home, but since he lived alone, and he had not required his servants to wait up for him, there was no one to corroborate his word. He might as easily have left again, had he chosen to.

As a matter of course Francis Standish, Susannah's brother-in-law, was also informed of her death, and probably asked if he would tell them where he had spent the evening. He replied that he had come home early, changed his clothes, and gone out to the theater alone. No, there was no one who could corroborate that.

What had he seen?

Esther Sandraz. He could describe the play in very general terms, but that meant nothing. A newspaper review would give him that.

Naturally every effort was made to find the driver of the hansom who had picked up Susannah Chancellor in Berkeley Square. He was the only one who knew what had happened to her after that, until she had met her murderer.

The constable deputed by Pitt spent all afternoon and all evening searching for him, and failed completely. The following day Pitt withdrew Tellman from the Colonial Office matter and put him to the task. He was equally unsuccessful.

"Perhaps it wasn't a real hansom?" Tellman said sourly. "Perhaps it was our murderer, dressed up to look like a cabby?"

It was a thought which had already occurred to Pitt. "Then find out where he got the hansom from," he instructed. "If that is the case, then it cuts down the possibilities for time. We know that most of the people we have suspected so far in the Colonial Office matter can account for themselves at half past nine."

Tellman snorted. "Did you really think it was one of them?" he said with contempt. "Why? Why would any of them kill Mrs. Chancellor?"

"Why would anybody at all kill her?" Pitt countered.

"Robbery. There are two rings missing, Bailey said. He checked with her maid."

"What about the locket? Why didn't they take that?" Pitt pursued it. "And did the maid say she was wearing her rings that night?"

"What?"

"Did the maid say she was wearing her rings that evening?" Pitt repeated patiently. "Ladies have been known to lose jewelry, even valuable pieces, or to pawn them, or sell them, or give them away."

"I don't think he asked." Tellman was annoyed because he had not thought of that. "I'll send him back."

"You'd better. But keep looking for that cabdriver all the same."

The last person Pitt found was Peter Kreisler. Three times the previous day Pitt had called upon him, and on each occasion he had still been absent, and his manservant had had no idea if he would be back at all that day. On the second occasion of Pitt's calling the footman informed him that Mr. Kreisler had been deeply upset by the news of Mrs. Chancellor's death, and had left the building almost immediately, without giving any indication as to where he was bound and when he intended to return.

When Pitt went again on the afternoon after Tellman's unsuccessful search for the cabdriver, Kreisler was at home, and received Pitt immediately and with some eagerness. His face was tired, as if he had slept little, and there was an intense nervous energy about him, but his grief, whatever its depth or extent, was well in control. But then Pitt imagined Kreisler was a man who masked his emotions at any time, and was used to both triumph and tragedy.

"Come in, Superintendent," he said quickly, showing him into a surprisingly charming room with a polished wooden floor and delicate African carvings on the mantel. There were no animal skins or horns, but one very fine painting of a cheetah. He waved to one of the chairs. "Dobson, bring the Superintendent a drink. What would you like, ale, tea, something stronger?"

"Have you cider?"

"Certainly. Dobson, cider for Superintendent Pitt. I'll have some too." He waved at the chair again, and himself sat opposite, leaning forward towards Pitt, his face earnest. "Have you found anything of importance yet? I have been studying the tides of the river to see where she could have been put in. That may help to discover where she was killed, and thus of course where she went from Berkeley Square, which I believe she left in the mid-evening, alone." His hands were clenched in front of him. "At least, alone as soon as Chancellor had called a cab for her and seen her into it. If she was bound for Upper Brook Street, she must have been waylaid almost immediately. Do you think it was meant to be an abduction, and somehow it went wrong?"

It was actually a thought which had not occurred to Pitt, and there was a glimmer of sense in it.

"For ransom?" he asked, aware that the surprise was in his voice.

"Why not?" Kreisler pointed out. "It seems to me to make more sense than to murder her, poor woman. Chancellor has both wealth and a great deal of power. So has her brother-in-law, Standish. Possibly it was intended to try to coerce him in some way. Which is an extremely ugly thought, but not an impossible one."

"No . . . indeed," Pitt agreed reluctantly. "Although it must have gone very badly wrong to end like this. She was certainly not killed by accident."

"Why?" Kreisler looked at him intently, his face tight with emotion. "Why do you say that, Superintendent?"

"The manner of her death made that apparent," Pitt replied. He did not intend to discuss it further with Kreisler, who was in many ways a principal suspect.

"Are you sure?" Kreisler pressed. "Whose good could her death serve? Surely it would . . ." His voice trailed off.

"If I knew whose good it served, Mr. Kreisler, I should

278

be a great deal further towards finding her murderer," Pitt answered. "You seem very profoundly concerned in the matter. Did you know her better than I had supposed?" He watched Kreisler closely, the pallor of his skin, the brilliance of his eyes, the tiny muscles flickering in his jaw.

"I have met her several times, and found her charming and intelligent, and a woman of great sensitivity and honor," he replied with a tensely loud voice. "Is that not more than enough reason to be horrified at her death and to wish passionately that her murderer should be found?"

"Of course it is," Pitt said very quietly. "But most people, however profound their feelings, are content to leave it to the police to bring that about."

"Well I am not," Kreisler stated fiercely. "I will do everything in my power to learn who it is, and make damned sure the world knows it too. And frankly, Superintendent, I don't care whether that pleases you or not."

9

P_{ITT} ARRIVED HOME late after a day which was exhausting both physically and emotionally. He was looking forward to putting the whole matter out of his mind for a space, and sitting in the parlor with his feet up and the doors to the garden open to let in the late spring evening air. It was fine and balmy, the sort of day when the smells of the earth linger heavily and overtake the awareness of a mighty city beyond the garden walls. One could think only of flowers, cut lawns, shady trees and moths drifting lazily in the stillness.

However as soon as he entered the hallway he knew that was not to be. Charlotte came out of the parlor, her face grave, a warning in her eyes.

"What is it?" he said with apprehension.

"Matthew is here to see you," she replied softly, aware of the open door behind her. "He looks very worried, but he wouldn't tell me anything about it."

"You asked him?"

"No, of course I didn't. But I made . . . listening noises."

He smiled in spite of himself, touched her gently as he passed and went into the parlor.

Matthew was sitting in Pitt's favorite chair, staring out of the open French windows across the lawn towards the apple tree. As soon as he felt Pitt's presence in the room, even though there had been no sound, he turned around and stood up. His face was pale and there were still shadows around his eyes. He looked as if he had suffered a long illness and was only barely well enough to be out of his bed.

"What's happened?" Pitt demanded, closing the door behind him.

Matthew seemed startled, as though the directness of the question had been unexpected.

"Nothing, at least nothing new. I . . . I wondered if you had been able to learn anything more about Father's death." He opened his eyes wide and stared at Pitt questioningly.

Pitt felt guilty, even though he had every reason for having been unable to even think of the matter.

"No, I . . . I am afraid not. The assistant commissioner has given me the murder of Susannah Chancellor, and it has driven—"

"I understand. Of course I do," Matthew interrupted. "You don't need to explain it to me, Thomas. I am not a child." He walked towards the French doors as if he meant to go outside into the evening air. "I just . . . wondered."

"Is that what you came for?" Pitt asked doubtfully. He joined Matthew in the doorway.

"Of course." Matthew stepped across the threshold and out onto the paved terrace.

Pitt followed, and together they walked very slowly over the grass towards the apple tree and the shaded section of the wall. There was deep green moss on the stones, rich as velvet, and low down near the ground a creeping plant with yellow starlike flowers.

"What else has happened?" Pitt repeated. "You look dreadful."

"I had a crack on the head." Matthew pulled a face and winced. "You were there."

"Is it worse? Have you had the doctor back?"

"No, no it's getting better. It's just slow. This is a fearful business about Chancellor's wife." He frowned and took another step across the soft grass. It was thick within the shade of the tree and spongy under the feet. The white drift of the apple blossom was faintly sweet in the air, a clean, uncloying smell. "Have you any idea what happened?"

"Not yet. Why? Do you know anything?"

"Me?" This time Matthew looked genuinely surprised. "Nothing at all. I just think it's a dreadful stroke of fate for a man so brilliant, and whose personal life was so unusually happy. There are many politicians who could have lost their wives and been little the worse for it at heart, but not Chancellor."

Pitt stared at him. The remark was curiously uncharacteristic, as if only half his mind were on his words. Pitt was becoming more and more certain that there was in fact something troubling him.

"Did you know Chancellor well?" he asked aloud.

"Moderately," Matthew replied, continuing to walk, and not looking at Pitt. "He's one of the most accessible men of high rank. Agreeable to talk to. He comes from a fairly ordinary family. Welsh, I believe, at least originally. They may have been in the Home Counties a while now. It wasn't political, was it?" He turned to Pitt, curiosity and puzzlement in his face. "I mean, it couldn't be, surely?"

"I don't know," Pitt replied candidly. "At the moment I have no idea at all."

"None?"

"What did you have in mind when you asked?"

"Don't play games with me, Thomas," Matthew said irritably. "I'm not one of your damned suspects!" Then a moment later he was struck with contrition. "I'm sorry. I don't know what I meant. I'm still plagued by Father's death. Part of my mind is convinced he was murdered, and by the Inner Circle, both to keep him from saying anything more about them and as a warning to other would-be traitors to the oaths. Loyalty's a hell of a thing, Thomas. How much loyalty can you demand of anyone? I'm not even sure I know what loyalty is. If you had asked me a year ago, or six months ago, I would have been quite convinced it was a stupid question, not even worth asking because the answer was so obvious. Now I can't answer it." He stood still on the grass, his face full of confusion, his eyes searching Pitt's. "Can you?"

Pitt thought for a long time before he replied, and even then it was tentative.

"I suppose it is honoring your promises," he said slowly. "But then it is also honoring your obligations, even if there have been no specific promises made."

"Exactly," Matthew agreed. "But who sets out what those obligations are, or to whom? Whose is the first claim? What when people assume you have some obligation to them, and you don't assume it? They can, you know."

"Sir Arthur and the Inner Circle?"

Matthew lifted his shoulders in a gesture of vague assent. "Anyone. Sometimes we take for granted things, and imagine that other people do too … and perhaps they don't. I mean … how well do we know each other, how well do we even know ourselves, until we are tested? You imagine you will behave in a certain way if you are faced with a choice, but when the time comes, you find you don't."

Pitt was even surer that Matthew had something specific in mind. There was too much passion in his voice for it to be mere philosophizing. But equally obviously, he was not yet ready to speak of it openly. Pitt did not even know if it was actually to do with Sir Arthur, or if he had merely mentioned that as something they had in common from which to begin.

"You mean a division of loyalties?"

Matthew moved a step away. Pitt knew he had touched a nerve, and it was too soon.

Matthew waited a moment before he replied. The garden was silent. Somewhere beyond the hedges a dog barked. A tortoiseshell cat walked along the wall and dropped soundlessly into the orchard.

"Some of those men at the inquest genuinely felt as if he had betrayed a trust," Matthew said at last. "A loyalty to their secret society, perhaps in a way to their class. Somebody in the Colonial Office is betraying their country, but perhaps they don't see it like that." He took a deep breath, his eyes on the wind in the apple leaves. "Father felt that to keep silent about the Inner Circle was to betray all that he felt most important in life, although he might never have thought to give it a name. I'm not sure I like giving things names. Does that sound like evasion? Once you give things a name and promise allegiance, you've given part of yourself away. I'm not prepared to do that." He looked at Pitt with a frown. "Can you understand that, Thomas?"

"Most things don't ask for an unlimited allegiance," Pitt pointed out. "That is what is wrong with the Inner Circle; it asks men to promise loyalty in advance of knowing what will be asked of them."

"A sacrifice of conscience, Father called it."

"Then you have answered your own question," Pitt pointed out. "You didn't need to ask me, and you shouldn't care what my answer would have been."

Matthew flashed him a sudden, brilliant smile. "I don't," he confessed, putting his hands into his pockets.

"Then what still troubles you?" Pitt asked, because the shadow and the tension were still in Matthew, and the smile faded as quickly as it had come.

Matthew sighed, turning away from the orchard wall and beginning to walk slowly along it. "Yes, you and I can say that comfortably because we have no issue between us that we see differently. But how would you feel if my course led me to do something which you felt betrayed you? Wouldn't you hate me for it?"

"Are you talking about all this in theory, Matthew, or is there something specific you are trying to find the courage to say?" Pitt fell in step beside him.

Matthew looked away, facing back towards the house. "I

don't even know of anything about which I believe all that differently from you. I was thinking of Father, and his friends in the Inner Circle." He glanced sideways for a moment at Pitt. "Some of them were his friends, you know? That is what he found so terribly difficult."

Nothing that Matthew said was untrue, but Pitt still had the feeling that in some way Matthew was lying. They walked up the lawn towards the house together but they did not touch on the subject again. Charlotte invited Matthew to stay and dine with them, but he declined, and took his leave, his face still shadowed with anxiety, and Pitt watched him go with a sadness he could not rid himself of all evening.

Charlotte looked at Pitt enquiringly when Matthew was gone. "Is he all right? He looked . . ." She searched for a word.

"Troubled," Pitt supplied it for her, sitting down in his chair and leaning back, stretching a little. "Yes, I am almost sure there is something else, but he cannot bring himself to say it."

"What sort of thing?" She looked at him anxiously. He was not sure whether she was concerned for Matthew or for both of them. He could see in her eyes the knowledge of his own regret mixed so heavily with his loss.

He turned his gaze away. "I don't know, something to do with loyalties. . . ."

She drew in her breath sharply, as if to speak, then changed her mind tactfully. He almost laughed, it was so unlike her, but it would too easily have broken into misery.

"I suppose it is to do with the Circle," he said, although he was not at all sure that was what had gnawed at Matthew so painfully. But either way, this evening he preferred not to think of it any further. "What is for dinner?"

"That's not much," Farnsworth said grimly when Pitt reported to him next. "The wretched man cannot have disappeared from the face of the earth." He was referring to the driver of the hansom cab which had picked up Susannah Chancellor in Berkeley Square. "Who did you say you had on it?"

They were in his own office rather than Pitt's room in Bow Street, and he stood by the window looking towards the Embankment of the river. Pitt sat in the chair opposite. Farnsworth had invited him to sit when he had first come in, and then a moment later had risen himself. It gave him a physical advantage he seemed to prefer.

"Tellman," Pitt replied, sitting back a little farther. He did not in the least mind looking up. "And I tried myself. I know the man may be crucial, but so far we have found no trace of him, which leads me to—"

"If you are going to say Chancellor was lying, then you are a fool," Farnsworth said irritably. "You surely cannot be so out of touch with reality as to imagine Chancellor would—"

"The whole question is irrelevant," Pitt interrupted in his turn. "Chancellor went straight back to his house and was seen within ten minutes of having put her in the hansom. I already know that from his own household staff. Not that I suspected him anyway. It is merely a matter of form to ascertain where everyone was at the relevant time."

Farnsworth did not reply to that.

"Which leads me to suppose," Pitt finished the sentence Farnsworth had broken into, "that the driver was in some way implicated. Possibly he was not a regular cabby at all, but someone dressed as one."

"Then where did he get the hansom from?" Farnsworth demanded. "Chancellor said it was a hansom. He would know the difference between a cab and a private carriage."

"I've got Tellman looking into that now. So far we don't know, but it must have come from somewhere, either hired or stolen. He's going around to all the companies."

"Good. Good. That could be the break we are needing."

"Kreisler thought it might have been an attempt at kidnapping that went wrong," Pitt suggested.

Farnsworth was startled and a flicker of irritation crossed his face.

"What? Who the devil is Kreisler?"

"Peter Kreisler. Something of an expert on African affairs." Pitt spoke thoughtfully. "He seems to be very concerned about the case. In fact he has spent a lot of time pursuing it himself."

"Why?" Farnsworth demanded, coming back to his desk and sitting opposite Pitt. "Did he know her?"

"Yes."

"Then he's a suspect, dammit!" His fist clenched. "I assume you are investigating him very thoroughly indeed?"

"Yes, of course I am." Pitt's voice rose in spite of his efforts to keep it level. "He says he was at home that evening, but he cannot prove it. His man had the evening off."

Farnsworth relaxed. "Well that may be all there is to it! It may be as simple as that, no abduction, nothing political, simply a jealous man, infatuated and rejected." There was considerable satisfaction in his voice. It would be an ideal solution.

"Possibly," Pitt agreed. "Lady Vespasia Cumming-Gould saw them in a heated discussion the previous night. But that is a long way from proving that Kreisler is violent and unstable enough to have murdered her simply because she refused him."

"Well find out, man!" Farnsworth said sharply. "Look into his past. Write to Africa, if you have to. He must have been attracted to other women at some time or another. See how he behaved then. Learn everything about him, his loves, hates, quarrels, debts, ambitions, everything there is to know about him! I am not going to allow the murder of a cabinet minister's wife to remain an unsolved case . . . and neither are you!"

It sounded like a dismissal. Pitt rose to his feet.

"And the Colonial Office," Farnsworth went on. "How are you progressing with that? Lord Salisbury asked me only yesterday if we had learned anything of use." His face tightened. "I did not inform him of your machinations to pass various different versions of false figures. God knows what he would have said if I had. I assume you have achieved nothing with that ploy or you would have told me?"

"It is too early yet," Pitt replied. "And the Colonial Office is in something of an upheaval with Chancellor himself not present."

"When do you expect that little piece of deception to bear fruit?" Farnsworth asked, not without sarcasm.

"In the next three or four days at the outside," Pitt replied.

Farnsworth frowned. "Well, I hope you are right. Personally I think you are a little too sanguine about it altogether. What do you propose to do next, if it fails?"

Pitt had not thought that far. His mind was taken up with Susannah Chancellor, and always at the back of his thoughts, intruding at every opportunity, was the death of Arthur Desmond—and, since he had seen Dr. Murray, the near certainty that he had been murdered by the Inner Circle. He still intended to prove that, as soon as the urgency of the Chancellor case allowed.

"I have no further ideas," he admitted. "Beyond continuing with usual police routine, to learn all I can of every possible suspect, in the hope that some fact, or lie, will prove who is guilty, both in the Colonial Office and in the Treasury. A connection that is not openly acknowledged would be indicative."

"Not very satisfactory, Pitt. What about this woman Pennecuick?" He stood up again and walked restlessly over towards the window. "It still looks to me as if Aylmer is your man."

"Possibly."

Farnsworth put his hands into his pockets and looked thoughtful. "You told me Aylmer could not account for his time that evening. Is it possible Mrs. Chancellor had in some fashion discovered his guilt, and that he was aware of this, and that he murdered her to protect himself? And had he, for example, any connection with Kreisler?"

"I don't know. . . ." Pitt began.

"Then find out, man! That shouldn't be beyond your wit to do." He looked at Pitt coldly, regret in his eyes.

Pitt was sure he was thinking of the Inner Circle, and how much easier such investigations might be with the help of a widespread, covert network to call on. But who would know, with all the interlocking covenants and obligations, the hierarchy of loyalties, who was bound to whom, what lies or silences were promised? Even which officers in the police might be involved, a thought which was peculiarly frightening. He met Farnsworth's stare with bland denial.

Farnsworth grunted and looked away.

"Then you had better be about it," he said, then turned to the river again, and the bright light on the water.

"There is another possibility," Pitt said quietly.

Farnsworth did not look around, but kept his back to the room and to Pitt.

"Yes?"

"That she did in fact visit the Thorne house," Pitt replied. "We are still looking for her cloak. She was wearing it when she left, but it was not with her body. If we find it, it may tell us something."

"Depending on where, I suppose," Farnsworth conceded. "Go on. What if she did visit the Thorne house?"

Farnsworth's shoulders tightened.

"Then either Thorne murdered her," Pitt answered, "or he and his wife did together, although I find that harder to believe. I think Mrs. Thorne was genuinely grieved and shocked when I told her."

"Why on earth would Thorne kill Mrs. Chancellor?

289

You're not suggesting an affair, are you?" This time there was mockery in Farnsworth's voice.

"No." Pitt did not bother to add how unlikely he thought it.

Farnsworth turned to look at him. "Then what?" His eyes widened. "The Colonial Office treason? Thorne?"

"Possibly. But there is another solution, which may not be unconnected. . . ."

"What do you mean, not unconnected?" Farnsworth frowned. "Explain yourself, Pitt. You are talking in circles. Do you mean it is connected, or don't you?"

Pitt gritted his teeth. "I think the death of Arthur Desmond may have been connected with his beliefs—"

He got no further. Farnsworth's face darkened and his eyes narrowed. "I thought we had already dismissed that, and put it to rest. Arthur Desmond was a good man who unfortunately, tragically if you like, became senile towards the end of his life and suffered from serious delusions. The kindest thing one can assume is that he accidentally took an overdose of his sleeping draft."

His lips tightened. "Less kindly, one might conclude that he knew he was losing his mind and had already seriously compromised his reputation and slandered many of his erstwhile friends, and in a moment of lucid realization of just what was happening to him, took his own life."

He swallowed. "Perhaps I should not say that is an unkind solution. On second thoughts it was a highly honorable thing to do, and most like him." His eyes met Pitt's for a moment. "Yes, I'm sure that is the man you knew also. It required a considerable courage. If you have the regard for him that you profess, you will leave it at that and let him rest in peace. By keeping on raking up the matter you are prolonging the pain for his family and seriously misadvising them. I cannot warn you more gravely that you are making a profound mistake. Do I make myself clear?"

"Perfectly," Pitt agreed, staring back at him, sensing the power of his resolve, and driven to ignore it. "But none of that is relevant to what Mrs. Chancellor may have thought, which is what we are concerned with."

"You didn't discuss this farrago of nonsense with Mrs. Chancellor, for God's sake!" Farnsworth was aghast. He was still standing with his back to the window, his face in his own shadow from the sunlight, throwing its lines and planes into sharp relief.

"No I didn't," Pitt replied steadily. "But I am aware that Mrs. Chancellor knew Sir Arthur and thought very highly of him, and that he discussed his beliefs about Africa with her. Lady Vespasia Cumming-Gould told me so."

Farnsworth pulled a face at the mention of Vespasia's name again. He was beginning to dislike her intensely.

"And how did she know that, pray? I suppose she is acquainted with Mrs. Chancellor? She is something of a busybody, and I think not to be taken seriously." The moment he had said that he regretted it. It was a mistake, and he not only saw it in Pitt's face, but his own social background was sufficient to have heard her name before, and to have recognized a true aristocrat when he met one. His temper had spoken before his intellect.

Pitt merely smiled, which was patronizing. Losing his own temper would have placed him in an equal position; this was superior.

"Well?" Farnsworth snapped. "Are you suggesting on the strength of that, that Mrs. Chancellor believed Mr. Thorne murdered Desmond, and that in fact he did, and felt compelled to murder her to keep her silent about it? Wouldn't simply denying it have been just as effective, and a great deal less trouble?" His voice was dripping sarcasm.

Put as baldly as that, it did sound absurd. Pitt felt the color rush up his face, and saw the satisfaction in Farnsworth's eyes. Farnsworth's shoulders relaxed and he turned back towards the window.

"You are losing your grip, Pitt. That was unworthy of you."

"That was your suggestion, not mine," Pitt denied it.

"What I am suggesting is that possibly Sir Arthur knew something about the missing information from the Colonial Office. After all, he often went in to the Foreign Office, and still had close connections there at the time of his death. He may not have realized the full importance of what he knew, but if he mentioned it to Susannah Chancellor, and she did understand it, because of Standish, and her family background in African finance, and Chancellor's knowledge in the Colonial Office, and her friendship with Mrs. Thorne, then . . ."

"She put it all together and tackled Thorne with it?" Farnsworth was staring at him with growing interest. "And if Thorne is the traitor after all . . . yes, yes, you have a possibility!" His voice lifted a little. "Look into that, Pitt, but very carefully. For heaven's sake remain discreet, both not to offend Thorne if he is innocent, and possibly more important, not to warn him if he is guilty."

He made an effort of will. "I apologize to you, Pitt. I should not have leapt to such a hasty conclusion as to what you were saying. This does indeed make sense. You'd better get to it straightaway. Go and see the servants at the Thorne household. And keep on looking for that cabdriver. If he delivered her there, then he has nothing to fear, and will be a witness at Thorne's undoing."

"Yes, sir." And Pitt rose from the chair to obey. It was what he had been intending to do anyway.

But the servants in the Thorne household could tell him nothing of use. He questioned them each, but no one had seen or heard Susannah Chancellor on the evening of her death. He pressed them as to the possibility of her having called without their knowledge. But it required a stretch of the imagination beyond reason to suppose that she had, unless she had specifically been asked to alight short of the house and not to present herself at the front door; instead to walk around the side, through the garden to the doorway to the back, and then make her way across the lawn to the

French doors of the study and let herself in that way. Or possibly someone had been waiting for her.

Of course that was perfectly possible, but why should she do such a thing? If anyone had asked her to come secretly, without any of the servants seeing her, what explanation could they give for such an extraordinary request? Had it been Thorne, or Christabel, or both?

If indeed they had anything to do with it, it seemed far more likely one of them had gone out and met her in the street and taken her to wherever she had been killed, then left and returned to the house through the side entrance.

But looking at Christabel Thorne's clear, wide eyes, full of intelligence, anger and grief, he could not imagine that she had taken part in anything so duplicitous.

But then again, if she loved her husband, perhaps he had persuaded her it was necessary, either for some higher good politically or morally, or simply to save him from discovery and disgrace.

"I really am sorry to be of so little assistance, Superintendent," she said earnestly. They were in the study, where the doors led into the garden and he could see the flowering shrubs beyond her from where he sat. "Believe me," she continued, "I have racked my brains to think of anything that could possibly be relevant. Mr. Kreisler was here, you know, and asked me all the same questions you are doing, and I could offer him nothing."

"Kreisler was here?" he said quickly.

Her eyes widened.

"You didn't know? He seems most concerned to learn the truth. I confess, I had not realized he cared so much for Susannah." Her expression was difficult to read; there was confusion, surprise, sadness, even a faint shred of wry, hurt amusement.

Pitt had other thoughts on the subject. He was beginning to wonder which motives lay behind Kreisler's enquiries. Was it a passion to avenge Susannah, either through assisting the police or privately? Or was it in order to learn

293

how much they knew, so he might guard either himself or someone else? Or was it to lay false information, to mislead and even further confuse the search? The more he knew of Kreisler, the less certain he was about him.

"No," he said aloud. "I think there is a lot yet to be learned on that matter."

She looked at him with a sudden quickening of interest. "Do you suspect him, Superintendent?"

"Of course, Mrs. Thorne."

There was a flash of humor across her face, this time undisguised. "Oh no," she replied. "I am not going to give words to any speculation. You must imagine what you will. I enjoy trivial gossip, but I abhor it when it touches on things that matter."

"And Mr. Kreisler matters?"

Her high eyebrows arched. "Not in the slightest, Superintendent. But accusations of complicity in murder matter very much." Her face darkened. "And Susannah mattered, to me. I liked her profoundly. Friendship matters, almost as much as honor."

She had spoken with intense seriousness, and he answered her in equal vein.

"And when the two conflict, Mrs. Thorne?"

"Then you have one of life's tragedies," she replied without hesitation. "But fortunately I am not placed in that situation. I know nothing about Susannah to her dishonor. Or about Linus either, for that matter. He is a man of deep conviction, and he always openly and honestly proclaimed both his intent and the means by which he would bring it to pass.

"And believe me, Superintendent, he has never entertained the slightest improper intentions towards another woman." It was a simple and rather obvious statement, one any friend might make in the circumstances, and frequently did. Normally it sounded trite, it was merely an exercise in loyalty, but looking at Christabel's face with its fierce intelligence and almost disdainful pride, he was unable to dismiss it so lightly. There was no sentimentality in her; it was not an emotional response, but one born of observation and belief.

They were both oblivious of the quiet room or the sunlit garden beyond, even of the wind moving the leaves to cast the occasional shadows on the glass.

"And Mr. Kreisler?" he asked.

"I have no idea. A contentious man," she said after a moment's consideration. "I had thought him attracted to Miss Gunne, which would be most understandable. But certainly he pursued Susannah as well, and even with his undoubted arrogance, I doubt he can have deluded himself he could achieve anything of a romantic nature with her."

Pitt was less certain. No matter how much Susannah might still be in love with her husband, people were capable of all sorts of strange acts where passion, loneliness and physical need were concerned. And Susannah had certainly gone somewhere she preferred not to tell anyone about.

"Then what?" he asked, watching her expression as she sought for an answer.

The veil came down over her thoughts again. Her eyes were bright and direct, but no longer revealing anything unguarded of herself.

"That is your profession to find out, Superintendent. I know nothing that would help you, or I should already have told it to you."

And Pitt learned nothing further from Thorne himself when he visited him at the Colonial Office. Garston Aylmer was more forthcoming.

"Absolutely frightful," he said with deep emotion when Pitt said that he was now here in connection with Susannah's murder. "Quite the most personally shocking thing I have ever heard." And indeed he looked very shaken. Seeing his pale face, slightly sunken eyes and yet the steadiness of his gaze when he met Pitt's, it would be difficult to imagine it was assumed, or indeed that it had anything to do with guilt.

"I knew her quite well, naturally," Aylmer went on, his short thick fingers playing absently with a pencil on the desk in front of him. "One of the most charming of women, and with an unusual integrity." He looked up gravely, the pencil frozen in mid-motion. "There was an inner honesty in her which was both very beautiful and at times quite disconcerting. I really am profoundly sorry she is gone, Superintendent."

Pitt believed him entirely, and felt naive even while he did so.

"What do you know of the relationship between her and Mrs. Thorne?" Pitt asked.

Aylmer smiled. "Ah—Christabel. A very rare type of lady ... thank goodness! A couple of dozen of her, and London would be revolutionized and reformed to within an inch of its life." He shrugged his heavy shoulders. "No, Superintendent, that is unfair. Christabel is charming at times, and always interesting. But women with quite such a driving force for good terrify me. It is a little like finding oneself accidentally in the path of a tornado."

"Tornados are destructive forces," Pitt pointed out, looking clearly at Aylmer to see if he intended the analogy.

"Only to one's peace of mind." Aylmer smiled ruefully. "At least as far as Christabel is concerned. She has a passion for educating women which is most disturbing. It genuinely frightens a great many people. And if you know her at all, you will know she does nothing in half measures."

"What is it she wishes to reform?"

Aylmer spread his hands in a gesture of abandonment. "Just about everything. Attitudes, beliefs, the entire role of women in the world, which of course means of men as well." He smiled. "Specifically? Improve radically the role of the odd women ..."

"The odd women?" Pitt was totally confused. "What odd women?"

Aylmer's smile grew broader. "All odd women. My dear fellow, odd women are all women who are not 'even,' that is to say, married. The women, of whom there are a large and ever-increasing number who have no man to provide for them financially, make them socially respectable and give them something to do, namely to care for him and whatever children there may be."

"What on earth does she propose to do about it?"

"Why, educate them! Have them join the professions, the arts, the sciences, anything they wish. The odd women, if that is where their abilities or their desires lead them. If Christabel succeeds, next time you call your dentist, your plumber, your banker or your architect, you may find it is a woman. Heaven help us when it is your doctor or your priest!"

Pitt was dumbfounded.

"Precisely," Aylmer agreed. "Apart from women's complete unsuitability both emotionally and intellectually—not to mention physically—for such tasks, that will throw thousands of men out of work. I told you, she is a revolutionary."

"And ... people allow it?" Pitt was amazed.

"No of course they don't. But have you ever tried to stop a truly determined woman? Any woman, never mind Christabel Thorne?"

Pitt thought of trying to stop Vespasia, and knew precisely what Aylmer meant.

"I see," he said aloud.

"I doubt it." Aylmer shook his head. "To see the full enormity of it, you would have to know Christabel. Incredible courage, you know. Doesn't give a damn about the scandal."

"Was Mrs. Chancellor also involved?" Pitt asked.

"Good gracious, what an appalling thought! I have no idea. I don't think so. No ... Susannah's interests were all to do with her family, banking, investment, finances and so on. If she had any radical ideas, it was about that sort of

297

thing. But she was far more conventional, thank God." His brow darkened suddenly. "That is what she quarreled with Kreisler about, so far as I can recall. Curious man. He was here, you know, asking me questions about her. In fact, Superintendent, he was rather more pressing than you are!"

Pitt sat a little farther upright. "About Mrs. Chancellor's death?"

"Yes. Yes, he seemed most concerned. I couldn't tell him anything I haven't told you . . . which is almost nothing at all. He also wanted to know about both Mr. and Mrs. Thorne." He laughed a little self-consciously. "And about me. I am not sure if he suspected I might have some involvement, or if he was simply desperate enough to pursue anything at all."

Pitt was wondering the same thing, both about Aylmer and about Kreisler. This information that he had been to see Aylmer was most disquieting.

He was further disturbed when he saw Ian Hathaway, ostensibly to ask if there had been any progress with the falsified figures, but also to see if he could learn anything more about either Mr. or Mrs. Thorne and their possible connection with Susannah or with Arthur Desmond.

Hathaway looked puzzled. He sat in his quiet, discreet office with its slightly faded good taste and solidity.

"No, Superintendent. That is what is so very curious, and, I admit, beyond me to understand. I would have called you this afternoon had you not come here to see me. We do have information from the German Embassy. . . ."

Pitt drew in his breath involuntarily, his heart beating a little faster, in spite of his effort to remain perfectly composed.

Hathaway saw it and smiled, his small, clear blue eyes steady.

"The message includes figures quite specifically, and this is what is incomprehensible. They are not any of those which I distributed, nor are they the genuine figures which I retained and passed to Lord Salisbury."

"What?" Pitt could scarcely believe what he had heard. It made no sense whatever. "I beg your pardon?"

"Precisely," Hathaway agreed. "I can see no sense in it at all. That is why I delayed contacting you." He sat motionless. Even his hands on the desk were quite still. "I made doubly sure that I had received the message correctly. It was my first thought that somehow figures had been transposed or misunderstood; but it was not so. The message was clear and correct, the figures are quite different, and indeed if acted upon, seriously misleading. I have no desire whatever to disabuse the German Embassy of its error. I am also, at this stage, at a loss to understand what has happened. I did take the liberty of informing Lord Salisbury of the matter, to be sure he had the correct figures himself. I need hardly say that he has."

Pitt sat in silence, digesting what Hathaway had told him and trying to think of some explanation. None came to his mind.

"We have failed, Superintendent, and I confess to total confusion," Hathaway said ruefully, leaning back in his chair again and regarding Pitt steadily. "I am perfectly prepared to try again, if you think there is any purpose to it?"

Pitt was more disappointed than he cared to admit. He had been counting on this producing some result, however small or difficult to follow. He had no idea where to turn next, and he dreaded confessing to Farnsworth that what had seemed such an excellent plan had failed so completely. He could already imagine his response, and the contempt with which it would be delivered.

"About the death of Mrs. Chancellor," Hathaway said quietly. "I fear I can be of little help there either. I wish I knew something of service to you. It seems such a pointless tragedy." He looked totally sincere, a decent man expressing a profoundly felt regret for grief, and yet Pitt also sensed in him a reasoning in his brain that superseded emotion. Was he distinguishing between pointless tragedies and those which were necessary, and had meaning?

"Did she ever mention Sir Arthur Desmond to you, Mr. Hathaway?" Pitt asked.

Not a flicker crossed Hathaway's face.

"Sir Arthur Desmond?" he repeated.

"Yes. He used to be at the Foreign Office. He died recently at his club."

"Yes, yes I know who you mean." He relaxed so slightly it was barely noticeable, a mere shift of the muscles in his shoulders. "Most unfortunate. I suppose such things tend to happen from time to time, when a club's membership is on the elderly side. No, I cannot recall her having mentioned him. Why? Surely he can have nothing whatever to do with this latest business? His death was a very ordinary sort of misfortune. I was at the club that afternoon myself, in the writing room with a business colleague."

He let out his breath in a very gentle sigh. "As I understood it from the newspapers, Mrs. Chancellor was attacked very violently, presumably while in her hansom cab, and then put in the river afterwards. Is that so?"

"Yes, that is correct," Pitt conceded. "It is simply that Sir Arthur was vehemently against the development of Central Africa as planned by Mr. Rhodes, and so is Mr. Kreisler, who . . ." He stopped. Hathaway's face had changed noticeably.

"Kreisler?" Hathaway said slowly, watching Pitt very closely. "He came to see me, you know? Also regarding Mrs. Chancellor's death, although that was not the reason he gave. He concocted some story about mineral rights and leases and so on, but it was Mrs. Chancellor and her opinions which seemed to concern him. A most unusual man. A man of powerful passions and convictions."

He had a curious habit of stillness which conveyed an intense concentration. "I assume you have naturally considered him as a possible suspect, Superintendent? I don't mean to tell you your business, but anyone who asks as many questions as to detail as does Mr. Kreisler has a far more than passing interest in the outcome."

"Yes, Mr. Hathaway, I have considered him," Pitt replied with feeling. "And by no means discounted the possibility that they quarreled, either about Africa and Mr. Chancellor's backing of Mr. Rhodes, or about something else, possibly more personal, and that that quarrel became a great deal more savage than either of them intended. I imagine Mr. Kreisler is well able both to attack and to defend himself as the situation may require. It is possible he may do either instinctively when aroused to uncontrolled rage, and far too late to realize he has committed murder."

Hathaway's face pinched with distress and distaste.

"What a very grave and uncivilized way to behave. Temper of such violence and complete lack of control is scarcely a characteristic of a human being, let alone a man of honor or intellect. What a dismal waste. I hope that you are not correct in your assumption, Superintendent. Kreisler has real possibilities for better ends than that."

They spoke a little further, but ten minutes later Pitt rose to leave, having learned nothing about Susannah Chancellor, and in a state of confusion about the information from the German Embassy.

"And what has that to do with anything at all?"

Charlotte was paying a duty call upon her grandmother, who, now that Charlotte's mother was recently remarried (a fact which Grandmama disapproved of with almost apoplectic fury), was obliged to live with Charlotte's sister and her husband. Emily and Jack found this arrangement displeasing; the old lady was of an exceedingly difficult temperament. But she could no longer remain at Cater Street with Caroline and Joshua—in fact she had refused point-blank to do so, not that the opportunity had been offered. And there was certainly no room in Charlotte's house, although in fact she had refused to consider that either. She would not dream of living in the house of a person of the police, even if he was recently promoted and now on the verge of respectability. That, when all was said and done, was only marginally better than being on the stage! Never in all the history of the Ellison family had anyone married an actor until Caroline had lost her wits and done so. But then of course she was an Ellison only by marriage. What poor Edward, Charlotte's father, would have said could only be guessed at. It was a mercy he was in his grave.

Charlotte had pointed out that were he not, the question of Caroline's remarrying anyone would not have arisen. She was told curtly not to be impertinent.

Now since Emily and Jack were on holiday in Italy, and Grandmama was thus alone, apart from the servants, Charlotte felt duty-bound to call upon her at least once a fortnight. She had kept a treat for herself after honor was satisfied. She was going out with Harriet Soames to visit the flower show.

Grandmama was keen to hear all the gossip Charlotte could think of. In fact, with Caroline living in Cater Street and seldom calling (being newly married and much occupied with her husband), and Emily and Jack abroad, she was starved for something to talk about.

Charlotte had idly mentioned Amanda Pennecuick and Garston Aylmer's pursuit of her, and that Mr. Aylmer was unusually homely.

"It has quite a lot to do with many things, if one is to consider marrying him," Charlotte replied candidly. They were sitting in Emily's large, airy, rather ornate withdrawing room. There were portraits of past Ashworths on all the walls and an Aubusson carpet specially woven for the room.

"Stuff and nonsense!" the old lady snapped. "That just goes to show how light-minded you are! A man's looks do not matter in the slightest." She glared at Charlotte. "Anyway, if they did, why on earth did you marry Thomas? He is hardly handsome, or even graceful. Never seen a man so badly dressed in my life! He could make the best Saville

Row suit look like a rag bag, once he had it on his back. His hair is too long, he keeps enough to stock a curiosity shop in his pockets, and I've never seen him with his tie on straight since the day he arrived."

"That is not the same thing as being homely!" Charlotte argued.

"Then I should like to know what the difference is," Grandmama retorted. "Except, of course, that a man cannot help his features, whereas he can most certainly help his dress. Untidy clothes are the sign of a slovenly mind, I always say."

"You don't always say it. In fact you've never said it before."

"Only to save your feelings, but since you raised the matter, you have brought it upon yourself. Who is this Amanda Shilling, or Sixpence, or whatever her name is?"

"Pennecuick."

"Don't quibble. That is not an answer. Who is she?" the old lady demanded.

"I don't know, but she's extremely pretty."

"That also is totally immaterial. Who are her family? Has she any breeding, any manners, any money? Does she know how to behave? Has she any relations worth mentioning?"

"I don't know, and I don't suppose Mr. Aylmer cares. He is in love with her, not her relatives," Charlotte pointed out. "He will make quite sufficient money of his own. He is a senior official in the Colonial Office, and much is expected of him."

"Then you have answered your own question, you stupid girl. What on earth does it matter what he looks like? He has good breeding and excellent prospects. He is a very good catch for the Penny-whatever girl, and she has enough sense to see it. Is he of agreeable temperament?" Her small, black eyes were bright with interrogation. "Does he drink to excess? Does he keep bad company?"

"He seems very agreeable, and I have no idea whether he drinks or not."

"Then as long as he is satisfactory in those areas, he is not to be dismissed." She spoke as if that were an end to the matter. "I don't know why you mentioned it. It is not remarkable in any way."

Charlotte tried again. "She is interested in astronomy."

"In what? Why can you not speak plainly? You are mumbling badly these days. You have become slipshod in your speech since you married and left home. It must be associating with poor types. You can always tell a person's breeding by their speech."

"You have just contradicted yourself," Charlotte pointed out, referring to the fact that the old lady was her direct ancestor.

"Don't be impudent!" the old lady said tartly, but from the flush of annoyance in her face, Charlotte knew that she had perceived the flaw in her argument. "Every family has its occasional black sheep," she added with a vicious glare. "Even our poor dear Queen has her problems. Look at the Duke of Clarence. I ask you. He doesn't even choose well-bred women to keep as his mistresses, or so I've heard. And you come here wittering on about some wretched girl, who is nobody at all, marrying a man who is well bred, has an excellent position, and even better prospects. Just because he is unfortunate enough to be a little plain. What of it?"

"She is not marrying him."

The old lady snorted fiercely. "Then she is a fool, that is all I can say! Now why don't you talk about something sensible? You have barely asked me how I am. Do you know that that wretched cook of Emily's sent me boiled fowl for my dinner last night. And baked mackerel the night before. And there was no forcemeat stuffing, and very little wine. It tasted of fish, and precious little else. I should have liked baked lobster. We have that when Emily is at home."

"Perhaps there were no good lobsters at the fishmongers'," Charlotte suggested.

"Don't tell me she tried, because I shan't believe you. I should have liked a little jugged hare. I am very partial to a well-jugged hare."

"It is out of season," Charlotte pointed out. "Jugged hare doesn't begin until September."

The old lady looked at her with acute disfavor and dropped the subject. She returned instead to Amanda Pennecuick. "What makes you suppose she is a fool, this Moneyfast girl?"

"You said she was a fool, not I."

"You said she was not marrying the man because he was homely, in spite of being in every way that matters an excellent catch. That makes her a fool, on your description. How do you know she is not marrying him? That she may have said so is neither here nor there. What else would she say, I ask you! She can hardly say that she is. That would be premature, and vulgar. And vulgarity, above all things, is unforgivable. And extremely unwise."

"Unwise?" Charlotte questioned.

The old lady looked at her with open disgust. "Of course it would be unwise, you stupid girl. She does not wish him to take her lightly." She sighed noisily with impatience. "If she allows him to undervalue her now, it will set the pattern for the rest of their lives. Let him think her reluctant. Let him woo her so diligently that when he finally wins her he feels he has achieved a great victory, not merely picked up something no one else wished for anyway.

"Really, there are times when I despair of you, Charlotte. You are clever enough at book learning, but what use is that to a woman? Your career is in your home, married to the best man you can find who will have you. You should make him happy, and see that he rises as high in his chosen profession as his abilities, and yours, will allow him. Or if you are clever enough to marry a gentleman, then see that he rises in Society and does not run into debt."

305

She grunted, and shifted her position with a rustle of skirts and creak of stays. "No wonder you had to settle for a policeman. A girl as naturally unintelligent as you are was fortunate to find anyone at all. Your sister Emily, on the other hand, has all the brains for both of you. She takes after her father, poor man. You take after your fool of a mother."

"Since you are so clever, Grandmama, it is really a great misfortune we don't have a title, an estate in the country and a fortune to match," Charlotte said waspishly.

The old lady looked at her with malicious delight. "I had not the advantages of your good looks."

It was the first compliment Charlotte could ever recall the old lady paying her, especially on such a subject. It quite robbed her of a reply, which—she realized a moment later—had been the intention.

Nevertheless in leaving her and riding in a hansom to Harriet Soames's house, in order to go together to the flower show, she did wonder if Amanda Pennecuick was doing what the old lady had suggested, and actually intended in due course to accept Mr. Aylmer's attentions.

She mentioned it to Harriet as they admired some magnificent early blooms arranged in a crystal bowl.

At first Harriet looked amazed, then as the thought took firmer hold in her mind, her attitude changed.

"You know . . ." she said very slowly. "You know that is not as absurd as it sounds. I have noticed in Amanda a certain inconsistency in disclaimers about Mr. Aylmer's attentions. She says she has nothing in common with him but an interest in the stars. But I never before suspected it was powerful enough to induce her to accept the company of anyone she genuinely disliked." She giggled. "What a delicious thought. Beauty and the Beast. Yes, I do think you might be right. In fact I hope so." She was beaming with pleasure as they walked in to admire a bowl of gaudy tulips whose petals opened like lilies in brilliant scarlets, oranges and flames.

306

* * *

Pitt arrived home late and tired to find Matthew Desmond there waiting for him, pale faced, his fair streaked hair flopping forward as if he had been running his fingers through it in nervous distraction. He had declined to sit in the parlor with Charlotte but had begged to be allowed to walk alone in the garden, and seeing his distress so plainly in his face, she had not tried to dissuade him. This was obviously not a time for the usual rigors of courtesy.

"He has been here nearly an hour," she said quietly when Pitt stood in the parlor looking out of the French doors at Matthew's lean figure pacing back and forth under the apple tree. Obviously he had not yet realized Pitt was there.

"Did he say what has happened?" Pitt asked. He could see that it was something that caused Matthew keen torment of mind. Had it been merely grief he would have sat still in the parlor; probably he would have shared it with Charlotte, knowing Pitt would certainly tell her afterwards anyway. He knew Matthew well enough to be certain that this was no longer the indecision which he felt had touched him last time he had been there, but something far stronger, and as yet unresolved.

"No," Charlotte replied, her face puckered with concern, probably for Matthew, but also for Pitt. Her eyes were tender and she seemed on the verge of saying something else, and then realized it would not help. Whatever the matter was, it could not be avoided, and to make suggestions that it could or should would make it harder, not easier.

He touched her gently in a silent acknowledgment, then went out through the door and over the lawn. The soft grass masked his footsteps so that Matthew did not know he was there until he was only three yards away.

Matthew turned suddenly. His face for an instant registered something close to horror, then he masked his feelings and tried to compose himself to his more usual courtesy.

"Don't," Pitt said quietly.

307

"What?"

"Don't pretend. Something is very seriously wrong. Tell me what it is."

"Oh. I ..." Matthew made an attempt to smile, then closed his eyes. His face flooded with pain.

Pitt stood by helplessly, filled with apprehension and the sort of fierce protectiveness one feels only towards a younger child whom you have watched and known through all the vulnerable years. Standing together under the apple tree it was as if all the intervening time had fled away and left them as they were a quarter of a century ago, when his single year's advantage had meant so much. He ached to do something, even as elemental as reaching out his arms to hold him, as if they were still children. But there were too many years between them, and he knew it would be unacceptable. He could only wait.

"The Colonial Office ..." Matthew said at last. "You don't know who it is yet, do you?"

"No."

"But some of the information comes ..." He stopped as if even now he hesitated on the verge of whatever it was he was compelled to say, and could not bear to.

Pitt waited. A bird was chirping in the apple tree. Somewhere beyond the wall a horse whinnied.

"From the Treasury," Matthew finished.

"Yes," Pitt agreed. He was about to add the names of the men to whom Ransley Soames had narrowed it down, then he realized that would be an intrusion, and not helpful. Better to allow Matthew to say uninterrupted whatever it was.

Matthew stared at a twig of apple blossom which had fallen on the grass, his back half turned towards Pitt.

"Two days ago Harriet told me that she had overheard her father, Ransley Soames, in a conversation. She went to speak to him in his study, not aware that he was using the telephone." Again Matthew stopped.

Pitt did not speak.

Matthew took a deep breath and continued in a quiet, husky voice, as if his throat were so tight he could barely get the words through it.

"He was speaking to someone about government finances for the exploration and settlement of Zambezia, and as Harriet recounted it, it concerned several aspects, from Cecil Rhodes to MacKinnon, Emin Pasha and the Cape-to-Cairo possibilities, and the importance of a naval base at Simonstown. What it might cost Britain if we were to lose it."

So far what Matthew was saying was what Soames might have been expected to say to a colleague, and not of itself remarkable.

Matthew was still staring at the apple twig on the grass.

"Then he went on to say, 'This is the last time I can tell you anything. That man Pitt from the police has been here, and I dare not continue. You will have to do all you can with what you already have. I'm sorry.' And then apparently he replaced the receiver. She did not realize what she was telling me—but I knew." At last Matthew turned and faced Pitt, his eyes agonized, as if waiting for a blow to be struck at him.

Now it was only too obvious why. Ransley Soames was the traitor in the Treasury. Unwittingly his daughter had betrayed him to Matthew, and after torment of indecision, Matthew had come to Pitt. Only he had not come in ignorance; he knew all that it meant, and could foresee the consequences of his act, and yet he felt unable to do otherwise.

Pitt did not speak. It was not necessary to say that he must use the knowledge he had. Matthew had known that when he came. It was also pointless to say that he would keep Matthew's name, or Harriet's, out of the issue, because Matthew knew that was impossible also. Nor did he need to make any sympathetic sounds of understanding. He knew what it meant. What Matthew was feeling, or what it would cost him, no one would know, or ever do more than guess.

He simply held out his hand in companionship for a brother, and in admiration for a man whose integrity was brighter than any comfort of his heart.

10

P_{ITT} *COULD NOT SLEEP.* At first he lay silently in bed, uncertain whether Charlotte was also awake and loath to disturb her, but eventually he decided she was asleep and would not be aware if he got up and left the room.

He crept downstairs and stood in the parlor looking at the soft light of the quarter moon over the garden. He could dimly see the pale drift of the apple blossom and the dark shadow of the tree on the grass. There were shreds of cloud in the sky, masking some of the stars. Others he could see in tiny pinpoints of light. The night air was warm. In a few weeks it would be midsummer and there were hardly any fires lit in all the million houses, only the cooking ranges, the gasworks and factory chimneys. Even the slight wind smelled clean.

Of course it was nothing like Brackley, where you could breathe in the scent of hay and leaves and damp woods and turned earth all in one great gasp. But it was better than usual, and there was a stillness that should have brought a sense of calm. In other circumstances it would have.

But tomorrow he would have to go and confront Ransley Soames. There really was no alternative. He knew all the information which had been passed from the Treasury. Matthew himself had given him that. Soames had been privy to all of it. So had several others, but he could recount precisely what he had overheard him say, and the specific reference to Simonstown and the Boers, even the exact words he had used regarding Pitt himself.

It would be an ugly scene; it was bound to be. Tomorrow was Saturday. Pitt would find him at his home, which was about the only good thing in the whole matter. He could be arrested and charged discreetly, not in front of his colleagues.

Of course for Harriet it would be close to unbearable. But then, anyone's fall hurt others. There was always a wife, a child or a parent, someone to be horrified, disillusioned, torn with amazement and grief and shame. One could not allow it to impinge too far, or one would be so racked with pity it would be impossible to function.

It was after nine o'clock when Pitt stood in Ransley Soames's hallway. The butler looked at him with curiosity.

"I am afraid it is a matter which cannot wait," Pitt said gravely. He had brought Tellman with him, in case the scene became uglier than he could handle alone, but he had left him outside, reluctant to call him unless it became unavoidable.

"I will see if Mr. Soames is able to receive you," the butler replied. It was not the customary euphemism, but it served the same purpose.

He was gone only a few moments and returned with an expressionless face.

"If you care to come this way, sir, Mr. Soames will see you in the study."

But actually it was a further ten minutes before Soames appeared. Pitt waited in the quiet, pale green room set with ornate furniture, too many pictures and photographs, and a potted plant which had been overwatered. Normally he might have looked at the bookcases. They were usually indicative of a man's character and interests. But today he could not concentrate his mind on more than the immediate future. He saw two rather idealistic books concerning Africa. One was a novel by H. Rider Haggard, the other a collection of letters from a missionary.

The door opened and Soames came in, closing it behind him. He looked mildly irritated, but not concerned.

"How may I help you, Mr. Pitt?" he said tersely. "I imagine it is urgent, or you would not have come to my home on a Saturday morning."

"Yes, Mr. Soames, it is," Pitt acknowledged. "There is no pleasant way of dealing with this, so I shall be direct. I have cause, sir, to know that it is you who has been passing financial information from the Treasury to someone in the Colonial Office, for them to pass on to the German Embassy."

The blood rushed scarlet to Soames's face, and then after a moment of terrible silence, fled, leaving him pasty white. He opened his mouth to say something, perhaps a denial, but the words died on his tongue. He might have had some conception of the guilt in his face, and how futile, even ridiculous, such a denial would be.

"It—it's not . . ." he began, and then faltered to a stop. "You don't understand," he said wretchedly. "It's not . . ."

"No," Pitt agreed. "I don't."

"It is not accurate information!" Soames looked as if he were in danger of fainting, his skin was so white, and there was a chill sweat standing out on his lip and brow. "It was to mislead Germany!"

Pitt hovered for a moment on the edge of believing him, then realized how easy that was to say, and how unlikely.

"Indeed," he said coldly. "Perhaps you will give me the names of the government ministers who are aware of this. Regrettably they do not include the Foreign Secretary, the Colonial Secretary, or the Prime Minister."

"It was not done . . . like . . . like that." Soames looked agonized and his eyes were desperate, and yet there was somewhere a shred of honesty in them. Was it a terrified last attempt to convince himself?

"Then you had better explain precisely how it was done, and who else is involved," Pitt suggested.

"But you know . . ." Soames stared at him, for the first time realizing that he did not know just how much Pitt was aware of, nor had he so far explained how he had learned it.

"If it is not what I think, Mr. Soames, then you will have to tell me precisely what it is," Pitt said, retrenching his position quickly. "It looks to me like simple treason, the handing over of privileged government information to someone you knew would pass it to Britain's enemies, or at best rivals. What consideration you received in return is a matter yet to be discovered."

"None!" Soames was indignant. "Good God, there is . . . that is a heinous suggestion! I passed on information to a man of subtlety and brilliance who distorted it just sufficiently to be misleading, but not so much as to be unbelievable. Not against Britain's interests, but very much to preserve them, in both East and Central Africa, but also in the North Sea. I would not expect you to understand. . . ."

"Heligoland," Pitt said succinctly.

Soames was transparently surprised. "Yes. Yes, that is right."

"You gave this man correct information for him to distort it?"

"Precisely."

Pitt sighed. "And how do you know he did that?"

"What?"

"How do you know that he distorted it before he passed it on?"

"I have his word. . . ." He stopped, his eyes sick with sudden comprehension. "You don't believe me. . . ."

"I think the kindest thing I can say for you, Mr. Soames," Pitt said wearily, "is that you are naive." Soames pushed backwards into the chair behind him.

"Who is it?" Pitt asked.

"I . . . I can't believe it." Soames made one last effort to cling to his innocence. "He . . . was . . ."

"Plausible," Pitt finished for him. "I find it hard to credit that you were so easily duped." Although even as he said it, it became a lie. Looking at Soames's face, ashen and wretched, he thought he was indeed naive.

"His reasons were . . ." Soames began again, still struggling. "His reasoning was so logical. They are not fools, the Germans." He brushed his hand across his sweating lip. "The information had to be very close to accurate. Inventions would not do."

"That I can easily accept," Pitt agreed. "Even the need to give misinformation is understandable. They are acutely involved with East Africa, Zambezia, Zanzibar especially, and I know we are in negotiations with them over a major treaty."

Soames's face brightened a little.

"But we have a secret service for that kind of thing," Pitt went on.

"Which works through the Foreign and Colonial offices!" Soames sat forward, his eyes brighter. "Really, Superintendent, I think you have misjudged the affair."

"No I have not, Mr. Soames," Pitt replied sharply. "If that kind of information were required of you, for that purpose, then you would have been asked for it by either Mr. Chancellor or Lord Salisbury. You would not have been required to do it covertly, and to be afraid of my enquiries. In fact I would have had no enquiries, because they were instigated by the Foreign Office, as you must recall, and assisted by the Colonial Office, who were most worried by the information passing to the Germans, and quite unaware that it is not correct."

Soames sat on the edge of the chair, his body slack in a moment's despair. Then he straightened up and shot to his feet, lunging at the telephone, and picked it out of its cradle, staring at Pitt defiantly. "I can explain!" He spoke to the operator and asked to be connected with Lord Salis-

315

bury's home, giving the number. All the time his eyes were on Pitt.

A part of Pitt felt pity for him. He was arrogant and gullible, but he was not an intentional traitor.

There was a crackle at the other end of the line.

Soames drew in his breath to speak, then realized the futility of it.

Slowly he replaced the receiver.

There was no need for Pitt to make a comment. Soames looked as if his knees would buckle under him.

"Who did you give the information to?" Pitt asked again.

"Jeremiah Thorne," Soames replied with stiff lips. "I gave it to Jeremiah Thorne."

Before Pitt had time to respond, even to wonder if it were the truth, the door opened and Harriet Soames stood in the entrance, her face pale, her eyes wide and ready to accuse. She looked first at her father and saw his extreme distress, bordering on the edge of collapse, and then she glared at Pitt.

"Papa, you look ill. What has happened? Mr. Pitt, why have you come here, and at this hour of the day? Is it to do with Mrs. Chancellor's death?" She came in and closed the door.

"No, Miss Soames," Pitt answered her. "It is a matter, so far as I know, quite unconnected. I think it would be better if you were to permit us to conclude it privately, and then Mr. Soames can tell you afterwards, as seems good to him."

She moved closer to her father, her eyes blazing, in spite of the alarm in her which was rapidly turning to fear.

"No. I will not leave until I know what has happened. Papa, what is wrong?" Her voice was rising with fear. He looked so desperate, so drained of all the buoyancy and confidence he had had only an hour ago. It was as if the vitality had bled out of him.

"My dear . . . I . . ." He attempted some explanation, but the test was too great for him. The truth weighed on him till it drove out everything else. "I have made a terrible

316

mistake," he tried again. "I have been very . . . naive. . . . I have allowed someone to use me, and to deceive me with a very plausible lie, a man whose honor I never questioned."

"Who?" Her voice rose close to panic. "Who has used you? I don't understand what you mean. Why is Mr. Pitt here? Why did you call in the police? If someone has defrauded you, can he help? Would it not be better to . . . I don't know . . . to deal with it privately?" She looked from her father to Pitt, and back again. "Was it much money?"

Soames seemed incapable of a coherent explanation. Pitt could not bear the agony any longer. To see him at once struggling and despairing was an intrusion into the man's shame which was unnecessary. A clean blow would be more merciful.

"Mr. Soames has been passing secret information to a spy," he said to Harriet, "in his belief that the man was using it to help Britain's interests in Africa by falsifying it before relaying it to the Germans. However the plan was not approved by either the Colonial Office or the Foreign Office. On the contrary, they had called me and empowered me to investigate where the information was coming from."

She looked at him with disbelief.

"You are wrong! You must be wrong." She swung around to her father, her mouth open, to ask him to explain; then she saw the full depth of his distress. Suddenly she knew that in some terrible way there was truth in it. She turned back to Pitt. "Well whatever happened," she said furiously, "if my father has been deceived by someone, it was not a dishonorable act, and you should be very careful what you say to him." Her voice shook and she stepped closer to Soames, as if he needed some physical protection and she would give it.

"I have not made an accusation of dishonor, Miss Soames," Pitt said gently. "At least not on your father's part."

"Then why are you here? You should be looking for

317

whoever it is that lied to him and passed on the information."

"I did not know who, until your father told me."

Her chin came up. "If you didn't know who it was, then how could you know it had anything to do with my father? Perhaps it hasn't. Have you thought of that, Superintendent?"

"I had thought of it, Miss Soames, and it is not so."

"Prove it," she challenged, staring at Pitt with brilliant eyes, her face set, jaw tight, her remarkable profile as stiff as if carved in almond-tinted stone.

"It's no use, Harriet," Soames interrupted at last. "The Superintendent overheard my conversation when I was passing the information. I don't know how, but he was able to recite it back to me."

She stood as if frozen. "What conversation? With whom?"

Soames glanced at Pitt, a question in his eyes.

Pitt shook his head.

"With the man at the Colonial Office," Soames replied, avoiding using his name.

"What conversation?" Her voice was strangled in her throat. "When?"

"On Wednesday, late afternoon. Why? What difference can it make now?"

She turned very slowly to look at Pitt, horror in her eyes and disgust so absolute and so terrible her face was made ugly with it.

"Matthew," she whispered. "Matthew told you, didn't he?"

Pitt did not know what to say. He could not deny it, and yet neither could he bear to confirm that her charge was true. It would be fatuous and unbelievable to suggest that Matthew might not have understood the meaning of what he said, or what the result would be.

"You can't deny it, can you!" she accused him.

"Harriet . . ." Soames began.

318

She swung around to him. "Matthew betrayed you, Papa ... and me. He betrayed both of us for his precious Colonial Office. They'll promote him, and you'll be ruined." There was a sob in her voice and she was so close to tears she barely had control.

Pitt wanted to defend Matthew, even to plead his cause, but he knew from her face that it would be useless, and anyway, Matthew had the right to say what he could to explain himself. Pitt should not preempt that, no matter how intensely he felt. He met Harriet's eyes, full of overwhelming hurt, anger, confusion and the passion to protect. He understood it far more deeply than reason or words could have conveyed. He wanted to protect Matthew from the hurt he knew was inevitable, and with the same fierce instinct to save the weaker, the more vulnerable, that burned in her.

And both of them were powerless.

"It is despicable," she said, catching her breath and almost choking "How could anyone be so ... so beneath contempt?"

"To give away their country's secrets, with which they had been entrusted, or to report that treason to the authorities, Miss Soames?" Pitt said quietly.

She was white to the lips. "It ... it is not ... treason." She found it difficult to say the word. "He ... he ... was deceived. ... That is not treason ... and ... and you will not excuse Matthew to me—not ever!"

Soames climbed to his feet with difficulty. "I shall resign, of course."

Pitt did not demur, nor point out that he would be extremely unlikely to have any option.

"Yes sir," he agreed. "In the meantime, I think it would be advisable if you were to come to the Bow Street station and make a statement in respect of what you have just told me."

"I suppose that is inevitable," Soames agreed reluctantly. "I'll ... I'll come on Monday."

"No, Mr. Soames, you will come now," Pitt said firmly. Soames looked startled.

Harriet moved closer to her father, putting her arm through his. "He has already told you, Superintendent, he will go on Monday! You have had your victory. What else do you need? He is ruined! Isn't that enough for you?"

"It is not I who has to be satisfied, Miss Soames," Pitt replied with as much patience as he could muster. He was not sure whether she was so naive. "Your father is not alone in this tragedy. There are other people to arrest. . . ."

"Then go and arrest them! Do your duty! There's nothing more to keep you here!"

"The telephone." Pitt looked at the instrument where it sat on its cradle.

"What about it?" She regarded it with loathing. "If you want to use it, you may!"

"So may you," he pointed out. "To warn others, and when I arrive there, they will be gone. Surely you can see the necessity for action now, and not Monday morning?"

"Oh . . ."

"Mr. Soames?" He waited with growing impatience.

"Yes . . . I er . . ." He looked confused, broken, and for that moment at least, Pitt was almost as sorry for him as Harriet, even though he also felt a contempt for his foolishness. He had been arrogant enough to think he knew better than his colleagues, and no doubt a little self-importance had played its part, the knowledge that he knew secrets others did not. But he was going to pay an uncommon price for a very common sin.

Pitt opened the door for him.

"I'm coming with him!" Harriet declared defiantly.

"No, you are not," Pitt said.

"I . . ."

"Please!" Soames turned to look at her. "Please . . . leave me a little dignity, my dear. I should rather face this alone."

She fell back, the tears spilling over her cheeks, and Pitt

escorted Soames out, leaving her standing in the doorway, her face filled with anger and overwhelming grief.

Pitt took Soames to Bow Street and left him there with Tellman, to take all the details of precisely what information he had passed to Thorne and when. He had hesitated to take him directly to the police station; it was a sensitive matter and he had been directly commissioned from higher up. But he could not take him to Matthew, the person who had originally instigated the investigation, because of the relationship between them. Nor could he take him to Linus Chancellor, who would be at home at this hour on a Saturday, and in no frame of mind to deal with such a matter. And he did not entirely trust any of the other people concerned, nor was he certain to find them in the Colonial Office, even if he had.

He had not the power to go directly to Lord Salisbury, and certainly not to the Prime Minister. He would arrest Thorne, and then make a complete report of the matter for Farnsworth.

He took two constables with him, just in case Thorne should prove violent. It was not beyond possibility. Secondly they would be necessary to conduct a search of the premises and prevent any destruction of further evidence which would no doubt be required if the matter came to trial. It was always possible the government might prefer to deal with it all discreetly, rather than expose its error and vulnerabilities to public awareness.

He arrived by hansom with the constables, and posted one at the back door, just in case of attempted flight. That would be undignified and absurd, but not beyond possibility. All kinds of people can panic, sometimes those one least expects.

A footman opened the front door, looking extremely sober—in fact the pallor of his face suggested he had already received some kind of shock and was still reeling from its effects.

"Yes sir?" he enquired without expression.

"I require to see Mr. Thorne." Pitt made it a statement, not a request.

"I'm sorry sir, he is not at home," the footman replied, still no emotion whatever in his face.

"When are you expecting his return?" Pitt felt a surprising frustration, probably because he had liked both Thorne himself and Christabel, and he loathed having to come on this errand. Being faced with postponing it made it even worse because it prolonged it.

"I am not, sir." The footman looked confused and distressed, his eyes meeting Pitt's directly for the first time.

"What do you mean, you are not?" Pitt snapped. "You mean you don't know at what hour he will return? What about Mrs. Thorne? Is she at home?"

"No, sir, both Mr. and Mrs. Thorne left for Portugal yesterday evening, and my information is that they are not returning to England."

"Not . . . at all?" Pitt was incredulous.

"No, sir, not at all. The household staff have been dismissed, except myself and the butler, and we are here only to take care of things until Mr. Thorne's man of affairs can dispose of the house and its effects."

Pitt was stunned. Thorne had fled. And if Thorne had gone last night, then it was not Soames's doing. In fact Thorne had left without warning Soames, and he could have.

"Who was here yesterday?" he said sharply. "Exactly who called at this house yesterday?"

"Mr. Aylmer, sir. He came in the afternoon shortly after Mr. Thorne returned from the Colonial Office, about four o'clock, and half an hour after that, a Mr. Kreisler—"

"Kreisler?" Pitt interrupted immediately.

"Yes sir. He was here for about half an hour, sir."

Pitt swore under his breath. "And when did Mr. Thorne inform you he was leaving for Portugal? When were those arrangements made?"

A delivery cart rumbled along the street behind them and fifty yards away a maid came up the area steps with a mat and began to beat it.

"I don't know when he made the arrangements, sir," the footman answered. "But he left about an hour after that, maybe a little less."

"Well, when did he pack? When did he give the servants notice?"

"They only took two large cases with them, sir, and so far as I know, they were packed just after Mr. Kreisler arrived. Mr. Thorne gave us notice at the same time, sir. It was all very sudden—"

"Last night?" Pitt interrupted. "They gave you all notice last night? But the other staff cannot all have gone last night. Where would they go to?"

"Oh no sir." He shook his head. "One of the upstairs maids was at her sister's anyway, there being a death in the family, like. So the other one went this morning. They were sisters. Mrs. Thorne's ladies' maid had been sent on holiday. . . ." He sounded surprised as he said it. It was an extraordinary thing to do. Servants did not have holidays. "And the cook is going this afternoon. She is a very good cook indeed, and much sought after." He said that with some satisfaction. "Lady Brompton'll be only too glad to have her. She's been angling after her for years. They need a new bootboy next door, and Mrs. Thorne said as she'd called someone for the scullery maid and found her a place."

So it was not completely sudden! They had been prepared for the eventuality. Kreisler had merely told him the time was come. But why? Why did Kreisler warn him instead of allowing him to be caught? His part in it, and in Susannah Chancellor's death, was becoming less clear all the time.

The footman was staring at him.

"Excuse me, sir, but you are Superintendent Pitt, aren't you?"

"Yes."

"Then, sir, Mr. Thorne left a letter for you. It is on the mantelpiece in the withdrawing room. If you'll wait a moment, sir, I'll fetch it."

"There's no need," Pitt said quickly. "I am afraid I am obliged to search the house anyway."

"Search the house?" He was startled. "What for? I don't know that I can allow that . . . except . . ." He stopped, uncertain what he meant. Now that his master was gone, apparently never to return, he was about to be without a position, although he had been given handsome notice and an excellent reference. And Pitt was the police.

"A wise decision," Pitt said, reading his face. He called the constable standing just beyond the step. "Fetch Hammond from the back, and then begin to look through the house. I shall be in the withdrawing room."

"What about Mr. Thorne, sir?"

Pitt smiled ruefully. "I am afraid that Mr. and Mrs. Thorne left London bound for Portugal last night. And they are not expected to return."

The constable's face fell; he made as if to say something, then changed his mind. "Yes, sir. I'll fetch Hammond, sir."

"Thank you." Pitt came into the hall and then followed the footman to the withdrawing room.

It was a comfortable room, unostentatious, with dark green curtains and pale, damasked walls. The pictures were arranged oddly, and it was only after a moment or two he realized that it was because three or four had been removed. Presumably they were either the most valuable or those of greatest sentimental worth. The furniture was old; the mahogany bookcase shone with generations of polishing, and one of its glass panes was cracked. The chairs were a trifle scuffed, as if sat in for long evenings beside the fire; the fender around the hearth had a dent in it and there was a tiny brown mark on the carpet where a spark had caught it. A vase of late tulips, gaudy and wide open like lilies, gave a heart and a perfume to the room.

A very small marmalade-and-white kitten lay curled into a ball on one of the cushions, apparently sound asleep. Another kitten, equally small, perhaps only nine or ten weeks old, lay in the seat of the chair, but he was smoky black, his shadowy, baby stripes still visible. He lay not curled up but stretched out his full length, and he was equally fast asleep.

The letter caught Pitt's eye straightaway. It was propped up on the mantelpiece, and his name was written on the front.

He picked it up, tore it open and read.

My dear Pitt,

By the time you read this, Christabel and I shall be on the boat across the Channel on our way to Portugal. Which will, of course, mean that you are aware that it is I who have been passing information from the Colonial Office and the Treasury to the German Embassy.

What you do not know is my reason for doing so. Nor, I think, do you know that it was almost all false. Naturally to begin with, it had to be genuine, and then later, when I had earned their trust, it was false only to a very minor degree, but sufficient to do them a considerable disservice.

I have never been to Africa myself, but I know a great deal about it from my years in the Colonial Office. I know from letters and dispatches more assuredly than you can appreciate, just what atrocities have been committed by white men in the name of civilization. I am not speaking of the occasional murder, or even massacre. That has occurred throughout history, and possibly always will. Certainly the black man is quite as capable of atrocities of that order as anyone else. I am speaking of the greed and the stupidity, the rape of the land and the subjugation, even the destruction of a nation of people, the loss of their culture and their beliefs, the degrading of a race.

I do not hold out great hope that Britain will settle either wisely or fairly. I am certain we shall do neither. But there will be those among us who will make the attempt, and we have a certain humanity, standards of conduct and honor which will mitigate the worst of it.

If, on the other hand, Germany takes East Africa, Zanzibar and the whole of that coast—which they are quite capable of doing, especially in our undecided state—then there will certainly be war between Britain in Central Africa and Germany in the east. Belgium in the west will be drawn in, and no doubt what is left of the old Arab Sultanates as well. What was once only tribal skirmishes with spears and assegais will become a full-scale war of machine guns and cannons as Europe turns Africa into a bloodbath to settle its own old rivalries and new greeds.

One European power dominant enough to prevent that is a better alternative, and quite naturally, I wish it to be Britain, for both moral and political reasons. To that end I have sent to the German Embassy misinformation regarding mineral deposits, endemic disease and its spread, the areas affected, the cost of various expeditions, their losses, the enthusiasm or disillusion of financial backers. I think you now see my purpose?

Is it necessary to explain to you why I did not do this through the Colonial Office's official channels? Surely not! Apart from the obvious danger that the more people who knew of it, the less likely it was to remain undetected and have any chance of success, I am quite sure Linus Chancellor would have had no part in such a scheme. I did sound him out, very tentatively.

Also Lord Salisbury is, as you well know, very ambivalent in his attitude towards Africa, and not to be trusted to remain in his present ebullient mood.

Poor Ransley Soames is very gullible, as easily duped as any man I know. But he has no worse sin than an overbearing vanity. Do not be too hard upon him. The fact that he is a fool will be punishment enough for him. He will not recover from that.

I have no knowledge as to who murdered poor Susannah, or why. Had I, I should most certainly have told you.

Be careful of the Inner Circle. Their power is wider than you know, and their hunger is insatiable. Above all they never forgive. Poor Arthur Desmond is witness to that, and one you will not forget. He betrayed their secrets and paid with his life. But again, I know that only because he spoke to me of his convictions, and I know enough of the Circle to be convinced his death was not accidental. He knew he was in danger. He had been threatened before, but he considered the game worth the stake. He was one of the best of men, and I miss him sorely. I do not know who contrived his death, nor how . . . only why.

I have given all my servants notice, a month's pay and good references. My man of affairs will dispose of the house and its contents, and the proceeds are to be given to Christabel's charity. It will do much good. Since you cannot prove treason against her, I think you will not interfere with that bequest?

My household staff are good, but they will be confused and alarmed. Therefore I have a personal favor to ask of you. Christabel's two kittens, Angus and Archie, have perforce been left behind. I do not feel at ease that they will be taken with any of my staff, who have no facilities to care for them. Will you please take them with you and see that they are found a good home . . . together, if you don't mind. They are devoted to each other. Archie is the marmalade one, Angus the black. I am greatly obliged to you. To say 'yours' seems absurd, when I am most patently not! But I write candidly, as one man of conviction to, I believe, another.

Jeremiah Thorne

Pitt stood with the paper in his hands as if he could scarcely comprehend what was written. And yet now that he saw it, it all made excellent sense. He could not condone what Thorne had done, nor could he entirely condone the means he had employed. His battle was as much against the Inner Circle as against Germany, yet there he was helpless. All he could do was warn as explicitly as possible.

He had known Sir Arthur. If there had been even a vestige of doubt lingering, that would have swept it away.

Yet he still believed British dominion of Africa was better than German, or a divided nation. What he said about war was almost surely true, and that would be a disaster of immeasurable proportions.

Why had Kreisler warned him? Their beliefs were not the same. Or was it not deliberate? Had Kreisler asked his questions and Thorne understood the meaning behind them?

It was all academic now. It explained why none of Hathaway's figures had reached the German Embassy. Thorne had altered them all anyway.

He looked around him at the gracious, comfortable room: the ormolu clock ticking on the mantelshelf from which he had taken the letter, the pictures on the walls, mostly dark Dutch scenes of landscapes with animals and water. He had never before appreciated how beautiful cows were, how a body with so many protruding bones could still have about it such an air of peace.

On the chair beside his elbow, Archie, the orange kitten, uncurled himself, stretched out a silken paw with claws spread, gave a little squeak of satisfaction and began to purr.

"What on earth am I going to do with you?" Pitt asked, unconsciously admiring the perfection of the creature. It had a star-shaped face with bright, sea-blue–green eyes and enormous ears. It was watching him with curiosity, and no fear whatever.

He put out his hand and rang the bell. The footman appeared immediately. He had obviously been waiting in the hall.

"Mr. Thorne has requested that I take these two cats," Pitt said with a frown.

"Oh, I am glad," the footman responded with relief. "I was afraid we were going to have them disposed of. That would be a terrible shame. Nice little things, they are. I'll get a basket for you, sir. I'm sure there'll be one suitable."

"Thank you."

"Not at all, sir. I'll do it right away."

Pitt took them home because he had very little alternative. Also he wanted to tell Charlotte about Soames, and knew it would devastate Matthew. Last night he had not told her of it, hoping in some way it would prove mistaken, although she knew there was something deeply wrong. Matthew had left without waiting to eat, or to speak with both of them, and she had watched him leave with anxious face and troubled eyes.

First he presented her with the cats. They were angry in the basket and in a considerable temper to be out, which took precedence over news of any other thought.

"They're beautiful," she exclaimed with delight, putting the basket on the kitchen floor. "Oh, Thomas, they're exquisite! Where on earth did you get them? I wanted a cat as soon as we moved, but no one has had any." She looked up at him with delight filling her face, then immediately turned back to the basket. Archie was playing with her finger, and Angus was staring at her with round, golden eyes. "I shall think of names for them."

"They are already named," he said quickly. "They belonged to Christabel Thorne."

"Belonged?" She jerked her head up. "Why do you say that? What has happened to her? You said she is all right!"

"I expect she is. Jeremiah Thorne is the traitor at the Colonial Office, if *traitor* is the right word. I'm not sure that it is."

"Jeremiah Thorne?" She looked crushed, her face filled

with sudden sadness. The kittens were temporarily forgotten, in spite of the fact that Archie was quietly biting her finger, and then licking it, holding it between his paws. "I suppose you are sure? Have you arrested him?"

He sat down on one of the wooden chairs beside the kitchen table.

"No. They have both gone to Portugal. They left last night. I think Kreisler's constant questions warned them."

"They've got away?" Then her expression sobered. "Oh. I'm sorry. I . . ."

He smiled. "There's no need to apologize for feeling relieved. I am myself, for a lot of reasons, not least because I liked them."

Her face was filled with a mixture of curiosity, guilt and confusion. "What other news? Is it not bad for you, for England, that they escaped?"

"For me, possibly. Farnsworth may be angry, but he may also come to realize that if we had caught them there would have been a considerable conflict as to what to do with them."

"Try them," she said instantly. "For treason!"

"And expose our own weakness?"

"Oh. Yes, I see. Not very good, when we are busy negotiating treaties. It makes us look incompetent, doesn't it?"

"Very. And actually all the information he gave was inaccurate anyway."

"On purpose? Or was he incompetent too?" She sat down opposite him, temporarily leaving the kittens to explore, which they did with enthusiasm.

"Oh, no, definitely on purpose," he replied. "So if he defended himself by saying that, then we ruin the good he has done, as well as making ourselves look stupid. No, on the whole, I think it is best he goes to Portugal. Only he left his cats behind, and asked me if I would look after them so their servants don't dispose of them. Their names are Archie and Angus. That is Archie, presently trying to get into the flour bin."

Her face softened into pure pleasure again as she looked down at the little animal, then at the other one, whose soft, black face was wide-eyed and filled with interest. He moved a step closer, then jumped back, then took another step forward, tail high.

It was hard to spoil the moment.

"I shall probably go and see Matthew this evening. . . ." he began.

She froze, her fingers motionless above the kitten, then she looked up at him, waiting for him to tell her.

"Soames was the traitor in the Treasury," he said. "Matthew knew it."

Her face filled with pain. "Oh, Thomas! That's dreadful! Poor Harriet. How is she taking it? Did you have to arrest him? Can Matthew be with her? Wouldn't it be better if . . . if you didn't go?" She leaned across the table, putting her hand over his. "I'm sorry, my dear, but he is not going to find it easy to understand that you had to arrest Soames. In time, I expect he will realize . . ." She stopped, seeing from his face that there was something she had not understood. "What? What is it?"

"It was Matthew who told me," he said softly. "Harriet Soames confided to him, in ignorance, a telephone call she had overheard her father make, not understanding its meaning, and he felt honor-bound to repeat it to me. I am afraid she will not forgive him for it. In her eyes he has betrayed both herself and her father."

"That's not fair!" she said instantly, then closed her eyes and shook her head from side to side in a sharp little movement of denial. "I know it is natural to feel that way, but it is still not fair. What else could he do? She cannot expect him to deny his own life's work and belief and be party to Mr. Soames's treason! It's not Matthew!"

"I know that," he said softly. "And perhaps there is part of her which knows it too, but that doesn't help. Her father is disgraced, ruined. The Colonial Office won't prosecute,

331

or the Treasury either, because of the scandal, but it will become known."

She looked up. "What will happen to him?" Her face filled with a cold, bleak sadness. "Suicide?" she whispered.

"It's not impossible, but I hope not."

"Poor Harriet! Yesterday she had everything and the future looked endlessly bright. Today there is nothing at all, no marriage, no father, no money, no standing in Society, only the few friends who have the courage to remain by her, and no hope for anything to come. Thomas, it's sad, and very frightening. Yes, of course, she cannot forgive Matthew, and that will be a wound he will never be healed of either. What a terrible, terrible mess. Yes, go to Matthew; he will need you more than ever before."

Pitt had stopped by at Matthew's office and found him white to the lips, hollow-eyed and barely able to function in his duty. He had known the danger of such rejection when he had first gone to Pitt, but part of him had clung to the hope that it would not be so, that somehow Harriet would, in her despair and shame, turn to him, in spite of what he had done, what he had felt compelled to do. Given his own sense of honor he had had no choice.

He had begun to tell Pitt some of this, but Pitt had understood it without the necessity of words. After a few moments Matthew had ceased trying to explain, and simply let the subject fall. They sat together for some time, occasionally speaking of things of the past, happy, easy times remembered with pleasure. Then Pitt rose to leave, and Matthew returned to his papers, letters and calls. Pitt took a hansom to Farnsworth's office on the Embankment.

"Soames?" Farnsworth said with confusion, anger and distress conflicting in his face. "What a damn fool thing to have done. Really, the man is an ass. How could he credit anything so—so totally beyond belief? He is a cretin."

"The curious thing," Pitt said flatly, "is that it is largely true."

332

"What?" Farnsworth swung around from the bookshelf where he was standing, his eyes wide and angry. "What are you driveling on about, Pitt? It's an absurd story. A child wouldn't have accepted that explanation."

"Probably not, but then a child would not have the sophistication . . ."

"Sophistication!" Farnsworth grimaced with disgust. "Soames is about as sophisticated as my bootboy. Although even he wouldn't have swallowed that, and he's only fourteen."

". . . to be misled by an argument about the results of a clash of European powers in black Africa, and the need to prevent it in the interests of morality in general, and the future of all of us," Pitt finished as if he had not been interrupted.

"Are you making excuses for him?" Farnsworth's eyes widened. "Because if you are, you are wasting your time. What are you doing about it? Where is he?"

"At Bow Street," Pitt replied. "I imagine his own people will deal with him. It is not my domain."

"His own people? Who do you mean? The Treasury?"

"The government," Pitt answered. "It will no doubt be up to them to decide what to do about it."

Farnsworth sighed and bit his lip. "Nothing, I imagine," he said bitterly. "They will not wish to admit that they were incompetent enough to allow such a thing to happen. That is probably true of the whole issue. To whom did he give his information? You haven't told me that yet. Who is this altruistic traitor?"

"Thorne."

Farnsworth's eyes widened.

"Jeremiah Thorne? Good heavens. I had my money on Aylmer. I knew it wasn't Hathaway, in spite of that lunatic scheme to disseminate false information to all the suspects. Nothing ever came of that!"

"Yes it did, indirectly."

"What do you mean, indirectly? Did it, or didn't it?"

"Indirectly," Pitt repeated. "We got the information back from the German Embassy, and it was none of the figures Hathaway had given, which supports what Soames said of Thorne. He was giving misinformation all the time."

"Possibly, but I shall want proof of that before I believe it. Is he at Bow Street as well?"

"No, he's probably in Lisbon by now."

"Lisbon?" A range of emotions fought in Farnsworth's face. He was furious, contemptuous, and at the same time aware of the embarrassment saved by the fact that Thorne could not now be tried.

"He left last night," Pitt went on.

"Warned by Soames?"

"No. If anyone, Kreisler . . ."

Farnsworth swore.

". . . but I imagine unintentionally," Pitt went on. "I think Kreisler was more concerned with finding out who murdered Susannah Chancellor."

"Or finding out how much you knew about the fact that he killed her," Farnsworth snapped. "All right, well at least you have cleared up the treason affair—not very satisfactorily, I might add, but this is better than nothing. And I suppose it could have been very ugly if you had arrested Thorne. You are due some credit for it."

He sighed and walked over to his desk. "Now you had better return to the tragedy of Mrs. Chancellor. The government, not to mention the press, want to see a solution to that." He looked up. "Have you anything at all? What about the cabdriver? Do you have him yet? Do you know where she was put into the river? Have you found her cloak? Do you even know where she was killed? I suppose it would be by Thorne, because she discovered his secret?"

"He said he knew nothing about it."

"Said? You just told me he had left for Portugal last night, and you got there this morning!"

"He left me a letter."

"Where is it? Give it to me!" Farnsworth demanded.

Pitt passed it across and Farnsworth read it carefully.

"Cats!" he said at the end, putting it down on his desk. "I suppose you believe him about Mrs. Chancellor?"

"Yes, I do."

Farnsworth bit his lip. "Actually, I am inclined to myself. Pursue Kreisler, Pitt. There is a great deal that is not right about that man. He has made enemies. He has an unreliable temper and is acquainted with violence. Seek out his reputation in Africa; nobody knows what he stands for or where his loyalties are. That much I have learned for myself." He jerked his hand sharply. "Forget the connection with Arthur Desmond. That's nonsense, always was. I know it is painful for you to accept that he was senile, I can understand that, but it is incontrovertible. I'm sorry. The facts are plain enough. He cadged brandy from everyone he knew, and when he was too fuddled to have any clarity of thought at all, he took an overdose of laudanum, probably by accident, possibly intending to make an honorable end of it before he became even more uncontrolled and finally said something, made some accusation or slander he could not live down."

Pitt froze. Farnsworth had used the word *cadged*. How did he know Sir Arthur had not ordered every brandy himself in the usual way? There was one answer to that— because he knew what had happened that afternoon in the Morton Club. He had not been there. It had not come out in testimony at the inquest; in fact the opposite had been said, that Sir Arthur had ordered the drinks himself.

Pitt opened his mouth to ask Farnsworth if he had spoken to Guyler himself, then just in time, with the words on the edge of his tongue, he realized that if he had not, the only way he could have known would be if he were part of the same ring of the Inner Circle which had ordered Sir Arthur's death.

"Yes?" Farnsworth said impatiently, his blue-gray eyes staring at Pitt. It seemed at a glance as if he spoke in temper, but behind the surface emotion, the exterior that Pitt could see—and had seen so often before he could picture it with his eyes closed, so familiar was it—he saw for a moment that colder, cleverer mind, far more watchful, waiting for Pitt to betray himself.

If Pitt asked the question, Farnsworth would know exactly what he suspected, how far he had moved already. He would know Pitt was looking for the executioner and that he knew Farnsworth was part of that ring.

Pitt veiled his eyes and lied, the fear breaking out in a cold sweat on his skin. Someone could so easily brush against him and push him in front of the oncoming wheels of a carriage, or pass their hand over his mug of cider in a tavern, and he would drink a fatal dose.

"Well?" Farnsworth said with something close to a smile.

Pitt knew if he gave in too easily Farnsworth would see through it and know he had understood. Suddenly he was aware of the possibility that Farnsworth was far cleverer than he had thought. He had never excelled at police procedure; he was too arrogant to take the pains. But he knew how to use the men whose skill it was: Tellman, Pitt, even Micah Drummond in his time. And how many had he inducted into the Circle? Who were they? Probably Pitt would never know; even when it was too late, he might not know who had struck the blow.

He was waiting, the afternoon sunlight shining through the windows on his fair hair.

"Do you really think that it could have been suicide?" Pitt asked as if he were accepting the idea with deep reluctance. "A matter of death rather than dishonor . . . to himself, I mean?"

"Would you prefer that?" Farnsworth countered.

"Not prefer, I don't think." Pitt forced himself to say the words, to act the part, even to believe it himself while he spoke. He was cold inside. "But it is easier to fit into the facts we know."

"Facts?" Farnsworth was still staring at him.

"Yes . . ." Pitt swallowed. "Taking a dose of laudanum at all in the afternoon, in your club. One would have to be

336

very fuddled indeed to do it by accident, it's . . . it's bad form. But a suicide would be more understandable. He wouldn't want to do it at home." He knew he was rambling, saying too much. He felt a little dizzy; the room seemed enormous. He must be careful. "Where his servants would find him," he went on. "And perhaps be distressed. A woman servant—maybe that was when the realization came to him of just how ruinous his behavior had been?"

"I should think that it was like that," Farnsworth agreed. His body relaxed indefinably. Once again he looked irritable and impatient. "Yes, I daresay you have it, Pitt. Well, let go of it, man. Get back to work on the Chancellor case. That is your absolute priority. Do you understand me?"

"Yes sir. Of course I do." Pitt rose to his feet and found his knees unaccountably weak. He was forced to stand still for several seconds before he could master himself and take his leave, closing the door behind him and starting down the stairs holding on to the banister.

11

N*OBBY GUNNE WAS* deeply distressed by the death of Susannah Chancellor, not only because she had found her a charming and unique person, but also, with an intense sense of guilt, because she was terrified that Peter Kreisler had some involvement in it. In her worst moments she even feared he might have been directly responsible.

She did not see him for at least three days, and that only added to her anxiety and the hideous ideas that danced in her head. His presence might have been reassuring. She might have looked at his face and seen the ultimate sanity in it, and known her fears were ugly and unjust. She would have been able to speak with him and hear his sorrow for Susannah. Perhaps he might even say where he had been that night and prove his innocence.

But all she received from him was a short note saying how grieved he was, and that business to do with it kept him occupied to the exclusion of all else, at least for the present. She could not imagine what business he could have as a result of Susannah's death, but possibly it concerned African finance and the banking which so involved her family.

When she did see him it was because he had called upon her in the afternoon. It was a most unconventional thing to do, but then convention had never bothered either of them. He found her in the garden picking early roses. Most of them were still in bud, but there were one or two open. She had already chosen some leaves from a copper beech tree which were a deep purply red and set off the pink petals in a way no ordinary green leaf could.

He was walking across the lawn, unannounced, a fact over which she would have words with her maid later on. Now all she could think of was her pleasure in seeing him and the brooding anxiety which made her heart beat faster and tightened her throat.

He did not bother with formal greetings, enquiries for health or remarks about delightful weather. He stopped in front of her, his eyes direct and troubled, but his delight in her company undisguised.

For a moment her fears were swallowed up in the inner surge of happiness at the sight of his face and the confidence in him which she had in part forgotten.

"I'm sorry to intrude on you uninvited," he said, holding out his hands, palms upwards.

She placed her own in his and felt the warmth of his fingers close over hers. For an instant she forgot her fears. They were absurd. He would never have done anything so appalling. If he had been involved at all, then there would be some innocent explanation of it, whether she ever heard it or not.

She did not reply with the cliché she might have said to anyone else.

"How are you?" She searched his face. "You look very tired."

He let go of her hands and fell into step beside her, walking very slowly along the herbaceous border. "I suppose I am," he admitted. "I seem to have slept very little in the last few days, since the death of Mrs. Chancellor."

Although the subject was at the forefront of her thoughts, yet still she was startled to hear him raise it so soon, too soon for her to have prepared what she meant to say, in spite of having turned it over in her mind through every wakeful hour since it had happened.

She looked away from him, as if to some point on the far side of the garden, although nothing was happening more important than a small bird hopping from one twig to another.

"I had not realized you were so fond of her." She stopped, afraid that she sounded petulant and he would misunderstand. Or was it misunderstanding? Was she not jealous? How absurd, and worse than that, how ugly. "She was indeed extremely charming." That sounded trite and flat. "And so very alive. I find it painful to acknowledge that she is gone. I should very much have liked to know her better."

"I liked her," he replied, staring at the spires of the delphiniums. They were already in bud heavily enough to tell which were the dark blue, which sky blue, and which either white or pink. "There was an honesty in her which is all too rare. But that is not why I lie awake over her death." He frowned, turning to face her. "Which I thought you knew. You are less direct than goes with your intelligence. I shall have to remember that. It is most feminine. I think I like it."

Now she was thoroughly confused, and felt the color burning up her cheeks. She avoided his eyes. "I am not at all sure I know what you mean. Why are you so distressed by her death, if it is not offensive to ask? I cannot believe it is pain for Linus Chancellor. I formed the distinct impression you did not care for him at all."

"I don't," he agreed. "At least, I have no objection to the man himself. In fact I admire him intensely. He has energy, intelligence, talent and the will to harness them to a purpose, which is the key to it all. Many men have all the attributes for success except that. Will and discipline can make a man." He walked another few steps before continuing, his hands thrust into his pockets. "But I disagree passionately with his beliefs and plans for Africa. But you already know that."

"So why are you so distraught?" she asked.

"Because I quarreled with her the evening before the night she died."

Nobby was startled. She had not believed him a man to have such a tender, even superstitious conscience. It sat ill with everything else she knew of him. Of course there were incongruities in people's characters, sudden traits that seemed quite contradictory, but this caught her completely by surprise.

"That's foolish," she said with a smile. "I doubt you were so unpleasant as to give you cause to feel guilty, just because it was not resolved. You differed in view about settlement in Zambezia. It was an honest difference. I am sure she would not—"

"For heaven's sake!" he interrupted with a laugh of derision. "I will stand by what I said to God himself! Certainly to Susannah Chancellor, dead or alive! No—it was a public place, and I am quite certain I was thoroughly observed, and the matter will have been reported to the police. Your diligent friend Pitt will be very aware of it. He has already been to see me. He was polite, of course, but also, underneath the good manners, very suspicious. It would suit a good many people if I were charged with murdering her. It would . . ." He stopped, seeing the alarm in her face.

He smiled self-mockingly. "Oh come, Nobby. Don't pretend you don't know that. The sooner the matter is settled, the greater honor there will be for the police, the press will leave them alone, and no one will need to look too exhaustively into poor Susannah's life. Although I am sure it was as pure as most people's; still it is an unpleasant exercise, and bound to offend a few whose lives touched hers, perhaps less than honorably."

" 'Less than honorably'?" She was surprised, and not sure what he meant.

He smiled ruefully. "Mine to begin with," he confessed. "The quarrel was innocent enough, not personal, a matter of conviction; but viewed by others who did not know what was said, it might look otherwise. I have no doubt there

341

will be other people who would not care to have every word or gesture examined by the prurient and unkind." He looked at her with a gentleness touched with humor which set her pulses racing. "Have you not been guilty of foolishness now and then which you would rather remained private? Or a word or an act that was hasty, shabbier than you wished?"

"Yes of course I have." She did not need to add more; the understanding was complete, without the necessity of words.

They walked a few paces farther and then turned along the path towards the stone wall and the early roses spilling over it. The archway was in dappled sunlight, picking out the flat surfaces of the individual stones, and the tiny plants in the crevices low down where it was moist, ferns and mosses with flowers like pinprick stars. Above them there was a faint rustle in the leaves of the elm trees as a breeze moved, laden with the smell of grass and leaf mold.

She looked at his face and knew he was thinking of the pleasures of being home in England, the timeless grace of old gardens. Africa with its savagery, its gaudy vegetation, so often seared and withered by relentless sun, its teeming wildlife, all seemed unreal in this ancient certainty where the seasons had come and gone with the same nurturing pattern for a hundred generations.

But Susannah's death would not go away. Law was also a thing more certain here, and Nobby knew Pitt well enough to have no doubt that he would pursue it to the end, no matter what that end might be. He did not bow to coercion, expediency or even emotional pain.

If the truth were unbearably ugly, she did not know if he would make public all the evidence. If the answer proved to be too desperately tragic, if it would ruin others for no good cause, if the motive caught his pity hard enough, he might relent. Although she could not imagine a reason that could ever mitigate the murder of someone like Susannah.

But that argument was pointless. It was not Pitt she was

afraid of, or prosecution or justice, it was truth. It would be equally terrible to her if Kreisler were guilty, whether he were charged or not.

But why did she even entertain the thought? It was hideous, terrible! She felt guilty that it even entered her mind, let alone that she let it remain there.

As if reading her thoughts, or seeing the confusion in her face, he stopped just beyond the arch in the small shade garden with its primroses and honesty and arching Solomon's seal.

"What is it, Nobby?"

She was abashed to find an answer that was neither a lie nor too hurtful to both of them.

"Did you learn anything?" She seized upon something useful to ask.

"About Susannah's death? Not much. It seems to have happened late in the evening and when she was alone in a hansom cab, no one knows where. She had said she was going to visit the Thornes, but never arrived, as far as we know. Unless, of course, the Thornes are lying."

"Why should the Thornes wish her harm?"

"It probably goes back to the death of Sir Arthur Desmond—at least that is what Pitt has apparently suggested. It makes little sense to me."

They were standing so still a small, brown bird flew out of one of the trees and stood on the path barely a yard from them, its bright eyes watching curiously.

"Then why?" she said quietly, the fear still large within her. She knew enough of men who traveled the wild places of the earth to understand that they have to have an inner strength in order to survive, a willingness to attack in the need to defend themselves, the resolve to take life if it threatened their own, a single-mindedness that brooked nothing in its way. Gentler people, more circumspect, more civilized at heart, all too often were crushed by the ferocity of an unforgiving land.

He was watching her closely, almost searchingly. Slowly

the happiness and the sense of comfort drained out of him, replaced by pain.

"You are not convinced that I did not do it, are you, Nobby?" he said with a catch in his voice. "You think I could have murdered that lovely woman? Just because . . ." He stopped, the color washing up his face in guilt.

"No," she said levelly, the words difficult to speak. "Not just because she differed with you over settlement in Africa, of course not. But then we both know that would be absurd. If you had, it would be because of the shares she has in one of the great banking houses and the influence she might have over Francis Standish, and of course because of her husband's position. She supported him fully, which meant she was against you."

He was very pale, his features twisted with hurt.

"For God's sake, Nobby! How would my murdering her help?"

"It is one supporter less. . . ." She trailed off, looking away from him. "I am not supposing you killed her, only that the police might think so. I am afraid for you." That was the truth, but not the whole truth. "And you were angry with her."

"If I killed everyone I was angry with, at one time or another, my whole career would be littered with corpses," he said quietly, and she knew from the tone in his voice that he had believed only the truth she had spoken; the lies and the omissions he understood for what they were.

The bird was still on the path close to them, its head cocked to one side.

He put his hands on her arms and she felt the warmth of him through the thin sleeves of her dress.

"Nobby, I know that you understand Africa as I do, and that at times men are violent in order to survive in a violent and sudden land, where the dangers are largely unknown and there is no law but that of staying alive, but I have not lost my knowledge of the difference between Africa and England. And morality, the underlying knowledge of good

344

and evil, is the same everywhere. You do not kill people simply because they stand in your way, or believe differently over an issue, no matter how big. I argued with Susannah, but I did not hurt her, or cause her to be hurt. You do me an injustice if you do not believe that . . . and you cause me deep pain. Surely I do not need to explain that to you? Do we not understand each other without the need for speeches and declarations?"

"Yes." She answered from the heart, her head ignored, silenced in a deeper, more insistent certainty. "Yes of course we do." Should she apologize for even having entertained the thought? Did he need her to?

As if he had read it in her eyes, he spoke, smiling a little. "Good. Now let us leave it. Don't go back over it. You had to acknowledge what passed through your mind. Don't let there be dishonesty between us, the need to hide behind deceit and politeness for fear of the truth."

"No," she agreed quickly, a ridiculous smile on her face in spite of all that common sense could tell her. "Of course I won't."

He leaned forward and kissed her with a gentleness that took her by blissful surprise.

Pitt was sitting at the breakfast table slowly eating toast and marmalade. The toast was crisp and the butter very mildly salted. Altogether it was something to be savored to the last crumb.

And he had been out until nearly midnight the previous evening, so if he were late at Bow Street this morning, it was justifiable. The children had left for school and Gracie was busy upstairs. The daily woman was scrubbing the back steps, and would presently put black lead on the range, after cleaning it out, a job which Gracie was delighted to have got rid of.

Charlotte was making a shopping list.

"Are you going to be late again this evening?" she asked, looking up at him.

"I doubt it," he replied with his mouth full. "Although we still haven't found the hansom driver yet. . . ."

"Then he's involved," she said with certainty. "If he were innocent he would have come forward by now. If he doesn't want to be found, how will you get him?"

He finished the rest of his tea. "By the long, slow process of questioning every driver in London," he assured her. "And proving whether they were where they say. And if we are lucky, by someone informing. But we don't know where she went into the water. It could have been upriver or down. All we do know is that she seems to have been dragged some distance by her clothes being caught in something." Charlotte winced. "I'm sorry," he apologized.

"Have you found her cloak?" she asked.

"No, not yet."

He ate the last of his toast with satisfaction.

"Thomas . . ."

He pushed out his chair and stood up. "Yes?"

"Do bodies often wash up at Traitors Gate?"

"No—why?"

She took a deep breath and let it out.

"Do you think it is possible that whoever it was intended her to end up there?"

The idea was puzzling, and one which had not occurred to him before.

"Traitors Gate? I should doubt it. Why? It's more likely that he cared where he put her in, close to where he killed her, and unobserved. It would be chance, tide and the currents which took her to the slipway at the Tower. And, of course, whatever dragged her."

"But what if it wasn't?" she insisted. "What if it was intended?"

"It doesn't honestly make a lot of difference, except that he would have had to find the right place to put her in, which might have meant moving her. But why would anyone care enough to take the risk?"

"I don't know," she confessed. "Only because she betrayed someone."

"Who? Not her husband. She was always loyal to him, not as a matter of course, but because she truly loved him. You told me that yourself."

"Oh, yes," she agreed. "I didn't mean that kind of betrayal. I thought perhaps it might be back to the Inner Circle again."

"There are no women members anyway, and I'm convinced Chancellor is not a member either."

"But what about her brother-in-law, Francis Standish?" she pressed. "Could he not be involved in Sir Arthur's death, and somehow she found out? Susannah was very fond of Sir Arthur. She wouldn't keep silent, even to protect her own. Perhaps that was what troubled her so much."

"Family loyalty . . . and betrayal," Pitt said slowly, turning the idea over in his mind. Harriet Soames's face was sharp in his inner eye, in passionate defense of her father, even knowing his guilt. "Possibly . . ."

"Does it help?"

He looked at her. "Not a lot. Intentional or not, she will have been put in at the same place." He pushed his chair back in, kissed her cheek before going to the door. His hat was on the rack in the hall. "It's something I shall search for with more diligence today. I think it is time I forgot the hansom driver and concentrated on finding a witness to her body being put into the water."

"Nothing except what didn't happen," Tellman said with disgust when Pitt asked him to report his progress so far. They were standing in Pitt's office in the early light, the noise from the street drifting up through the half-open window.

Tellman was tired and frustrated. "No one has seen the damned hansom, either in Berkeley Square or Mount Street, or anywhere else," he went on. "At least, no one who has it in mind to tell us. Of course all London is crawling with cabs, any one of which could have had Mrs. Chancellor in it!" He leaned against the bookcase behind him. "Two were seen in Mount Street about the right time, but both of them have been accounted for. One was a Mr. Garney going out to dine with his mother. His story is well vouched for by his servants and hers. The other was a Lieutenant Salsby and a Mrs. Latten, going to the West End to dine. At least that is what they said."

"You disbelieve them?" Pitt sat down behind his desk.

" 'Course I disbelieve them!" Tellman smiled. "Seen his face, and you would have too. Seen hers, and you'd know what they were going to do! She's no better than she should be, but not party to abducting a cabinet minister's wife. That's not how she makes her living!"

"You know her?"

Tellman's face registered the answer.

"Anything else?" Pitt asked.

"Don't know what else to look for." Tellman shrugged. "We've spent days trying to find the place she went in. Most likely Limehouse. More discreet than upriver. It'd be eleven or so before he put her into the water, maybe. That'd be four hours before she was found. Don't really matter whether she hit the slipway on the incoming tide or went past farther into the current and was washed up on the outgoing. Still means she put in somewhere south." He breathed out slowly and pulled a face. "And that's a long stretch of river with a dozen wharves and steps, and as many streets that lead to them. And you'll get no help from the locals. The people that spend their time waiting around there aren't likely to speak to us if they can help it. Slit your throat for the practice."

"I know that, Tellman. Have you a better idea?"

"No. I tried them all and they don't work, but I'm known 'round there. Used to be at that station. You might do better." His expression and his voice both denied it.

But Pitt was not satisfied. According to the river police, if she had been put into the water within an hour or so of

348

having been killed, which the medical examiner had said could be no later than eleven, or at a stretch half past, then the incoming tide could only have carried her from the Limehouse area, at the farthest. It was more likely to have been closer, except that that made it Wapping, right on the Pool of London.

Tellman had already tried the Thames police, whose station was on the river's edge. They were extremely helpful, in an utterly negative way. Their patrols were excellent. They knew every yard of the waterfront, and they were sure no woman of Susannah Chancellor's description and status had been put into the river there that night. It was an extravagant claim, but Pitt was inclined to believe them. The Port of London was always busy, even as late as midnight. Why should anyone take such a risk?

Which always brought him back to the question as to why anyone should murder Susannah Chancellor anyway. Was it an abduction that had gone tragically wrong?

Then was it simply greed, imagining Chancellor would pay a fine ransom? Or was the motive political . . . which brought him back to Peter Kreisler again.

Tellman had already spent fruitless days in Limehouse and learned nothing of use. If anyone had seen a body put into the water, they were not saying so. If they had seen a hansom, and a man carrying a woman, they were not saying that either. He had even been south of the river to Rotherhithe, but that yielded no conclusion, except that it was not impossible that someone could have taken a small boat from one of the hundred wharves or stairs and carried a body in it. He had even considered if Tellman could be part of the conspiracy, a subtle and brilliant Inner Circle member. But looking at the anger in his face, hearing the brittle edge in his voice, he could not believe his own judgment to be so wrong.

"What now?" Tellman said cynically, interrupting Pitt's thoughts. "You want me to try the Surrey Docks?"

"No, there's no point." An idea was forming in Pitt's

mind from what Charlotte had said about betrayals and Traitors Gate. "Go and see what you can find out about her brother-in-law."

Tellman's eyebrows rose. "Mrs. Chancellor's brother-in-law—Francis Standish? Why? Why in the name of Hell would he want to murder her? I still think it was Kreisler."

"Possibly. But look at Standish anyway."

"Yes sir. And what will you be doing?"

"I shall try upriver, somewhere like the stretch between Westminster and Southwark."

"But that would mean someone'd waited with her after she was dead and before they put her into the water," Tellman pointed out incredulously. "Why would anyone do that? Why take that risk?"

"Less chance of being seen, closer to midnight," Pitt suggested.

Tellman gave him a look of total scorn. "There's people up and down the river all the time. Anything after that'd be as good. Better get rid of it as soon as possible. Easier to travel about in a hansom when they're all over the streets," he said reasonably. "Who'd notice one in the many? Notice one at one o'clock in the morning. Too late for theaters. People who go to late parties and balls have their own carriages."

Pitt was uncertain whether to share Charlotte's idea with Tellman or not. On the face of it, it sounded absurd, and yet the more he thought of it, the more it seemed possible.

"What if he intended her to be washed ashore at Traitors Gate?"

Tellman stared at him. "Another warning to anyone minded to betray the Circle?" he said with a spark of fire in his eyes. "Maybe. But that'd take some doing! No reason why she should come ashore at all. Often they don't. And even if he knew the tides, she could have been dragged; as it happens, she was! He'd have to wait for the ebb, in case she washed off again." His voice was gathering enthusiasm. "So he waits somewhere, and puts her in at

350

high water, then he'd be certain positive she'd not go off again."

Then his face darkened. "But there's no way, even if he put her in above the Tower, that she'd be sure to go ashore there. She could have gone all the way down to the next big curve, around Wapping, or further, to the Surrey Docks." He shook his head. "He'd have to put her there himself, by boat, most likely. Only a madman would risk carrying her there down at Queen's Steps, the way we went to find her."

"Well he wouldn't come from the north bank upriver," Pitt thought aloud. "That's Custom House Quay, and then the Billingsgate Fish Market. He'd have been seen for sure."

"Other side of the river," Tellman said instantly, standing upright, his thin body tense. "Horsley Down. Nobody 'round there! He could have put her in a small boat and ferried her across. Just left her more or less where we found her. Outgoing tide wouldn't touch her."

"Then I'm going to the south bank," Pitt said decisively, standing up and moving away from the desk.

Tellman looked doubtful. "Sounds like a lot of trouble, not to say danger, just to make sure she fetched up at the Tower. Can't see it, myself."

"It's worth trying," Pitt answered, undeterred.

"The medical examiner said she was dragged," Tellman pointed out, the last shreds of reluctance still clinging. "Clothes caught on something! He couldn't have just put her there!"

"If he brought her from the other side, perhaps he dragged her?" Pitt replied. "Behind his boat, to make it look as if she'd been in the water some time."

"Geez!" Tellman sucked his breath in between his teeth. "Then we're dealing with a madman!" He caught sight of Pitt's face. "All right—even madder than we thought."

* * *

Pitt took a hansom. It was a long ride. He went south and east along the river, crossed at London Bridge and then turned east again immediately into Tooley Street.

"What ezac'ly are yer lookin' fer?" the cabby asked dubiously. It was not that he objected to a fare that lasted several hours, and was willing to pay him to stand around, but he liked to know what was wanted of him, and this was a most peculiar request.

"I'm looking for a place where someone could have waited in a carriage until a quiet time just after the tide had turned, and then rowed a body across the river and left it on the slipway at Traitors Gate," Pitt replied.

The cabby let out an incredulous blasphemy under his breath. "Sorry, guv," he apologized the moment after. "But you ain't 'alf got a nasty turn o' mind." He looked nervously around at the quiet bank and the empty stretch of river in the sun.

Pitt smiled sadly. "The murder of Mr. Chancellor's wife," he explained, showing the man his card.

"Oh! Oh, yeah! That was terrible, poor lady." The man's eyes widened. "Yer reckon as she was killed over 'ere, and taken across after, like?"

"No, I think she was brought over here in a carriage, someone waited until the tide turned, and then rowed across and left her on the slipway at the Tower."

"Why? That don't make no sense! Why not just stick 'er in the water and scarper! Daft ter be seen. 'Oo cares where she fetches up?"

"I think he may have cared."

"Why wait for the tide to turn? I'd just a' put 'er in there as quick as possible and got goin' afore anyone saw me." He shivered. "You looking for a madman?"

"A man with an insane hatred, perhaps, but not mad in any general sense."

"Then he'd a' gone ter 'Orsley Steps and rowed up a fraction on the incoming tide and left 'er there," the cabby said with decision. "An' rowed back ter Little Bridge, further up, ter keep goin' with the tide, like, instead o' rowin' agin it." He looked satisfied with his answer.

"If he'd left her on the incoming tide," Pitt reasoned, "she might have been floated off again, and finished up somewhere else."

"True," the cabby agreed. "Still an' all, I'd a' taken the chance."

"Perhaps. But I'll see if anyone saw a carriage standing waiting that night. Horsley Down Steps and Little Bridge Stairs, you said?"

"Yes, guv. Yer want ter go there ter them places?"

"I do."

"It would take an awful long time!"

"It probably will," Pitt agreed with a tight smile. "Don't worry, I'll take you to lunch. Do you know a good pub close by?"

The cabby's face brightened. " 'Course, I do! Bin 'ere before, or 'ereabouts. There's the Black Bull up over London Bridge, bit over the other side. Or the Triple Plea down Queen Elizabeth Street, just over there." He pointed with a gnarled hand. "Or over the railway line" he swiveled far ther around—"yer could go into Bermondsey and find anything yer like."

"We'll try the Triple Plea," Pitt promised. "First we'll go to the Horsley Down Steps."

"Right, guv. Right y'are." And he urged his horse forward with something almost close to anticipation.

They went down Tooley Street at a brisk trot until it became Queen Elizabeth Street, then the cab turned sharply left towards the river. There was a large building on the right side of the road which looked like a school. The street bore the dismal name of Potters' Fields. Pitt wondered if it struck the cabby's macabre sense of humor. They followed it a hundred yards or so until it ended at the road, little more than a path, which ran along the riverbank. There was only a sloping margin between them and the water, and it was deserted, even at this time of day. They passed two more roads leading up towards Queen Elizabeth Street before they came to the Horsley Down Steps, from where it would have been easy enough to get into a boat.

There was a small open area, less than a square, at the end of Freeman's Lane. A couple of men stood around idly, watching whoever might pass, mainly the traffic along the water.

Pitt got out of the hansom and approached them. Several possible opening gambits occurred to him; the one he least favored was admitting who he was. It was one of those occasions when his sartorial inelegance was an advantage.

"Where would I get a boat around here?" he asked bluntly.

"What kind of a boat?" one of them asked, removing the clay pipe from between his teeth.

"Small one, only to cross the river," Pitt replied.

"London Bridge, jus' up there." The man gestured with his pipe. "Why don't yer walk?"

The other one laughed.

"Because I might meet someone I don't wish to," Pitt replied without a flicker of humor. "I might be taking something private with me," he added for good measure.

"Might yer, then?" The first man was interested. "Well I daresay as I could rent yer a boat."

"Done it before, have you?" Pitt asked casually.

"Wot's it ter you?"

"Nothing." Pitt affected indifference and turned as if to leave.

"Yer want a boat, I'll get yer one!" the man called after him.

Pitt stopped. "Know the tides, do you?" he enquired.

" 'Course I know the tides! I live 'ere!"

"What tide's best for going across to the Tower?"

"Geez! Yer planning to rob the Tower? After the crown jools, are yer?"

Again the second man laughed uproariously.

"I want to take something, not fetch it back," Pitt answered, hoping he had not gone too far.

"Slack water," the first man replied, watching him closely. "Stands ter reason. No current pullin' yer."

"Is the current strong?"

"'Course it's strong! It's a tidal river, ain't it! Geez, w'ere you bin? Yer stupid or summink?"

"If I got here early, where could I wait?" Pitt ignored the insult.

"Well not 'ere, if yer don't want to be seen, that's fer sure," the man said dryly, and clasped his pipe between his teeth again.

"Why? Who'd see me?"

"Well I would, fer a start!"

"Slack water's in the middle of the night," Pitt argued.

"I know when slack water is! I come down 'ere middle o' the night often enough."

"Why?"

"'Cause there ain't much right 'ere, but a hundred yards or so"—he pointed along the bank—"there's dozens o' wharfs. There's Baker's Wharf, Sufferance, Bovel and Sons, Landells, West Wharf, the Coal Wharf and a lot o' steps. And that's before yer gets to Saint Saviour's Dock. There's always summink ter be 'ad down there."

"In the middle of the night?"

"'Course in the middle o' the night. Look, guv, if yer wants to take summink across the river as yer shouldn't, this in't the right place for yer. If yer got to get to the Tower, then go upstream, the Little Bridge Stairs. That's quieter, and there's often the odd boat moored up there as yer could take fer nuffink, if yer brought it back again. No trouble. I'm surprised yer didn't see it from London Bridge if yer came over that way. Only a quarter of a mile or so. Yer can see if there's a boat."

"Thank you," Pitt said with a lift in his voice he could barely control. "That's excellent advice." He fished in his pocket and found a shilling. "Have a pint each. I'm obliged to you."

"Thanks, guv." The man took the shilling and it disappeared into his pocket. He shook his head as Pitt turned away. "Nutter," he said to himself. "Right nutter."

"Back to Little Bridge Stairs," Pitt told the cabby.

"Right y'are."

They went back up to Tooley Street and then down Mill Lane towards the river. This time there was no road beside the water. Mill Lane ended abruptly at the bank and Little Bridge Stairs. There was a narrow dock a few yards upriver, and nothing else but the water and the bank. Pitt alighted.

The cabby wiped the side of his nose and looked expectantly at him.

Pitt looked around him, then down at the ground. Nothing would pass that way, except to go to the steps and the water. A carriage could wait here for hours without necessarily being remarked.

"Who uses these stairs?" Pitt asked.

The cabby looked affronted.

"Y'askin' me? 'Ow the 'ell would I know? Be fair, guv, this ain't my patch."

"I'm sorry," Pitt apologized. "Let's have luncheon at the nearest public house, and they may be able to tell us."

"Now that sounds like a very sensible idea," the cabby agreed with alacrity. "I saw one jus' 'round the corner. Called the Three Ferrets, it were, and looked quite well used, like."

It proved to be more than adequate, and after a meal of tripe and onions, followed by steamed spotted dick pudding and a glass of cider, they returned to the stairs armed with even more information than Pitt had dared hope for. It seemed very few people used the stairs, but one Frederick Lee had passed by that way on the night in question and had seen a carriage waiting sometime before midnight, the coachman sitting on his box, smoking a cigar, the carriage

356

doors closed. On his way home, more than an hour later, the man had seen it again. He had thought it odd, but none of his business, and the coachman had been a big fellow, and Lee was not inclined to make trouble for no good reason. He believed in minding his own business. He despised nosiness; it was uncivil and unhealthy.

Pitt had thanked him heartily, treated him to a glass of cider, then taken his leave.

But at the narrow, riverside end of Mill Lane, overlooking the water and the stairs down, Pitt walked back and forth slowly, eyes downcast, searching the ground just in case there were any signs of the carriage that had waited there so long, while the tide reached its height, hung slack, and then began the ebb. The surface of the road bore no trace; it was rutted stone sloping away to gutters at the side.

But it was summer. There had been only a brief shower or two of rain in the last week, nothing to wash away debris. He walked slowly up one side, and was partway down the other, about twenty yards from the water, when he saw a cigar butt, and then another. He bent down and picked them up, holding them in the palm of his hand. They were both coming unraveled from the leaf at the charred end, the tobacco loose and thready. He pulled it gently. It was distinctive, aromatic, certainly costly, not the sort of a cigar a cabdriver or waterside laborer would smoke. He turned it over carefully, examining the other end. It was curiously cut, not by a knife but by a specifically designed cigar clipper, the blades meeting equidistantly from either side. There was a very slight twist to it, and the mark of an uneven front tooth where someone had clenched a jaw on it in a moment of emotional tension.

He took out his handkerchief and wrapped them both carefully and placed them in his pocket, then continued on his way.

But he found nothing else of interest, and returned to the hansom, where the cabby was sitting on the box, watching every move he made.

"Got summink?" he asked with excitement, waiting to be told what it was and what it meant.

"I think so," Pitt replied.

"Well?" The man was not going to be shut out of the explanation.

"A cigar butt," Pitt said with a smile. "An expensive one."

"Gawd . . ." The cabby let out his breath in a sigh. " 'Er murderer sat an' smoked, with 'er corpse in his carriage, awaiting to take 'er across the river. 'E's a cool bastard, in't 'e?"

"I doubt it." Pitt climbed into the cab. "I rather think he was in the grip of a passion possibly greater than ever before in his life. Take me to Belgravia please, Ebury Street."

"Belgravia! Yer never thinking 'im what done it lives in Belgravia, are yer?"

"Yes I am. Now get started will you!"

It was a long ride back across the river and westwards, and in places the traffic was heavy. Pitt had plenty of time to think. If Susannah's murderer had thought of her as a traitor, and felt it so passionately he had killed her for it, then it could only be someone to whom she could be considered to owe an intense loyalty. That must be either her family, represented by Francis Standish, or her husband.

What betrayal could that be? Had she believed Arthur Desmond and Peter Kreisler, after all? Had she questioned Standish's investment with Cecil Rhodes, the whole manner in which the Inner Circle was involved? If Standish were a member, possibly a prominent one, could he even be the executioner? And had Susannah known, or guessed that? Was that why she had to be killed, for her knowledge, and because she was bent on sharing it rather than remaining loyal to her family, her class, and its interests?

That made a hideous sense. Standish could have met her in Mount Street. She would have expected a quarrel, a plea, but not violence. She would have been quite unafraid of anything but unpleasantness, and climbed into his carriage without more than a little coercion on his part. It satisfied all the facts he knew.

Except for what had happened to her cloak. Now that he was sure she had not been put in the river at all, simply made to look as if the receding tide had left her there by chance, it was no longer a reasonable explanation that her cloak had become lost as the current took her one way and then another.

Had he dropped it in the river for that purpose? Why? It proved nothing. And if he had, why had it not been washed up somewhere, or tangled in some rudder or oar? It would not have sunk with no body in it to carry it down. Anyway, it was a stupid thing to do; simply one more article for the police to search for, and meaning nothing one way or the other.

Unless, of course, the cloak did mean something! Could it be in some way marked, which would incriminate Standish?

Pitt could think of nothing. No one was pretending it was suicide or accident. The method and means were plain enough, even the motive was plain. He had defiantly and unnecessarily drawn attention to it!

The more he thought about it, the more sense it made. Sitting in the hansom, in spite of the mildness of the day, he shivered as he felt the power of the Inner Circle everywhere around him, not only making threats of financial and political ruin, but when betrayed, ruthlessly murdering its own, even a woman.

"Ebury Street, guv!" the cabby called out. "What number do you want?"

"Twelve," Pitt replied with a start.

" 'Ere y'are then, twelve it is. D'yer want me to wait for yer?"

"No thank you," Pitt replied, climbing out and closing the door. "I could be some time." He looked in his pocket for the very large sum he now owed for having had the cab out most of the day.

The cabby took it and counted it. "No offense," he apologized before putting it into his pocket. "That don't matter," he said, referring back to the time. "I'd kinda like to see this to the end, if yer don't mind, like?"

"As you please." Pitt gave a slight smile, then turned and went up the steps.

The door was opened by a tall footman in livery. "Yes sir?"

"Superintendent Pitt, from Bow Street. Is Mr. Standish at home?"

"Yes sir, but he has a gentleman with him. If you care to wait, I will ask if he is able to see you." He stood aside to allow Pitt in, and then showed him to the study. Apparently Standish and his visitor were in the withdrawing room.

The study was a small room by the standards of houses in Belgravia, but graciously proportioned and furnished in walnut wood with a red Turkey carpet and red curtains, giving it an air of warmth. It was obviously a room in which work was carried out. The desk was functional as well as handsome; and there were inkwells, pens, knives, blotting powder and seals neatly placed ready for use. And there was paper splayed out, as if only recently left. Perhaps Standish had been interrupted by the arrival of his present visitor. A large red jasper ashtray sat on one corner of the desk, a heavy coil of ash lying in the center, and one cigar stub, burned right down to within half an inch of the end.

Gingerly Pitt picked it up and put it to his nose. It was quite unlike the one from Little Bridge Stairs, both in aroma and texture of tobacco. Even the end was different—cut with a knife—and the faint teeth marks were very even.

He reached for the bell rope and pulled it.

The footman came, looking a little startled at being summoned by a guest whom he knew to be a mere policeman. "Yes sir?"

"Does Mr. Standish have any cigars other than these?" Pitt asked, holding up the butt for the man to see.

The footman hid his distaste for such a display of peculiar manners as well as he was able, but some shadow of it was visible in his eyes.

"Yes sir, I believe he does keep some others for guests. If you care to have one, sir, I shall see if I can find them."

"Yes please."

With raised eyebrows the footman went to a drawer in the desk, opened it and produced a box of cigars which he offered to Pitt.

Pitt took one, although he knew before smelling it that it was not like the butt in his pocket. It was narrower, darker in color and of a bland, unremarkable odor.

"Thank you." He replaced it in its box. "Does Mr. Standish ever drive his own carriage, say a four-in-hand?"

The footman's eyebrows were so high they furrowed his brow. "No sir. He has a touch of rheumatism in his hands, which makes it most uncomfortable, indeed extremely dangerous, when trying to control horses."

"I see. What are the symptoms of the rheumatism?"

"I think he is better placed to tell you such things, sir, than I. And I am sure that he will not be above an hour or so with his present business."

"What are the symptoms?" Pitt persisted, and with such urgency in his voice that the footman looked taken aback. "If you can tell me, I may not need to bother Mr. Standish."

"I'm sure, sir, it would be much better if you were to consult a physician. . . ."

"I don't want a general answer," Pitt snapped. "I want to know precisely how it affects Mr. Standish. Can you tell me or not?"

"Yes sir." The footman backed away a step. He regarded Pitt with considerable apprehension. "It shows itself with a sudden, sharp pain in the thumbs, and loss of strength."

"Enough to lose grip upon whatever he is holding, for example, the reins of the carriage?"

"Precisely. That is why Mr. Standish does not drive. I thought I had explained that, sir."

"You have, indeed you have." Pitt looked towards the door. "I shall not now have to bother Mr. Standish. If you feel it necessary to say I called, tell him you were able to answer my questions. There is no cause for alarm."

"Alarm?"

"That's right. None at all," Pitt replied, and walked past him to the hallway and the front door.

It was not Standish. He did not believe it was Kreisler—he had no cause for the passion in it—but he had to make certain. He found the cabdriver waiting for him, surprised to see him back so soon. He offered no explanation, but gave him Kreisler's address and asked him to hurry.

"Mr. Kreisler is out," the manservant informed him.

"Does he have any cigars?" Pitt asked.

"I beg your pardon, sir?"

"Does he have any cigars?" Pitt repeated tartly. "Surely the question is plain enough?"

The man's face stiffened. "No he does not. He does not smoke, sir. He finds the smell of tobacco offensive."

"You are quite sure?"

"Of course I am sure. I have worked for Mr. Kreisler for several years, both here and in Africa."

"Thank you, that is all I needed to know. Good day."

The manservant muttered something under his breath along the general lines of a parting, but less polite than he would have wished to be heard.

It was now early evening. Pitt got back into the hansom. "Berkeley Square," he ordered.

"Right y'are, guv."

It was not far, and Pitt rode deep in thought. There was one more thing he wanted to find, and if it was as he now expected, then there was only one conclusion that fitted all he knew, all the material evidence. And yet emotionally it was a tragedy out of proportion to anything he had foreseen or imagined. The thought of it saddened him, even touched him with a dark fear of the mind, a confusion of ideas and beliefs, as well as a very immediate apprehension about his own actions and the course that lay before him now.

The cabby peered in. "What number, guv?"

"No number. Just stop by the nearest manhole down into the sewers."

"What did yer say? I didn't 'ear yer right. Sounds like yer said the sewers!"

"I did. Find me a manhole," Pitt agreed.

The cab moved forward thirty or forty yards and stopped again.

"Thank you." Pitt climbed out and looked back at the hansom. "This time I definitely want you to wait. I may be a little while."

"I wouldn't leave yer now if yer paid me to go," the cabby said vehemently. "I never 'ad a day like this in me life before! I can get free dinners on this fer a year or more. Yer'll want a light, guv?" He scrambled down and detached one of his carriage lamps, lit it and gave it to Pitt.

Pitt took it and thanked him, then pulled up the manhole lid and very carefully climbed into the hole down the rungs into the bowels of the sewer system. The daylight decreased to a small round hole above him, and he was glad of the lamp and its pool of light. He turned to make his way along through the round brick-lined tunnel, moisture dripping onto the path and echoing eerily as it struck the rancid waterway between. Tunnel led off tunnel, down steps and over sluices and falls. Everywhere was a sound of water and the sour smell of waste.

"Tosher!" he called out, and his voice echoed in all directions. Finally he fell silent and there was no more sound than the incessant dripping, broken by the squeak of rats, and then nothing again.

He walked a dozen more yards, and then shouted again. "Tosher" was the general cant term for the men who made their living scavenging the sewers. He was close to a great sluice that must have spilled water over a drop of a dozen feet onto a lower level. He moved on, and called a third time.

"Yeh?"

The voice was so close and so harsh it startled him and he stopped and nearly fell into the channel. Almost at his elbow a man in thigh-high rubber boots came out of a side tunnel, his face grimy, his hair smeared across his forehead.

"Is this your stretch?" Pitt jerked his arm backwards towards the way he had come.

"'Course it is. What d'yer think I'm doin' 'ere, lookin' for the source o' the Nile?" the man said with contempt. "If yer lookin' fer a stretch o' yer own, this ain't it. It's not fer sale."

"Police," Pitt said succinctly. "Bow Street."

"Well, yer off yer beat," the man said dryly. "Watcher want 'ere?"

"A woman's blue cloak, maybe put down a manhole almost a week ago."

In the dim light the man's face had a guarded look, devoid of surprise. Pitt knew he had found it, and felt a sudden breathlessness as the reality of his belief swept over him.

"Maybe," the man said cautiously. "Why? What's it werf?"

"Accessory after the fact of murder, if you lie about it," Pitt replied. "Where is it?"

The man drew in his breath, whistling a little between his teeth, looked at Pitt's face for several seconds, then changed his mind about prevaricating.

"There weren't nothing wrong with it at all, not even wet," he said with regret. "I gave it to me woman."

"Take it to Bow Street. Maybe if you're lucky you'll get it back after the trial. The most important thing is your evidence. Where did you find it, and when?"

"Tuesd'y. Early mornin'. It were 'ung up on the stairs up inter Berkeley Square. Someone must a' dropped it in and

364

not even waited to see if it fell all the way down. Though why the devil anyone'd want ter do that I dunno."

"Bow Street," Pitt repeated, and turned to find his way back. A rat scuttered past him and plopped into the channel. "Don't forget," he added. "Accessory to murder will get you a long stretch in the Coldbath. Helpfulness will get you an equally long stretch of undisturbed prosperity."

The man sighed and spat, muttering something under his breath.

Pitt retraced his steps back to the ladder and daylight. The cabby was waiting for him with burning curiosity in his eyes.

"Well?" he demanded.

Pitt replaced the light in its bracket.

"Wait for me outside number fourteen," he replied, breathing in deeply and looking for his handkerchief to blow his nose. He set out at a brisk walk across the square to Chancellor's house, mounted the steps and knocked at the door. The lamplighter was busy at the far side and a carriage swept past, harness jingling.

The footman let him in with a look of surprise and distaste, not only at his appearance but also at the distinctive and highly unpleasant odor surrounding him.

"Good evening, Superintendent." He opened the door wide and Pitt stepped inside. "Mr. Chancellor has just returned from the Colonial Office. I shall tell him you are here. May I say, sir, that I hope you have some good news?" It seemed he had not read the shadows in Pitt's face.

"I have much further information," Pitt replied. "It is necessary that I speak with Mr. Chancellor. But perhaps before you bother him, I might have another word with the maid—Lily, I think her name is—who saw Mrs. Chancellor leave."

"Yes sir, of course." He hesitated. "Superintendent, should I know . . . er . . . should I have Mr. Richards present this time?" Perhaps after all he had seen something of

365

the emotions Pitt felt with such intensity, the sadness, the knowledge that he was in the presence of overwhelming passions of violence and tragedy.

"I think not," Pitt replied. "But thank you for the thought." The man had served Chancellor for fifteen years. He would be confused, torn with horror and conflicting loyalties. There was no need to subject him to what was bound to ensue. He would be little likely to be of any use.

"Right sir. I'll get Lily for you. Would you like to see her in the housekeeper's sitting room?"

"No thank you, the hall would be better."

The footman turned to leave, hesitated for a moment, perhaps wondering if he should offer Pitt some opportunity to wash, or even clean clothes. Then he must have considered the situation too grave for such small amenities.

"Oh—" Pitt said hastily.

"Yes sir?"

"Can you tell me what happened to Bragg's arm?"

"Our coachman, sir?"

"Yes."

"He scalded it, sir. Accident, of course."

"How did it happen, exactly? Were you there?"

"No sir, but I got there just after. In fact we were all there then, trying to clean up, and to help him. It was a pretty right mess."

"A mess? Did he drop something hot?"

"Not exactly. It was Mr. Chancellor himself who dropped it. It just sort of slipped out of his hands, so Cook said."

"What did?"

"A mug o' hot cocoa. Boiling milk is awful hot, makes a terrible scald, it does. Poor George was in a right state."

"Where did it happen?"

"Withdrawing room. Mr. Chancellor had sent for George to harness up the brougham and come and tell him when it was done. He wanted to know something about one o' the horses, so he wanted George hisself, like, not just the message. He was having a mug o' cocoa—"

"Warm weather for cocoa, isn't it?"

"Yes, it is. I would sooner have had a lemonade, myself," the footman agreed. His face was puzzled, but he still obediently answered every question.

"Is Mr. Chancellor fond of cocoa?"

"Never 'eard that he was. But he certainly had cocoa that evening. I'd swear to that. I've seen poor George. Anyway, seems Mr. Chancellor's foot slipped, or summink, and George moved rather sudden like, and got himself scalded. Mr. Chancellor rang the bell immediately, and Mr. Richards came and saw what had happened. Then before you know what's what, we're all in the kitchen trying to help poor George, getting his coat off, ripping his shirtsleeves, putting this and that on his arm, Cook and the housekeeper arguing fit to bust whether butter's best, or flour, maids shrieking and Mr. Richards saying as we should get a doctor. Housemaids is upstairs in bed, in the attic, so they didn't know a thing, and nobody even thought of them to clean up. And with Mr. Chancellor needing to go out."

"So he drove himself?"

"That's right."

"What time did he get home?"

"Don't know, sir. Late, because we went to bed just before midnight, poor George being in state, and the mistress not home yet. . . ." His face fell as he remembered all that he had learned since the panic of that night.

"Where was Lily during this upheaval?"

"In the kitchen with the rest of us, till Mr. Chancellor sent her to the landing to tear up the old sheets to make bandages for George."

"I see. Thank you."

"Shall I get Lily, sir?"

"Yes please."

Pitt stood in the fine hallway, looking about him, not at the pictures and the sheen on the parquet flooring, but at the stairway and the landing across the top, and then at the chandelier hanging from the ceiling with its dozen or so lights.

Lily came through the green baize door looking anxious and still profoundly shaken.

"Y-you want to see me, sir? I didn't know anything, I swear, or I'd have told you then. I don't know where the mistress went. She never said a thing to me. I didn't even know she was going out!"

"No, I know that, Lily," he said as gently as he could. "I want you to think back very carefully. Can you remember where you were when you saw her leave? Tell me exactly what you saw . . . absolutely exactly."

She stared at him. "I just came along the landing after turning down the beds an' looked down to the hallway. . . ."

"Why?"

"Beg pardon, sir?"

"Why did you look down?"

"Oh—I suppose 'cause I saw someone moving across towards the door. . . ."

"Exactly what did you see?"

"Mrs. Chancellor going to the front door, sir, like I said."

"Did she speak to you?"

"Oh no, she was on 'er way out."

"She didn't say good night, or tell you when she expected to come back? After all, you would have to wait up for her."

"No sir, she didn't see me 'cause she didn't turn 'round. I just saw her back as she went out."

"But you knew it was her?"

"O' course I knew it was her. She was wearin' her best cloak, dark blue velvet, it is, lined with white silk. It's the most beautiful cloak. . . ." She stopped, her eyes filling with tears. She sniffed hard. "Yer didn't ever find it, did you, sir?"

"Yes, we found it," Pitt said almost in a whisper. He had never before felt such a complex mixture of grief and anger about any case that he could recall.

She looked at him. "Where was it?"

"I don't think you need to know that, Lily." Why hurt her unnecessarily? She had loved her mistress, cared for her in her day-to-day life, been part of it in all its intimacies. Why tell her it had been pushed down into the sewers that wove and interwove under London?

She must have understood his reasons. She accepted the answer.

"You saw the back of Mrs. Chancellor's head, the cloak, as she went across the hall towards the front door. Did you see her dinner gown beneath it?"

"No sir, it comes to the floor."

"All you could see would be her face?"

"That's right."

"But she had her back to you?"

"If you're going to say it weren't her, sir, you're wrong. There weren't no other lady her height! Apart from that, there weren't no other lady here, sir, then nor ever. Mr. Chancellor isn't like that with other ladies. Devoted, he was, poor man."

"No, I wasn't thinking that, Lily."

"I'm glad. . . ." She looked uncomfortable. Presumably she was thinking of Peter Kreisler, and the ugly suspicions that had crossed their minds with regard to Susannah.

"Thank you, Lily, that's all."

"Yes sir."

As soon as Lily had gone the footman appeared from the recess beyond the stairs. No doubt he had been waiting there in order to conduct Pitt to his master.

"Mr. Chancellor asked me to take you to the study, Superintendent," he instructed Pitt, leading the way through a large oak door, along a passage into another wing of the house, and knocking on another door. As soon as it was answered, he opened it and stood back for Pitt to enter.

This was very different from the more formal reception rooms leading off the hall where Pitt had seen Chancellor before. The curtains were drawn closed over the deep windows. The room was decorated in yellows and creams, with touches of dark wood, and had an air of both graciousness and practicality. Three walls had bookcases against them, and there was a mahogany desk towards the center, with a large chair behind it. Pitt's eyes went straight to the humidor on top.

Chancellor looked strained and tired. There were shadows around his eyes, and his hair was not quite as immaculate as when Pitt had first known him, but he was perfectly composed.

"Further news, Mr. Pitt?" he said with a lift of his eyebrows. He only glanced at Pitt's grimy clothes and completely disregarded the odor. "Surely anything now is academic? Thorne has escaped, which may not be as bad as it first appears. It will save the government the difficulty of coming to a decision as to what to do about him." He smiled with a slight twist to his mouth. "I hope there is no one else implicated? Apart from Soames, that is."

"No, no one," Pitt replied. He hated doing this. It was a cat-and-mouse game, and yet there was no other way of conducting it. But he had no taste for it, no sense of achievement.

"Then what is it, man?" Chancellor frowned. "Quite frankly, I am not in a frame of mind to indulge in lengthy conversation. I commend you for your diligence. Is there anything else?"

"Yes, Mr. Chancellor, there is. I have learned a great deal more about the death of your wife. . . ."

Chancellor's eyes did not waver. They were bluer than Pitt had remembered them.

"Indeed?" There was a very slight lift in his voice, an unsteadiness, but that was only natural.

Pitt took a deep breath. His own voice sounded strange in his ears when he spoke, almost unreal. The clock on the Pembroke table by the wall ticked so loudly it seemed to echo in the room. The drawn curtains muffled every sound from the garden or the street beyond.

"She was not thrown into the river and washed up by chance of tide at Traitors Gate. . . ."

Chancellor said nothing, but his eyes did not leave Pitt's.

"She was killed before, early in the evening," Pitt went on, measuring what he was saying, choosing his words, the order in which he related the facts. "Then taken in a carriage across the river to a place just south of London Bridge, a place called Little Bridge Stairs."

Chancellor's hand closed tight above the desk where he was sitting. Pitt was still standing across from him.

"Her murderer kept her there," Pitt continued, "for a long time, in fact until half past two in the morning, when the tide turned. Then he placed her in the small boat which is often tied up at the steps, the boat he had seen when crossing London Bridge. It is a few hundred yards away."

Chancellor was staring at him, his face curiously devoid of expression, as if his mind were on the verge of something terrible, hovering on the brink.

"When he had rowed out a short way," Pitt went on, "he put her over the stern, tied across her back and under her arms with a rope, and rowed the rest of the way, dragging her behind, so her body would look as if it had been in the water a long time. When he got to the far side, he laid her on the slipway at Traitors Gate, because that was where he wished her to be found."

Chancellor's eyes widened so imperceptibly it could have been a trick of the light.

"How do you know this? Do you have him?"

"Yes, I have him," Pitt said softly. "But I know it because the carriage was seen."

Chancellor did not move.

"And during the long wait, he smoked at least two cigars," Pitt went on, his eyes going for a moment to the humidor a few inches from Chancellor's hand, "of a curiously aromatic, pungent brand."

Chancellor coughed and caught his breath. "And you . . . worked all this out?"

"With difficulty."

"Was ..." Chancellor was watching Pitt very closely, measuring him. "Was she killed in the hansom cab? Was she ever really going to Christabel Thorne's?"

"No, she was never going to Christabel Thorne's," Pitt replied. "There was no hansom cab. She was murdered here in this house."

Chancellor's face tightened, but he did not move. His hand on the desk opened and closed, but he did not touch the cigar box.

"Her maid saw her leave," he said, swallowing with difficulty.

"No, Mr. Chancellor, she saw you leave, wearing Mrs. Chancellor's cloak," Pitt corrected him. "She was a very tall woman, as tall as you are. You walked along the street to the manhole at the corner of the square, then you opened it and pushed the cloak down. You returned here and went upstairs saying you had put her in the hansom. You rang the bell and ordered your own carriage. Shortly after that you contrived an accident in which you scalded your coachman's arm, and while everyone was attending to that, you carried Mrs. Chancellor's body downstairs and put it into your own carriage, which you drove east and south until you crossed the river, as I have already said, and waited until the tide turned, so you could leave her at Traitors Gate, when the water would not rise any further and take her away again."

Pitt reached forward and opened the cigar box, taking out one of the rich cigars. The aroma of it was sickeningly familiar. He held it to his nose, and looked over it at Chancellor.

Suddenly the pretense was gone. A passion flooded Chancellor's face that was so savage and so violent it altered him utterly. The assurance, the urbanity, were vanished, his lips drawn back revealing his teeth, his cheeks white; there was a burning outrage in his eyes.

"She betrayed me," he said harshly, his voice still high

with the incredulity of it. "I loved her absolutely. We were everything to each other. She was more than just my wife, she was my companion, my partner in all my dreams. She was part of everything I did, everything I've admired. She always believed exactly as I did . . . she understood . . . and then she betrayed me! That's the worst sin of all, Pitt . . . to betray love, to betray trust! She fell away, she couldn't trust me to be right. A few rambling, ill-informed, hysterical conversations with Arthur Desmond, and she began to doubt! To doubt me! As if I didn't know more about Africa than he did, than all of them! Then Kreisler came along, and she listened to him!" His voice was rising with the fury which consumed him till it was close to a shriek.

Pitt moved a step forward but Chancellor ignored him. The wound he felt engrossed him so he was barely aware of Pitt as anything more than an audience.

"After all I had told her, all I had explained," he went on, risen to his feet now behind the desk, staring at Pitt, "she didn't trust me, she listened to Kreisler—Peter Kreisler! A mere adventurer! He sowed a few seeds of doubt in her, and she lost her faith! She told me she was going to have Standish remove his backing from Rhodes's venture. That in itself wouldn't have mattered. . . ."

He laughed savagely, a wild note of hysteria rising in it. "But when people knew about it . . . that my own wife no longer supported me! Dozens would have withdrawn— hundreds! Soon everyone would have doubted. Salisbury's only looking for an excuse. I would have looked a complete fool, betrayed by my own wife!"

He threw himself back into the chair and pulled the desk drawer open, still staring at Pitt. "I never thought you'd work it out! You liked her . . . you admired her! I didn't think you'd ever believe she was a traitor to her husband, to all we had both believed, even though I left her at Traitors Gate. It was the perfect place . . . she deserved that."

Pitt wanted to say that if he had not, he might never have found the truth, but it was pointless now.

"Linus Chancellor—"

Chancellor pulled his hand out of the desk drawer. There was a small black pistol in it. He turned the barrel on himself and pulled the trigger. The shot was like a whip crack in the room and exploded in his head, splattering blood and bone everywhere.

Pitt was numb with horror. The room rocked like a ship at sea; the light from the chandelier seemed to splinter and break. There was a terrible smell in the air, and he felt sick.

He heard a running of feet outside. A servant threw open the door and someone screamed, but he did not know if it was a man or a woman. He stumbled over the other chair, bruising himself violently as he made his way out, and heard his own voice like a stranger's sending someone for help.

12

"WHY?" Nobby Gunne stood in Charlotte's front parlor, her face twisted with anxiety. Of course the newspapers had been full of the tragedy of Linus Chancellor's death. Whatever discretion or pity may have dictated, it was impossible to conceal the fact that he had taken his life suddenly and violently in the presence of a superintendent of the police. No euphemistic explanation would have satisfied even the most naive person. It had to be because the police had brought him some news which was not only unbearable, but so threatening that his response was immediate.

Were it a normal tragedy, some solution to his wife's death which destroyed the faith and trust he had had in her, or which implied some further disaster, he might well have felt there was no alternative but to take his own life; but he would have done it later, after contemplation, and in the privacy of his own company, perhaps late at night. He would not have done it in the police superintendent's presence unless he had not only brought shattering news but also a threat to arrest him and place him under such immediate restraint as to make instant action the only possible way of escape.

There might have been other answers, but no one thought further than the murder of Susannah and that Chancellor himself was guilty.

"Why?" Nobby repeated, staring at Charlotte with urgency and mounting distress. "What did she do that he could not possibly have forgiven her? He did love her, I would have sworn to that. Was it—" she swallowed with great difficulty, as though there were something blocking her throat "—another man?"

Charlotte knew what she feared, and wished intensely that she could have given an answer which would have been painless. But lies were no use.

"No," she said quickly. "No, it was not another man. You are quite right, I believe they did love each other, each in their own way. Please ..." She indicated the closest chair. "It seems ..."

"Yes?"

"I was only going to say that it seems so ... formal, so cold, to stand here face-to-face across the carpet discussing something so terribly important."

"Is it ... important?" Nobby asked.

"People's feelings are always important."

Reluctantly Nobby sat down, a matter of perching on the edge of one of the chairs. Charlotte sat in another opposite her, but farther back in it, less uncomfortably.

"You do know why, don't you?" Nobby pressed. "Superintendent Pitt will have told you. I remember you used to be most involved in his cases ... at the time of ..."

"Yes, he told me."

"Then please, it is of the utmost importance to me. Why did Mr. Chancellor kill Susannah?"

Looking at Nobby's earnest face, Charlotte was deeply afraid that the answer she had to give was not the one Nobby most feared, but one that would in a way be every bit as hard.

"Because he felt she betrayed him," she said gravely. "Not with another man! At least not in the way one would usually take that to mean: with another man's ideas. And he found that intolerable. It would have become public, because she was intending to withdraw her support, and that of the part of the family banking business which was still in her influence. That could not remain private." She looked at Nobby's pale face. "You see, she had been one of his most fervent supporters and admirers all the way along. Everyone would know, and would talk about it."

"But .., if she felt . . differently . . ." Nobby started a train of thought, but it died even as she tried to give it words. It was indefinable, something no one had even bothered to express because it was taken for granted. Women owed their husbands their loyalty, not only of supporting them in all they aspired to do, but more subtly than that, going far deeper into the assumptions of man and woman, of trusting their judgment in all matters that lay in the male domain, matters of thought, philosophy, politics and finance. It was taken for granted married women did not require a vote since they were naturally represented by their husbands. It was not open to question, even in the privacy of the home. To challenge publicly was a betrayal of all unspoken agreements everyone assumed, even in a marriage where there was no love, let alone in one where there was love both long-standing and still intense.

"It was a matter of conscience with her," Charlotte added. "She was not willingly disloyal. I even remember seeing her try to argue with him once. He simply did not hear her, because the idea that she thought differently was inconceivable to him. Heaven knows how many times she tried."

Nobby looked almost as if it had been she who was bereaved. She seemed stunned, her eyes focusing far away, her attention inward. She even swayed a little when she stood up.

"Yes . . . yes, of course. I know she did nothing out of malice, or lightly. Thank you. You have been most generous to me. Now, if you will excuse me . . . I think I have a further call to make. . . ."

Charlotte hesitated on the brink of asking her if she was all right, but she knew the wound was an emotional one and must be endured. No one else could help. She murmured some sort of farewell and watched Nobby go, very upright and fumbling a little, out of the parlor and to the front door.

Nobby rode home barely aware of where she was going. Half of her wanted to go now to see Kreisler, to speak to him in the shadow-thin hope there was some other answer. A far larger part knew it was not only pointless but also absurd. She would only embarrass them both. One did not call upon a man in his rooms to inform him that you were . . . What? Disillusioned? Heartbroken? That you loved him, which subject had never been discussed between you, never given such words, but that you could not condone what he had done.

He had not asked her to.

She went home engulfed in misery, and it was late in the afternoon, after the time when social calls of a formal nature were paid, when the maid told her that Mr. Kreisler was there to see her.

She considered receiving him in the withdrawing room. The thought of the garden was too painful, too full of memories of a different mood, a closeness and an hour of intimacy and hope.

And yet the withdrawing room—any room in the house—was too small. They would have to stand too close to each other; turning away would be obvious.

"I shall be in the garden," she replied, and walked quickly out of the door as if, even before he entered, it could be some kind of escape.

She was standing by the border, the roses now in bloom, when he reached her. He did not bother with preamble. They had never spoken to each other in trivialities.

"I imagine you have heard about Linus Chancellor?" he said quietly. "All London has. I wish I could be sure it would mean some space, some interim of relief for Africa, but the treaty will go ahead, and by now I daresay Rhodes is already in Mashonaland."

She kept her back towards the lawn and did not turn sideways to face him.

"Is that why you did it?"

"Did what?" He sounded genuinely puzzled. There was no evasion in his voice, no pretense.

She had expected to sound querulous, even tearful, but her question, when it came, was level and surprisingly strong.

"Drove Susannah until she broke."

He was startled. There was a moment's silence. She was acutely aware of his physical presence beside her.

"I didn't!" he said with amazement. "I just . . . just argued my case!"

"Yes, you did," she replied. "You pressed her relentlessly, tearing away Chancellor's reasoning, painting word pictures of greed and ruin in Africa, the ultimate immorality of the destruction of a whole race of people. . . ."

"You know that's true!" he challenged her. "That is what will happen. You, of all people, know as well as I do what will happen to the Mashona and the Matabele when Rhodes settles there. Nothing can make them obey Lobengula's laws! It's laughable . . . at least it would be if it were not so bloody tragic."

"Yes I do know that, but that is not the point!"

"Isn't it? I think it's precisely the point!"

She turned to face him. "It is not your beliefs I challenged. I wouldn't even if I didn't share them. You are entitled to believe as you will. . . ."

His eyebrows rose and his eyes widened, but she ignored him. Sarcasm was beneath the passions and the seriousness of her argument.

"It is the methods you used. You attacked Chancellor where he was vulnerable."

"Of course," he retorted with surprise. "What would you have me do, attack him where he is best defended? Give

379

him a sporting chance? This is not a game, with chips to be won or lost at the end. This is life, with misery and destruction the price of losing."

She was quite sure of what she meant. She faced him without a flicker.

"And the destruction of Susannah, pressing her heart and her loyalties until they broke, and broke her with them, was it a fair price?"

"For God's sake, Nobby! I didn't know he was going to kill her!" he protested, his face aghast. "You surely cannot imagine I did. You know me better than that!"

"I don't imagine you knew it," she continued, the ache of misery inside her temporarily subsiding under the force of her certainty. "I think you didn't particularly care."

"Of course I care!" His face was white to the lips. "I wouldn't have had it this way. I didn't have options."

"You did not have to press her till she had no way out but to choose between her loyalty to the husband she loved or to her own integrity."

"That's a luxury. The stakes are too high."

"Central Africa, against the turmoil and death of one woman?"

"Yes . . . if you like. Ten million people against one."

"I don't like. What about five million against twenty?"

"Yes . . . of course." There was no wavering in his eyes.

"One million against a hundred? Half a million against a thousand?"

"Don't be absurd!"

"When does it even out, Peter? When does it stop being worth it? When the numbers are the same? Who decides? Who counts?"

"Stop it, Nobby! You are being ridiculous!" He was angry now. There was no apology in him, no sense that he had to defend himself. "We are talking about one person and a whole race. There is no counting to be done. Look, you want the same things for Africa that I do. Why are we quarreling?" He put his hands up as if to touch her.

She stepped back.

"You don't know, do you?" she said with slow under-standing, and a sadness that tore at her emotions and left her reason like a shining, solitary light. "It is not what you want I cannot tolerate, it is what you are prepared to do to attain it, and what that doing makes of you. You spoke of the end and the means as if they were separate. They are not."

"I love you, Nobby. . . ."

"I love you also, Peter. . . ."

Again he made a move towards her, and again she stepped back, only a few inches, but the gesture was unmistakable.

"But there is a gulf between what you believe is acceptable and what I believe, and it is one I cannot cross."

"But if we love each other," he argued, his face pinched with urgency and incomprehension, "that is enough."

"No it isn't." There was finality in her voice, even a bitter irony. "You counted on Susannah's love of honor, her integrity, to be greater than her love for Chancellor . . . and you were right. Why is it you do not expect mine to be also?"

"I do. It's just that . . ."

She laughed, a funny, jerky sound, harshly aware of the irony. "It's just that, like Linus Chancellor, you never thought I could disagree with you. Well I do. You may never know how much I wish I did not."

He drew in his breath to speak, to argue one more time, and then saw in her eyes the futility of it, and saved himself the indignity and her the additional pain of refusing him again.

He bit his lip. "This is a price I did not expect to have to pay. It hurts."

Suddenly she could not look at him. Humility was the last thing she had expected. She turned to the roses, and then right around towards the apple tree, so he would not see the tears on her face.

"Good-bye, Nobby," he said softly, his voice husky, as if he too were in the grasp of an emotion almost beyond his bearing, and she heard his footsteps as he walked away, no more than a faint whispering over the grass.

Charlotte's mind was preoccupied with Matthew Desmond and the terrible, consuming loneliness he felt because Harriet could not forgive him for having repeated the telephone conversation she had overheard. She would not even have him received in the house. There was no way he could plead his case or offer any comfort or explanation to her. She had shut herself away with her shame, her anger and her sense of being unforgivably betrayed.

Charlotte turned it over and over in her mind; never for a moment did she doubt that what Matthew had done was right. If he made that choice, he lost Harriet, but had he not done so, had he kept silent against his own conscience, to please her, he could not have kept faith with himself. He would have lost what was best in him, that core of truth which in the end is the key to all decisions, all values, the essence of identity. To deny the knowledge of right is something one does not forgive oneself. Ultimately that would have destroyed their love anyway.

But all the time she was about her own chores, simple or complicated, kneading bread or cutting pastry frills for a pie, watching Gracie peel the vegetables, sorting the linen and mending Pitt's frayed shirt cuffs, finding buttons to replace the lost ones, every time her mind could wander, she could think of nothing but Matthew's pain, his loneliness and the sense of utter bereavement he must be feeling. Even watching Archie and Angus careering around the kitchen floor after each other brought only a brief smile to her face.

In the few evenings they had together she watched Pitt's face in repose, and saw the tension which never left him lately, even after the solution to Susannah's death, and she knew the pity for that ached within him, and the remnants of guilt which still shadowed his thoughts of Arthur Desmond. She longed to be able to help, but putting her arms around him, telling him she loved him, were only palliative, on the surface, and she knew better than to pretend they reached the hurt.

It was the same day that Nobby had called, when she realized what had really hurt her, and what Charlotte was convinced she was going to do about it, that she determined to go and see Harriet herself. Whatever happened, she could hardly make matters any worse, and Harriet, just as much as Matthew, deserved to be told the truth. Her happiness, however much was possible—and that could be a great deal in time—depended on the decision she must make now. She could choose courage, understanding and forgiveness; or she could retreat behind blame, consume herself with anger and outrage, and become a bitter and lonely woman, unloving and unlovely.

But she had the right to know what her choice was in its reality, not the reassuring words of lying comfort.

Charlotte dressed accordingly in a modest but becoming gown of forest green muslin trimmed with blue. It was unusually dark for the summer, and therefore the more striking. She took a hansom to Matthew's rooms, whose address she had found in Pitt's desk, and asked the cabby to wait.

He was startled to see her, but made her welcome. He still looked ill and profoundly unhappy.

Briefly she told him her plan and asked him to accompany her, not into Harriet's home, but at least as far as the street outside.

"Oh no!" He rejected her plan immediately, pain and defeat filling his face.

"If I cannot persuade her, she will never know you were there," she pointed out.

"You won't succeed," he said flatly. "She'll never forgive me."

"Were you wrong?" Charlotte challenged.

"I don't know. . . ."

"Yes you do! You did the only possible thing that was honorable, and you should never doubt it. Think of the alternative. What would that be? To have lied by silence to cover Soames's treason, not because you believed it was right but because you were afraid Harriet would reject you. Could you live with that? Could you keep your love for Harriet if you had paid that price for it?"

"No . . ."

"Then come with me and try. Or are you absolutely sure she is too shallow to understand?"

He smiled thinly and picked up his jacket. There was no need to say anything.

She led the way out and this time gave the cabby Harriet Soames's address. When they arrived she gave Matthew's hand a quick squeeze, then alighted, leaving him inside the cab, and climbed the steps. She did not intend to allow herself to be turned away if it was humanly possible, short of creating a scene. She knocked, and when the door was opened, looked the maid very directly in the eye and announced her name, adding that she had something of importance of which she wished to inform Miss Soames, and would be greatly obliged if Miss Soames would consent to receive her.

The maid was gone rather a long time, about five minutes, before returning and saying that she regretted that Miss Soames was unwell and would not be receiving today. If Mrs. Pitt cared to leave a note, she would take it to her mistress.

"No thank you," Charlotte said briskly, but forcing a rather desperate smile. "The matter is personal and very delicate. I shall call again, and again, until Miss Soames is well enough to receive me. I am not prepared to pass it through a third person, nor to commit it to paper. Would you please inform her of that? I am sure Miss Soames is a lady of courage. She could not have the countenance she does and wish to hide from the world forever. To the best of my knowledge, she has not yet anything whatsoever of which to be ashamed—only shame itself, and the desire to run away."

The maid blanched. "I—I can't tell her that, ma'am!"

"Of course you can't." Charlotte smiled even more encouragingly. "But you can tell her that I said so. And if you have any regard for her at all, which I am sure you have, then you will wish her to face the world and defy it. Everyone who is worth anything at all will admire her for it. People take you largely at your own estimation, you know. If you think yourself unworthy, they will assume that you know what you are about, that you are indeed unworthy. Carry your head high and look them in the eye, and unless the evidence is overwhelming, they will assume you are as innocent as you seem. Now please go and tell her what I have said."

"Yes ma'am. Yes, right away, ma'am." And she retreated hastily to do so, her heels clicking on the polished floor.

Charlotte let her breath out in a sigh of momentary relief. That had been a speech worthy of Great-Aunt Vespasia! What she said she believed to be true, but she had spoken with an incredible arrogance and a confidence in herself she was far from feeling.

She stood just inside the entrance in the sunlight, declining to take a seat in the handsome hall, although there were several provided. It seemed an age until the maid returned, although it was probably no more than ten minutes.

"Yes ma'am," the maid said, coming back almost at a trot, her face pink, her manner showing considerable respect. "Miss Soames said that she would make the effort to see you. If you will come this way, please."

Charlotte followed her to a small private sitting room at the back of the house where Harriet was lying on a gold-colored velvet chaise longue, looking dramatically wan, in an afternoon gown of white muslin, her dark hair around her shoulders in undress. It would have been more becoming had there been color in her skin, instead of the rather

385

sallow look it had, indicating a real malady, even if one born of despair.

She looked up at Charlotte and invited her to be seated, dismissing the maid. She made no pretense of offering refreshment.

"Your message was candid to the point of offense, Mrs. Pitt. It is remarkable of you to have felt you had any right to insist upon seeing me. We had the slightest of acquaintance; a few pleasant occasions together do not give you the right to intrude on my grief with threats of harassing me, or calling me a coward. What is it you wish to say that you think warrants such behavior? I cannot imagine what it can be."

Charlotte had thought long and hard about what she would say, but now that the moment was come, it was far more difficult than her worst thoughts had foreseen.

"You have an extremely important choice to make," she began, her voice low and gentle. "One which will affect the rest of your life . . ."

"I have no choice whatsoever," Harriet said bluntly. "Matthew Desmond has removed them all from me. There is only one path open to me now. But that does not concern you, Mrs. Pitt. I suppose I cannot blame your husband for what has happened. After all, he is a policeman and bound to follow his duty. However, I cannot like him for it, nor you, because you are his wife. If we are to speak so plainly, which seems to be your wish, then I will be plain."

"The matter is far too important to be anything less than plain," Charlotte agreed, changing her mind suddenly as to how she would say what she had to. "But if you think I agree with my husband's actions out of loyalty to him, you are mistaken. There are certain things we must believe for ourselves, regardless of what any others may think, be they fathers, husbands, political leaders or men of the church. There is an inner self, a soul, if you like, which is answerable to God, or if you do not believe in Him, then to history, or to life, or merely to yourself, and loyalty to that

386

must supersede all other loyalties. Whatever light of truth you have glimpsed, that must never be betrayed, whatever or whoever else must fall because of it."

"Really, Mrs. Pitt, you—"

"That sounds extreme?" Charlotte cut across her. "Of course there are ways of doing things. If you have to let someone down, deny their beliefs, you owe it to them to do it openly and honorably, to their faces and not their backs, but no one has the right to demand of you a loyalty to them above that to your own conscience. . . ."

"No, of course not, I mean . . . I . . ." Harriet stopped, unsure where her agreement was leading her.

"I used to know a poem at school, written during the Civil War," Charlotte went on. "By Richard Lovelace. It was called 'To Lucasta, Going to the Wars.' There was a line in it—'I could not love thee, dear, so much,/Loved I not honor more.' I laughed at it then. My sister and I would ask, 'Who is Honor Moore?' But I am beginning to understand what it means; at least in my better moments I have a glimpse of it."

Harriet frowned at her, but she was listening.

"The finer a person is," Charlotte continued, "then the more integrity, compassion, and courage they have, and the finer the love they can give you, and I honestly believe also the deeper the love. A shallow vessel holds less, has less from which to give, and you can reach the bottom a lot sooner than you expect or wish to."

Harriet's eyes had not moved from Charlotte's face.

"What are you trying to tell me, Mrs. Pitt?"

"Do you admire a man who does what he believes to be right, indeed knows to be, only when it does not cost him anything?"

"Of course not," Harriet replied quickly. "Anyone can do that. Most people do. Indeed it is in one's own interest to do so. It is only when there is cost involved that there is any nobility, any honor."

"Then your answer in words is quite different from the

answer in your acts," Charlotte pointed out, but gently, and with a look of sadness that held no criticism.

"I don't understand you," Harriet said slowly, but her very hesitation showed that perhaps she was beginning to.

"Don't you? Would you have had Matthew do something he knew to be wrong in order to please you? Would you have admired that, loved him for it? If he could do something wrong, betray his country's trust and his colleagues' honor to please you, what else would he betray, to save himself pain or loneliness, if the occasion arose?"

Harriet's face pinched with distress and a terrible conflict of decision.

"Would he lie to you," Charlotte went on, "to save himself from your anger or rejection? Where does he make a stand? What truths or promises are sacred? Or can anything be broken if the pain of keeping it is sharp enough?"

"Stop it!" Harriet said. "You don't need to go on. I know what you mean." She drew in a long breath, twisting her fingers in her lap. "You are telling me I am wrong to blame Matthew for doing what he believed was right."

"Don't you believe it was right?" Charlotte pressed.

Harriet was silent for a long time.

Charlotte waited.

"Yes . . ." Harriet said at last, and Charlotte could guess how much it hurt her. She was in a sense turning her back on her father, admitting he was wrong. And yet it was also a kind of release from the effort of trying to maintain a fiction that tore her reason from her emotion in a conflict which would erode her as long as it lasted. "Yes, yes you are right." She looked at Charlotte through a frown of anxiety. "Do you think he will . . . forgive me for my hasty judgment . . . and anger?"

Charlotte smiled with absolute certainty.

"Ask him," she replied.

"I . . . I . . ." Harriet stammered.

"He is outside." Charlotte smiled in spite of herself. "Shall I ask him to come in?" Even as she said it she

388

moved towards the door. She barely waited to hear Harriet's husky assent.

Matthew was sitting hunched up in the hansom, peering out, his face haggard. He saw Charlotte's expression and eagerness and hope fought with reason in his eyes.

Charlotte stopped beside him. "Harriet says will you please come in," she said gently. "And Matthew . . . she . . . she has realized her mistake. I think the less that is said of it, the more easily will it have some chance to heal."

"Yes. Yes, of course. I . . ." He gulped. "Thank you!" And then he forgot Charlotte and strode to Harriet's front door and through it without bothering to knock or wait for any answer.

Charlotte walked back down the pavement and quite unashamedly stared in through the front window, where she could just make out the shadows of two figures face-to-face, and the moment after they moved so close they seemed but one together as if never to let go.

When she had returned after seeing Harriet Soames and Matthew, Charlotte was in a buoyant mood, full of elation that the matter had gone so well; but there were other visions to be dealt with, which she was much less certain even as to how to approach, let alone what their resolution might be. It had all begun with the death of Arthur Desmond. Susannah's murder was a tragedy she felt keenly, having known her; but Sir Arthur's death was the one which hurt Pitt, and his grief was interwoven through everything because it was part of his life and could never be set aside or forgotten. And she knew, even through his silences, that there was still guilt in it.

She had the framework of a plan in her mind, but it needed someone to help, someone with access to the Morton Club, who would not in any way be associated with the police but could go there as an innocent and curious member. That person would also, of course, have to be willing to conduct such an enquiry.

The only one she knew who fitted even part of that description was Eustace March, and she was very uncertain if he could ever be persuaded to satisfy the last requirement. Still, there was only one possible way to find out.

Accordingly she sat down and wrote a letter.

"Dear . . ."

She hesitated, confounded as to whether she should address him as "Uncle Eustace" or "Mr. March." The first seemed too familiar, the second too stiff. Their relationship was unique, a mixture of distant kinship, acute guilt and embarrassment, and finally antagonism over the tragedies at Cardington Crescent. Now it was a sort of truce, nervous and extremely wary on his part.

She wanted his help, needed it. His own estimation of himself was such that he would always leap to assist a woman in distress; it fitted his conception of the respective roles of male and female, and his vision of a righteous and powerful Christian, as well as a beneficent gentleman.

"Dear Mr. March," she wrote.

"Forgive my approaching you so forthrightly, and without any preamble, but I need help with a matter of the utmost moral gravity." She smiled as she continued. "I can think of no one else to whom I could turn with the assurance both of their ability to help, and their willingness to do so with the courage it would require, and the supreme tact. Quick judgment may be called for, great perception of men, and their motives as well as their actual honesty, and possibly even a certain physical presence and authority."

If that did not appeal to him, nothing would! She hoped she had not overstated her case. Pitt would instantly be suspicious of a letter like that. But then Pitt had a sense of humor, and Eustace had not.

"If I may call upon you this evening," she continued, "I shall explain precisely what the trouble is, and how I believe we may solve it to the satisfaction of both honor and justice.

"I have a telephone, the number of which is at the top of the page. Perhaps you would be kind enough to let me know whether it would be convenient for me to call ... that is, if you are willing to come to my assistance?

"Yours with affection and hope, Charlotte Pitt."

She sealed it and stamped it and sent Gracie to put it in the post. It would be delivered that afternoon.

She received the answer by telephone. It was an enthusiastic affirmative, delivered with gravitas and considerable self-assurance, not to say satisfaction.

"Well, my dear lady," he said to her as she was shown into his withdrawing room at Cardington Crescent. "What may I do to be of assistance to you?" He stood in front of the fireplace, even though on such a balmy summer evening there was no fire lit. It was simply a matter of habit and the prerogative of the master of the house to warm himself there all winter, and he did it without thought. "Perhaps if you were to tell me the precise problem?"

She sat in the seat he had offered and tried not to think of the past associations of this place and all the memories of tragedy.

"It is to do with a terrible death," she said, meeting his gaze frankly and endeavoring to look as appealing as possible without any shred of flirtation. "But it is a matter which the police, by virtue of their social standing, or lack of it, are unable to solve. At least, Thomas knows a great deal about it, but the final answer is beyond him, because he has not access to the place where it happened, except as a policeman. So everyone will be on their guard, and observing them will be no good at all." She smiled very slightly. "Besides, some people need to see the authority and natural status of a gentleman before they will respond with the truth. Do you understand what I mean, Mr. March?"

"Of course I do, my dear lady," he said immediately. "It is one of the great drawbacks of being of the social ..." Just in time he realized he was about to be offensive. His dilemma was plain in his face. "Occupation," he finished, with a flourish at his fortunate extrication. "People are forewarned," he added for good measure. "Where is it that you believe I have entrance?"

"To the Morton Club," she said sweetly. "I know you are a member, because I recall your saying so. Besides, it is the most distinguished gentleman's club, and I am sure you would find yourself welcome there, even as a visitor, were that necessary. No one would question your presence or think you out of place, and I know of no one else who could do that, and who would also have the . . . forgive me, I do not know how to phrase this without sounding fulsome."

"Please, just be frank with me," he urged. "I shall not criticize either what you say or the way in which you say it. If this is a matter as serious as you intimate, then it would be an unfortunate time to find fault in so small a subject."

"Thank you, you are most understanding. It will take a love of justice and a courage which puts that love before comfort and convenience. Such people are not as common as one would wish."

"Just so," he said sadly. "It is a grim reflection of our times. What, precisely, is it you wish me to do?"

"To find out what happened to Sir Arthur Desmond the afternoon he died . . ."

"But surely that was either an accident, or a suicide." He pulled a very slight face. "To take one's own life was not the act of a Christian, or of a gentleman, unless he had debts he could not pay or had committed a grave dishonor. Or suicide," he finished.

"No, no, Mr. March! That is exactly the point, it was most certainly murder . . . for reasons I shall not go into now." She leaned forward, facing him with an intense look. "It is not unconnected with the death of Mrs. Chancellor." She ignored his look of amazement.

"And with members of the Colonial Office I am not free to name. Indeed, I only know the veriest fraction which I have overheard, but matters where England's interest, and those of the Empire, may have been jeopardized." Now his face was agog and his round eyes wide.

"Sir Arthur was murdered because he drew attention to matters which exposed certain people to suspicion and eventually ignominy," she finished.

"Good gracious! You don't say so!" He drew a deep breath. "Dear lady, are you perfectly sure you have this quite right? It seems . . ."

"Mrs. Chancellor is dead," she pointed out. "And now Mr. Chancellor also. Can you doubt the matter is profoundly serious?"

"No. No, of course not. But the connection . . . ?"

"Is to do with Africa. Will you help me?"

He hesitated only a moment. How could he refuse, and deny himself the opportunity for such gallantry, a noble part in such a matter, perhaps a small place in history?

"Of course," he said enthusiastically. "When shall we begin?"

"Tomorrow, about lunchtime?" she suggested. "Of course, I cannot come into the club. . . ."

"Good gracious no!" he agreed with a look of alarm. Such a thing would be tantamount to sacrilege.

"So I shall be obliged to wait outside in the street," she said with as little irritation as she could manage, although it called for more self-control than she thought she possessed. It was absurd. Why on earth should they all be so appalled at the idea of a woman coming into the club? Anyone would think that they were all sitting around naked! That idea was so amusing she contained her laughter only with difficulty.

He noticed her expression, and his face filled with alarm. "I hope you are not considering . . ."

"No!" she said sharply. "No, of course not. I shall wait in the street, I assure you. If nothing else will convince you, remember that Thomas has been promoted. I have every interest in behaving with the most perfect decorum to see that

393

I do not in any way embarrass him." That was a major stretching of the truth, but she felt Eustace would believe it.

"Of course, of course." He nodded sagely. "I apologize for having doubted you. Now tell me what information it is you wish?"

"To begin with, to know precisely who was there that afternoon, and where they were sitting, or standing, or whatever it is gentlemen do in their clubs."

"That sounds very simple. Surely Thomas would have learned that from the stewards," he said with satisfaction.

"No, apparently they are so terribly busy waiting on people they don't notice," she responded. "Anyway, people tend to avoid speaking to the police if they can, especially if they fear it might compromise their friends unjustly."

"I quite see the point. . . ." He was dubious.

"But you will not be talking to the police, you will simply be telling me," she pointed out.

She wondered whether she ought to mention Farnsworth's opposition to Thomas's working on the case at all, and decided it was too big a risk to take. Eustace was very impressed by authority. Apart from that, he might conceivably be in the same ring of the Inner Circle, and that would never do.

"Yes, that is certainly true," he agreed, apparently calmed by the thought. After all, who was she, that anyone should mind? "Right." He rubbed his hands together. "Then we shall begin tomorrow morning, shall we say outside the Morton Club at eleven o'clock?"

She rose to her feet. "I am enormously grateful to you, Mr. March. Thank you very much. I have taken the liberty of writing a short description of the principal suspects," she added hastily, passing him a piece of paper. "I am sure it will be helpful. Thank you so much."

"Not at all, dear lady, not at all," he assured her. "In fact I am quite looking forward to it!"

* * *

He was not nearly so certain that that was how he felt at ten minutes past eleven the following day when he was actually in the main sitting room of the Morton Club, looking for a place to sit down and wondering how on earth he was to begin such an extraordinary undertaking. To start with, in the cold light of a public place, he realized it was in the most appallingly bad taste. One did not question a fellow member about his acts, whatever they were. It simply was not done. The very essence of the purpose of having a club was in order to remain unquestioned, to have both company and privacy, to be among people of one's own thought, who knew how to behave.

He sat down where Charlotte had told him Sir Arthur had died, feeling a complete fool, and quite sure that his face was scarlet, even though no one took the slightest notice of him. But then people never did in a decent club. He should not have undertaken this, whatever Charlotte Pitt had said! He should have declined politely and kindly, pointing out the impossibility of it, and sent her on her way.

But it was too late now. He had given his word! He was not cut out to be a knight errant. For that matter, Charlotte was not really his choice of a damsel in distress. She was too clever to be satisfactory, much too sharp with her tongue.

"Good morning, sir. May I bring you something?" a discreet voice said at his elbow.

He started in surprise, then saw the steward.

"Oh, yes, er, a small whiskey would be excellent, er . . ."

"Yes sir?"

"Sorry, I was trying to recall your name. Seems I know you."

"Guyler, sir."

"Yes, that's right. Guyler. I, er . . ." He felt hopelessly self-conscious, a complete ass, but it had to be done. He could not possibly go back to Charlotte and tell her he had failed, that he had not even had the courage to try! No shame here could be worse than that. To confess such cow-

ardice to any woman would be appalling; to her it would b
intolerable.

"Yes sir?" Guyler said patiently.

Eustace took a deep breath. "Last time I was here, ver
end of April, I was talking to a most interesting chap, bee
all over the place, especially Africa. Knew the devil of a lc
about settlement there, and so on. But can't remember hi
name. Don't think that he ever said. Sometimes on
doesn't, you know?"

"Quite, sir," Guyler agreed. "And you were wishing t
know who it was?"

"Exactly!" Eustace said with intense relief. "See you un
derstand completely."

"Yes sir. Where were you sitting, sir? That might hel
And perhaps if you could describe the gentleman a li
tle. Was he elderly? Dark or fair? A large gentleman, c
not, sir?"

"Er . . ." Eustace racked his brains to think of how Cha
lotte had described the main suspects. Unfortunately the
were quite unalike. Then a brilliant idea occurred to hin
"Well, the gentleman in question was quite bald, with
powerful nose and very clear, pale blue eyes," he said wi
sudden conviction. "I remember his eyes especially. Mo
arresting . . ."

"Africa, you said?" Guyler asked.

"That's right. You know who I mean?"

"Would you have been in the reading room, sir?"

"Yes, yes, possibly." Deliberately he looked uncertain.

"Then that was likely Mr. Hathaway, sir."

"He was here that day?"

"Yes sir. Not for very long though." Guyler's fa
clouded. "He was taken unwell, as I recall. He went to t
cloakroom, and then I think he went home without comi
back into the reading room, and was never in this room
all. Most unfortunate. So maybe it wasn't him, sir. Did y
speak with him for long, this gentleman who knew so mu
about Africa?"

"Well, I rather thought it was a while." Eustace let his imagination loose. He had never lied about anything before. He had been brought up to tell the exact truth about everything, regardless of how unpleasant, or how completely tedious it might be. To invent, with a free conscience, had the sweet taste of forbidden fruit. It could be rather fun! "Actually I think there was another gentleman there with considerable knowledge. In fact he had only lately returned from his travels. Very sunburned, he was. Fair hair, don't you know, but weathered complexion. Tall, lean fellow, military type of bearing. German name, I think, or possibly Dutch, I suppose. Sounded foreign to me, anyway. But English fellow, naturally!"

"Would that be Mr. Kreisler, sir? It sounds uncommonly like him. He was here. I recall it especially because that was the day poor Sir Arthur Desmond died, right here in his very chair you are sitting in. Very sad, that was."

"Oh very," Eustace agreed with alarm. "And yes, you are right, that sounds like the name I recall. Did he know Sir Arthur?"

"Ah, no sir. Sir Arthur was only in this room, and as far as I know, Mr. Kreisler never came out of the reading room. Actually he was there quite a short while anyway. Came to see someone, and then left just after luncheon."

"Never came in here?" Eustace said. "Are you quite sure?"

"Absolutely, sir," Guyler replied with conviction. "Nor Mr. Hathaway either, so I suppose it must have been neither of those two gentlemen. It doesn't seem as if I can be of much assistance, sir. I'm very sorry."

"Oh, don't give up yet," Eustace said urgently. "There were one or two other fellows around who might know him. One was remarkably well read, as I recall, could quote anything, but as plain as you like, short, heavyset, face melted right into his neck." He was using Charlotte's words, and felt artificial doing it. It was not a description he would have chosen. "Round eyes, fat hands, excellent hair,"

he gabbled, feeling the heat burn up his cheeks. "Goo
voice."

Guyler looked at him curiously. "Sounds not unlike M
Aylmer, sir. And he certainly knows about Africa. He work
in the Colonial Office."

"That'd be him!" Eustace said eagerly. "Yes, sounds ex
actly right!"

"Well he was here that day...." Guyler said though
fully. "But seems to me he only came in and went right o
again...."

"Ah, but at what time?" Eustace demanded.

"About ... about noon, sir. Could that not have bee
him?"

Eustace was warming to this. He was really rather goo
at it. The evidence was piling up. Come to think of it,
seemed he had something of a talent for it. Pity it was a
negative, so far.

"Well, there was another fellow there," he said, looki
at Guyler with wide eyes reflecting absolute cando
"Speaking to you reminds me of him. Tall fellow, da
wavy hair, distinguished looking. Gray a bit." He touch
the sides of his own graying head. "Can't quite think of h
name."

"I'm sorry, sir, that description fits rather a lot of o
gentlemen," Guyler said regretfully.

"His name was ..." Eustace furrowed his brow as if tr
ing to remember. He did not want to lead Guyler too ob
ously. Lying, of course, was sinful, but invention was rath
fun. "Something to do with feet, I think ..."

"Feet, sir?" Guyler looked confused.

"Reminded me of feet," Eustace elaborated. "N
sounded like feet, you understand?"

Guyler looked utterly confounded.

"Understand ..." Eustace repeated the word as if it we
deeply significant in itself. "Understand ... stand .
stand ..."

"Standish!" Guyler said excitedly, and so loudly that s

eral of the somnolent gentlemen in nearby chairs turned and glared at him. He blushed.

"Astounding!" Eustace said with admiration. "By jove, that's exactly it. How clever of you." Flattery was also a sin, but it was a remarkably useful tool, and it was surprising how the ordinary chap responded to it. And women, of course, were slaves to it. Flatter a woman a trifle, and she could swallow it like cake and do anything for you. "That's absolutely right," he went on. "Standish was his name. Indubitably."

"Well, Mr. Standish was in and out that day, sir," Guyler said with a flush of pleasure at being praised so heartily. "Can't say that I have seen him since then. But if you would care for me to find him, sir, I am sure Mr. Hathaway is in the club today. He does occasionally come in for luncheon."

"Ah ..." Eustace was momentarily caught. "Well ..." His brain raced. "Er, before you trouble Mr. Hathaway, was Mr. Standish in this room on that day, would you know?"

Guyler hesitated.

"Rather a difficult question, I know," Eustace apologized. "Long time ago now. Hate to press you. Asking rather a lot."

"Not at all, sir," Guyler denied it instantly. His memory for gentlemen's faces was part of his stock in trade. "Difficult day to forget, sir, with poor Sir Arthur being found dead, like. I was the one who found him, sir. Dreadful experience."

"It must have been," Eustace sympathized. "Most unnerving for you. Amazing you recovered yourself so rapidly."

"Thank you, sir." Guyler squared his shoulders.

"Er ... was he? Standish, I mean?" Eustace pressed.

"No sir, I rather think he played a game of billiards with Mr. Rowntree, and then left and went home to dinner," Guyler said with concentration.

"But he was here in the late afternoon?" Eustace tried to keep the excitement out of his voice, and felt he failed.

"Yes sir, I remember that, because of poor Sir Arthur. Mr. Standish was here at the time. Saw him in the hall as he was leaving, just as the doctor arrived. I recall that plainly now you mention it."

"But he didn't come into this room?" Eustace was disappointed. For a moment it had looked as if he had the answer he was seeking.

"No sir," Guyler replied with increasing certainty. "No sir, he didn't. It must have been Mr. Hathaway you spoke to, sir, and you must have been mistaken about the place, if you will forgive me saying so. There is a corner of the green room not unlike this, the arrangement of the chairs and so on. Could it have been there that you had your discussion?"

"Well . . ." Eustace wanted to leave himself open for a rapid redeployment if necessary. "I daresay you could be right. I'll try to clarify my memory. Thank you so much for your help." He fished out a crown and offered it to a delighted Guyler.

"And the whiskey, sir? I'll fetch it immediately," Guyler said.

"Thank you . . . yes, thank you." Eustace had no choice but to wait until the whiskey came, and then drink it without indecent haste. To do anything else would draw attention to himself as a man without taste or breeding, a man who did not belong. And that he could not bear. All the same, he was bursting to go and tell Charlotte what he had learned, and in such a remarkably short time. He felt very pleased with himself. It had been accomplished completely and without raising the least suspicion.

He finished the whiskey, rose to his feet and sauntered out.

Charlotte was on the steps in the sun and quite a sharp breeze.

"Well?" she demanded as soon as he was out of the door

and before he was halfway down to the street. "Did you learn anything?"

"I learned a great deal." He grasped her arm and linked it to his, then half dragged her to walk side by side with him up the pavement, so to a passerby they would look like a respectable couple taking a stroll. There was no point whatever in making a spectacle of oneself. After all, he was a member of the Morton Club and would wish to return one day.

"What?" Charlotte said urgently, threatening to stop.

"Keep walking, my dear lady," he insisted out of the corner of his mouth. "We do not wish to be observed as out of the ordinary."

To his surprise the argument seemed to sway her. She fell into step beside him.

"Well?" she whispered.

Glancing at the expression on her face, he decided to be brief.

"Mr. Standish was present that afternoon, and at the appropriate time, but the steward is positive he did not go into the room where Sir Arthur was seated."

"Are you sure it was Standish?"

"Beyond doubt. Kreisler was also there, but left too early, as did Aylmer." They were passed by a man in a pinstripe suit and carrying an umbrella, in spite of the pleasantness of the day.

"However," Eustace went on, "Hathaway was present, but also not in the same room. He was apparently taken ill, and went to the cloakroom, from where he sent for a cab and was helped into it. He never went anywhere near the room where Sir Arthur was either. I am afraid it appears that none of your suspects can be guilty. I'm sorry." Actually he was sorry, not for her, but because although it was far more suitable answer, it was also an anticlimax.

"Well someone must be guilty," she protested, raising her voice against the noise of the traffic.

401

"Then it cannot be any of them. Who else might it be?" he asked.

"I don't know. Anyone." She stopped, and since she was still clinging to his arm, he was pulled to a sudden halt also. A middle-aged lady on the arm of an elderly man looked at them with suspicion and disapproval. From her expression it was obvious she had supposed some domestic quarrel which no dutiful wife would have allowed to happen in public.

"Stop it!" Eustace hissed. "This is most unseemly. You are causing people to look at us."

With a great effort Charlotte bit back the response that came to her lips.

"I'm sorry." She proceeded to walk again. "We shall just have to go back and try harder."

"Try harder to do what?" he said indignantly. "None of the people you mentioned could possibly have passed by Sir Arthur and put laudanum in his brandy. Not one of them was even in the same room."

"Well where did the brandy come from?" She did not even think of giving up. "Perhaps they passed it on the way."

"And poisoned it?" His eyes were round and full of disbelief. "How? Passing by and slipping something into it while it was on the steward's tray? That would be ridiculous. No steward would permit it, and he would certainly remember it afterwards and testify to it. Besides, how would anyone know it was meant for Arthur Desmond?" He straightened his back and lifted his chin a little. "You are not very logical, my dear. It is a feminine weakness, I know. But your ideas are really not practical at all."

Charlotte was very pink in the face. It did cross his mind to wonder for a moment if it was suppressed temper. Not very attractive in a woman, but not as uncommon a trait as he would have wished.

"No," she agreed demurely, looking down at the pavement. "I cannot manage without your assistance. But

402

there is a flaw in the argument, I know you will find it, or a lie in anyone's testimony, perhaps? You will go back, won't you? We cannot allow injustice to triumph."

"I really cannot think what else I could learn," he protested.

"Exactly what happened, even more exactly than now. I shall be so very grateful." There was a slight quaver in her voice, as of some intense emotion.

He was not certain what it was, but she really was a very handsome woman. And it would be immensely satisfying to place her in his debt. Then he would be able to face her without the almost intolerable embarrassment he felt now. It would wash out the hideous memory of the scene under the bed!

"Very well," he conceded graciously. "If you are convinced it would be of service."

"Oh I am, I am!" she assured him, stopping and turning around, ready to return the way they had come. "I am so obliged to you."

"At your service, ma'am," he said with considerable complacency.

Once inside the Morton Club again he had profound misgivings. There was nothing to find out. He began to feel exceedingly foolish as once more he approached Guyler.

"Yes sir?" Guyler said helpfully.

"Forgive me," Eustace began, feeling the color flush up his cheeks. Really, this was too bad of Charlotte. And he was a fool to have agreed to it. "I fear I am being extremely tedious. . . ."

"Not at all, sir. What can I do for you?"

"Is it not possible that Mr. Standish could have come through here that afternoon, after all?"

"I can make enquiries for you, sir, if you wish, but I think it most unlikely. Gentlemen don't usually leave a game of billiards, sir. It is considered bad form to leave one's opponent standing waiting for one."

"Yes, yes of course. I know that!" Eustace said hastily.

403

"Please don't trouble yourself. I should not like Mr. Standish to imagine I thought him discourteous."

"No sir."

"And, er . . ." He could have sworn under his breath and cursed Charlotte, only the steward would have heard him. He could not get out of it now. This was appalling. "Mr., er . . . Hathaway. You said he was taken ill. That is most unfortunate. When was that? What hour? I don't think I recall that happening."

"Oh it did, sir, I remember it quite plainly. Are you sure you have the right day yourself, sir, if you'll pardon me, sir? Perhaps you were here the day before, or the day after? That would account for a lot."

"No, no, I have the day right. I recall it because of Sir Arthur's death, just as you do," Eustace said hastily. "What was it you said happened to Mr. Hathaway?"

"He was took a bit queer, sir, and went to the cloakroom. Then he must have decided to go home. He'd been there a while, no doubt hoping he'd get to feel better, but seems he didn't, so he rang for assistance, poor gentleman, and one of the stewards went to him. And when he asked for a cab, the cloakroom attendant called him one, and helped him out into the hall and down the steps into it. He never came back into any of the club rooms at all, sir, that is for certain."

"I see. Yes, I see. That wasn't you, by any chance?"

"No sir. Tell you the truth, don't know who it was. Saw him go, but only out of the corner of my eye, so to speak and I didn't recognize him. Might have been Jones; it looked a lot like him, sort of heavyset and with very little hair. Yes, I think it might have been Jones."

"Thank you, yes I expect it was. Thank you very much." Eustace wanted to end the pointless conversation. Charlotte would have to unravel the meaning of this, if there was any. There was no more for him to learn. He must escape. This was getting worse by the moment.

"Mr. Hathaway is here this afternoon, sir," the steward persisted. "If you like I can take you across to him, sir."

"No . . . no thank you," Eustace said vehemently. "I . . . I think I shall go to the cloakroom myself, if you will excuse me. Yes, yes indeed. Thank you."

"Not at all, sir." Guyler shrugged and went about his errands.

Eustace made his escape and fled to the cloakroom. It was really a very agreeable place, suitably masculine, set out with all the comforts: washbasins with plenty of hot water, clean towels, mirrors, spare razors and strops, shaving soap in two or three different brands, lotions, Macassar oil for the hair, fresh cloths for buffing one's boots, and polish, brushes for its application and removal, and overall a pleasant aroma like sandalwood.

He had no requirement for the water closet, and instead sat down on one of the wooden bench seats that were rather like well-shaped pews. He had had occasion to come here only twice before, but it still seemed pleasantly familiar. Hathaway must have sat here, feeling ill and wondering if he would be able to get home without assistance. Eustace glanced around. There was an ornate bell pull near the door. Nothing was written on it or under it, but its purpose was obvious. Without premeditation he stood up, crossed the couple of steps to it and pulled.

Almost immediately it was answered by an elderly man in a uniform which was less than livery but more than merely a steward.

"Yes sir?" he said quietly. "Is there something I can do for you?" Eustace was taken aback. There really was nothing at all. He thought of Hathaway.

"Are you a steward? You wear a different . . . uniform."

"Yes sir," the man agreed. "I'm the cloakroom attendant. If you wish for a steward I can send for one, but perhaps I can help you, sir. It would be more regular. Stewards attend to gentlemen in the drawing rooms and reading rooms, and so on."

Eustace was confused.

"Doesn't this bell ring on the steward's board in the pantry?"

"No sir, only in my room, which is quite separate, sir. Can't I be of assistance? Are you not feeling well, sir?"

"What? Oh, yes, yes I am perfectly well, thank you. Always well." Eustace's brain raced. Was it possible he was on the brink of discovery? "It is just that a friend of mine, more of an acquaintance, told me that he had been taken unwell here in the cloakroom and had summoned a steward from the drawing room who had called him a hansom." He waited, almost holding his breath.

"No sir," the attendant said patiently. "That is not possible, sir. The bell here doesn't ring in the steward's pantry. It only leads to my board, sir, nowhere else."

"Then he was lying!" Eustace said in triumph.

The attendant looked at him with as much amazement as his duty and position allowed, not at the conclusion—which was unavoidable—but at Eustace's delight in it.

"That seems a harsh judgment, sir. But he was certainly mistaken."

"It was Hathaway," Eustace said, plunging in where only moments before he would not have dared to be so blunt. "The day Sir Arthur Desmond died. Didn't you call him a hansom?"

"Yes sir. One of the temporary stewards told me he was unwell, but I don't know how he knew that."

"You mean one of the attendants? Someone junior to yourself," Eustace said.

"No sir, I mean a temporary steward, from one of the main rooms. Though, come to think of it, I don't know how he knew, if Mr. Hathaway was in here!" He shook his head in denial of the impossible.

"Thank you, thank you! I am most obliged to you!" Eustace fished in his pocket and brought out a shilling. was excessive; still, it would look so paltry to put it bac and hand over a threepenny bit instead, and he was feeling in a highly generous mood. He gave it unstintingly.

"Thank you, sir." The attendant masked his surprise and took it before Eustace could change his mind. "If I can be of any further assistance, please let me know."

"Yes, yes of course." Eustace only glanced at him, then strode out into the foyer and down the front steps to the street.

Charlotte was a few paces away; apparently she had been walking back and forth, maybe in her impatience, perhaps to make her waiting less obvious. She saw the expression of jubilation on his face and ran towards him.

"Yes? What have you found?" she demanded.

"Something quite extraordinary," he said, his excitement fighting his normal manner and the condescension he considered appropriate when speaking to women. "The cloakroom bell does not connect with the steward's pantry or any part of the rest of the club!"

She was confused. "Should it?"

"Don't you see?" He caught her by the arm and began walking. "Hathaway said he called the steward from the cloakroom to fetch him a cab when he was taken ill. The drawing room steward told me that. He saw the steward go. But he couldn't have, because the bell doesn't ring there." He was still gripping her arm firmly as he paced the pavement. "The cloakroom attendant said a steward from the drawing room told him that Hathaway was ill and wanted a cab. Hathaway lied!" Quite unconsciously he shook her gently. "Don't you see? He said he did not come back into the main rooms. At least the steward said he didn't . . . but he must have, if he called one of the ordinary stewards to get his cab!" He stopped abruptly, the satisfaction fading a little in his eyes. "Although I'm not quite sure what that proves. . . ."

"What if . . ." Charlotte said, then stopped.

A lady with a parasol passed by, pretending not to look at them, a smile on her face.

"Yes?" Eustace urged.

"I don't know . . . let me think. And please don't grip me quite so hard. You're hurting my arm."

"Oh! Oh . . . I'm sorry." He blushed and let go of her.

"An extra steward . . ." she began thoughtfully.

"That's right. It seems they hire one or two now and then, I suppose if someone is ill or otherwise absent."

"And there was one that day? Are you sure?"

"Yes. The steward I spoke to said he saw one."

"What like?" She ignored two women carrying pretty boxes of millinery and chatting to each other.

"What like?" Eustace repeated.

"Yes! What did he look like?" Her voice was rising with urgency.

"Er . . . elderly, squarish, very little hair . . . why?"

"Hathaway!" she shouted.

"What?" He ignored the man passing by them who looked at Charlotte in alarm and disapproval, and increased his pace.

"Hathaway!" she said, grasping him in turn. "What if the extra steward was Hathaway? What a perfect way to murder someone. As a steward he would be practically invisible! As himself, he goes to the cloakroom saying he is not feeling well. Once in there he changes into a steward's jacket, then returns to the pantry, collects a tray and brandy into which he puts the laudanum, serves it to Sir Arthur, saying it is a gift from someone. Then he says that Mr. Hathaway has been taken unwell in the cloakroom and has rung for assistance, so he establishes that Hathaway was in the cloakroom all the time." Her voice was rising with excitement. "He goes out, changes back into himself, then further to establish that, he leaves directly from the cloakroom. He calls the attendant and has him fetch a hansom and assist him out into it. He has established his own whereabouts, with witnesses, and become invisible long enough to give Sir Arthur a fatal dose of laudanum, virtu-

408

ally unseen. Uncle Eustace, you are brilliant! You have solved it!"

"Thank you." Eustace blushed scarlet with pleasure and satisfaction. "Thank you, my dear." For once he was even oblivious of the giggles and words of a group of ladies in an open landau. Then the brilliance of his smile faded a little. "But why? Why should Mr. Hathaway, an eminent official of the Colonial Office, wish to poison Sir Arthur Desmond, an erstwhile eminent official of the Foreign Office?"

"Oh—" She caught her breath. "That is regrettably easy. By a process of deduction, he must be the executioner of the Inner Circle. . . ."

Eustace's expression froze. "The what? What on earth are you talking about, my dear lady?"

Her face changed. The victory fled out of it, leaving only anger and a terrible sense of loss. It alarmed him to see the fierceness of the emotion in her.

"The executioner of the Inner Circle," she repeated. "At least one of them. He was detailed to kill Sir Arthur, because—"

"What absolute nonsense!" He was appalled "The Inner Circle, whose name you should not even know, is a group of gentlemen dedicated to the good of the community, the protection of the values of honor and wise and beneficent rule, and the well-being of everyone."

"Balderdash!" she retorted vehemently. "The junior new recruits are told that, and no doubt sincerely believe it. You do, Micah Drummond did, until he learned otherwise. But the inner core of it is to gain power and to use it to preserve their own interests."

"My dear Charlotte . . ." He attempted to interrupt, but she overrode him.

"Sir Arthur was speaking out against them before he died."

"But what did he know?" Eustace protested. "Only what he may have imagined."

"He was a member!"

"Was he? Er . . ." Eustace was confounded, a worm of doubt creeping into his mind.

"Yes. He found out about their intentions to use the Cecil Rhodes settlement of Africa to gain immense wealth for their own members, and he tried to make it public, but no one would listen to the little he could prove. And before he could say any more, they killed him. That's what they do to members who betray their covenants. Don't you know that?"

With a sudden sickening return of memory, Eustace thought of the covenants he had been obliged to make, the oaths of loyalty he had taken. At the time he had thought them rather fun, a great adventure, something like the vigil of Sir Galahad before receiving his spurs, the weaving of good and evil that belongs to high romance, the ordeals of those who dare the great adventures. But what if they had meant them truly? What if they really did mean that the Circle was to come before mother or father, wife or brother or child? What if he had pledged away the right to choose on pain of his life?

She must have seen the fear in his eyes. Suddenly there was gentleness, almost pity, mixed with her anger. Neither of them was even aware of the world around them, the pedestrians who passed within a yard of them on the pavement, or the carriages in the street.

"They count on your secrecy to protect them," she said more softly. "They count on your not breaking your promises, even when you gave them without being aware what they would lead to, or that you might compromise yourself, and betray what you most believe in, your own honor, in their keeping." Her expression hardened into contempt and the anger returned. "And of course they also count on fear. . . ."

"Well, I'm not afraid!" he said furiously, turning back towards the steps up into the club. He was too angry to be frightened. They had taken him for a fool, and even worse than that, they had betrayed his belief in them. They had pretended to espouse all the things in which he most dearly believed, honor and openness, candor, high-minded courage, valor to defend the weak, the true spirit of leadership which was the Englishman's heritage. They had shown him an Arthurian vision, made him believe something of himself, and then they had perverted it into a thing that was soiled, dangerous and ugly. It was an insupportable outrage, and he would not be party to it!

He strode up the steps, hardly aware of Charlotte behind him, swung the doors open and made his way across the foyer without a word to the doorman. He pushed his way through the drawing room doors and accosted the first steward he saw.

"Where is Mr. Hathaway? I know he is here today, so don't prevaricate with me. Where is he?"

"S-sir, I—I think . . ."

"Don't trifle with me, my good man," Eustace said between his teeth. "Tell me where he is!"

The steward looked at Eustace's gimlet eyes and rapidly purpling cheeks and decided discretion was definitely the better part of valor.

"In the blue room, sir."

"Thank you," Eustace acknowledged him, turning on his heel to march back into the foyer. Only then did he remember he was not sure which way the blue room was. "The blue room?" he demanded of a steward who appeared at the pantry door with a tray held up above his head in one hand.

"To your right, sir," the steward answered with surprise.

"Good." Eustace reached the door in half a dozen steps and threw it open. The blue room might once have lived up to its name, but now it was faded to a genteel gray, the heavy curtains blue only in the folds away from the sunlight which streamed in from four long, high windows looking onto the street. Through the decades the brilliance had bleached out of the carpet also, leaving it pink and gray and a green so soft as to be almost no color at all. Portraits of distinguished members from the past decorated the walls in discreet tones of sepia and umber, many of them from the seventeenth and eighteenth centuries. In some the whiteness of a powdered wig was the only distinguishable feature.

Eustace had not been in here before. It was a room reserved for senior members, one of which he only aspired to be.

Hathaway was sitting in a large leather armchair reading the *Times*.

Eustace was too enraged even to consider the impropriety of what he was doing. Greater decencies had been blasphemed against. No one was going to be permitted to hide behind the conventions of a gentleman's club. He stopped in front of Hathaway's chair, put his hands on the *Times* and tore it away, dropping it to one side in a heap of crackling paper.

Every head in the room looked up at the noise. A whiskered general snorted with offense. A banker cleared his throat ostentatiously. A member of the House of Lords (who actually attended now and then) put down his glass in amazement. A bishop dropped his cigar.

Hathaway looked up at Eustace with considerable surprise.

"I am making a citizen's arrest," Eustace announced grimly.

"I say, old chap . . ." the banker began.

"Somebody robbed you, old boy?" the bishop asked mildly. "Pickpocket, what? Cutpurse?"

"Bit high-handed, taking a fellow's newspaper," the earl said, regarding Eustace with disfavor.

Hathaway was perfectly composed. He sat quite still in the chair, ignoring the wreck of his paper.

"What is it that has disturbed you so much, my dear fellow?" he said very slowly. At another time Eustace might not have noticed the hard, unflinching quality of his eyes, but all his senses were sharpened by his outrage

Now he felt almost as if Hathaway might offer him physical violence, and he was poised, ready to react, even to
welcome it.

"Yes I have been robbed," he said fiercely. "Of trust, of
. . . of . . ." He did not know how to express the feeling he
had of having been used, insulted, then suddenly it came to
him in a rush of words fraught with pain. "I have been
robbed of my belief in my fellows, of those I admired and
honored, even aspired to be like! That's what you've taken.
You've destroyed it, betrayed it."

"My dear fellow!" the banker protested, rising to his feet.
"You are overemotional. Sit down and calm yourself. You
are making a mistake. . . ."

"You are making a damned noise!" the general said angrily, his whiskers bristling. "I know that, sir!" He shook
his newspaper with a snap and buried his head in it again.

"Come on, old chap." The banker took another step towards Eustace and put his hands forward as if to restrain
him. "A good douse of cold water and you'll feel better.
I—"

"I am as sober as a judge," Eustace said between his
teeth. "And if you touch me, sir, if you put one hand on
me, I swear by God I shall lay you flat. This man"—he was
still looking at Hathaway—"has committed murder. I am
not speaking figuratively but quite literally. He cold-
bloodedly and intentionally took the life of another man by
poison."

This time no one interrupted him. Hathaway sat smiling
very slightly, composed, tolerant.

"Poisoned his brandy right here in the club. . . ."

"Really . . . Come now," the bishop spluttered.
"That's . . ."

Eustace glared at him and he faded into silence.

"You are the executioner!" Eustace swung back to
Hathaway. "And I know now how you did it! You went to
the cloakroom and changed into a steward's jacket, then
came back into the main room, gave poor Sir Arthur his

413

poisoned drink, which you had prepared, then went back to the cloakroom. . . ." He stopped. He could see by the sudden whiteness of Hathaway's face that he was no longer sure of himself. He was shaken; for the first time he was afraid. The secret he had trusted to protect him was not secret anymore. Eustace saw the fear in his eyes, and now he saw also the violence. The mask was gone.

"I am arresting you for the poisoning to death of Arthur Desmond. . . ."

"Absolute nonsense," the earl said levelly. "You are drunk, sir. Arthur Desmond took his own life, poor devil. We shall forget this appalling behavior of yours, March, if you withdraw this on the spot and resign your membership."

Eustace turned to face him, recognizing another member of the Circle, by act if not by feature. "If that is what you wish, sir," he said without giving an inch, "then it must be that you are equally guilty with Hathaway. You have perverted your power, sir, and betrayed all that is best in England, the people who trusted you and whose labor and belief gave you the very position you now abuse."

Hathaway had risen to his feet and made to move past Eustace. The earl took Eustace's arm in a tight grip and pulled him sideways.

Eustace was outraged. He was of a robust physique, and a disciple of good health. He landed a powerful and well-placed punch on the jaw of the earl and sent him crashing backwards into one of the armchairs.

Hathaway lunged past to escape, swinging a hard kick at Eustace which landed on his shin with acute pain. Eustace swung around and dived after him, catching him in a tackle which would have been cheered to the echo in his rugby playing days. They both went down onto the floor in a crash, kicking over a small table, splintering one of its legs and sending a tray of cups and saucers flying to break in shards all over the carpet.

The door was thrust open and a horrified steward stared

with utter dismay at the earl spread-eagled across the chair, and Eustace and Hathaway locked in desperate combat on the floor, thrashing around grunting and gasping, arms flailing and legs kicking. He had never witnessed a scene like it in all his life and he had no idea what to do. He stood in an agony of indecision.

The general was shouting out commands no one was obeying. The bishop was making noises of disapproval and muttering something about peace and wisdom, and was totally ignored.

Out in the hallway, a judge of the Queen's Bench demanded to know what was going on, but no one would tell him.

Someone sent for the manager. Someone else sent for a doctor, assuming that one of the members had taken a fit and was being restrained, with difficulty. An advocate of temperance was delivering a monologue, and one of the stewards was praying.

"Police!" Eustace shouted as loudly as his lungs would bear. "Send for the police, you fool! Bow Street . . . Inspector Pitt." And with that he hit Hathaway as hard as he could on the point of the jaw, and his left foot caught the table on the other side and sent it hurtling sideways into the trolley. There was a final crash as a decanter of brandy and half a dozen glasses smashed on the wooden floor at the edge of the carpet.

Hathaway subsided into unconsciousness, his body limp, his eyes closed.

Eustace did not entirely trust him. "Get the police," he ordered again, struggling upright to sit astride Hathaway's chest.

The steward in the doorway hastened to obey. That at least was an order he both understood and agreed with. Whatever was going on, the police were obviously needed, even if it was only to remove Eustace himself.

Then he was face-to-face with the impossible, the worst

offense of all. There was a woman standing in the doorway staring into the blue room and watching the appalling scene, a young woman with chestnut-colored hair and a very handsome figure, and—although her eyes were wide with amazement—she was also on the verge of laughter.

"Madam!" the bishop said in horror. "This is a gentleman's club! You are not permitted in here. Please, madam, observe the decencies and take your leave."

Charlotte looked at the debris of broken china and crystal, spilled coffee and brandy, the splintered furniture, the overturned chair, the earl with his collar askew and a bruise fast purpling on his cheek, and Eustace sitting astride the still-senseless form of Hathaway on the floor.

"I always wondered what you did in here," she said mildly, but there was a lift in her voice, and a slight huskiness that threatened to erupt in giggles. She arched her eyebrows very high. "Extraordinary," she murmured.

The bishop said something completely unholy.

Eustace was beyond embarrassment. He was flushed with victory both moral and physical. "Has anyone sent for the police?" he asked, looking at each in turn.

"Yes sir," one of the stewards said immediately. "We have a telephone. Someone is on their way from Bow Street right now."

Charlotte was bundled out and persuaded to wait in the foyer, and that only on sufferance. The blue room was out of bounds. For goodness' sake, it was out of bounds even to junior members!

Eustace refused to leave Hathaway, especially when he regained consciousness (albeit with a profound headache), although he remained silent and made no protest or defense.

When Pitt arrived he found Charlotte first of all, who told him that Eustace had solved the case, adding modestly that she had given him some assistance and direction, and that he had the murderer under citizen's arrest.

"Indeed," Pitt said dubiously, but when she explained to

416

him precisely how it had come about, he was generous in his praise, both of her and of Eustace.

Some fifteen minutes later Hathaway, under arrest and manacled, was put in a hansom cab to the Bow Street station, and Eustace emerged to receive the praise of his fellows. Charlotte was sent home, under protest, in a hansom.

On the journey towards Bow Street, Pitt sat in the cab beside Hathaway. Hathaway was manacled and unarmed, but still in his quiet face with its long nose and small, round eyes there was a sense of strength. He was afraid—he would be a fool not to be—but there was nothing of weakness in his expression, no suggestion that he would break the covenants by which he too was bound to the Inner Circle.

This was the man who had murdered Arthur Desmond. It was Hathaway who had slipped the laudanum into the brandy and passed it to him, and then discreetly left, knowing what would happen. But it was the whole senior hierarchy who was guilty of his death. Hathaway had carried out the sentence. But who had pronounced judgment, who had given the orders that Hathaway had obeyed?

That was the man Pitt wanted. That was the only justice which would be enough to take to Matthew, and more importantly still, to ease the ache of guilt within himself and allow him to rest with the memory of Sir Arthur.

He believed he knew who it was, but even certainty was futile without proof.

He glanced sideways at the silent, almost motionless figure of Hathaway. The small blue eyes looked back at him with biting intelligence and hard, ironic humor. Pitt knew in that moment that whatever fear Hathaway might have, whatever beliefs of death or what lay beyond it, loyalty to the Inner Circle would supersede them all, and would remain unbroken.

He shivered, cold with a new perception of the power of the oaths that bound the society, far more than a club or an association. It was mystic, almost religious, the vengeance

417

for betrayal more than merely human. Hathaway would hang alone rather than speak even a word that would lead to another.

Or did he imagine that even now some other member, someone as high as a judge, would somehow contrive his escape from the rope?

Was even that possible?

He must not allow it, for Arthur Desmond's sake, if nothing else. Pitt looked at him again, meeting his eyes and holding them in a long, steady stare. Neither of them spoke. It was not words, arguments, he was seeking, it was emotion and beliefs.

Hathaway did not flinch or look away, and after several seconds the corners of his mouth turned upwards in a very tiny smile.

In that moment Pitt knew what he must do.

When they reached Bow Street they alighted. Pitt paid the cabby and with Hathaway still manacled, led him inside past the openmouthed desk sergeant who leapt to attention.

"Is Mr. Farnsworth there yet?" Pitt demanded.

"Yes sir! I sent the message to 'im like you told me, sir—that you was off to make an arrest for the murder of Sir Arthur Desmond. . . ."

"Yes?"

"And he came straightaway, sir. He's been here about ten minutes, maybe. And Mr. Tellman is here, sir, as you said, sir."

"Is Mr. Farnsworth in my office?"

"Yes sir. And Mr. Tellman's in his room too."

"Thank you." Pitt felt a sudden surge of excitement, and at the same time a hardening of fear inside him, as if a hand had closed into a fist in his chest. He turned and strode up the stairs, almost pushing Hathaway ahead of him. At the top he flung his office door open and Farnsworth swung around from where he had been standing at the window. He saw Hathaway and although his expression did not flicker, the blood drained from his skin, leaving it blotched, white around the eyes and mouth.

He parted his lips as if about to speak, then changed his mind.

"Good morning, sir," Pitt said calmly, as if he had noticed nothing. "We've got the man who murdered Sir Arthur Desmond." He smiled and nodded at Hathaway.

Farnsworth's eyebrows rose. "He did?" He allowed his surprise to border on incredulity. "Are you sure?"

"Absolutely," Pitt said calmly. "We know precisely how he did it, and have all the witnesses. It is just a matter of piecing it together. Very clever and very efficient."

"Are you," Farnsworth said coldly.

"No sir, I meant Hathaway's means and method." Pitt allowed himself to smile. "Only a chance observation of stewards' bells on a board caught him. But it's enough." He looked at Farnsworth guilelessly.

Farnsworth came forward and took Pitt by the arm, guiding him towards the door.

"Speak to you privately, Pitt," he said tersely. "Call a constable to wait in here and keep guard."

"Of course," Pitt agreed. "I'll get Tellman." It was what he had intended anyway, and would have contrived if Farnsworth had not.

"Yes sir?" he asked as soon as they were in an adjoining office with the door closed, and Tellman with Hathaway.

"Look, Pitt, are you sure you have the right man?" Farnsworth said seriously. "I mean, Hathaway's a respected official in the Colonial Office, a thoroughly decent man, father in the church . . . son too. Why on earth would he wish Desmond any harm? He didn't even know the man, except by sight as a fellow club member. Maybe you have the right means and method, but the wrong man?"

"No sir. It was not a personal motive. Knowing him by sight was all that was needed."

"What on earth . . ." He trailed off, staring at Pitt's face.

"Quite simple." Pitt met his eyes, keeping all subtlety out of his own. Not a thread of suspicion must enter Farnsworth's mind. "Sir Arthur was killed because he broke the oath of the Inner Circle and betrayed them."

Farnsworth's eyes widened almost imperceptibly.

"And Hathaway was the executioner deputed to deal with the matter," Pitt went on. "Which he did, with coldness and precision."

"Murder!" Farnsworth's voice rose with disbelief, a high, hard note in it. "The Inner Circle doesn't murder people! If Hathaway did indeed kill him, then there must have been some other reason."

"No sir, as you just pointed out, he did not even know him in any personal sense. It was an execution, and we can prove it." He hesitated only an instant. Please God he could trust Tellman. But if there were any man in the police force he would stake his life on as not being a member of the Inner Circle, it was Tellman. He took precisely that chance now, facing Farnsworth squarely. "But it will all come out in the trial."

"If the society were what you say, Pitt, then Hathaway would die without telling anyone what you charge," Farnsworth said with certainty and faint derision.

"Oh, I don't expect Hathaway to admit it," Pitt replied with the shadow of a smile. "I am sure you are right. He will go to the gallows without betraying his fellow members. We may never know who they are," he said slowly, meeting Farnsworth's eyes. "But every man and woman in London who can read a newspaper will know what they are! That we can prove, and we will do, in open court."

"I see." Farnsworth took a very deep breath and let it out. He looked at Pitt with something like surprise, as if he had done more than he had foreseen. "I would like to speak to him myself for a few moments, alone, if you don't mind." It was delivered with courtesy, but it was an order. "I find all this ... distressing ... hard to believe."

"Yes sir, of course. I've got to go back to the Morton Club anyway, and make sure of the steward's evidence, and see what happened to the other witnesses."

"Yes, by all means do that." And without waiting any further, Farnsworth went out of Tellman's room and back along the passage to Pitt's office. A moment later Tellman came out and looked questioningly at Pitt.

Pitt held his finger to his lips, walked noisily down the stairs half a dozen steps, then crept back up to stand motionless beside Tellman.

They waited for what seemed an endless five minutes, ears straining, hearts thumping so violently Pitt could feel his body shake.

Then the faint murmuring of voices ceased from behind the office door and there was a very soft thud.

Pitt flung the door open, Tellman barely a step behind him.

Farnsworth was on the floor almost astride the prone figure of Hathaway. The paper knife from Pitt's desk was protruding from Hathaway's chest and his manacled hands were just below it, but it was Farnsworth's fingers which were now clenched around it, and his body's weight behind the blow.

Tellman gasped.

Farnsworth looked up, his face slack with disbelief for an instant, then horror. He started to speak.

"He . . . he took the paper knife. . . ." he began. "I tried to stop him. . . ."

Pitt stepped a little aside.

"You murdered him!" Tellman said with amazement and fury. "I can see it!"

Farnsworth turned from Pitt to Tellman, and recognized the incorruptible outrage in his eyes. He looked back at Pitt.

"Giles Farnsworth," Pitt said with satisfaction he had seldom felt in the solution of any case, "I arrest you for the murder of Ian Hathaway. I must warn you that anything

421

you say will be taken down, and may be given in evidence at your trial ... which I will make very sure you live long enough to face, for Arthur Desmond's sake."

Don't miss this novel
featuring Charlotte and Thomas Pitt

SEVEN DIALS

by Anne Perry

"An Anne Perry novel is a delight to read."
—*Chicago Tribune*

"A master of crime fiction."
—*The Baltimore Sun*

Thomas Pitt, mainstay of Her Majesty's Special Branch, is summoned to Connaught Square mansion where the body of a junior diplomat lies huddled in a wheelbarrow. Nearby stands the tenant of the house, the beautiful and notorious Egyptian woman Ayesha Zakhari, who falls under the shadow of suspicion. Pitt's journey to uncover the truth takes him from Egyptian cotton fields to the insidious London slum called Seven Dials, to a packed London courtroom where shocking secrets will at last be revealed. . . .

Published by Ballantine Books.
Available wherever books are sold.

Don't miss this New York Times *bestselling novel featuring Charlotte and Thomas Pitt*

SOUTHAMPTON ROW
by Anne Perry

"COMPELLING AND PROVOCATIVE ...
VINTAGE PERRY: A GRAND, SWEEPING
MYSTERY OF MANNERS."
—*Pittsburgh Tribune-Review*

In Victorian England, a divisive election is fas
approaching. Passions are so enflamed that Thoma
Pitt, shrewd mainstay of the London police, ha
been ordered to prevent a national disaster. Th
Liberal candidate is Aubrey Serracold, whose wife'
dalliance with spiritualism threatens his chances
Indeed, she is one of the participants in a late-nigh
séance that leads to a brutal murder on Southampto
Row. Meanwhile, Pitt's wife, Charlotte, and thei
children are enjoying a country vacation—unawar
that they, too, are deeply endangered by the sam
fanatical forces hovering over the steadfast Pitt. . .

Published by Ballantine Books.
Available wherever books are sold.

THE HYDE PARK HEADSMAN

by Anne Perry

"A corking good story . . .
Anne Perry continues at the top of her form
as a pre-eminent writer of Victorian mysteries."
—*Chicago Sun-Times*

Not since the bloody deeds of Jack the Ripper have Londoners felt such terror as that aroused by the gruesome beheadings in Hyde Park. And if newly promoted Police Superintendent Thomas Pitt does not quickly apprehend the perpetrator, he is likely to lose his own head, professionally speaking. Yet even with the help of Charlotte Pitt's subtle investigation, the sinister violence continues unchecked. And in a shocking turn of events that nearly convinces the pair of sleuths that they have met their match, the case proves to be Pitt's toughest ever. . . .

Published by Fawcett Books.
Available wherever books are sold.